Student Study Guide and Map Exercise Workbook

to accompany

Traditions and Encounters
Volume I

Jerry H. Bentley
University of Hawaii

Herbert F. Ziegler
University of Hawaii

Prepared by
Lynda S. Bell
University of California

Guangyuan Zhou
University of Baltimore

Boston Burr Ridge, IL Dubuque, IA Madison, WI New York San Francisco St. Louis
Bangkok Bogotá Caracas Lisbon London Madrid
Mexico City Milan New Delhi Seoul Singapore Sydney Taipei Toronto

McGraw-Hill Higher Education 🐝

A Division of The McGraw-Hill Companies

Student Study Guide and Map Exercise Workbook to accompany
TRADITIONS AND ENCOUNTERS, VOLUME I

2 3 4 5 6 7 8 9 0 QPD/QPD 9 0 3 2 1 0 9

ISBN 0-07-005360-X

www.mhhe.com

Introduction

This study guide is designed to help students improve their understanding of the world history textbook, *Traditions and Encounters: A Global Perspective on the Past, Volume 1: From the Beginning to 1500*, by Jerry H. Bentley and Herbert F. Ziegler. It aims to promote good learning habits and analytical skills. The central concerns of the guide are two-fold: to provide a concise overview of each chapter of the textbook and to enhance students' comprehension and analytical ability through exercises of various kinds. Each chapter of the guide is divided into the following sections:

Introduction and Learning Objectives

This section highlights the central themes and major events presented in the corresponding chapter of the textbook. It is designed not to supplant the reading of the textbook but to direct students' attention to the questions the textbook seeks to raise. It asks students to read the text and grasp the most important details that are essential in understanding the chapter. A number of important issues listed in the bulleted learning objectives at the end of this section serve as hints on how to understand the history presented in the text.

Chapter Outline

The chapter outline uses the textbook's chapter structure and summarizes the information presented in each major section. Students are often overwhelmed with the amount of material and divergent nature of information presented in a chapter, and they sometimes feel lost while reading from section to section. The chapter outline requires students to grasp the organizing principles of the chapter and to see how important details fit into the big structure instead of memorizing various details in an unrelated or unorganized manner. Students may use the outline before they read the textbook chapter, or use it to review the textbook chapter after reading. Moreover, since the outline includes all the important information and concepts presented, students can use it to help answer some of the self-test questions that follow. Finally, for those students who do not have good habits in taking notes, the outline also serves as an example of note-taking.

Significant Individuals and Chapter Glossary

These two sections contain brief accounts for all significant individuals, important terms, and vital concepts included in the textbook chapter. The primary purpose of these two sections is to help students review each chapter's specific factual information and to prepare for possible identification questions on exams. A good understanding of these individuals and terms will also help students write essay questions and answer some of the self-test multiple choice questions.

Map Exercises

This section asks students to understand historical events in geographical context through reading and analyzing maps presented in the textbook. It is designed to stimulate students' interest in historical inquiry through visual and spatial means. The guide provides a great variety of map exercises. Some ask students to locate specific places, rivers, mountains, trade routes, and so on, on a map provided. Some require students to make connections between certain geographical features and historical developments such as migration, commercialization, colonization, and so on. Still others involve comparison of different maps which reveal historical change within a certain geographical context. Exercises of these sorts encourage regular use of maps and provide a visual means for students to enhance their knowledge of world history.

Self-Test/Student Quiz

This section contains approximately twenty multiple choice questions designed to enhance students' reading comprehension. All the questions focus on important details—events, opinions, concepts, significant individuals, chronology, and terms. We have tried to compose questions that are informative, challenging, interesting, and closely tied to the narrative account of the textbook chapter, with a strong concern for avoiding trivial, tricky, and obfuscating questions (a little humor is thrown in for good measure as well). There is an answer key at the end of the study guide and students will find it easy to locate the pertinent material in the textbook for each question by using the page numbers given there. Instead of giving a simple "yes" or "no" answer, we have tried to make the answer key an important learning tool by offering explanations as to why a given answer is right, wrong, or the "best" among several choices.

Textual Questions for Analysis

Each chapter includes several textual questions for analysis designed to help students explore broader historical themes that can form the basis for essay questions on exams. Unlike the multiple choice questions which focus on single matters, the textual questions require students to bring together several blocks of historical knowledge into a coherent theme. The textbook provides the factual basis for answering these questions, but not ready-made answers. Questions in this section mostly focus on issues of causation at moments of major historical change, interpretations of important events, and comparisons or contrasts among cultures, religions, or political ideas. Because questions in this section require a short essay-type response, students should work out an outline before answering each question.

Documentary Evidence

Believing that one of the best ways to learn history is to expose students to primary sources, we include in each chapter a piece of original text followed by a number of questions to consider. The primary purposes of this section are to provide students with a sense of how historians use primary sources to form their opinions and conclusions, and to satisfy students' curiosity about the personal voices of historical actors. The documents are selected for their informative and interesting nature and are closely tied to issues discussed in the textbook. Each document is introduced with a brief discussion of the author of the piece, and, as appropriate, the historical circumstances in which the document was written or produced. Reading of primary sources not only requires students to communicate directly with the ideas, values, and perspectives of people in the past, it also demands that students evaluate the credibility or bias of the maker of the piece. Hence, the questions at the end of this section seek to guide students toward a critical reading of the documents and a recognition of their historical significance.

PLEASE NOTE: A pronunciation guide and comprehensive, comparative timelines are provided in the textbook. They are not repeated here but students are advised to use them in conjunction with the study guide.

Contents

Chapter 1

Before History

Introduction and Learning Objectives

This chapter deals with the long period of prehistory from the age of *Australopithecus* in east Africa (between 4 million and 1 million years ago) to the emergence of the earliest cities in the valley of the Tigris and Euphrates Rivers (between 4000 and 3500 B.C.E.). Overall, it discusses two interrelated themes—the evolution of the human species and the transition from paleolithic society to neolithic society. The authors also stress the importance of the prehistoric legacy to our understanding of world history.

The authors point out that the human species was not endowed with great strength nor equipped with natural means of attack and defense as many other animals were. What, then, made the human species a successful competitor in the natural world? How could human beings stand out as the most distinctive of the primate species? The authors emphasize the remarkable intelligence of the human brain that provided a powerful edge in the contest for survival. It was the high order of intelligence that enabled human beings to devise tools, technologies, language skills, and other means of communication and cooperation. Whereas other animal species adapted physically and genetically to their natural environment, human beings altered the natural environment to suit their own needs and desires. This point can be illustrated by the evolution from *Australopithecus* to *Homo erectus* and from *Homo sapiens* to modern man.

High intelligence also endowed humans with immense potential for social and cultural development. The most significant development, of course, was the transition from hunting and gathering society to settled agricultural society. The authors argue that the term "agricultural revolution" is rather misleading, because the transition was a long process unfolding over many centuries, leading from paleolithic experiments with cultivation to early agricultural societies in the neolithic era. Moreover, the shift from foraging to agriculture was not a voluntary choice. As humans spread throughout the habitable world, they placed enormous pressure on animal populations and on the capacity of the land to support them. As they hunted large game animals into scarcity, and sometimes into extinction, human groups were forced to find new supplies of food. They found agriculture to be a workable solution.

Differing from the economy of hunting and gathering, agriculture produced a surplus, which, in turn, laid the economic foundation for the development of villages, towns, and cities as well as for cultural development. Already in the paleolithic era, Neandertal peoples began to display their reflective thought by deliberate burials, while Cro-Magnon peoples showed their deep interest in fertility and successful hunting as revealed in their figurines and cave paintings. As society became more complex in the neolithic era, various gods and goddesses were celebrated for favoring the rhythms that governed agricultural society—birth, growth, death, and regeneration of life.

1

After reading this chapter, students should understand and be able to discuss the following issues:

- the evolution of the human species

- the transition from hunting and gathering society to agricultural society

- cultural development from the paleolithic to the neolithic era

Chapter Outline

I. **The Evolution of *Homo Sapiens***

  A. The Hominids
    1. *Australopithecus*
      a) Appeared in east Africa about 4 million to 1 million years ago
      b) The term means "the southern ape," but it belongs to hominids
      c) Walked upright on two legs, well-developed hands
      d) Fashioned stone tools, probably knew how to use fire later
    2. *Homo erectus*
      a) Flourished 1.5 million to 200,000 years ago, east Africa
      b) The term means "upright walking human"
      c) Large brain, sophisticated tools, definitely knew how to control fire
      d) Developed language skills in well-coordinated hunts of large animals
    3. Migrations of *Homo erectus*
      a) First migrated to north Africa
      b) Between 500,000 and 200,000 years ago migrated to Asia and Europe
  B. *Homo sapiens*
    1. *Homo sapiens*
      a) The term means "consciously thinking human"
      b) Evolved as early as 250,000 years ago
      c) Brain with large frontal regions for conscious and reflective thought
      d) The advantages of intelligence over other species
    2. Migrations of *Homo sapiens*
      a) Beginning more than 100,000 years ago, spread throughout Eurasia
      b) Several ice ages between 120 and 25 thousand years ago
      c) Land bridges enabled them to populate islands of Indonesia and New Guinea
      d) Arrived in Australia at least 60,000 or perhaps as long as 120,000 years ago
      e) Between 40,000 and 25,000 years ago, migrated to North America
    3. The natural environment
      a) *Homo sapiens* used knives, spears, bows, and arrows
      b) Brought tremendous pressure on other species

II. Paleolithic Society

    A. Economy and Society of Hunting and Gathering Peoples
        1. Economic life
            a) Prevented individuals from accumulating private property
            b) Lived an egalitarian existence
            c) Social equality probably extended to relations between sexes
            d) Lived in small bands, about 30 to 50 members in each group
        2. Big game hunting
            a) Large animals included elephant, mastodon, rhinoceros, bison, wild cattle
            b) Paleolithic hunters used special tools and tactics for hunting large animals
    B. Paleolithic Culture
        1. Neandertal peoples
            a) Named after the site of the Neander valley in S.W. Germany
            b) Flourished in Europe and S.W. Asia between 100 and 35 thousand years ago
            c) Careful, deliberate burials—evidence of a capacity for emotion and feelings
        2. Cro-Magnon peoples
            a) The first human beings of fully modern type, appeared 40,000 years ago
            b) Classified as *Homo sapiens sapiens*
            c) A noticeable interest in fashion and artistic production
        3. Venus figurines
            a) Besides jewelry and furniture, there were also Venus figurines and paintings
            b) The figurines reflect a deep interest in fertility
        4. Cave paintings
            a) Best known are Lascaux in France and Altamira in Spain
            b) Subjects: mostly animals
            c) Purposes: aesthetic, "sympathetic magic"

III. The Neolithic Era and the Transition to Agriculture

    A. The Origins of Agriculture
        1. Neolithic era
            a) "New stone age"—refined tools and agriculture
            b) Time period: from about 12,000 to 6,000 years ago
            c) Most likely, paleolithic women began systematic cultivation of plants
            d) Paleolithic men began to domesticate animals
            e) "Agricultural transition" is better than "agricultural revolution"
        2. Early agriculture
            a) The earliest evidence found between 10,000 to 8000 B.C.E.
            b) Slash-and-burn cultivation involved frequent movement of farmers
            c) About 5000 B.C.E., agriculture was well-established in Asia and Americas
        3. The spread of agriculture
            a) Advantages of cultivation over hunting and gathering
            b) Agriculture provided a surplus
    B. Early Agricultural Society
        1. Population explosion caused by surplus

2. Emergence of villages and towns
   a) Jericho, earliest known neolithic village, site north of the Dead Sea
   b) Agricultural society, supplemented by hunting and limited trade
   c) Mud huts and defensive walls
3. Specialization of labor
   a) The neolithic site of Çatal Hüyük (south-central Anatolia)
   b) Developed into a bustling town with 8000 inhabitants
   c) Three prehistoric craft industries—pottery, metallurgy, and textile production
4. Social distinctions
   a) Agriculture brought about private land ownership
   b) Social classes emerged, as seen in Çatal Hüyük site
C. Neolithic Culture
   1. Paleolithic communities had already honored Venus figurines
   2. Neolithic peoples celebrated deities associated with life cycle
D. The Origins of Urban Life
   1. Emergence of cities
      a) Cities were larger and more complex than neolithic villages and towns
      b) Cities influenced political, economic and cultural life of large regions
   2. Earliest cities in the valley of the Tigris and Euphrates Rivers, 4000 to 3500 B.C.E.

Significant Individuals

Lucy (pp. 7, 9) — Best known prehistoric individual; lived about 3.5 million years ago in east Africa, and her skeleton was discovered by archaeologists in 1974 in modern-day Hadar, Ethiopia; belongs to *Australopithecus* and classified as AL 288-1; her name "Lucy" was given by archaeologists.

Chapter Glossary

Australopithecus (p. 9) — "Southern ape," earliest species of hominids; flourished in east Africa between four million and one million years ago; walked upright on two legs; fashioned crude stone tools by well-developed hands with opposable thumbs; had limited ability to communicate verbally; might have used fire in later ages.

Çatal Hüyük (p. 24) — One of the best known neolithic towns; located in south-central Anatolia (modern-day Turkey) and dated from 7250 to 6150 B.C.E.; had about eight thousand inhabitants; various products found in this site indicate specialization of labor.

cave paintings (p. 18) — prehistoric art of Cro-Magnon peoples dating from about 35 to 12 thousand years ago; mostly found in caves in southern France and northern Spain; most of the subjects were animals, which reflect the artists' interest in successful hunting expeditions.

Cro-Magnon peoples (pp. 17-18) — Paleolithic peoples; the first human beings of the fully modern type; appeared about 40 thousand years ago; displayed a noticeable interest in fashion, artistic expression, and a strong concern about fertility.

hominids (p. 9) — Human and humanlike species, one of the most distinctive of the primate species; share some remarkable similarities with large apes, but small differences in genetic makeup and body chemistry led hominids to develop an extraordinarily high order of intelligence.

Homo erectus (pp. 10-11) — "Upright walking human"; species of hominids; flourished in east Africa between 1.5 million and two hundred thousand years ago; possessed brains larger than that of *Australopithecus*; fashioned more sophisticated tools; knew how to control fire; had effective language skills; between five hundred and two hundred thousand years ago spread to north Africa and Eurasian landmass.

Homo sapiens (pp. 12-13) — "Consciously thinking human"; species of hominids; possessed a large brain with a broad frontal region for conscious and reflective thought; used refined tools for hunting and gathering; remarkable intelligence and language skills enabled them to adapt to widely varying environments; beginning more than one hundred thousand years ago, spread throughout the eastern hemisphere.

Homo sapiens sapiens (pp. 13, 17) — Human beings of fully modern type; first appeared on the earth about 40,000 years ago (Cro-Magnon peoples).

Jericho (pp. 23-24) — One of the earliest known neolithic villages; site of a fresh-water oasis north of the Dead Sea in present-day Israel; dates from about 8000 B.C.E.; had about two thousand residents; cultivated wheat and barley and engaged in a limited amount of trade.

Neandertal peoples (p. 16) — *Homo sapiens* who flourished in Europe, southwest Asia, Africa, and east Asia between about 100 thousand to 35 thousand years ago; named after the site of the Neander valley in southwest Germany; known for their careful, deliberate burial accompanied by ritual observances.

neolithic (pp. 19-20) — "New stone age"; early stages of agricultural society, from about 12 thousand to 6 thousand years ago.

paleolithic (p. 14) — "Old stone age"; extended from the evolution of the first hominids (4 million years ago) until about 12 thousand years ago; societies typified by using crude stone tools, hunting and gathering for subsistence.

prehistory (p. 8) — Period of human history before the invention of writing.

Shanidar cave (pp. 16-17) — A Neandertal site located north of modern-day Baghdad; known for its ritual of burying the dead in beds of flowers.

Venus figurines (pp. 17-18) — Small sculptures of women found in many Cro-Magnon sites; exaggerated sexual features reflect a deep interest in fertility.

Map Exercises

1. Study Map 1.1 on pp. 10-11 in your textbook, read the related portions of the chapter, and fill in the missing information in the following table:

Hominids	Migrated to:	Time of migration
Australopithecus	East and south Africa	_____
Homo erectus	_____	500,000 years ago
Homo sapiens	Eurasia, Australia, and North America	_____

2. Mark the six origins of agriculture and their outward spread on the following map (consult Map 1.2, pp. 22-23 of your textbook):

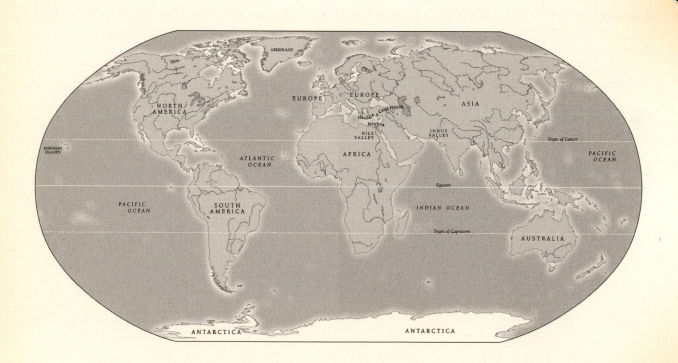

3. Match each place of agricultural origin with its crops and domesticated animals in the following table:

Origins	Crops and domesticated animals
Southwest Asia	Maize, beans, squash
East Asia	Yams, sorghum
Southeast Asia	Wheat, barley, cattle, sheep, goat, pig
West Africa	Maize, beans, potato, tomato, squash, llama, alpaca
Mesoameria	Millet, rice, wheat, soybean, sorghum, pig, chicken
South America	Banana, yam, pea, rice, pig, oxen, chicken

Self-Test/Student Quiz

1. By scholarly convention, *prehistory* refers to the period

    a. before the emergence of cities.
    b. before modern man was born.
    c. before the invention of writing.

2. Human beings and large apes are slightly different in

    a. genetic makeup and body chemistry.
    b. level of intelligence.
    c. the structure of the brain.

3. The famous Lucy was

    a. a female ape.
    b. an *Australopithecus*.
    c. a *Homo erectus*.

4. The family of hominids includes all of the following species except

    a. apes and monkeys.
    b. *Australopithecus* and *Homo erectus*.
    c. *Homo sapiens* and *Homo sapiens sapiens*.

5. A *Homo erectus* might have taught an *Australopithecus* how to

    a. walk upright on two legs.
    b. domesticate animals.
    c. communicate through language.

6. *Homo sapiens* were better hunters than *Australopithecus* and *Homo erectus* because they

    a. organized larger hunting bands than their ancestors did.
    b. were smaller in body size but swifter in action.
    c. had larger brains and higher intelligence.

7. The principal defining characteristic of the paleolithic era was that

    a. human beings used stone and bone tools in their cultivation of crops.
    b. peoples relied on hunting and gathering for subsistence.
    c. men and women engaged in the same economic activities.

8. In hunting and gathering society,

    a. individuals who accumulated more animals would dominate others.
    b. men and women were more or less equal.
    c. peoples organized themselves through family and clan.

9. Neandertal peoples developed a capacity for emotion and feelings, which can be seen from their

    a. elaborate burials.
    b. cave paintings.
    c. ancestor worship.

10. Cro-Magnon peoples were

    a. *Homo sapiens*.
    b. *Homo sapiens sapiens*.
    c. *Homo erectus*.

11. The prominent sexual features of Venus figurines at Cro-Magnon sites indicate that the Cro-Magnon peoples

    a. worshipped the goddess of love 40 thousand years ago.
    b. had a deep interest in love-making activities.
    c. were strongly concerned with fertility and the generation of new life.

12. All of the following were purposes of Cro-Magnon cave paintings except

    a. to beautify living space.
    b. to practice telepathy.
    c. to exercise "sympathetic magic."

13. The term *neolithic era* refers to

    a. the early stages of agricultural society.
    b. the agricultural revolution.
    c. the era in which the peoples began to use polished stone tools.

14. By about 5000 B.C.E., agriculture had displaced hunting and gathering societies in several regions of the world primarily because

    a. cultivation required much less work than hunting and gathering.
    b. cultivation provided a relatively stable and regular supply of food.
    c. human beings had mastered agricultural knowledge and technique.

15. All of the following social changes were brought about by agriculture except

    a. population growth.
    b. the emergence of villages and towns.
    c. the invention of writing.

16. The site of Jericho was the earliest known

    a. village.
    b. town.
    c. city.

17. Three neolithic industries that illustrate the greatest potential of specialized labor include

    a. stone tool making, leather, and jewelry.
    b. wood carving, beads, and baskets.
    c. pottery, metallurgy, and textiles.

18. Çatal Hüyük is an archaeological site in Anatolia from neolithic times in which one can readily see evidence of

    a. social distinctions.
    b. iron production.
    c. long-distance trade.

19. "Neolithic religious thought clearly reflected the natural world of early agricultural society." This point is based on observation of

    a. religious texts.
    b. gods and goddesses.
    c. cave paintings.

20. Cities first emerged from agricultural villages and towns in

    a. the valleys of Tigris and Euphrates Rivers.
    b. Egypt.
    c. China.

Textual Questions for Analysis

1. Compare and contrast the following hominids—*Australopithecus*, *Homo erectus*, and *Homo sapiens*. What accounts for their success in the contest for survival in the natural world?

2. Describe paleolithic hunting and gathering society.

3. What were the advantages of agricultural society over hunting and gathering society? Why was agriculture important to the development of complex society?

4. What were the beliefs of the paleolithic and neolithic peoples? How were these beliefs related to their daily lives?

Documentary Evidence

Because this chapter deals with prehistory, there is no documentary evidence provided. The reason for this is that students typically will have had too little experience to evaluate the sorts of archaeological materials used to construct the narrative of prehistory as presented in this chapter.

Chapter 2

Early Societies in Southwest Asia and North Africa

Introduction and Learning Objectives

The two earliest complex societies, Mesopotamia and Egypt, emerged in the valley plains of big rivers, and their irrigated agriculture supported urban centers, where new and specialized vocations emerged along with the developments of complex political and cultural institutions. In both societies, the urban-centered government not only ruled surrounding agricultural settlements, but also established regional empires and spread their cultures and technologies to less developed societies of the surrounding areas. What accounted for the emergence of these complex societies? How complex were they in comparison with neolithic societies? What were the characteristics of the two societies? How did they influence surrounding smaller societies? These are the major issues addressed by the authors in this chapter.

The authors emphasize the importance of big rivers to the development of the two societies. Mesopotamia literally means "the land between the rivers," which specifically refers to the valleys of the Tigris and Euphrates Rivers in modern-day Iraq, while Egypt was called "the gift of the Nile." In both cases, fertile soil of the river valleys supported settled agriculture and complex societies represented by the rise of cities, the emergence of states, and invention of writing. The authors argue that the sense of private property, regional coordination among those who used the water supply, as well as the need to maintain peace and order, all led to emergence of political and economic organizations larger than those that existed during Neolithic times. Important in Mesopotamia, however, were independent city-states and nobility, while in Egypt the state government was formed through conquest and unification. In comparison with Mesopotamia, Egypt had few cities and its administrative activities were highly centralized.

Finally, the authors also point out that the significance of the above two societies was not restricted to their cultural achievements and imperial expansion, but also manifested in their influence on a number of smaller societies surrounding them. By interacting with the above two cultural centers, the smaller societies began to produce important innovations of their own. The alphabetic writing of Phoenicians and monotheism of Hebrews, for instance, had great significance for world history, while the Nubians changed African history by spreading the technology of iron metallurgy in sub-Saharan Africa.

After reading this chapter, students should understand and be able to discuss:

- the origins of the two complex societies in Mesopotamia and Egypt

- similarities and differences between the two in terms of politics, economy, culture, and society

- influences of the two societies on the peoples of adjacent territories and the latter's contributions to historical change

11

Chapter Outline

I. **The Quest for Order**

   A. Mesopotamia: "The land between the rivers"
      1. Sumer
         a) Sumerians migrated to Sumer, 5000 B.C.E., built irrigation networks
         b) Became dominant by 3000 B.C.E.
         c) Other inhabitants, mostly Semites—Akkadian, Hebrew, Aramaic, Phoenician
      2. Sumerian city-states
         a) A dozen cities dominated the area from 3200 to 2350 B.C.E.
         b) Internal and external pressures promoted cities to become states
         c) Importance of government in irrigation and self-defense
      3. Sumerian Kings
         a) Earliest governments: assemblies of prominent men
         b) 3000 B.C.E., all cities were ruled by kings in cooperation with nobles
         c) All cities were city-states, autonomous one to another
   B. Egypt: "The Gift of the Nile"
      1. The Nile River
         a) Reliable water supplies and rich mulch: Beneficial conditions for agriculture
         b) Agriculture began before 5000 B.C.E.
         c) Agricultural communities appeared along the Nile, 4000 B.C.E.
      2. Unification of Egypt
         a) State emerged through Menes' conquest, 3100 B.C.E.
         b) Important cities: Memphis, Thebes, Tanis
         c) Centralized state ruled by the pharaoh, the god-king
      3. The pyramids
         a) Royal tombs, mostly constructed during the Old Kingdom
         b) Enormous monuments, can be seen today at Giza, near Cairo
         c) The largest is the pyramid of Khufu
   C. The Course of Empire
      1. Sargon of Akkad (2370-2315 B.C.E.)
         a) Leader of the Semitic people from northern Mesopotamia
         b) Organized a coup against the king, 2334 B.C.E.
         c) Conquered Sumerian cities of Mesopotamia
         d) Sargon's empire lasted for several generations, collapsed in 2100 B.C.E.
      2. Hammurabi (re. 1792-1750 B.C.E.) and the Babylonian Empire
         a) Babylonian Hammurabi, "King of the four quarters of the world"
         b) His dynasty dominated Mesopotamia until 1600 B.C.E.
         c) Devised the most extensive Mesopotamian law code
         d) Empire fell under the invasion of the Hittites, 1595 B.C.E.
      3. The Egyptian New Kingdom
         a) Ahmosis, founder of New Kingdom, expelled the Hyksos, 1550 B.C.E.
         b) Expanded to Palestine and Syria
         c) Pharaoh Tuthmosis III, launched 17 campaigns in Palestine and Syria

4. The Assyrian empire
    a) A hardy people from northern Mesopotamia, began conquest by 1000 B.C.E.
    b) Empire included Mesopotamia, Syria, Palestine, much of Anatolia, and most of Egypt, 8th-7th centuries B.C.E., collapsed in 612 B.C.E.
5. Nebuchadnezzar and the New Babylonian empire
    a) After Assyrian empire, Mesopotamia fell under New Babylonian empire
    b) Babylon, the most luxurious city

II. The Development of Complex Societies

A. Economic Specialization and Trade
  1. Bronze metallurgy
      a) Alloy of copper and tin, discovered about 3000 B.C.E.
      b) Bronze weapons were developed first, bronze farming tools appeared later
      c) Egyptians embraced bronze after the 17th century B.C.E.
  2. Iron metallurgy: discovered after 1000 B.C.E. by Mesopotamian craftsmen
  3. The wheel: Used by Sumerians probably for centuries before 3200 B.C.E.
  4. Shipbuilding: Sumerians and Egyptians built watercraft by 3500 B.C.E.
  5. Long-distance trade
      a) Trade between Mesopotamia and Egypt, as early as 3500 B.C.E.
      b) 2300 B.C.E., Sumerian trade with Harappan society (north India)
      c) In Babylonian times, Mesopotamians traded with peoples in all directions
      d) Surviving evidence shows great volume of trade
B. The Emergence of Stratified Societies
  1. Social distinctions: much more sharply defined than in neolithic times
  2. Mesopotamian kings
      a) Royal status became hereditary
      b) Legends portray some kings as offsprings of gods (e.g., Gilgamesh)
  3. Temple communities
      a) Priestly elites: intervened with gods to ensure good fortune of communities
      b) Received offerings from city inhabitants
      c) Owned large tracts of lands and workshops
      d) Functioned as banks and charities
  4. Other social classes
      a) Free commoners: peasants, craftsmen, or other professionals
      b) Dependent clients: worked on other people's lands
      c) Slaves: mostly domestic servants, some worked in fields
  5. Egyptian society
      a) Pharaoh as a supreme central ruler
      b) Military elite and bureaucrats were more important than nobles
      c) Also had priests, commoners, and slaves
C. The Construction of Patriarchal Societies
  1. Patriarchal societies as seen from Hammurabi's laws
  2. Women's roles
      a) Despite their subordinate legal status, women had their influence
          (1) Women as regents for young rulers, e.g., Queen Hatshepsut
          (2) A few women served as high priestesses and scribes
          (3) Women as midwives, shopkeepers, brewers, bakers, textile makers

b) Mesopotamia saw decline of women's status in the 2nd millennium B.C.E.
    (1) Virginity of brides and chastity of women were emphasized
    (2) Married women began to wear veils from 1500 B.C.E.

III. Writing and the Formation of Sophisticated Cultural Traditions

A. The Origins of Writing
  1. Cuneiform writing appeared in Mesopotamia around 2900 B.C.E.
  2. Hieroglyphic and hieratic scripts were used in Egypt

B. Education, Literacy, and Learning
  1. Education and literacy were essential for smooth functioning of societies
    a) Educated individuals became scribes or government officials
    b) Priests, physicians, or some other professionals were also literate
    c) *The Satire of the Trades*, described privileged life of a scribe
  2. Astronomy and mathematics
    a) Both sciences were important for agricultural societies
    b) Mesopotamian conventions: 12 months in a year, sixty minutes in an hour
  3. *The Epic of Gilgamesh*, the best known reflective literature of Mesopotamia
    a) Adventure story about Gilgamesh and his friend Enkidu
    b) Themes: friendship, human relation to gods, meanings of life and death

C. The Origins of Organized Religion
  1. Community gods of Mesopotamian cities
    a) Each city held one deity in especially high esteem
    b) Temples were prominent features of urban landscapes, e.g., the ziggurats
  2. Amon-Re of Egypt
    a) Combined cult of Re, the sun god, and Amon, the air god
    b) The massive temple at Heliopolis (near Memphis)
  3. Akhenaten
    a) The god Aten, a challenge to Amon-Re, championed by Pharaoh Amenhotep IV, who renamed him self Akhenaten in honor of his preferred deity
    b) Aten might represent the world's first monotheism
    c) After Pharaoh Amenhotep IV died, Amon-Re regained domination
  4. The quest for immortality and mummification
    a) Egyptians' practice of mummification
    b) Common to pharaoh, officials, and wealthy individuals
  5. Cult of Osiris
    a) Associated with immortality
    b) Individuals who observed high moral standards deserved immortality
    c) After death, individuals faced judgments of Osiris

IV. The Broader Influence of Mesopotamian and Egyptian Societies

A. Mesopotamian Influence on the Hebrews and the Phoenicians
  1. The Hebrews
    a) Pastoral nomads, between Mesopotamia and Egypt, 2000 B.C.E.
    b) Close relation with Sumerians, part of Mesopotamian tradition
  2. Moses and monotheism
    a) Hebrews migrated to Egypt, 18th century B.C.E.
    b) Moses led Hebrews to Palestine, and established a kingdom, 1300 B.C.E.
    c) From 1000 to 930 B.C.E., dominated Syria and Sinai peninsula

    d) Built the cosmopolitan capital city at Jerusalem
    e) Moses taught only one supreme god, Yahweh, the creator of the world
    f) A single god, scriptures, and moral concerns became Hebrews' identity
  3. The Phoenicians
    a) Lived between the Mediterranean and Lebanon
    b) Turned to industry and trade because of their meager lands
    c) By 2500 B.C.E., dominated trade in the Mediterranean basin
    d) Established colonies in Cyprus, Sicily, Spain, north Africa from 1200 B.C.E.
    e) Adopted Mesopotamian cultural traditions
  4. Alphabetic writing of the Phoenicians
    a) Simplified cuneiform by devising 22 symbols, about 1500 B.C.E.
    b) Spread alphabetic writing throughout the Mediterranean
    c) Greeks modified Phoenician alphabet and added vowels
    d) Romans later adapted Greek alphabet and passed it to European peoples
    e) Egyptians also learned alphabetic writing from the Greeks
B. Egyptian Influence in Sub-Saharan Africa
  1. Nubia
    a) Located in the southern part of sub-Saharan Africa
    b) Poor in agriculture but rich in gold, ivory, ebony, gems
    c) Adopted Egyptian cultural traditions
  2. Kush
    a) Nubians established the kingdom of Kush, the 1st millennium B.C.E.
    b) Invaded Egypt and imposed Nubian rule, 750 B.C.E.
    c) Assyrian conquerors drove the Kushites out of Egypt, 664 B.C.E.
    d) Moved to the south, received less Egyptian influence
  3. Iron metallurgy
    a) Nubians forged iron tools and weapons as early as the 9th century B.C.E.
    b) Iron metallurgy soon spread throughout much of Africa

Significant Individuals

Ahmosis (p. 39) — Pharaoh and founder of the New Kingdom in Egypt; expelled the Hyksos and reunited Egypt by 1550 B.C.E.; began imperial expansion by leading armies into Palestine and Syria.

Akhenaten (p. 49) (reigned 1353-1335 B.C.E.) — Egyptian Pharaoh Amenhotep IV, who named himself Akhenaten to honor the god Aten. He considered Aten to be the only true god, thus issuing in a short-lived era of monotheism in Egypt, perhaps the world's first.

Gilgamesh (p. 48) — Legendary king of the Sumerian city, Uruk, shortly after 3000 B.C.E.; hero in *Epic of Gilgamesh*.

Hammurabi (pp. 38-39) (reigned 1792-1750 B.C.E.) — Creator of Babylonian empire; styled himself "king of the four quarters of the world," relied on centralized bureaucratic rule and levied regular tax; especially known for his codification of laws.

Menes (also known as **Narmer**) (p. 36) — Egyptian king, unified Egypt through conquest about 3100 B.C.E. and brought about the first centralized state ruled by the pharaoh; also founded the capital city Memphis.

Moses (pp. 50-51) — Leader of the Hebrews who led them from Egypt around 1300 B.C.E. to Palestine, where they built a regional kingdom.

Nebuchadnezzar (p. 40) (reigned 605-562 B.C.E.) — King of the New Babylonian Empire; known for his construction of the enormous capital city, Babylon.

Queen Hatshepsut (p. 46) (reigned 1503-1482 B.C.E.) — Regent of a young pharaoh, claimed the title of pharaoh for herself.

Sargon of Akkad (p. 38) (2370-2315 B.C.E.) — Founder and emperor of the Akkadian empire; seized power through a coup in 2334 B.C.E.; conquered other Sumerian city-states and controlled all of Mesopotamia.

Tuthmosis III (p. 39) (reigned 1490-1436 B.C.E.) — Pharaoh of the New Kingdom; continued imperial expansion and personally launched seventeen campaigns against Palestine and Syria; eventually dominated the coastal regions of the eastern Mediterranean.

Chapter Glossary

alphabet (p. 52) — Writing first invented by the Phoenicians by about 1500 B.C.E.; consisted of twenty-two symbols representing consonants (the Phoenician alphabet did not have vowels).

Amon-Re (pp. 48-49) — Composite of the sun god Re and the air god Amon around which the most important cult of ancient Egypt developed; honored at a massive temple complex in Heliopolis by Egyptian priests.

Assyrian empire (p. 40) — Empire in Mesopotamia built by the Assyrians, a hardy people from northern Mesopotamia who extended their authority south after 1000 B.C.E. At its high point, during the eighth and seventh centuries B.C.E., the Assyrian empire covered Mesopotamia, Syria, Palestine, much of Anatolia, and most of Egypt. Internal unrest and external assaults brought it down in 612 B.C.E.

Aten (p. 49) — Egyptian god whose cult flourished during the reign of Pharaoh Amenhotep IV (reigned 1353-1335 B.C.E.). The pharaoh changed his name to Akhenaten in honor of his preferred deity. Aten was considered to be one and only true god, but this monotheism was only short-lived in Egypt. After the pharaoh died, the cult of Amon-Re soon replaced the cult of Aten.

Babylonian empire (pp. 38-39) — A regional empire built by Hammurabi in 1792 B.C.E. that dominated Mesopotamia until about 1600 B.C.E.; collapsed due to foreign invasions.

bronze (p. 41) — Discovered by Mesopotamian craftsmen around 3000 B.C.E. A strong alloy of copper and tin, bronze enabled the specialized production of much more effective weapons. Eventually, it was also used for agricultural tools.

chariots (pp. 36-37) — Drawn by horses and developed by foreign peoples (e.g., the Hyksos and the Assyrians) as a powerful new military technology; used to invade Egypt around the time of the Middle Kingdom (2080-1640 B.C.E.)

city-state (pp. 33-35) — Form of government typical in ancient Mesopotamia; urban-based kingdom ruled by kings and nobles.

Cult of Osiris (p. 49) — Popular cult of ancient Egypt; Osiris, the lord of the underworld, was associated with immortality as an afterlife reward for individuals observing high moral standards.

cuneiform (pp. 46-47) — Writing system developed by the Sumerians beginning about 2900 B.C.E., using a wedge-shaped stylus to impress symbols on wet clay tablets. The symbols represented not only physical objects, but also sounds, syllables, and ideas.

Epic of Gilgamesh (pp. 43, 48) — First reflective literature in Western civilization, compiled after 2000 B.C.E. during the days of Babylonian empire; recounted the experiences of Gilgamesh, king of Uruk, who lived shortly after 3000 B.C.E.; explored themes of human friendship, relations between humans and the gods, and especially the meaning of life and death; also included the story of the Great Flood.

Hammurabi's laws (pp. 38-39) — The most extensive and complete Mesopotamian law code; used by Hammurabi to maintain his empire. Criminal laws established high standards of behavior through stern punishments for violators, and civil laws regulated prices, wages, commercial dealings, marital relationships, and the conditions of slavery; relied heavily on the principle of *lex talionis*—the "law of retaliation," whereby offenders suffered punishments resembling their violations.

Hebrews (pp. 33, 50-51) — Semitic speaking people who lived between Mesopotamia and Egypt during the second millennium B.C.E. Migrated first to Egypt and then to Palestine, where they established a regional kingdom that dominated the territory between Syrian and Sinai peninsula during the tenth century. Especially known for their monotheistic belief in Yahweh.

hieroglyphs (p. 47) — Writing system developed in ancient Egypt; pictographs supplemented with symbols representing sounds and ideas. The term *hieroglyphs* came from two Greek words meaning "holy inscriptions."

Hittites (p. 39) — Based in Anatolia, they brought down the Babylonian empire around 1595 B.C.E.

Hyksos (pp. 36-37) — Foreign invaders who brought down Egypt's Middle Kingdom in 1640 B.C.E. They were later expelled but their success prompted later pharaohs to seize control of regions that might pose future threats.

iron (p. 41) — After about 1000 B.C.E., Mesopotamians used iron to make tools and weapons. Assyrians made particularly effective use of iron weapons in building their empire.

Kush (p. 53) — African kingdom established by Nubians in the northern part of sub-Saharan Africa by about 1000 B.C.E. Invaded Egypt about 750 B.C.E. and imposed Nubian rule there until Assyrian conquerors drove them out in 664 B.C.E.; especially known for their spreading iron metallurgy in sub-Saharan Africa.

Mesopotamia (pp. 32-33) — Literally, "the land between the rivers," referring to the alluvial valley plain of the Tigris and Euphrates Rivers in modern day Iraq. The world's first complex society emerged in this area in about 3200 B.C.E.

mummification (pp. 31, 49) — Custom of preserving bodies of the dead with a belief in afterlife, especially developed in ancient Egypt; process was complicated and costly.

New Babylonian empire (p. 40) — Also known as the Chaldean empire; dominated Mesopotamia from 600 to 550 B.C.E. Built by King Nebuchadnezzar after the collapse of Assyrian empire.

The Nile (p. 35) — River of northeast Africa; runs more than 6,400 kilometers (3,978 miles) from its source at lake Victoria to its outlet through the delta to the Mediterranean Sea. Annual floods left alluvial deposits on the valley and supported productive agriculture in ancient Egypt.

Nubians (pp. 52-53) — People of northern sub-Saharan Africa who established the kingdom of Kush during the first millennium B.C.E., and invaded Egypt imposing their rule in 750 B.C.E. Known for their spread of iron metallurgy in sub-Saharan Africa.

patriarchal society (pp. 44-46) — A system of social organization in which men have vested authority over all public and private affairs. Both Mesopotamia and Egypt built patriarchal societies; Hammurabi's laws reflected the importance of patriarchal organization.

pharaoh (p. 36) — Kings of ancient Egypt, claimed to be gods living on the earth in human form, owners and absolute rulers of all the land.

Phoenicians (pp. 51-52) — Semitic speaking people who lived between the Mediterranean and the mountains of Lebanon. By 2500 B.C.E., they dominated trade in the Mediterranean basin. Between 1200 and 800 B.C.E., the Phoenicians established colonies in Cyprus, Sicily, Spain, and north Africa; they are known especially for their invention of alphabetic writing.

pyramids (p. 36) — Monumental royal tombs, typical of Old Kingdom Egypt (2660-2180 B.C.E.).

Sargon's empire (p. 38) — First regional empire in Mesopotamia, created by Sargon, the ruler of the city-state of Akkad, in about 2334 B.C.E. At its high point, the empire embraced all of Mesopotamia, and its armies had ventured as far afield as the Mediterranean and Black Sea; the empire lasted only for a few generations.

Sumerians (pp. 32-33) — People who migrated to the land of Sumer (in the southern half of Mesopotamia) as early as about 5000 B.C.E., where they created the first complex society in about 3200 B.C.E.

temple communities (p. 43) — Communities of priests and priestesses in ancient Mesopotamian cities; wealthy and powerful institutions that served many social and economic functions beyond those of religion.

Yahweh (p. 51) — God of the Hebrews, believed to be the creator and sustainer of the world and all within it; demanded that the Hebrews, his chosen people, observe high moral and ethical standards. Monotheism represented by belief in Yahweh had a deep influence on the development of Christianity and Islam.

Map Exercises

1. Place the following labels on the map below (review Map 2.1, p. 33 of your textbook):

- Rivers: Nile, Tigris, and Euphrates
- Societies: Mesopotamia, Lower Egypt, Upper Egypt
- Cities: Babylon, Jericho, Uruk, Ur, Heliopolis, Memphis
- Seas: Mediterranean, Red Sea, Black Sea, Aegean Sea, Caspian Sea
- Desert: Sahara

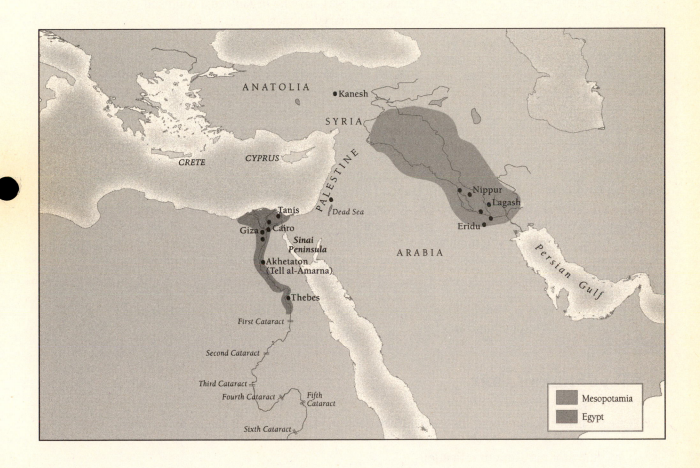

2. Match each empire on the left with the statement that best describes it on the right:

Empire	Description
Akkadian empire	Created by Hammurabi in the 18th century B.C.E.
Babylonian empire	Established by Ahmosis, who expelled the Hyksos, and led his armies north to Palestine and Syria
New Kingdom	Had a magnificent capital city occupying 850 hectares, thick city walls, enormous palaces and numerous temples
Assyrian empire	Founded by Sargon, who organized a coup and resorted to constant military conquests
New Babylonian empire	Used horse-drawn chariots and other advanced military skills to conquer all of Mesopotamia, Syria, and Palestine, much of Anatolia, and most of Egypt

3. Review Map 2.2 (p. 37) in your textbook and the portion of the chapter that discusses expansion of complex societies in early Mesopotamia. Then answer the following questions as best you can: Assume that you are the leader of nomadic herders seeking a place to settle down in Mesopotamia during the fourth millennium B.C.E. How do you persuade your group that you have chosen the best location? Would you prefer to reclaim the land in the wilderness or to invade the agricultural settlements of other groups? After your settlement, how would you interact with the surrounding environment? How do you maintain order and defend the wealth accumulated in your settlement? Use concrete examples to describe what kind of political system you would prefer for the best interests of your group.

4. How can geography help to explain differences between the political, social, and cultural development of Mesopotamia and Egypt?

Self Test/Student Quiz

1. Egyptian funerary customs reveal a wealthy agricultural society, which can be discerned by

    a. the process of mummification.
    b. the food offerings and scenes painted on tomb walls.
    c. the enormous pyramids.

2. Increased food supply, which was caused by settled agriculture and artificial irrigation, was crucial to the formation of the two complex societies, Mesopotamia and Egypt, because

    a. it supported population growth and encouraged trade and specialization.
    b. it gave a group of professional scholars enough time and leisure to invent a writing system.
    c. it encouraged craftsmen to experiment with iron metallurgy.

3. The two major ethnic groups of ancient Mesopotamia were

    a. Hebrews and Phoenicians.
    b. Semites and Akkadians.
    c. Sumerians and Semites.

4. The Sumerian cities were all city-states, so called because

    a. the state government was located in cities.
    b. each city was an autonomous kingdom.
    c. each city was economically self-sufficient.

5. The ancient Greek historian Herodotus proclaimed Egypt "the gift of the Nile" because, in his account,

    a. the process of desiccation forced paleolithic human groups to migrate from the Sahara to the valley of the Nile.
    b. the Egyptians depended on the Nile for drinking water.
    c. the reliable rhythm of the Nile created fertile land, which supported a remarkably productive agricultural economy.

6. The centralized state of Egypt first came into being through

    a. constant fighting against external threats and invasions.
    b. building enormous pyramids which demanded a great amount of labor.
    c. unification by a powerful man.

7. Mummification, pyramids, and funerary rituals in ancient Egypt were extremely costly and troublesome. The customs prevailed for several thousand years because

    a. the ruling elites perceived a need for demonstrating their power and wealth.
    b. Egyptians believed in an afterlife.
    c. the pharaohs tried to solve the problems of population pressure and unemployment.

8. In ancient Egypt, the largest pyramid was that of

    a. Khufu.
    b. Menes.
    c. Horus.

9. Hammurabi's laws

    a. were not concerned with justice but merely subjected people to severe punishments.
    b. comprised the first code of law ever promulgated in Mesopotamia.
    c. relied heavily on the principle of *lex talionis*—the "law of retaliation."

10. Technologically, Mesopotamia was more advanced than Egypt, seen by the fact that

    a. bronze and iron metallurgy appeared in Mesopotamia much earlier than in Egypt.
    b. the city walls of Babylon were more significant then the pyramids of Egypt.
    c. Mesopotamians mastered shipbuilding skills much earlier than Egyptians did.

11. The political structures of Mesopotamia and Egypt were very different seen from the facts that

    a. a Mesopotamian state had a king, priests, commoners, and slaves, while the Egyptian state had a pharaoh, religious specialists, farmers, and war prisoners.
    b. Egyptian pharaohs relied on divine power to rule while Mesopotamian kings did not.
    c. the city-states of Mesopotamia meant the joint rule of urban kings and a noble class, while in Egypt the pharaoh was the supreme central ruler who relied on military officers and bureaucrats to rule.

12. According to Hammurabi's laws,

    a. men had the power to sell their wives and children to satisfy their debts.
    b. wives caught in adultery deserved death by drowning, while their partners would be aquitted.
    c. both men and women could be heads of households, depending on who had the ability and power to make major decisions.

13. If you could travel back to ancient Mesopotamia and Egypt, it is most UNLIKELY that you would see

    a. a Sumerian man divorcing his wife shortly after marriage because he discovered that she was not a virgin.
    b. a powerful Egyptian lady dreaming of becoming a pharaoh herself someday.
    c. young Mesopotamian girls wearing veils when they went out.

14. *Cuneiform* writing in Mesopotamia and *hieroglyphic* writing in Egypt were very much the same in the sense that

    a. both writing systems were pictographic.
    b. both writing systems combined pictographs and other graphic symbols to represent sounds and ideas.
    c. both were alphabetic systems.

15. Astronomy and mathematics were important sciences in Mesopotamia and Egypt because

    a. the rulers needed celestial power to justify their secular authority.
    b. both sciences were noble professions that brought handsome rewards to scientists.
    c. the people needed accurate calendars and measurements of land.

16. *The Epic of Gilgamesh* is a

    a. a story about how Gilgamesh built the city walls.
    b. a reflection on the meanings of life and death.
    c. a text explaining religious practices.

17. As for organized religions in Mesopotamia and Egypt, the difference is that

    a. in Egypt the pharaohs were above the gods, while in Mesopotamia the gods were above the kings.
    b. the Egyptians believed only in one god, while Mesopotamians believed in several deities.
    c. Egyptians had national gods, while each Mesopotamian city had its own god.

18. Despite the frequent cultural contact between Egypt and Mesopotamia, mummification was practiced only in Egypt, not in Mesopotamia, because

    a. Egyptians kept their skills and techniques of mummification secret from the Mesopotamians.
    b. unlike Egyptians, Mesopotamians believed that death was inevitable.
    c. Mesopotamians did not yearn for immortality as much as Egyptians did.

19. The cult of Osiris, the lord of the underworld in ancient Egypt,

    a. expressed a practical concern for immortality regardless of high moral standards.
    b. rewarded immortality only to those who held high moral standards.
    c. was a cult to the god of fertility.

20. The Hebrews

    a. had always honored many of the same gods as their Mesopotamian neighbors.
    b. honored only one god.
    c. first established the religions of Christianity and Islam.

21. The Phoenicians were best known for their

    a. skills of industry and trade.
    b. ability to adapt all elements of the cultures with which they had contact.
    c. invention of alphabetic writing.

22. Nubia exercised a profound influence on African history by

    a. spreading the technology of iron metallurgy.
    b. spreading Egyptian culture to other parts of Africa.
    c. invading Egypt and imposing Nubian rule there between 750 and 664 B.C.E.

Textual Questions for Analysis

1. What do the authors mean by the term "complex society"? Based on the evidence provided by the societies of Mesopotamia and Egypt, describe the differences between neolithic societies and complex societies.

2. The complex societies of both Mesopotamia and Egypt emerged in river valleys. How do you explain this common phenomenon?

3. The peoples in ancient Mesopotamia and Egypt had already begun to strive for the meanings of life, immortality, and social order. In these respects, were they fundamentally different from us? Write a short essay to express your opinion. The essay should focus on either reflective literature, longevity, or law.

4. Both Mesopotamia and Egypt built patriarchal societies. Given the surviving evidence, what do we know about the roles and social status of women in these two societies? In your opinion, what factors may have contributed to the domination of men over women?

5. Briefly describe the differences of the four writing systems—pictograph, cuneiform, hieroglyph, and alphabet—and answer the following question: how important were writing systems to the development of complex societies?

6. The city-states of Mesopotamia and highly centralized authority of pharaohs in Egypt seem to represent two distinctive types of political systems. Explain.

7. Organized religions were an essential part of complex societies. What were the differences among the Sumerian community cults, Egyptians' Amon-Re, and Hebrews' Yahweh?

Documentary Evidence

A Babylonian Manumission Agreement

The following document is a simple agreement from the city of Nippur, religious capital of the Babylonian state, announcing the manumission (freeing from slavery) of Ishtar-utari. It was written in Sumerian cuneiform, pressed into a clay piece about 4 inches long and 3 inches wide. (From Edward Chiera, ed., *Old Babylonian Contracts.* University of Pennsylvania, University Museum, Publications of the Babylonian Section, vol. 8, no. 2 [1922], pl. 137 and p. 132.)

The Original Sumerian cuneiform document:

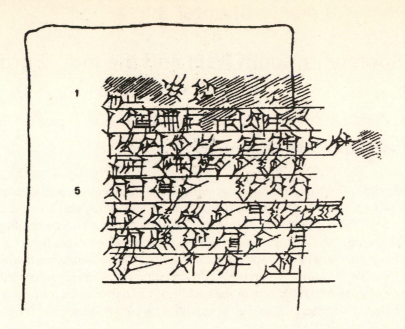

English translation:

Ishtar-utari, a female slave, Nudubtum, the daughter of Sili-Shamash, has set free. Her forehead she has cleansed. The mark (?) of her slavery she has destroyed. A manumission document she has given her.

QUESTIONS TO CONSIDER

1. Describe the similarities and differences between cuneiform writing and English writing (the forms of symbols, the ways of writing, the popularity of written language, social functions of writing, etc.).

2. According to Hammurabi's laws, those who sheltered runaway slaves deserved the death penalty. But how could one identify whether a person was a slave or not? As part of the exercise, you are required to add the information obtained from the above document into the section on slavery in the textbook (Chapter 2, p. 44, second paragraph). In so doing, you must keep the same writing style of the paragraph to gain a sense of how historians use primary sources, no matter how scattered or obscure, to construct history.

Chapter 3

Early Society in South Asia and the Indo-European Migrations

Introduction and Learning Objectives

In this chapter the authors explain how a group of Indo-Europeans called the Aryans migrated into the Indian subcontinent where the Dravidians had lived for millennia, and how the combined legacies of these two peoples led to the development of a distinctive society and a rich cultural tradition in India. Without being able to decipher the written records of the Dravidians, historians have called their complex society Harappan society (named after Harappa, one of two major Dravidian cities), which began around 3000 B.C.E. in the Indus River valley. When the Aryans accelerated their migration into India around 1500 B.C.E., however, Harappan society was in the middle of rapid decline, a process that had begun about five centuries before. The merging of the two traditions took a millennium, from 1500 to 500 B.C.E., a period that is called the Vedic Age.

In the newly formulated Indian society, large cities and a centralized state were absent, and regional kingdoms dominated agriculture and herding communities throughout most parts of the subcontinent. One of the most important issues discussed by the authors is the formation and function of the caste system. The authors argue that such a rigid hierarchical system originated through the development of class, occupational, linguistic, and skin-color distinctions between the Dravidians and the increasingly dominant Aryan migrants. As the four castes took the shape, however, they not only functioned to distinguish social classes, but served as a system of social organization, political domination, and religious order. In the end, the authors point out that the blending of Aryan and Dravidian values accounted for the development of the Upanishads, a set of religious texts that deeply influenced the development of Indian religions in later centuries.

After studying this chapter, students should understand and be able to discuss the following issues:

- archaeological discoveries that show the rise and fall of Harappan society

- the migration of Indo-Europeans throughout Eurasia

- distinctive characteristics of the Dravidian and Aryan traditions

- formation of Indian society in the Vedic age

- spiritual speculation and religious beliefs of Aryan India

Chapter Outline

I. Harappan Society

A. Foundations of Harappan Society
1. The Indus River
   a) Runs through north India, sources at Hindu Kush and the Himalayas
   b) Rich deposits, but less predictable than the Nile
   c) Wheat and barley were cultivated in Indus valley
   d) Cultivated cotton before 5000 B.C.E.
   e) Complex society of Dravidians, 3000 and 2500 B.C.E.
2. Harappa and Mohenjo-daro
   a) Harappa and Mohenjo-daro: possibly served as twin capitals
   b) Each city had a fortified citadel and a large granary
   c) Broad streets, market places, temples, public buildings
   d) Standardized weights, measures, architectural styles, and brick sizes
3. Specialized labor and trade
   a) Domestic trade, items included pottery, tools, gold, silver, copper
   b) Trading with Mesopotamians about 2300 to 1750 B.C.E.

B. Harappan Society and Culture
1. Social distinctions as seen from living styles
2. Religious beliefs strongly emphasized fertility
3. Harappan society declined from 2000 B.C.E. onward
   a) Ecological degradation led to a subsistence crisis
   b) Another possibility: natural catastrophes—floods or earthquakes
   c) Population began to abandon their cities by about 1700 B.C.E.
   d) Almost entirely collapsed by about 1500 B.C.E

II. The Indo-European Migrations and Early Aryan India

A. Indo-European Peoples and Early Aryan India
1. Indo-European languages
   a) Linguistic similarities among languages of Europe, Persia, and India
   b) Indo-European family of languages: Indo-Iranian, Greek, Balto-Slavic, Germanic, Italic, and Celtic
   c) Migrations as the key to explain linguistic similarities
2. Indo-European origins: North of the Black Sea and Caspian Sea, modern-day Ukraine and southern Russia
3. Indo-European migrations
   a) To Tarim Basin, fourth millennium B.C.E.
   b) To Anatolia (the Hittites), 3000 B.C.E.
   c) By 2nd millennium, established communities in central and western Europe

B. The Aryans and India
1. The early Aryans
   a) Depended heavily on a pastoral economy
   b) No writing system, but had orally transmitted works called the Vedas
   c) Sacred language (Sanskrit) and daily-use language (Prakit)
2. The Vedic Age: 1500 to 500 B.C.E.
   a) A boisterous period, conflict with indigenous peoples
   b) Called indigenous people *dasas*—"enemies" or "subject people"
   c) Indra, the Aryans' war god and military hero
   d) Aryan chiefdoms fought ferociously among themselves
3. Aryan migrations in India
   a) First settled in the Punjab, the upper Indus River valley
   b) Spread east and south from their base
   c) After 1000 B.C.E. settled between Himalayan foothills and Ganges River
   d) Used iron tools and developed agriculture
   e) By 500 B.C.E. migrated as far south as the northern Deccan
   f) Lost tribal organizations but established regional kingdoms

III. Vedic Society

A. Origins of the Caste System
1. Caste and *varna*
   a) The meaning of *caste*: hereditary, unchangeable social classes
   b) The Sanskrit word *varna,* "color," referring to social classes
   c) Social distinctions based on racial differences
2. Social distinctions in the late Vedic Age
   a) Four main varnas, recognized after 1000 B.C.E.
      (1) *brahmins* (priests)
      (2) *kshatriyas* (warriors and aristocrats)
      (3) *vaishyas* (cultivators, artisans, and merchants)
      (4) *shudras* (landless peasants and serfs)
   b) Later, the category of the untouchables was added
3. Subcaste or *jati*
   a) Represents more elaborate scheme of social classification, developed after the 6th century B.C.E.
   b) *Jati*, or subcastes, were determined by occupations
   c) The elaborate rules of *jati* life
4. Caste and social mobility
   a) Caste system was capable of accommodating social change
   b) Social mobility was very difficult but still possible
   c) Foreign peoples could find a place in society of the castes
B. Development of Patriarchal Society
1. Patriarchal and patrilineal society
   a) Men served as priests, warriors, and tribal chiefs
   b) Family lines based on male descendants (the patriline)
   c) Only males could inherit property
   d) Men learned the Vedas and received formal education

2. *The Lawbook of Manu*
   a) Prepared by an anonymous sage, 1st century B.C.E.
   b) Dealt with moral behavior and social relationships
   c) Advised men to treat women with honor and respect
   d) Subjected women to the control and guidance of men
   e) Women's duties: to bear children and maintain the household
3. *Sati* as a social custom

IV. Religion in the Vedic Age

A. Aryan Religion
   1. The Aryan gods
      a) The war god, Indra
      b) The gods of the sun, the sky, the moon, fire, health, disease...
      c) The god Varuna—an ethical concern
   2. Ritual sacrifices
      a) Importance of ritual sacrifices
      b) Priests were specialists of the ritual sacrifices
      c) Ritual sacrifices for rewards from the divine power
   3. Spirituality
      a) Many Aryans were dissatisfied with ritual sacrifices in late Vedic age
      b) A shift to spiritual contemplation
      c) Thoughtful individuals retreated to forests as hermits
      d) Dravidian notions of transmigration and reincarnation were adapted
B. The Blending of Aryan and Dravidian Values
   1. The Upanishads
      a) Works of religious teachings, 800 to 400 B.C.E.
      b) The religious forums: dialogues between disciples and sages
   2. Brahman: the universal soul
      a) Brahman was the only genuine reality
      b) Highest goal: to escape reincarnation and join with Brahman
   3. Teachings of the Upanishads
      a) *Samsara*: An individual soul was born many times
      b) *Karma*: specific incarnations that a soul experienced
      c) *Moksha*: permanent liberation from physical incarnation
   4. Religion and Vedic Society
      a) *Samsara* and *karma* reinforced social hierarchy
      b) Upanishads were also spiritual and intellectual contemplations
      c) Taught to observe high ethical standards
      d) Respect for all living things, a vegetarian diet

Significant Individuals

There are no significant individuals discussed in this chapter. Numerous written records of Harappan society have been uncovered, but since no one can decipher the writing, we simply know nothing about significant individuals or events that might have been recorded in these written materials. As for the writing of the Vedic Age, such writings were not records of historical events and individuals but spiritual speculations, religious teachings, and literary reflections.

Chapter Glossary

Aryans (pp. 57, 66-67) — A group of Indo-European nomadic pastoralists who migrated to India in large numbers after 1500 B.C.E.; they integrated with the indigenous Dravidians and created a new society in India.

Brahman (p. 73) — the "universal soul" described in the Upanishads, sacred texts of Aryan India; believed to be an eternal, unchanging, permanent foundation for all things that exist, hence the only genuine reality. The highest goal of an individual soul was to escape the cycle of birth and rebirth and enter into permanent union with Brahman.

caste (pp. 67-69) — Comes from the Portuguese word *casta*, referring to a social class of hereditary and usually unchangeable status. The caste system as a rigid system of social classification was first introduced into Indian society by the Aryans.

Dravidians (pp. 58-59) — Indigenous people from the valley of the Indus River. Established Harappan society by about 3000 B.C.E.

Harappa and Mohenjo-daro (pp. 59-60) — Two major cities of Harappan society, well-planned and precisely laid out, that dominated the valley of the Indus River until its collapse about 1500 B.C.E.

Harappan society (pp. 60-62) — First complex society of the Indian subcontinent. Harappan society emerged in the Indus River valley about 3000 B.C.E. and was replaced by a new society developed under Aryan influence from 1500 B.C.E. onward.

Harappan writing (p. 58-59) — Writing of the Dravidians; it used about four hundred symbols to represent sounds and words and survives on clay seals, copper tablets, and other Harappan artifacts. Scholars have not yet succeeded in deciphering these scripts.

Himalayas (pp. 59-60) — Mountains located at the northeastern edge of the Indian subcontinent. They form a natural barrier between India and China and are one of the sources of the Indus River.

Hindu Kush (pp. 59-60) — Mountains in the northern portion of the Indian subcontinent, one of the sources of the Indus River.

Indo-Europeans (pp. 63-65) — Nomadic people whose original homeland was probably the steppe region of modern-day Ukraine and southern Russia; developed their earliest communities there between about 4500 and 2500 B.C.E., and migrated to many other regions of Eurasia beginning about 4000 B.C.E.
Indo-European migrations (pp. 63-65) — Migrations of Indo-European speaking people, which continued from about 4000 to 1000 B.C.E. throughout Eurasia.

Indra (pp. 57, 71) — Aryan god, primarily a war god; depicted as a boisterous, hard-drinking warrior.

Indus River (p. 59) — One of the major rivers of the world, flowing from its sources in the Hindu Kush and the Himalayas to the Arabian Sea. The first complex society of the Indian subcontinent, Harappan society, was located in its valley.

jati (p. 68) — Subcastes of Indian society, largely determined by occupations.

karma (p. 73) — One of the important concepts in the teachings of the Upanishads; accounts for the specific incarnations that souls experienced.

Lawbook of Manu (p. 70) — Manuscript prepared by an anonymous sage of India during the first century B.C.E. or perhaps somewhat later; dealt with proper moral behavior and social relationships, including sex and gender relationships.

moksha (p. 73) — The religious goal taught by the Upanishads; a state of deep, dreamless sleep that came with permanent liberation from physical incarnation.

Prakrit (p. 65) — Language of Aryan India, not sacred but used for everyday communication.

raja (p. 66) — Title for leaders of chiefdoms of early Aryan society who governed in collaboration with a council of village elders. *Raja* was a Sanskrit term related to the Latin word *rex* ("king").

reincarnation (p. 72) — Typical of religious beliefs of Dravidians that an individual soul could depart from one body at death and become associated with another body through a new birth.

samsara (p. 73) — One of the important doctrines of the Upanishads; held that upon death, individual souls go temporarily to the World of the Fathers and then return to earth in a new incarnation.

Sanskrit (pp. 63, 65) — Sacred language of Aryan India, used only for religious purposes.

sati (p. 70) — Indian custom by which a widow voluntarily threw herself on the funeral pyre of her deceased husband to join him in death.

soma (p. 72) — Hallucinogenic concoction that produced sensations of power and divine inspiration, used in ritual sacrifices of Aryan Indians.

Upanishad (pp. 72-73) — Literally means "a sitting in front of," which referred to the practice of disciples gathering before a sage for discussion of religious issues in Aryan India. The written works that contained such discussions appeared between about 800 and 400 B.C.E., and were called the *Upanishads*.

varna (pp. 67-68) — Sanskrit word meaning "color," used by Aryans to refer to social classes. There were four main *varnas*: priests (*brahmins*); warriors and aristocrats (*kshatriyas*); cultivators, artisans, and merchants (*vaishyas*); and landless peasants and serfs *(shudras)*; all four *varnas* were above the untouchable caste.

Varuna (pp. 71-72) — Aryan god, believed to preside over the sky and oversee the behavior of mortals, who also inflicted malefactors with severe punishments.

Vedas (pp. 65-66) — Literally, *veda* in Aryan Sanskrit meant "wisdom" or "knowledge" needed by priests to carry out their functions. Refers to orally transmitted works of early Aryan priests. There are altogether four Vedas, the earliest and the most important of which is the *Rig Veda*; compiled between 1400 and 900 B.C.E., written down beginning in about 600 B.C.E.

Vedic age (p. 66) — The millennium between 1500 and 500 B.C.E. in ancient Indian history. So-called because of the importance of the Vedas as historical sources.

Map Exercises

1. Label the map below with the following information (review Map 3.1 on p. 60 of your textbook):

Indus River	Ganges River
Himalayas	Hindu Kush
Harappa	Mohenjo-daro
Iranian Plateau	Deccan Plateau

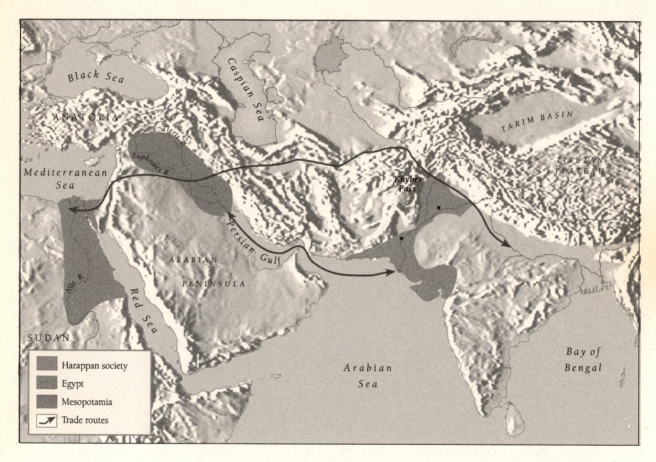

2. Write a short essay describing the Indus River and explain how it contributed to the rise of Harappan society.

3. To place the Indo-European migrations in geographical and historical context, provide dates in the following table. In some cases, dates are not available (review pp. 66-67 of your textbook).

From	To	Date
Indo-European homeland	Tarim Basin	
" " "	Persia	

			Anatolia
"	"	"	Russia
"	"	"	Indus River
"	"	"	Europe

4. Explain the importance of horses to Indo-European migrants and their interactions with other peoples.

Self Test/Student Quiz

1. Our understanding of Harappan society depends entirely on

    a. written records uncovered in Harappa and other Dravidian cities.
    b. archaeological discoveries of Harappan physical remains below the water table.
    c. archaeological discoveries of Harappan physical remains above the water table.

2. The inhabitants of Harappan society enjoyed a rich variety of diet. Their food included

    a. wheat, barley, chicken, cattle, sheep, goats
    b. soybeans, sorghum, rice, pigs, fish
    c. sweet potatoes, tomatoes, maize, cacao beans

3. In the sites of Harappa and Mohenjo-daro, archaeologists have found a high degree of standardization of weights, measures, architectural styles, and even brick sizes. Such standardization may suggest that

    a. the Harappan state was very oppressive, forcing different racial groups to adopt the same standards.
    b. there might have been a central authority powerful enough to reach all corners of society.
    c. there was a high degree of commercialization in the economy.

4. Archaeologists claim that there were sharp social distinctions in Harappan society, which can be illustrated by the people's

    a. houses, ovens, and wells.
    b. bathrooms, showers, and toilets.
    c. foods, clothes, and hairstyles.

5. Harappan religion reflected a strong concern for fertility. We know this because

    a. it was very common for the peoples in other early agricultural societies to honor fertility gods or goddesses.
    b. the bronze figurine of a dancing girl discovered at Mohenjo-daro reveals this point.
    c. of the similarities between the images of Harappan deities and the images of Hindu fertility deities.

6. By about 1700 B.C.E., the residents of Harappa and Mohenjo-daro began to abandon their cities because

    a. frequent epidemics made city-living impossible.
    b. deforestation of the Indus River valley brought about an ecological disaster.
    c. the horse-riding Aryans began to invade the cities.

7. The process of the Indo-European migrations was discovered primarily by

    a. historians.
    b. linguists.
    c. archaeologists.

8. When Indo-Europeans migrated to the Indian subcontinent, they called themselves *Aryan* or *aryo* ("noblemen" or "lords"). Based on the contexts of their migrations, possible reasons for this self-serving notion of superiority might be that

    a. they considered themselves to be the chosen people of Indra, being commissioned to conquer the world.
    b. they were at a higher level of civilization than that of the indigenous peoples.
    c. they had horse-riding advantages as well as bodily differences from the indigenous peoples.

9. From 1500 to 500 B.C.E., the period of Indian history is called the Vedic Age. It is so called because

    a. this was how the Aryans referred to this period.
    b. the four Vedas were compiled in this period.
    c. this was the period in which the Indians were particularly religious.

10. The Aryans' term for their four original castes was

    a. *jati.*
    b. *brahmins.*
    c. *varnas.*

11. The Indian caste system

    a. was a central institution that served as a principal foundation of social stability.
    b. was incapable of accommodating social changes.
    c. was actually not much of a restriction on the upward mobility of individuals.

12. One of the hymns in the *Rig Veda* offered a brief account of the origins of the four *varnas* (castes). It was said that

    a. the four castes were created according to the wills of Indra and Agni (the god of fire).
    b. Purusha, a primeval being, sacrificed himself in order to create the four castes.
    c. the four castes emanated from the four parts of Purusha when the gods sacrificed him.

13. All of the following show the subordination of women to men except

     a. the schist carving of *Mother and Child*.
     b. the *Lawbook of Manu*.
     c. the practice of *sati*.

14. Aryan religion during the early Vedic Age was relatively unconcerned with ethics, but concerned itself more with

     a. ritual sacrifices and the god of war.
     b. fertility and immortality.
     c. spirituality and meditation.

15. The Upanishads can be best characterized as

     a. the spiritual longing of the Aryans.
     b. the further development of the religious tradition of the Dravidians.
     c. the blending of Aryan and Dravidian values.

16. According to the teachings of the Upanishads, the highest goal of the individual soul was

     a. to attain the state of *samsara*.
     b. to attain the state of *moksha*.
     c. to avoid one's *karma*.

17. According to the authors, the Upanishads can be best understood as

     a. an ideology designed to justify social inequalities imposed by the caste system.
     b. a set of doctrines that concentrated on spiritual and intellectual problems.
     c. a combination of the above two.

18. In one portion of the *Chandogya Upanishad* (cited in Chapter 3 of your textbook, p. 74), a man explained to his son how

     a. bees made honey.
     b. the subtle essence of Brahman pervaded everything.
     c. individuals were separate in universal reality.

19. According to the teachings of the Upanishads, an individual should

     a. be attached to the material world as closely as possible.
     b. ignore ethical standards, since these standards were not the ultimate reality.
     c. observe high ethical standards.

20. Believers in the Upanishads respect all living things, including animals and insects, especially because

     a. human beings are not superior to animals and insects, which also participate in a large cosmic order and form small parts of the universal soul known as Brahman.

b.   animals and insects might well hold incarnations of unfortunate souls suffering the effects of a heavy debt of karma.

c.   none of the above are true.

Textual Questions for Analysis

1.   "If the Greek historian Herodotus had known of Harappan society, he might have called it 'the gift of the Indus,'" reminiscent of his views of Egypt (p. 59 of your textbook). In what ways did Harappan society resemble Egyptian society?

2.   Should scholars one day be able to decipher the Harappan writings, how might the Dravidians have described the decline of their society? What were the possible causes of the decline that you might expect to find in Dravidian records?

3.   What facts contributed to the successful migrations of the Indo-Europeans throughout Eurasia?

4.   Without a powerful centralized government, large military forces, and fortified citadels, how did Vedic India achieve its high level of social stability?

5.   In what sense can we say that the teachings of the Upanishads were the blending of Aryan and Dravidian values?

6.   What were the basic doctrines of the Upanishads? How would you evaluate these doctrines?

Documentary Evidence

I. The Rig Veda

The *Rig Veda* contained 1,028 hymns addressed to Aryan gods, which were orally transmitted between about 1400 and 900 B.C.E. They were eventually compiled in written form (along with the three later Vedas) in about 600 B.C.E. The following hymn is taken from the *Rig Veda*. Apparently intended to be humorous and entertaining, this hymn probably was used as a work song by priests engaged in the pressing of "soma," a psychoactive drug used in Vedic ritual. (From *The Rig Veda: An Anthology*. Translated by Wendy Doniger O'Flaherty [New York: Penguin Books, 1981], p. 235).

Our thought brings us to diverse callings, setting people apart: the carpenter seeks what is broken, the physician a fracture, and the Brahmin priest seeks one who presses Soma. O drop of Soma, flow for Indra.

With his dried twigs, with feathers of large birds, and with stones, the smith seeks all his days a man with gold. O drop of Soma, flow for Indra.

I am a poet; my dad's a physician and Mum a miller with grinding stones. With diverse thoughts we all strive for wealth, going after it like cattle. O drop of Soma, flow for Indra.

The harnessed horse longs for a light cart; seducers long for a woman's smile; the penis for the two hairy lips, and the frog for water. O drop of Soma, flow for Indra.

QUESTIONS TO CONSIDER

1. How many occupations can you identify from this hymn? Can you put them into the categories of the four castes?

2. What was the author's attitude toward life? How do you compare the values expressed in this hymn with the Upanishads' emphasis on spirituality and asceticism?

Chapter 4

Early Society in East Asia

Introduction and Learning Objectives

This chapter opens with the legends of three sage kings venerated by the Chinese throughout their history. One of the legends was about the heroic figure of flood control who founded the first dynasty of China, a story that relates well to the recurrent theme of the origins of complex societies discussed in previous chapters. Having little contact with the peoples of Mesopotamia or India, the Chinese developed a distinctive complex society and cultural tradition of their own in the valley of the Yellow River. From neolithic settlements to the development of a complex society, the story of China once again demonstrates the potential of settled agriculture to support urbanization and large-scale political organization.

Through discussion of the rise and fall of the three successive dynasties established along the valley of the Yellow River, the authors raise a number of important questions: Why did China adopt decentralized administration? How did bronze and iron technologies affect the political organization of the Shang and Zhou states respectively? How did the Zhou rulers use the theory of the mandate of heaven to justify their overthrow of the Shang instead of adopting a theory of Darwinian justice (might is right)? Why was the veneration of ancestors important to the Chinese? What might have caused change from matrilineal society to patrilineal society in China? How did the practice of divination lead to the Chinese writing system, which in turn led to the flourishing of Chinese literature? After discussing these issues, the authors end the chapter with an exploration of China's expansion through interactions with the indigenous peoples to their north, west, and south. These interactions led to different consequences conditioned by environmental factors: the people in the south, where natural conditions were suitable for agriculture, rapidly adopted Chinese ways of life while the peoples in the steppelands of the north and west developed nomadic societies.

After studying this chapter, students should understand and be able to discuss the following issues:

- the strengths and weaknesses of ancient Chinese political organization

- the importance of Chinese family and kinship

- Chinese writing and cultural development

- China's expansion and its interactions with the surrounding indigenous peoples

Chapter Outline

I. Introduction

A. Ancient Chinese Legends: The Three Sage Kings
   1. King Yao: a virtuous ruler bringing harmony to society
   2. King Shun: regulating the four seasons, weights, measures, and units of time
   3. King Yu: rescued China from raging floods of the Yellow River
   4. Legends reflected the values of the society

B. The Appearance of Humans in East Asia
   1. Beginnings were over two hundred thousand years ago
   2. Domesticated rice around 7000 B.C.E. in the valley of the Yangzi River
   3. Millet cultivation in the valley of the Yellow River
   4. Wheat and barley became staple foods of north China by 2000 B.C.E.

C. Emergence of a Complex Society: Second Millennium B.C.E.
   1. Agricultural villages appeared in the valleys of the two rivers
   2. Cities and states appeared in north China during the second millennium B.C.E.
   3. The three dynastic states in the valley of Yellow River: Xia, Shang, and Zhou

II. Political Organization in Early China

A. Early Agricultural Society and the Xia Dynasty
   1. The Yellow River
      a) Water source at high plateau of Tibet
      b) Loess soil carried by the river's water, hence "yellow"
      c) The river was "China's Sorrow"
      d) Loess provided rich soil, soft and easy to work
   2. Neolithic societies after 5000 B.C.E.
      a) Yangshao society, 5000-3000 B.C.E.
      b) Excavations at Banpo village: fine pottery, bone tools
   3. The Xia dynasty
      a) Archeological discovery of the Xia is still in its preliminary stage
      b) Established about 2200 B.C.E.
      c) Legendary King Yu, the dynasty founder, a hero of flood control
      d) Erlitou: possibly the capital city of the Xia

B. The Shang Dynasty: 1766-1122 B.C.E.
   1. Arose in the southern and eastern areas of the Xia realm
   2. Many written records and material remains discovered
   3. Bronze metallurgy, monopolized by ruling elite
   4. Agricultural surpluses supported large troops
   5. A vast network of walled towns
   6. The Shang capital moved six times
   7. Lavish tombs of Shang kings
      a) Thousands of objects—chariots, weapons, bronze goods
      b) Sacrificial human victims, dogs, horses

C. The Zhou Dynasty: 1122-256 B.C.E.
  1. The rise of the Zhou
      a) The last Shang king was a bad ruler
      b) The Zhou forces toppled the Shang
  2. Mandate of heaven—the right to rule
      a) The Zhou needed to justify the overthrow
      b) Ruler as "the son of heaven"
      c) Mandate of heaven only given to virtuous rulers
  3. Political organization
      a) Adopted decentralized administration
      b) Used princes and relatives to rule regions
      c) Consequence: weak central government and rise of regional powers
  4. Iron metallurgy
      a) Iron metallurgy spread in China, the 1st millennium B.C.E.
      b) Iron weapons helped regional authorities to resist the central power
  5. The fall of the Zhou
      a) Nomadic invasion sacked Zhou capital in 711 B.C.E.
      b) Territorial princes became more independent
      c) The Warring States (403-221 B.C.E.)
      d) The last king of the Zhou abdicated his position in 256 B.C.E.

III. Society and Family in Ancient China

A. The Social Order
  1. The ruling elites
      a) Royal family and allied noble families at the top
      b) Their lavish consumption of bronze products
      c) Hereditary aristocrats with extensive landholding
  2. Specialized labor
      a) Free artisans and craftsmen highly demanded
      b) Also served the needs of the ruling elites
  3. Merchants and trade were important
      a) Jade from central Asia
      b) Military technologies came through central Asia from Mesopotamia
      c) Tin from southeast Asia
      d) A few pieces of pottery from Mohenjo-daro
  4. Peasants, the majority of population
      a) Landless peasants provided labor
      b) Lived in small subterranean houses
      c) Women's work—wine making, weaving, silkworm raising
      d) Wood, bone, stone tools before iron was spread in the 6th century B.C.E.
  5. Slaves
      a) Mostly war prisoners
      b) Performed hard work
      c) Became sacrificial victims, especially during the Shang

B. Family and Patriarchy
  1. Early dynasties ruled through family and kinship groups
  2. Veneration of ancestors
     a) Belief in ancestors' presence and their continuing influence
     b) Burial of material goods with the dead
     c) Offering sacrifices at the graves
     d) Family heads presided over rites of honoring ancestors' spirits
  3. Patriarchal society
     a) During neolithic times, Chinese society was matrilineal
     b) The rise of large states brought focus on men's contribution
     c) After the Shang, not even queens and empresses merited temples

IV. Early Chinese Writing and Cultural Development

A. The Secular Cultural Tradition
  1. Absence of organized religion and priestly class
  2. Believed in the impersonal heavenly power—*tian*
  3. Oracle bones and early Chinese writing
     a) Oracle bones
        (1) Primary instruments of fortune-tellers
        (2) Discovery of the "dragon bones" in 1890s
        (3) Bones recorded day-to-day concerns of the Shang royal court
     b) Early Chinese writing
        (1) Earliest form was the pictograph
        (2) From pictograph to ideograph
        (3) Absence of alphabetic or phonetic component
        (4) More than two thousand characters identified on oracle bones
        (5) Modern Chinese writing is direct descendant of Shang writing
B. Thought and Literature
  1. Zhou literature
     a) *The Book of Change*, a manual of diviners
     b) *The Book of History*, the history of the Zhou
     c) *The Book of Rites*, the rules of etiquette and rituals for aristocrats
     d) *The Book of Songs*
        (1) The most notable of the classic works
        (2) Verses on themes both light and serious
        (3) Reflected social conditions of the early Zhou
  2. Destruction of early Chinese literature
     a) Most Zhou writings have perished
     b) The first Qin emperor ordered the destruction of most writings

V. The Broad Influence of Ancient Chinese Society

A. Chinese Cultivators and Nomadic Peoples of Central Asia
  1. Steppelands
     a) Foragers domesticated herds of animals on grassy lands
     b) Became nomads, the ancestors of Turks and Mongols

2. Nomadic society
    a) Little farming, but relied on herding animals
    b) Exchange of products between nomads and Chinese farmers
    c) Nomads frequently invaded rich agricultural society
    d) Nomads did not imitate Chinese ways
    e) Nomadism relied on grains and manufactured goods of the Chinese
B. The Southern Expansion of Chinese Society
    1. The Yangzi valley
        a) The Yangzi, the longest river of China
        b) Two crops of rice per year in ancient China
        c) The Yangzi was dependable and beneficial to farmers
    2. The indigenous peoples of southern China
        a) Many were assimilated into Chinese agricultural society
        b) Some were pushed to hills and mountains
        c) Some migrated to Taiwan, Vietnam, Thailand
    3. The state of Chu
        a) Emerged in the central region of the Yangzi during the late Zhou
        b) Challenged the Zhou for supremacy
        c) Adopted Chinese ways

Significant Individuals

The chapter does not provide specific names of significant individuals other than the mythical founders of ancient China—Yao, Shun, and Yu (see Chapter Glossary below).

Chapter Glossary

Ao (p. 83) — Earliest capital of the Shang, near modern Zhengzhou. The most remarkable feature of this site is the city wall, with part of it still surviving today.

Banpo village (p. 81) — An entire neolithic village of Yangshao society, discovered in 1952 at Banpo, near modern Xi'an. The site contained a large quantity of finely painted pottery and bone tools used by early cultivators in the sixth and fifth millennia B.C.E.

Book of Changes (p. 95) — A diviners' manual, a Chinese classic, written during Zhou times, still influential today among diviners and geomancers of east Asia.

Book of Etiquette (p. 95) — A manual of aristocrats regarding the art of polite behavior and the proper way of conducting rituals. One of classics of ancient China; also known as the *Book of Rites*.

Book of History (p. 95) — A collection of documents that justified the Zhou state and called for subjects to obey their overlords. One of the Chinese classics.

Book of Songs (p. 95) — One of China's classic works; a collection of poems and folksongs on various topics. Compiled after 600 B.C.E., but reflected conditions of the early Zhou dynasty. Also known as *Book of Poetry* or *Book of Odes*.

"China's Sorrow" (p. 81) —Referring to the Yellow River for its frequent destruction brought by flooding.

Erlitou (p. 82) — Site of the excavation of an ancient city of China near Luoyang, possibly the capital of the Xia dynasty. Excavations have shown that the city featured a large, palace-type structure as well as more modest houses, pottery workshops, and a bronze foundry.

ideograph (p. 94) — Two or more pictographs combined into one character to express complex or abstract notions. Typical of Chinese writing.

loess (pp. 80-81) — Extremely fine, powderlike soil carried by the Yellow River and deposited on the plains of northern China; created fertile soil for Chinese agriculture. Found also in several other parts of the world.

mandate of heaven (pp. 84-85) — Political theory of ancient China, referring to divine source for political legitimacy of rulers. Heaven only gave the mandate, or the right to rule, to virtuous rulers. First advocated by the Zhou rulers to justify their overthrow of the Shang.

nomadic society (p. 96) — Society of steppelands to the north and west of China; the people had little agriculture but relied on herding animals; they depended on the agricultural society of China for grains and finished products.

oracle bones (p. 93) — Principal instruments used by fortune-tellers or diviners in ancient China. Questions were inscribed on broad bones of large animals or turtle shells, and when heated, the bones or shells would produce splits and cracks, which were interpreted by diviners to determine the answers.

Shang (pp. 82-83) — Second dynasty of China, changed its capitals six times along the valley of Yellow River. Famous for its bronze arts and writings on oracle bones. Lasted from 1766 to 1122 B.C.E.

Shun (p. 79-80) — One of the three sage kings in ancient Chinese legends; allegedly ordered the four seasons and issued uniform weights, measures, and units of time.

son of heaven (p. 85) — Title for a Chinese ruler; so called because he was supposed to serve as a link between heaven and earth, to govern conscientiously, to observe high standards of honor and justice, and to maintain order and harmony within his realm.

The state of Chu (p. 99) — A powerful state that emerged during the late Zhou in the central region of the Yangzi River; governed its affairs autonomously and challenged the Zhou for supremacy.

steppelands (p. 96) — Dry and grassy lands of central Asia, to the north and west of China; inhospitable to foragers and cultivators.

tian (p. 92) — Chinese word for "heaven"; an important concept referring to impersonal heavenly power, or an agent responsible for bestowing and removing the power of rulers; first appeared in the Zhou dynasty.

veneration of ancestors (p. 90) — Popular religion of China since neolithic times; based on the belief that spirits of one's ancestors passed into another realm of existence from which they had the power to support and protect their surviving families if the descendants displayed proper respect and ministered to the spirits' needs.

The Warring States (p. 86) — Period of Chinese history which lasted from 403 to 221 B.C.E. A number of states resorted to military campaigns against one another, struggling for hegemony over China, as the central government of the Zhou became powerless. The prolonged civil wars were finally brought to an end by the unification of the Qin state.

Xia (pp. 81-82) — First dynasty of China, founded by Yu in the valley of the Yellow River, 2200 to 1766 B.C.E. So far no certain archaeological sites have been connected to it.

Yangshao Society (p. 81) — Neolithic society of China, flourished from about 5000 to 3000 B.C.E. in the middle region of the Yellow River valley.

Yangzi River (p. 98) — River in the southern part of China, flowing from mountains of Tibet in the west to the East China Sea in the east. Very dependable for rice farmers and important for water transport.

Yao (p. 79-80) — One of the three sage kings in ancient Chinese legends. A towering figure, extraordinarily modest, sincere, and respectful, whose virtuous influence brought harmony to his own family and the larger society.

Yellow River (pp. 80-81) — River of north China; flows from the west starting at the high plateau of Tibet eastward into the Yellow Sea. The complex society of East Asia originated from the valley of this river.

Yin (p. 83) — Another capital of Shang, near modern Anyang. The site of this city includes a complex of royal palaces, archives with written documents, several residential neighborhoods, two large bronze foundries, several workshops of craftsmen, and burial grounds.

Yu (p. 79-80) — One of the three sage kings in ancient Chinese legends. Allegedly the founder of the Xia dynasty; possibly a real Chinese ruler. Revered for his deeds of bringing the Yellow River under control.

Zhou (pp. 84-86) — Third Chinese dynasty. Originally a vassal kingdom of Shang in the west region. Overthrew the Shang in 1122 B.C.E. and established a new dynasty that lasted until 256 B.C.E.

Map Exercises

1. On the following map, label the six capital cities of early China and its two major rivers (based on Map 4.1 on p. 82 of your textbook):

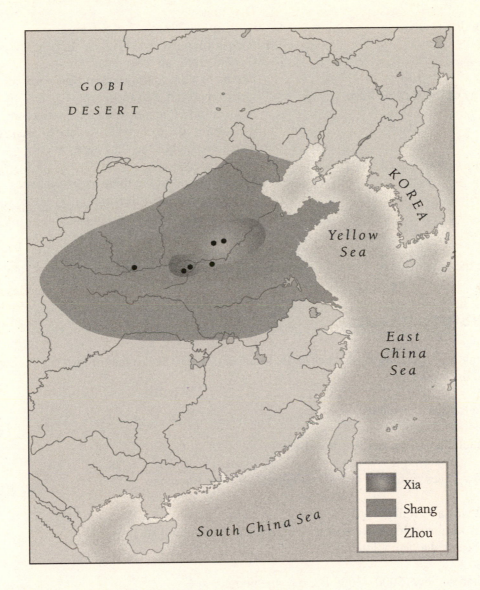

2. Match the dynasties on the left with their capitals on the right:

Dynasty	Capital
Xia	Ao, Yin
Shang	Erlitou
Zhou	Hao, Luoyang

3. Match the regions on the right with their descriptions on the left (consult Map 4.3, p. 97, of your textbook and the accompanying text):

Region	Description
	Loess soil, medium rain fall
	Dry, grassy
Steppelands	Cultivation of millet, wheat, barley
	Rice cultivation
	Copious rain fall
	Not hospitable for cultivators, but good for herding
The valley of the Yellow River	Great importance of irrigation
	Subject to frequent destruction by flooding
	The origin of the complex society of East Asia
	The homeland of the Chu state
The valley of the Yangzi River	Nomadic economy
	The homeland of the three early dynasties
	No city, state, or settled life
	Where oracle bones were found

4. Describe the expansion of China through interactions with peoples in the north, west, and south.

Self Test/Student Quiz

1. By exalting the legendary sage kings (Yao, Shun, and Yu) as exemplars of virtue, Chinese moralists promoted the values of

    a. agricultural society.
    b. political authority.
    c. social harmony, selflessness, hard work.

2. The Yellow River earned its nickname "China's Sorrow" because

    a. it was a turbulent river.
    b. its frequent floods were very destructive to agricultural society.
    c. it carried a heavy load of loess.

3. In Yangshao society (5000 - 3000 B.C.E.), the people

    a. had fine pottery and used bone tools.
    b. cultivated rice through irrigation.
    c. began to use bronze tools.

4. Many scholars believe that the first dynasty of China, Xia, was not a mere legend, but a real state, because

    a. Erlitou, the capital of Xia, has been excavated.
    b. the oracle bones of Shang mentioned the Xia kings.
    c. the Chinese legends associated the founder of Xia with flood control.

5. The Shang rulers monopolized bronze technology for no other purpose than

    a. making superior weapons against potential competitors.
    b. distributing bronze tools among the farmers.
    c. preventing proliferation of weapons.

6. All of the following were found in the tomb of Fu Hao, except

    a. bronzes, cowrie shells, pottery, ivory.
    b. human victims, dogs, bone carvings.
    c. mummification of the body, paintings on tomb walls.

7. According to Zhou political theory, the Zhou king overthrew the Shang dynasty because

    a. the Shang lost the mandate of heaven.
    b. the subjects of Shang shifted their loyalty to Zhou.
    c. the last Shang king was a criminal fool.

8. The Chinese king was called the "son of heaven" who served as

    a. an unchallengable ruler.
    b. a link between heaven and earth.
    c. a god king.

9. To rule an extensive territory without advanced transportation and communication technology, Zhou rulers relied on decentralized administration, which meant that

    a. they entrusted power to locally elected authorities.
    b. they entrusted their relatives to rule the regions of their kingdom.
    c. they divided powers into three parts: legislative, judicial, and administrative.

10. Unlike bronze technology that strengthened Shang rulers, iron technology undermined the power of the Zhou central government because

    a. the Zhou kings were not able to monopolize iron production.
    b. iron weapons were of such poor quality that they were no match for bronze weapons.
    c. the Zhou rulers spent too much money on iron weaponry.

11. All of the following were social classes of Xia, Shang, and Zhou, except

    a. hereditary aristocrats, scholars, bureaucrats.
    b. craftsmen, merchants, peasants, slaves.
    c. priests, emperor, monks.

12. The tradition of venerating ancestors was firmly established during the Xia, Shang, and Zhou dynasties. According to this tradition,

    a. one must treat the ancestors as gods or deities.
    b. one worshipped the departed ancestors for protection and good fortune.
    c. one only venerated those ancestors who performed good deeds for the family.

13. In practice, the veneration of ancestors reinforced the authority of the patriarchal head of the family because

    a. only male ancestors were the subjects of worship.
    b. female members of the family did not participate in honoring ancestors.
    c. he was the one who presided at the rites honoring ancestors.

14. During the Xia, Shang, and Zhou dynasties China experienced the shift from a matrilineal society to a patrilineal society. This was caused by

    a. settled agriculture.
    b. the rise of large states.
    c. bronze metallurgy.

15. During Shang times, Chinese diviners used oracle bones

    a. primarily to help kings make decisions.
    b. as drugs to cure people's diseases.
    c. primarily to record important events of the royal family.

16. From Shang times until today, Chinese writing is primarily

    a. ideographic.
    b. pictographic.
    c. phonetic.

17. All but one of the following were not part of Zhou culture:

    a. poems, art of foretelling the future.
    b. political history, art of polite behavior and performing rituals.
    c. art of god worship, religious teachings.

18. The nomadic peoples to the north and west of China did not imitate Chinese ways because

    a. they did not speak Chinese.
    b. the grassy steppelands were suitable for their pastoral nomadism.
    c. the Chinese were their enemies.

19. During the Zhou dynasty China expanded into the Yangzi River valley primarily through

    a. military conquest and colonization.
    b. migration and assimilation.
    c. inter-racial marriage.

20. The state of Chu

    a. was an autonomous state to the south of the Zhou state.
    b. refused to accept Chinese traditions and writing system.
    c. established a society radically different from that of north China.

Textual Questions for Analysis

1. Based on your understanding of the legend of the sage king Yu as well as the environmental conditions of the Yellow River, write a short essay on the development of river valley agriculture and the rise of the state in that region.

2. Why did Chinese rulers prefer decentralized administration? What were the strengths and weaknesses of this form of government?

3. What was the content of "the mandate of heaven"? What did the Zhou rulers intend to do by advocating such a political theory? Would this theory also put a check on the Zhou rulers themselves?

4. Explain the differential effects of bronze on the Shang and of iron on the Zhou.

5. How did the practice of veneration of ancestors reinforce the Chinese family as a central institution and the family head as an indisputable authority? How did the centrality of family influence political organization?

6. It seems that the development of large states was always accompanied by the deterioration of women's position. Write a short essay to argue that this was not a mere coincidence. You are encouraged to use comparisons with Mesopotamia, Egypt, and India to develop your answer.

7. From Xia to Zhou, China expanded rapidly. Explain the economic drive behind this territorial expansion.

Documentary Evidence

Oracle-Bone Inscriptions

As we now know, royal diviners of the Shang inscribed questions on shoulder blades of large animals or turtle shells, sometimes with alternative answers on both sides of a bone or shell. When heated with a piece of hot metal, the bone or shell would crack, and the patterns of cracks would be interpreted to determine an answer. The standard form for an oracle-bone inscription usually included the following parts:

a) Preface: a description of when the divination took place.
b) Charge: a statement of a potential prediction, sometimes presented as two charges, one for each possible outcome.
c) Prognostication: a statement of the outcome of the divination, predicting one or another charge.
d) Verification: a statement of whether the prediction came true.

The following is an example of an oracle-bone inscription asking about the advisability of attacking Zhou, a subordinate state of Shang at the time (From David N. Keightley, *Sources of Shang History: The Oracle-Bone Inscriptions of Bronze Age China*. Berkeley, Calf.: University of California Press, 1978, p. 43):

The Chinese Inscription:

Translation (with some rearrangement for convenience of reading):

(Preface:)	Crack-making on *guichou* (day 50), Zheng divined:
(Charge:)	"From today to *dingsu* (day 54) we will harm the Zhou."
(Prognostication:)	The king, reading the cracks, said: "(Down to) *dingsu* (day 54) we should not perhaps harm (them); on the coming *jiazi* (day 1) we will harm (them)."
(Verification:)	...On the eleventh day, *guihai* (day 60), (our) chariots did not harm (them); in the *tou* period between that evening and *jiazi* (day 1), (we) really harmed (them).

QUESTIONS TO CONSIDER

1. Who made the charge? Who interpreted the pattern of cracks? By using the oracle bone, was the king trying to convince himself or his generals? Add your answers or speculations to the section "Oracle Bones and Early Chinese Writing" on pp. 93-94 of your textbook.

2. Compare and contrast Chinese writing and cuneiform writing of ancient Mesopotamia (see the Documentary Evidence section of Chapter 2 in this study guide).

Chapter 5

Early Societies in the Americas and Oceania

Introduction and Learning Objectives

Who were the ancient peoples of the Americas and Oceania? Where were they from originally? What kinds of societies did they develop over the centuries? How did their cultural traditions and societies differ or resemble those developed in ancient Eurasia and north Africa? Despite the scarcity of written records, the authors nevertheless provide informative discussions on these issues. Common to these societies were their relative isolation, lack of iron metallurgy, and the absence of transportation by large animals and wheeled vehicles, which set limits for their development. The authors' discussion emphasizes relationships among migration, development of settled agriculture, and the rise of complex societies.

After the arrival of migrants to the Americas from northeast Asia, the Americas experienced a transition from hunting and gathering society to agricultural society as hunting big game became increasingly difficult. As a result, several distinctive cultures arose in Mesoamerica: the Olmecs, the Maya, and a northern Mexican city-state known as Teotihuacan. In the Andean region of the South American continent, agriculture also supported complex societies such as those of Chavín cult and Mochica state.

In Oceania, migrants from southeast Asia created settlements in Australia and New Guinea beginning somewhere in the period of 120,000 to 60,000 years ago. Agriculture was not developed in these islands, but in New Guinea agriculture was introduced around 3,000 B.C.E. by new groups of migrants called Austronesians. With their extraordinary navigational skills and agricultural expertise, these Austronesian-speaking peoples fanned out further to most islands in the Pacific. Because of the abundance of natural plants and game, the peoples in Australia maintained their foraging societies until modern times while the peoples in other Oceaniac islands began to settle in agricultural communities and develop their chiefly political organizations.

After reading this chapter, students should understand and be able to discuss:

- patterns of migration in the Americas and Oceania

- the significance of agriculture for the development of complex societies

- the cultural achievements of the Olmec, Maya, and Teotihuacan in Mesoamerica

- the Chavín cult and Mochican society in the Andean region of South America

- the impact of Austronesian-speaking peoples throughout Oceania

Chapter Outline

I. **Early Societies of Mesoamerica**

   A. The Olmecs
      1. Migration to Mesoamerica
         a) Humans traveled from Siberia to Alaska, 40,000 years ago, in search of big game
         b) By 7000 B.C.E., reached the southern-most part of South America
         c) As hunting became difficult, agriculture began, 7500 B.C.E.
      2. Early agriculture in Mesoamerica
         a) Beans, chili peppers, avocados, squashes, gourds were cultivated first
         b) By 5000 B.C.E., discovered potential of maize, the staple food
         c) Later, developed tomatoes
         d) Agricultural villages appeared after 3000 B.C.E.
         e) No large animals, no wheeled vehicles
      3. Ceremonial centers, by the end of the 2nd millennium B.C.E.
      4. Olmecs: The "rubber people"
         a) Earliest center, on the coast of Mexico Gulf, 1200 B.C.E.
         b) Built by Olmecs, the "rubber people"
         c) Served as the capital for 400 years
         d) The other two later centers: La Venta and Tres Zapotes
      5. Olmec society
         a) Authoritarian in nature
         b) The colossal human heads—possibly likenesses of rulers
         c) Rulers' power as shown in construction of huge pyramids
      6. Trade in jade and obsidian
      7. Decline and fall of Olmec society
         a) The cause remains a mystery
         b) The Olmecs systematically destroyed their ceremonial centers
         c) Most likely, civil conflict ruined their society
         d) By 400 B.C.E., other societies eclipsed the Olmecs
      8. Influence of Olmec traditions
         a) Maize, ceremonial centers were common to later societies
         b) Other legacies: Calendar, rituals of human sacrifice, ballgame
         c) Olmecs did not leave written records
   B. Heirs of the Olmecs: The Maya
      1. The Maya
         a) Earliest heir of the Olmecs, lived in highlands of Guatemala
         b) Kaminaljuyú, a ceremonial center, but not a full-fledged city
         c) Teotihuacan became dominant during the 4th century C.E.
         d) After the 4th century, society flourished in lowlands
         e) Besides maize, also cultivated cotton and cacao
      2. Tikal
         a) Most important Maya political center, 300 to 900 C.E.
         b) A bustling city of 40,000 people
         c) Enormous plazas, scores of temples, pyramids, palaces

3. Maya warfare
    a) Victorious warriors won enormous prestige
    b) War captives became slaves or sacrificial victims to gods
4. Chichén Itzá
    a) Rose as a power by the 9th century
    b) Organized a loose empire in the northern Yucatan
5. Maya decline
    a) Began in 800 C.E., the Mayas (except in Chichén Itzá) deserted their cities
    b) Causes of decline remain unclear
C. Maya Society and Religion
1. Maya society
    a) Kings, priests, and hereditary nobility at the top
    b) Merchants were from the ruling class, served also as ambassadors
    c) Professional architects and artisans were important
    d) Peasants and slaves were majority of population
2. The Maya calendar
    a) Maya priests understood planetary cycles and could predict eclipses
    b) Besides the solar year, also had a ritual year of 260 days and 20 months
    c) Combined attributes of the two calendars determined the fortune of activities
3. Maya writing
    a) Contained both ideographic elements and symbols for syllables
    b) Maya scribes used writing extensively
    c) Only 4 books survived the destruction by Spanish conquerors
4. Religious thought
    a) *Popol Vuh*, a Maya creation myth, taught that gods created humans out of maize and water
    b) Gods maintained agricultural cycles in exchange for honors and sacrifices
5. Bloodletting rituals
    a) The most important rituals, to honor the gods for rains
    b) Besides sacrificing captives, also voluntary bloodshedding
6. The Maya ballgame
    a) Played by two individuals or two teams
    b) Very popular, every ceremonial center had stone-paved courts
D. Heirs of the Olmecs: Teotihuacan
1. The city of Teotihuacan
    a) Built in the highlands of Mexico
    b) Colossal pyramids of sun and moon dominated the skyline
    c) High point between 400 and 600 C.E., the city had 200,000 inhabitants
    d) Paintings and murals reflect the importance of priests
2. Teotihuacan society
    a) Rulers and priests dominated society
    b) Two-thirds of the city inhabitants worked in fields during daytime
    c) Artisans were famous for their obsidian tools and orange pottery
    d) Professional merchants traded extensively throughout Mesoamerica
    e) No sign of military organization or conquest
3. Cultural traditions
    a) Inherited Olmecs' culture: ballgame, calendar, writing, human sacrifices
    b) Honored an earth god and a rain god

4. Decline of Teotihuacan
    a) Faced military pressure from other peoples since 500 C.E.
    b) Began to decline about 650 C.E.
    c) Invaders sacked and ruined the city, mid-8th century

II. Early Societies of South America

A. Early Andean Society and the Chavín cult
    1. Early migration
        a) By 12,000 B.C.E. hunting and gathering peoples reached South America
        b) By 8000 B.C.E. began to experiment with agriculture
        c) Complex societies appeared in central Andean region after 1000 B.C.E.
        d) Andean societies located in modern day Peru and Bolivia
        e) Geography hindered communication between Andeans and Mesoamericans as well as within the Andean region
    2. Early agriculture in South America
        a) Main crops: beans, peanuts, sweet potatoes, cotton
        b) Fishing supplemented agricultural harvests
        c) By 1800 B.C.E., produced pottery, built temples and pyramids
    3. The Chavín Cult
        a) Very popular around 900 to 800 B.C.E, but vanished completely by about 300 B.C.E.
        b) The rise of the cult was probably related to introduction of maize
        c) The cult left large temple complexes and elaborate art works
    4. Complexity of Andean society
        a) Devised techniques of producing cotton textiles and fishing nets
        b) Discovered gold, silver, and copper metallurgy
        c) Cities began to appear shortly after Chavín cult
        d) Early Andeans did not make use of writing
B. Early Andean States: Mochica (300-700 C.E.)
    1. The Mochica state—one of several early Andean states, located in northern Peru
    2. Mochica ceramics: lives of different social classes
    3. Like other Andean states, Mochica did not integrate the whole Andean region

III. Early Society of Oceania

A. Early Societies in Australia and New Guinea
    1. Early migrations
        a) Human migrants arrived in Australia and New Guinea at least 60,000 years ago
        b) By the mid-centuries of the first millennium C.E., human communities in all habitable islands of the Pacific Ocean
        c) About 10,000 years ago, rising seas separated Australia and New Guinea
        d) Australia: hunting and gathering until the 19th and 20th centuries C.E.
        e) New Guinea: Turned to agriculture about 3000 B.C.E.
    2. Early hunting and gathering societies in Australia
        a) Small communities, seasonal migrations for food
        b) Plant-based diet of the Australian peoples
        c) Animals and fish were also in their diet

3. Austronesian peoples
   a) From southeast Asia, spoke Austronesian languages
   b) Processed remarkable seafaring skills
   c) Settled in north New Guinea, 3000 B.C.E.
4. Early agriculture in New Guinea
   a) Austronesians introduced root crops and herding animals
   b) Indigenous peoples soon began to cultivate crops and keep animals
   c) Agriculture brought population growth and specialization
B. The Peopling of the Pacific Islands
   1. Austronesian migration to Polynesia
      a) Outrigger canoes enabled them to sail safely
      b) Agriculture and domesticated animals helped them to settle in new-found islands
   2. Austronesian migrations to Micronesia and Madagascar
      a) Early agriculture in the resource-poor Pacific islands
      b) Chiefly political organization
         (1) Strong chiefly societies found on large islands—Tonga, Samoa, Hawaii
         (2) Chiefs and their retinues claimed a portion of agricultural surplus
         (3) Oversaw irrigation systems, public rituals
         (4) Chiefs and aristocrats regarded themselves as divine or semidivine

Significant Individuals

Because very little writing survives from the early societies of America and Oceania, we cannot speak of certain significant individuals who contributed to the development of the two societies.

Chapter Glossary

Austronesians (p. 121) — Seafaring peoples from southeast Asia who first entered New Guinea and surrounding islands about 5,000 years ago. Their skills of navigation, agriculture, and raising domestic animals helped them to people most islands of the Pacific.

bloodletting rituals (pp. 103, 112) — Rituals practiced by Mayans with the belief that such sacrifices would please the gods who, in turn, would send rain to sustain agriculture.

cacao (p. 108) — Large beans first cultivated by the Mayans, which were the source of chocolate. Cacao was a precious commodity consumed mostly by nobles in Mayan society, and cacao beans were also used as money.

Chavín cult (pp. 117-18) — Popular religious cult of the Andeans, centered at the modern location of Chavín de Huantar in northern Peru.

Chichén Itzá (p. 109-10) — A city-kingdom of the Maya, located in the northern Yucatan peninsula. Between the ninth and eleventh centuries C.E., Chichén Itzá organized a loose empire that brought a measure of political stability to the Maya.

Kaminaljuyú (p. 108) — One of the most prominent ceremonial centers of the Maya, located on the site of modern Guatemala.

maize (p. 105) — Most important staple food crop of the early societies of the Americas.

Maya (pp. 108-14) — Complex society of Mesoamerica; inherited the Olmec cultural traditions; had agricultural settlements and grand ceremonial centers in southern Mexico (including the Yucatan peninsula), Guatemala, Belize, Honduras, and El Salvador.

Maya calendar (pp. 112-13) — Most elaborate calendar of the ancient Americas. It combined two kinds of years into one system: a solar year of 365 days governed the agricultural cycle, and a ritual year of 260 days governed daily affairs by organizing time into twenty "months" of thirteen days apiece.

Maya ballgame (p. 112) — Popular game of the Mayans who inherited it from the Olmecs; served not only sporting purpose but also figured in Maya political and religious rituals.

Mesoamerica (p. 105) — Region from the central portion of modern Mexico to Honduras and El Salvador.

Mochica Ceramics (p. 119) — Painted pottery vessels of the Mochican people of the Andean region; contained detailed and expressive depictions of early Andean society in all its variety.

Mochica (pp. 118-19) — One of the Andean states, located in the valley of the Moche River; dominated the coasts and valleys of northern Peru during the period from about 300 to 700 C.E.

Oceania (p. 120) — Designation refers to most of the islands in the Pacific Ocean; subdivisions include Melanesia, Micronesia, Polynesia, Australia and New Zealand.

Olmecs (pp. 105-106) — First complex society of the Americas, with its center located on the coast of the Gulf of Mexico, near the modern Mexican city of Veracruz; cultural traditions influenced all complex societies of Mesoamerica until the arrival of European peoples in the 16th century C.E.

outrigger canoes (p. 121) — Large canoes equipped with beams and sails; used by Austronesian peoples in their sailing to stabilize their crafts and reduce the risks of long voyages.

Popol Vuh (pp. 112-13) — A Maya creation myth; taught that the gods had created human beings out of maize and water, the ingredients that became human flesh and blood.

pyramid of the sun (pp. 114-15) — Largest building in Mesoamerica, occupying nearly as much space as the pyramid of Khufu in Egypt, though it stands only half as tall. It was built by 100 C.E., in the city of Teotihuacan.

San Lorenzo, La Aventa, Tres Zapotes (p. 105) — Three early Olmec ceremonial centers, dating from 1200 to 800 B.C.E., 800 to 400 B.C.E., and 400 to 100 B.C.E., respectively.

Teotihuacan (pp. 114-16) — Mesoamerican city northeast of modern Mexico city; inherited Olmec cultural traditions; flourished from 200 B.C.E. to 750 C.E.

Tikal (pp. 108-109) — Most important Maya city kingdom between the fourth and ninth centuries C.E; located in the lowland area of modern day Mexico City.

Map Exercises

1. Study Map 5.1 (p. 106), Map 5.2 (p. 117) and textual information in Chapter 5 of your textbook and match the societies on the left in the following table with the ceremonial centers or kingdoms on the right:

Societies	Ceremonial centers
ChavínCult	San Lorenzo
	Tikal
Olmec	Mochica
	Tres Zapotes
Maya	Teotihuacan
	Chichén Itzá
Teotihuacan	La Venta
	Kaminaljuyú
Andean	Palenque

2. Fill in the dates of migration on the following map. (This map is based on Map 5.3, p. 120, of your textbook):

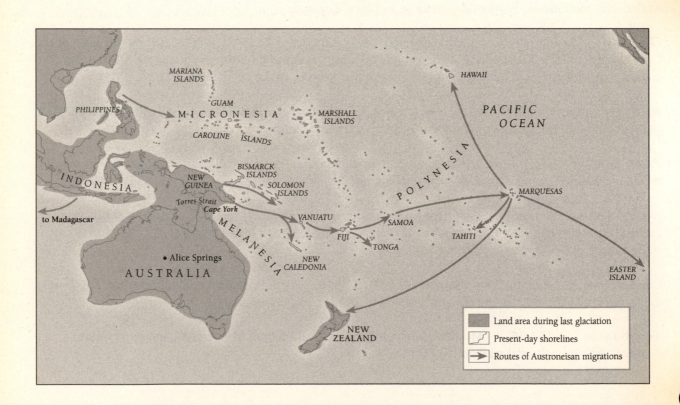

3. Study the map on the previous page and match the four regions of Oceania on the left in the following table with the islands on the right:

Regions	Islands
	New Caledonia
Indonesia	New Zealand
	Bismarck Islands
	Hawaii
Melanesia	Marshall Islands
	New Guinea
	Solomon Islands
Micronesia	Easter Island
	Philippines
	Tonga
Polynesia	Marquesas
	Fiji

Self Test/Student Quiz

1. By cutting slits onto his penis in a public ritual, the Maya prince Chan Bahlum intended to

    a. test his potency and power of fertility.
    b. please the goddess.
    c. imitate the gods' sacrifice.

2. The low sea levels during ice ages

    a. prohibited human migrations from Siberia to North America.
    b. exposed land bridges that linked Siberia with Alaska and Australia with New Guinea.
    c. enabled humans to migrate via floating glaciers.

3. All but one of the following is true regarding migrations to the Americas:

    a. small human groups came from Siberia to Alaska in search of big game.
    b. small human groups came from Siberia to Alaska via the Bering Straits.
    c. migrants were exclusively hunters and gatherers.

4. As for early agriculture in Mesoamerica, we can say that

    a. the settlers developed food crops brought from Siberia.
    b. horses and oxen played important roles in transportation and farming.
    c. the settlers developed maize as their staple food around 5000 B.C.E.

5. The Olmecs

    a. established the first complex society in Mesoamerica.
    b. referred to themselves as "rubber people" because of the importance of rubber in their lives.
    c. lived in modern day Peru where rubber trees flourished.

6. The authoritarian nature of Olmec society can be seen from

    a. Olmec paintings that depicted the daily lives of the ruling elite.
    b. Olmec books.
    c. the construction of ceremonial centers.

7. The decline of Olmec society might have been caused by

    a. civil conflicts.
    b. human sacrifice.
    c. calendrical miscalculation.

8. For the Olmecs, the ceremonial center at San Lorenzo was like

    a. Tikal to the Maya.
    b. Chichén Itzá to the Tikal.
    c. La Venta to the Tikal.

9. A traveler in Tikal might have seen all of the following except

    a. pyramids, plazas, temples, palaces, stone-paved courts for ball games.
    b. wild animals with names like "Curl Snout" and "Giant Jaguar."
    c. kings, priests, nobles, merchants, slaves, and war captives.

10. The Maya calendar

    a. contained a solar year and a ritual year
    b. contained a 60-year cycle.
    c. was devised by the kings.

11. The Maya script was

    a. exclusively ideographic.
    b. used exclusively for religious purposes.
    c. written on paper as well as on temples and monuments.

12. Compared with Maya society, Teotihuacan seemed to be

    a. less theocratic.
    b. more militaristic.
    c. equally complex.

13. After about 650 C.E., the city of Teotihuacan, another of the successor societies of the Olmecs, began to decline. The reasons for the downfall of Teotihuacan are

   a. military pressure and invasion from surrounding peoples.
   b. epidemic diseases, population pressure, and ecological destruction
   c. still unknown.

14. The heartland of early Andean society was

   a. the region now occupied by the states of Peru and Bolivia.
   b. the region now occupied by the states of Mexico, Honduras, and El Salvador.
   c. the islands of the Pacific ocean.

15. The Chavíncult
   a. honored god Chavín.
   b. was a popular Andean religion from 900 to 800 B.C.E.
   c. was associated with war gods.

16. Mochica was

   a. one of several large states of Andean society.
   b. one of several large ceremonial centers of Andean society.
   c. one of several large cults of the Andean region.

17. When the state of Mochica emerged, it

   a. coordinated the building of irrigation networks throughout the Andean region, and established trade and exchange networks that tied together the highlands, central valleys, and coastal regions.
   b. encouraged long distance trade with Mesoamerican peoples.
   c. consolidated its power primarily through religious rituals to which others also adhered.

18. If you were to go to a museum exhibition in which Mochican art works were displayed, what scenes, people, or objects from those listed below would be absent?

   a. A harem of court ladies; representations of beautiful paintings done on paper for hanging; warriors wearing horse-riding gear for combat.
   b. Hunting parties of aristocrats; women working in textile factories under the careful eye of a supervisor.
   c. Beggars looking for handouts on a busy streets; rulers receiving messengers or ambassadors from neighboring states.

19. The developments of early societies in Australia and New Guinea took different paths because

   a. the environments of the two islands were very different.
   b. the Austronesians introduced root crops and domesticated animals to New Guinea.
   c. the aboriginal peoples of Australia relied on kangaroo meat, which made agriculture unnecessary.

20. All of the following conditions helped the Austronesians to people the islands of the Pacific except

    a. their skills of navigation, agriculture, and raising domestic animals.
    b. population pressure and internal conflicts.
    c. their chiefly political organizations.

Textual Questions for Analysis

1. Migrations in the Americas and Oceania involved different patterns. Write an essay to describe and compare these patterns, including where the migrants came from, how they traveled, and what pushed them forward.

2. What do the ceremonial centers of the Olmecs and Mayas tell us about the nature and processes of social stratification among the early societies of Mesoamerica? What did agriculture have to do with these developments?

3. Much evidence suggests that trade was important among the early peoples of Mesoamerica. Describe the types of products traded, relative distances of trading networks, and other important characteristics of the trade.

4. A variety of cultural practices among the Mayans and the residents of Teotihuacan suggest societies of growing complexity and sophistication. Describe some of these practices, and comment on what they tell us about the evolution of complex societies.

5. What sort of evidence exists about the Mochica state and what can we say about the lives of the people who inhabited that state? How does this compare with forms of evidence we have for the study of other early complex societies in Mesoamerica?

6. When Austronesian-speaking peoples arrived in Oceania, they brought profound change throughout the region and beyond. Who were these peoples? Where did they come from and how did they travel? What sorts of societies did they produce as they migrated? You could comment on how we know these things in addition to spelling out what we know.

Documentary Evidence

Mayan Writing

The Mayans created the most sophisticated of all the early American systems of writing. The Mayan script contained both ideographic elements and symbols for syllables. Scholars began to decipher this script in the 1960s, making it clear that the Mayans used this script extensively in writing history, myth, poetry, and for keeping records of various sorts. The following text is taken from an inscription on the facade of the Temple of the Foliated Cross at Palenque, an archaeological site in eastern Mexico. It dates from around 700 C.E. (From Linda Schele and David Freidel, *A Forest of Kings: The Untold Story of the Ancient Maya*. New York: William Morrow and Co., 1990, pp. 250-51.)

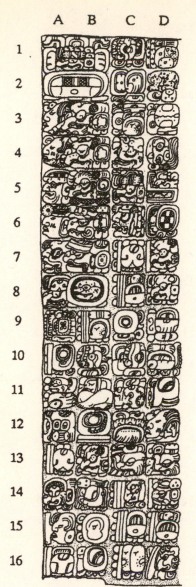

On October 25, 2360 B.C.
>the third Lord of the Night ruled,
>>it was 26 days after the moon was born,
>>>four moons had ended,
>>>>X was its name and it had 30 days...

It was 1 year, 46 days after
>God K set the north quadrant
>>on July 24, 2587 B.C.

On that day he was born,
Mah Kina Tah-Waybil-Ahau,
>Kin-tan "decapitated jaguar."
>>*Ti Nah, Zac-Bac-Na-Chan, Atin Butz,—-.*
>>*Mah Kina Ahau* [A1 to D6]

765 years, 3 months, 6 days after the *wac-chan*
>had been set,
>>and then the *matawil*, the child of Lady Deastie,
>>>Divine Palenque Lord, was born [C7 to D13]

3,858 years, 5 months, 16 days...[C1 to D16]
>...after the present epoch began on August 13, 3114 B.C.,
>>and then July 23, 690, came to pass.
>>>GIII came into conjunction [D16 to O6]

One day later on July 24, 690,
>the Kinich-Bahlum-Kuk Building was dedicated.
>>in the house of the *Bacel-Way*
>>>Lord Chan-Bahlum [N7 to O12]

Three days later he materialized the divinity
>through bloodletting.
>>He did it at the Waterlily Place,
>>>the Old God of *Kuk-Te-Witz* [N13 to N16]

146 years, 12 months, 3 days after November 20, 496,
>when Kan-Xul took office as the heir-designate.
>>It had come to pass at the *Toc-tan* Place.
>>>and then June 17, 641, came to pass.
>>>>He (Chan-Bahlum) became the heir.
>>>>>And on the fifth day after
>>>>>>Lord Chan-Bahlum became the sun
>>>>>>>In the company of GI [O16 to Q10]

6 years, 2 months, 17 days after he had been born
>on May 23, 635,
>>and then he was designated heir [P11 to Q13]

It was 1 year, 167 days until December 6, 642,
>when 10 years ended,
>>he warred as heir [P14 to Q16]

QUESTIONS TO CONSIDER

1. Compare the appearance of Mayan script with that of Phoenician alphabetic writing (see Chapter 2, p. 52, of your textbook). Which do you think was more effective in terms of keeping records, expressing ideas, decorativeness, and conveying mysterious feelings? Could Mayan writing have been invented by merchants? Why or why not?

2. How important was writing to the development of a complex society? Was it essential? How did it fit or relate to other elements of a complex society such as population growth, trade, specialization, city, social stratification, and state government?

3. Read the discussion on the Maya calendar on pp. 110-11 of your textbook and explain why the author(s) of the above excerpt put great emphasis on exact dates of events in the past and present.

4. The above text mentions that Chan Bahlum "materialized the divinity through bloodletting." How does the bloodletting ritual fit the Maya myth of human creation (read the selection from the *Popol Vuh* on p. 113 of your textbook)? Are you familiar with other rituals that helped to achieve legitimacy for political leaders in various societies?

Chapter 6

The Empires of Persia

Introduction and Learning Objectives

Medes and Persians, two closely related Indo-European-speaking peoples, migrated from central Asia to Persia during the centuries before 1000 B.C.E., where they lived in loose subjection to the Babylonian and Assyrian empires. What was amazing about these peoples was that beginning in the 6th century B.C.E., they built the largest empires the world had yet seen. For more than one millennium, there were four dynasties that successively maintained their imperial rule in much of southwest Asia. The theme of this chapter is the rise and fall of the four Persian empires, including the formation of classical Persian society and its relations with surrounding societies.

Empires always involved military conquests of other peoples. What accounted for the military might of the conquerors? After conquests, how did the imperial rulers control the vast territories of their empires? With their great military prowess, why did the empires inevitably fall, one after another? Were there any regularities governing the rise and fall of the empires? The authors' discussion of Persian empires lays solid ground for us to think through these issues. Most conquerors were not full-fledged agriculturalists, but rather tough peoples retaining certain nomadic traditions whose powerful cavalry forces gave them an edge in competing against long-established agricultural societies. But military prowess alone was not enough to govern far-flung empires. Vast systems of administration were needed, and the key was to organize and maintain communication and exchange among all parts of the empire under a single centralized rule. The wealth and glory of the empire might attract invasions of more formidable forces on the borders, but the longevity of an empire also depended on internal imperial policies toward the conquered peoples. Without a certain amount of cultural tolerance, accompanied by some measure of administrative efficiency, rebellions would have been more common, costing imperial governments dearly. As an example of what could happen, the Achaemenid empire was first undermined by rebellions in Mesopotamia and Egypt, then seriously wounded by rebellions of the Greek city states during the Persian Wars, and finally ruined by the invasion of Alexander's conquering force.

Cross-cultural exchanges were common in the vast Persian empires. The imperial administrative structure created a large commercial zone linking the different regions and peoples into an integrated economy, while the systems of communication also facilitated the cross-cultural traveling of religious faiths, art styles, and philosophical thought throughout the Persian realm. A new faith called Zoroastrianism, for instance, emerged as a reflection of the cosmopolitan society of the Persian empires, influencing the beliefs and values of Judaism, Christianity, and Islam in later centuries.

After studying this chapter, students should understand and be able to discuss the following issues:

- the advantages of the conquering peoples who founded the empires of classical Persia

- the nature of the administration of the Achaemenid empire

- decay and decline of the four Persian empires

- Zoroastrianism

Chapter Outline

I. **The Rise and Fall of the Persian Empires**

    A. The Achaemenid Empire
       1. The Medes and the Persians
          a) Migrated from central Asia to Persia before 1000 B.C.E.
          b) Indo-European speakers, sharing cultural traits with the Aryans
          c) Challenged the Assyrian and Babylonian empires
       2. Cyrus the Achaemenid (reigned 558-530 B.C.E.)
          a) A tough, wily leader, military strategist
          b) Became the king of the Persian tribes in 558 B.C.E.
          c) Brought all of Iran under his control by 548 B.C.E.
          d) Established a vast empire stretching from India to borders of Egypt
          e) Died in 530 B.C.E.
       3. Cyrus's son, Cambyses (re. 530-522 B.C.E.), conquered Egypt in 525
       4. Darius (re. 521-486 B.C.E.)
          a) A young kinsman of Cyrus
          b) Built the largest empire in world history so far
          c) Ruled more than 70 ethnic groups
          d) New capital at Persepolis, 520 B.C.E.
       5. Achaemenid administration
          a) Divided the empire into twenty-three satrapies
          b) Satraps (Persian governors) were appointed by the central government
          c) Local officials were from the local peoples themselves
          d) Satraps' power was checked by military officers and "imperial spies"
          e) Replaced irregular tribute payments with formal taxes
          f) Standardization of coins and laws
          g) Communication systems: Persian Royal Road and postal stations
    B. Decline and Fall of the Achaemenid Empire
       1. Xerxes (reigned 486-465 B.C.E.)
          a) Retreated from the policy of cultural toleration
          b) Caused ill will and rebellions among the peoples in Mesopotamia and Egypt
       2. The Persian Wars (500-479 B.C.E.)
          a) The rebellion of Ionian Greeks
          b) Aid from peninsular Greece
          c) Persian rulers failed to put down the rebellion
       3. Alexander of Macedon
          a) Invaded Persia in 334 B.C.E.
          b) The battle of Gaugamela, the end of Achaemenid empire, 331 B.C.E.
          c) Alexander burned the city of Persepolis

C. The Seleucid, Parthian, and Sasanid Empires
   1. The Seleucids
      a) Seleucus inherited most of the former Achaemenid empire
      b) The Seleucids retained the Achaemenid system of administration
      c) Met opposition from native Persians
      d) Lost control over northern India and Iran
   2. The Parthians
      a) Based in Iran, extended to wealthy Mesopotamia
      b) Retained some traditions of nomadic people
      c) Formidable power of Parthian heavy cavalry because of alfalfa diet of horses
      d) Rebellion against Seleucid overlords in 238 B.C.E.
      e) Mithradates I established a mighty empire through conquests
   3. Parthian government
      a) Portrayed themselves as restorers of the Persian tradition
      b) Followed the example of the Achaemenids in administration
      c) Clan leaders as satraps: potential threats for central government
      d) The pressure from the expanding Roman empire, 1st century C.E.
      e) Internal rebellion brought it down in the early 3rd century C.E.
   4. The Sasanids
      a) From Persia, claimed direct descent from the Achaemenids
      b) Toppled the Parthians in 224 C.E.
      c) Capital at Ctesiphon
      d) Merchants brought in various crops from India and China
      e) The empire stood against the Kushan empire in the east and the Roman and Byzantine empires in the west, 3rd century C.E.
      f) In 651 C.E., the empire was incorporated into the expanding Islamic empire

II. Imperial Society and Economy

A. Social Development in Classical Persia
   1. Nomadic character of early Persian society
      a) Similar to the Aryans in India
      b) Importance of family and clan relationships
   2. Imperial bureaucrats
      a) Imperial administration called for educated bureaucrats
      b) Shared power and influence with warriors and clan leaders
   3. Free classes
      a) In the city: artisans, craftsmen, merchants, civil servants
      b) In the countryside: peasants—building underground canals (*qanat*)
      c) Slaves in both cities and countryside
B. Economic Foundations of Classical Persia
   1. Agriculture was the economic foundation
      a) Main crops: Barley and wheat
      b) Supplemental crops: peas, lentils, mustard, garlic, onions, cucumber
      c) Large agricultural surplus
   2. Trade
      a) Commercial zone from India to Egypt
      b) Political stability promoted growth of trade

      c) Standardized coins, good trade routes

      d) Specialization of production in different regions

C. Religions of Salvation in Classical Persian Society

  1. Zarathustra and his faith

      a) Earliest Persian religion resembled that of the Aryans

      b) Zoroastrianism, emerged from the teachings of Zarathustra

  2. The Gathas

      a) Zoroastrian teachings, transmitted orally, many perished

      b) Preserved later in writing, by *magi*

      c) Compilation of the holy scriptures, Avesta, under Sasanid dynasty

      d) Zarathustra's own writing survived, known as *Gathas*

  3. Zoroastrian teachings

      a) Ahura Mazda as a supreme deity, with 6 lesser deities

      b) Cosmic conflict between Ahura Mazda and Angra Mainyu

      c) Heavenly paradise and hellish realm as reward and punishment

      d) The material world as a blessing

      e) Moral formula: good words, good thoughts, good deeds

  4. Popularity of Zoroastrianism

      a) Attracted Persian aristocrats and ruling elites

      b) Darius regarded Ahura Mazda as supreme God

      c) The faith was most popular in Iran

      d) Sizable followings in Mesopotamia, Anatolia, Egypt, and other regions

D. Religions of Salvation in a Cosmopolitan Society

  1. Suffering of Zoroastrian community during Alexander's invasion

  2. Officially sponsored Zoroastrianism during the Sasanid empire

  3. The Zoroastrians' difficulties

      a) Islamic conquerors toppled the Sasanid empire, seventh century C.E.

      b) Some Zoroastrians fled to India

      c) The remaining Zoroastrians converted to Islam

      d) A few thousand faithful Zoroastrians still exist in modern day Iran

  4. Other faiths: Buddhism, Christianity, and Manichaeism

  5. Influence of Zoroastrians

      a) Influence on Jewish religion: belief in future reward and punishment

      b) Influence on Christianity: concepts of heaven and hell

      c) The above concepts of Judaism and Christianity later influenced Islam

Significant Individuals

Alexander of Macedon (p. 138) — Often called Alexander the Great. Alexander invaded Persia in 334 B.C.E., decisively defeating a much larger Persian force with his Macedonian army. He proclaimed himself heir to the Achaemedids, and captured (and perhaps also purposely burned) their capital at Persepolis.

Cambyses (p. 134) — Cyrus's son, succeeded the throne of his father and expanded the Achaemenid empire by conquering Egypt in 525 B.C.E. Reigned from 530 to 522 B.C.E.

Croesus (p. 131) — Ruler of the powerful and wealthy kingdom of Lydia in southwestern Anatolia (modern-day Turkey). Launched an invasion in Persia in 546 B.C.E., but was badly defeated by the Persian armies led by Cyrus. Croesus was taken captive and afterward became an advisor to Cyrus.

Cyrus (pp. 131, 133-34) — Founder of the Achaemenid empire, extended it from India to the borders of Egypt through military conquests. Reigned 558-530 B.C.E.

Darius (pp. 134-35) — Third ruler of the Achaemenid empire, extended the empire to the Indus River in the east and the western coast of the Black Sea in the west. The central rule of the imperial administration was well-established during Darius's reign, which lasted from 521 to 486 B.C.E.

Gimillu (p. 143) — A slave of the Achaemenid empire, lived in mid- to late 6th century B.C.E. and served the temple community of Eanna in Uruk. Became known because records of his various misadventures survive in archives. By the records, he habitually defrauded his masters, pocketed bribes, and embezzled temple funds. With his personal talent and protection of some powerful individuals, however, he always managed to escape serious punishment.

Mithradates I (p. 139) — Parthians' greatest conqueror; came to the throne about 171 B.C.E. Under his rule, the Parthian state extended into a mighty empire covering Iran and Mesopotamia.

Seleucus (p. 138) (reigned 305-281 B.C.E.) — One of Alexander of Macedon's military commanders who took the choicest part of Alexander's realm upon his death in 323 B.C.E.; this included most of the former Achaemenid empire.

Shapur I (p. 140) — Ruler of the Sasanid empire, reigned 239-272 C.E. His rule stabilized the western frontier by creating a series of buffer states between the Sasanids and the Roman empire. Shapur even defeated several Roman armies and settled the prisoners in Iran, where they devoted their famous engineering skills to the construction of roads and dams.

Xerxes (p. 137) — Successor of Darius, reigned 486-465 B.C.E. Sought to impose his own values on conquered lands, retreated from Darius's policy of cultural toleration, and caused ill will and rebellions of the peoples under the rule of the Achaemenid empire.

Zarathustra (pp. 145-46) — Founder of Zoroastrianism. Born into an aristocratic family probably during late seventh or early sixth century B.C.E. After about ten years of travel and meditation, he experienced a series of visions and became convinced that the supreme god, Ahura Mazda ("the wise lord"), had chosen him to serve as his prophet and spread his message.

Chapter Glossary

Achaemenid empire (pp. 132-38) — First Persian empire, founded by Cyrus and Darius in southwestern Asia. By the late 6th century B.C.E., it was the largest empire the world had yet seen, with boundaries extending from the Indus River in the east to the Aegean Sea in the west, and from the Armenian hills in the north to the first cataract of the Nile in the south. Lasted from 558 to 330 B.C.E.

Ahura Mazda (p. 145) — "The wise lord," the supreme deity worshipped by Zoroastrians. In the compositions of Zarathustra, the founder of the Zoroastrian religion, Ahura Mazda engaged in a cosmic conflict with an independent adversary, an evil and malign spirit known as Angra Mainyu, a struggle that would continue for twelve thousand years.

Avesta (p. 146) — Holy scriptures of Zoroastrianism, compiled during the Sasanid empire.

Ctesiphon (p. 139) — Capital city of the Parthian, Sasanid, and Seleucid empires, located on the Euphrates River near modern Baghdad.

Gathas (pp. 145-46) — Zarathustra's own works, hymns that he composed in honor of the various deities that he recognized.

haoma (p. 145) — Hallucinogenic agent used by early Persian priests during the performance of their rituals, probably the same substance used by the early Aryan priests which they called *soma*.

magi (p. 146) — Term for Zoroastrian priests.

Medes and Persians (p. 132) — Two closely related Indo-European peoples who migrated from central Asia to Persia (the southwestern portion of modern-day Iran) before 1000 B.C.E., where they lived in loose subjection to the Babylonian and Assyrian empires. Mostly pastoralists, they organized themselves by clans. Persians overthrew their Median overlord and extended their territory to an enormous empire during the 6ᵗʰ century B.C.E.

Parthian empire (pp. 138-39) — Third Persian empire. Established by the Parthians, lasted from 247 B.C.E. to 224 C.E. Portrayed themselves as enemies of the foreign Seleucids and restorers of the Persian tradition. People's rebellions from within and Roman military pressure from without eventually brought the Parthian empire down.

Parthians (pp. 138-39) — Nomadic people who migrated from the steppes of central Asia to eastern Iran around Khurasan from Achaemenid times, famous for their heavy cavalry. Revolted against their Seleucid overlord in 238 B.C.E., and extended their state to a mighty empire covering Iran and Mesopotamia.

Persepolis (p. 135) — Capital of the Achaemenid empire, near Pasargadae. Structures at Persepolis included vast reception halls, lavish royal residences, and a well-protected treasury. Burned by Alexander of Macedon during the 4ᵗʰ century B.C.E.

Persian Royal Road (p. 136) — Built during Darius's reign, stretched some 2,575 kilometers (1,600 miles) from the Aegean port of Ephesus to Sardis in Anatolia, through Mesopotamia along the Tigris River, to Susa in Iran, with an extension to Pasargadae and Persepolis.

Persian Wars (p. 137) — Wars between the city states of the Greeks and the Achaemenid empire from 500 to 479 B.C.E. The Greeks successfully resisted Persian invasions and maintained their independence.

qanat (p. 142) — Underground canals of the Persian empires, built for irrigation purposes. *Qanat* enabled cultivators to distribute water to fields without losing large quantities to evaporation through exposure to the sun and open air.

Sasanid empire (pp. 140-41) — Fourth Persian empire. Toppled the Parthians in 224 C.E., and ruled until the year 651. The empire covered the lands from India to Mesopotamia, recreating much of the splendor of the Achaemenid empire.

satrapies (pp. 135-36) — Administrative and taxation districts of the Achaemenid empire, governed by satraps, or appointed governors who served as agents of the central government. The vast empire was divided into twenty-three satrapies during Darius's reign.

Seleucid empire (p. 138) (323-83 B.C.E.) — Second Persian empire, founded by Seleucus (see above, in Significant Individuals section). The Seleucids continued Achaemenid systems of administration, taxation, and transport; they also founded new cities to attract Greek colonists. Seleucid rule was often opposed by native Persians, and the empire lost its power finally to Roman conquerors in 83 B.C.E.

Zoroastrianism (pp. 146-49) — Persian religion that honored Ahura Mazda and six lesser deities; Zoroastrians believed in the cosmic conflict between Ahura Mazda and the Angra Mainyu ("the destructive spirit" or "the hostile spirit"). Zoroastrianism developed the concepts of future judgment and of heavenly paradise and hell as reward and punishment. It allowed followers to enjoy the world and its fruits, so long as individuals abided by the moral teachings of "good words, good thoughts, good deeds." Zoroastrian teachings had a substantial influence on Judaism, Christianity, and Islam.

Map Exercises

1. Fill in the following information on the map below (cf. Map 6.1, p. 133, of your textbook):

   - Cities: Persepolis, Pasargadae, Susa, Sardis, Ephesus
   - Regions: Macedonia, Greece, Lydia, Anatolia, Babylonia, Persia, Hindu Kush, Arabia
   - Roads: The Royal Road

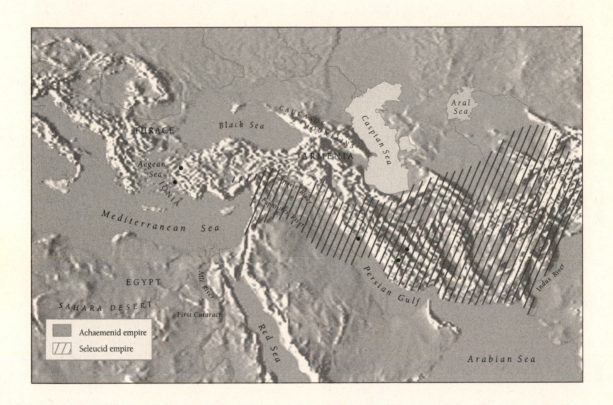

2. Study Map 6.1 (p. 133) and Map 6.2 (p. 140) in your textbook, and read the accompanying text. Link each empire on the left with two phrases on the right that describe the empire:

Empires	Descriptions
Achaemenid	built the capital city at Ctesiphon
	toppled by Arab army in 651 C.E
Seleucid	one of three realms conquered by Alexander
	established by Cyrus and Darius
Parthian	most territory lost to the Parthians
	engaged in the Persian Wars
Sasanid	established by Mithradates I
	rulers claimed direct descendent of the Achaemenids

3. Explain how environmental factors contributed to the rise of the Parthian empire.

Self Test/Student Quiz

1. The Medes and the Persians were

   a. Sumerians who migrated from Mesopotamia to Persia.
   b. Indo-Europeans who migrated from Anatolia to Iran.
   c. Indo-Europeans who migrated from central Asia to Persia.

2. All but one of the following sets of characteristics were true with regard to the Medes and Persians from the tenth to the sixth century B.C.E.:

   a. Expert agriculturalists, good at irrigation and rice cultivation.
   b. Expert archers, frequently raided the wealthy lands of Mesopotamia.
   c. Descendants of nomadic peoples, culturally close to the Aryans.

3. Cyrus's contemporaries called him Cyrus the Shepherd, referring to

   a. the fact that he treated the conquered people like animals.
   b. his conquests laid the foundation of the first Persian empire.
   c. his origins in a mountainous region where the people lived by herding animals.

4. Egypt was conquered by

   a. Cyrus.
   b. Cambyses.
   c. Darius.

5. To govern a far-flung empire consisting of more than seventy distinct ethnic groups, the Achaemenid rulers

   a. established lines of communication and centralized administration.
   b. forced the peoples to speak only the Persian language and believe only in the Persian religion.
   c. used imperial spies to control the conquered peoples.

6. The Persian Royal Road stretched some 2,575 kilometers (1,600 miles) from Sardis in Lydia to Susa in Iran. To travel from one end to the other, it would take

   a. four months for caravans.
   b. two weeks for Marathon runners.
   c. one week for imperial couriers.

7. The Persian Wars (500-479 B.C.E.) referred to

    a. the rebellions of Mesopotamia and Egypt against the Achaemenid overlord.
    b. the rebellions of the Greek city states, fighting for their independence.
    c. the wars between Alexander of Macedon and the Achaemenid empire.

8. Alexander's invasion of the Achaemenid empire met great success because

    a. his army outnumbered the Persian army.
    b. he proclaimed himself the heir to the Achaemenid rulers.
    c. his army was well-disciplined, heavily armed, and employed sophisticated military tactics.

9. The rulers of the Seleucid empire could not control the empire effectively primarily because

    a. they abandoned the Achaemenid systems of administration and communication.
    b. as foreigners, they were opposed by native Persians.
    c. they were not able to resist the military pressure of the Islamic empire.

10. All of the following were true about the Parthians except that

    a. they were primarily cultivators.
    b. they were seminomadic people.
    c. they had well-trained forces of heavily armed cavalry.

11. The Parthian empire was toppled by

    a. the Roman army.
    b. the Islamic army.
    c. the Sasanid army.

12. The centralized administration of the Persian empires called for a new class of educated bureaucrats who

    a. displaced the positions of the old warrior elite and clan leaders.
    b. shared power and influence with the old warrior elite and clan leaders.
    c. actually ruled the empires themselves through the running of governmental affairs.

13. The construction of numerous underground canals (known as *qanat*) required enormous human labor, which could be justified by

    a. a scarcity of land since crops could grow above the canals.
    b. plenty of slave labor used in such construction.
    c. a scarcity of water since the canals could keep water from evaporating.

14. In classical Persia, a slave

    a. could take on administrative chores involving considerable responsibility.
    b. could marry another slave at will so long as both consented.
    c. could choose to work either as a domestic servant or as a cultivator.

15. The economic foundation of classical Persian society was

    a. long-distance trade.
    b. herding domestic animals.
    c. agriculture.

16. Imperial rule during the classical Persian eras promoted growth of trade by

    a. linking the lands from India to Egypt into a vast commercial zone.
    b. enacting commercial laws to encourage commercial activities.
    c. establishing state-owned banks to facilitate commercial activities.

17. Zoroastrianism was

    a. an original contribution of the Persians.
    b. borrowed from various faiths of different peoples under Persian control.
    c. developed from the Upanishads.

18. To understand the original teachings of Zarathustra which have been preserved in hymns, one must study

    a. the Avesta.
    b. the *Gathas*.
    c. the *Vedas*.

19. Which of the following was not a Zoroastrian teaching?

    a. The cosmic conflict between Ahura Mazda and Angra Mainyu.
    b. Individual souls would undergo future judgment.
    c. Ascetic renunciation of the world in favor of a future heavenly existence.

20. From the mid-7th century, Zoroastrianism lost its popularity because

    a. most Zoroastrians eventually converted to Islam.
    b. it was no longer sponsored by the Persian government.
    c. more and more people turned to belief in Christianity.

Textual Questions for Analysis

1. Taking the Persians and Parthians as examples, explain what contributed to the successful expansion of empires in southwest Asia.

2. How did the Persians rule the Achaemenid empire? What measures were taken to bring the vast empire under a single, centralized rule?

3. What caused the Persian empires to decline and collapse? Compare the fall of the Achaemenid empire with the fall of the Chinese Zhou dynasty.

4. Imperial rule had an important impact on the social and economic lives of the peoples within the empires. Explain this statement.

5. Compare and contrast Zoroastrianism with the teachings of the Upanishads (see Chapter 3 of your textbook).

Documentary Evidence

Child Education in the Achaemenid Period (558-330 B.C.E.)

The following three passages are from the writings of three Greek writers—Herodotus, Xenophon, and Plato. Their descriptions of child education in the Achaemenid empire reveal the values of Persian society at large (From Mary Boyce, ed. and transl., *Textual Sources for the Study of Zoroastrianism*. Manchester: Manchester University Press, 1984, pp. 106-107).

A. From Herodotus, before 445 B.C.E.

After valor in battle it is most reckoned as manly merit to show the greatest number of sons.... They educate their boys [i.e. noblemen's sons] from five to twenty years old, and teach them three things only, riding and archery and truth-telling.... They hold lying to be foulest of all, and next to that debt; for which they have many other reasons, but this in especial, that the debtor must needs (so they say) speak some falsehood....

B. From Xenophon, written 365 B.C.E.

The boys go to school and give their time to learning justice and righteousness: They will tell you they come for that purpose, and the phrase is as natural with them as it is for us to speak of lads learning their letters. The masters spend the chief part of the day in deciding cases for their pupils.... There will be charges, we know, of picking and stealing, of violence, of fraud, of calumny, and so forth. The case is heard and the offender, if shown to be guilty, is punished.... The culprit convicted of refusing to repay a debt of kindness when it was fully in his power meets with severe chastisement. They reason that the ungrateful man is the most likely to forget his duty to the gods, to his parents, to his fatherland, and his friends.... Further, the boys are instructed in temperance and self-restraint.... Then they are taught obedience to authority manifested by their elders everywhere. Continence in meat and drink is another branch of instruction.

C. From Plato, after 374 B.C.E.

When the (Persian princes) are seven years of age they are given horses and have riding lessons, and they begin to follow the chase. And when the boy reaches fourteen years he is taken over by the royal tutors, as they call them there: these are four men chosen as the most highly esteemed among the Persians of mature age, namely the wisest one, the justice, the most temperate one, and the bravest one. The first of these teaches him...the worship of the gods: he teaches him also what pertains to a king. The justice teaches him to be truthful all his life long;

the most temperate, not to be mastered by even a single pleasure, in order that he may be accustomed to be a free man and a veritable king, who is first master of all that is in him, not the slave; while the bravest trains him to be fearless and undaunted, telling him that to be daunted is to be enslaved.

QUESTIONS TO CONSIDER

1. Through education, what values were instilled in Persian boys? How did these values serve the empire's needs for competent warriors, bureaucrats, and kings?

2. All of the above selections were written by foreigners whose observations or hearsay might not have been accurate or reliable. Find from these passages things that you think were unlikely to have been true, and give some explanations for your choices. For instance, is it possible for Herodotus to have mistakenly thought that the boys were learning about "debt" rather than Xenophon's "debt of kindness"? Do you believe that Persian boys learned nothing in school other than how to judge their own wrongdoings as Xenophon described it?

Chapter 7

The Unification of China

Introduction and Learning Objectives

In the midst of turmoil in China during the Warring States era (403-221 B.C.E.), the kings of different states struggled for survival and hegemony, and thoughtful scholars reflected on the nature of society to find ways for the people to get along in a civilized and orderly manner. The champion in the political arena was the Qin, a state in the rustic region of west China, which came to conquer one kingdom after another, eventually bringing China under the central rule of the Qin empire in 221 B.C.E. The champion in the intellectual arena was an individual called Confucius, whose ideas became influential throughout Chinese history thereafter. The central theme of this chapter, therefore, is the making of classical China, which was accomplished by the Qin and Han dynasties with the eventual triumph of Confucianism as the dominant ideology.

The First Emperor of Qin was a powerful and tyrannical individual who accomplished what most other imperial rulers desired: he established centralized rule through bureaucrats, built transportation and communication networks, and standardized weights, measures, and scripts. But he also did some things that were very unusual: he buried alive scholars who dared to utter criticisms against his regime, burned most books, enacted harsh laws, and built massive walls for defense against nomadic peoples in the northwest. Ironically, the ruthless Legalist approaches adopted by the Qin rulers made the Qin a formidable power but led to the downfall of the dynasty soon after the death of the First Emperor. After a short period of hesitation, the newly established Han dynasty adopted the centralized rule created by the Qin but discredited its worst policies. Although much of the glory of the Han dynasty was achieved by the "Martial Emperor" through his Legalist style of rule, he eventually adopted Confucianism as the state ideology. The imperial university of the dynasty, which was a training ground for bureaucrats, had its curriculum based on Confucianism alone. By the end of classical era, although Legalism lost political favor, it had contributed a set of central political institutions that would continue in later Chinese history. Confucianism became the state ideology, with all government offices to be filled by Confucian scholars. As a counterbalance to Confucian activism, however, Daoism was widely accepted and wielded profound influence on Chinese views toward nature, society, and man.

The Han ruled China for more than four centuries, during which time social stability and technological innovation led to the greatest prosperity China had yet seen. There were two central problems, however, that seemed beyond imperial resolution: uneven landholding between the rich and the poor, and factionalism at court. The two problems, which substantially weakened the Han dynasty, would persist throughout Chinese imperial history.

After studying this chapter, students should understand and be able to discuss the following issues:

- the basic ideas of Confucianism, Daoism, and Legalism

- the triumph of Legalism in the Qin

- the legacy of the Qin empire

- Han dynasty rule and its problems

Chapter Outline

I. **In Search of Political and Social Order**

  A. Confucius and His School
    1. Confucius (551-479 B.C.E.)
      a) A strong-willed man, from an aristocratic family
      b) Traveled ten years searching for an official post
      c) Ended up being an educator, with numerous disciples
      d) His sayings were compiled in the *Analects* by his disciples
    2. Confucian ideas
      a) Fundamentally moral and ethical in character
      b) Thoroughly practical: How to restore political and social order
      c) Concentrated on formation of *junzi*—"superior individuals"
      d) Edited and compiled the Zhou classics for his disciples to study
    3. The key Confucian concepts
      a) *Ren*—a sense of humanity
      b) *Li*—a sense of propriety
      c) *Xiao*—filial piety
      d) Cultivating of *junzi* for bringing order to China
    4. Mencius (372-289 B.C.E.)
      a) A principal spokesman for the Confucian school
      b) Firmly believed in the goodness of human nature
      c) Advocated government by benevolence and humanity
    5. Xunzi (298-238 B.C.E.)
      a) Served as a governmental administrator
      b) Cast doubt on the goodness of human nature
      c) Preferred harsh social discipline to bring order to society
      d) Also advocated moral education and good public behavior
  B. Daoism
    1. The most prominent critics of Confucian activism
      a) Preferred philosophical reflection and introspection
      b) To understand natural principles, to live in harmony with them
    2. Laozi and Zhuangzi
      a) Laozi, the founder of Daoism, allegedly wrote the *Daodejing*
      b) Zhuangzi, an influential Daoist philosopher, wrote *Zhuangzi*
    3. The *Dao*
      a) *Dao*—The way of nature, the way of the cosmos
      b) An elusive concept: an eternal principle governing all the workings of the world
      c) *Dao* is passive and yielding, does nothing yet accomplishes everything
      d) Humans should tailor their behavior to the passive and yielding nature of the *Dao*
      e) Ambition and activism had only brought the world to chaos

4. The doctrine of *wuwei*
   a) Disengagement from worldly affairs
   b) Called for simple, unpretentious life, living in harmony with nature
   c) Advocated small state, self-sufficient community
5. Political implications
   a) Served as a counterbalance to Confucian activism
   b) Individuals could live as Confucians by day, Daoists by night
C. Legalism
   1. The doctrine of statecraft
      a) Promoted a practical and ruthlessly efficient approach
      b) No concern with ethics and morality
      c) No concern with the principles governing nature
   2. Shang Yang (ca. 390-338 B.C.E.)
      a) A chief minister of the Qin state
      b) His policies were summarized in *The Book of Lord Shang*
      c) Was executed by his political enemies
   3. Han Feizi (ca. 280-233 B.C.E.)
      a) Student of Xunzi, became the most articulate Legalist
      b) A synthesizer of Legalist ideas
      c) Forced to suicide by his political enemies
   4. Legalist doctrine
      a) The state's strength was in agriculture and military force
      b) Discouraged commerce, education, and the arts
      c) Harnessing self-interest of the people for the needs of the state
      d) Called for harsh penalties even for minor infractions
      e) Advocated collective responsibility before the law
      f) Legalism was not popular among the Chinese, but practically effective

II. The Unification of China

A. The Qin Dynasty
   1. The Qin state
      a) Located in west China and adopted Legalist policies
      b) Encouraged agriculture, resulted in strong economy
      c) Organized a powerful army equipped with iron weapons
      d) Conquered other states and unified China in 221 B.C.E.
   2. The first emperor
      a) The king of the Qin proclaimed himself the First Emperor, 221 B.C.E.
      b) Established centralized imperial rule
      c) Project of connecting and extending the Great Wall
   3. Suppressing the resistance
      a) Buried 460 scholars alive because of their criticism against the Qin
      b) Burned all books except some with utilitarian value
   4. Policies of centralization
      a) Standardization of laws, currencies, weights, measures
      b) Standardization of scripts

5. Tomb of the First Emperor
   a) Died in 210 B.C.E.
   b) The tomb was an underground palace
   c) Excavation of the tomb since 1974
6. The collapse of the Qin dynasty
   a) Massive public works generated tremendous ill will among the people
   b) Waves of rebels overwhelmed the Qin court in 207 B.C.E.
   c) A short-lived dynasty, but left deep marks in Chinese history

B. The Early Han Dynasty
   1. Liu Bang
      a) A general, a persistent man, a methodical planner
      b) Restored order and established the Han dynasty, 206 B.C.E.
   2. Han was a long-lived dynasty: Former Han and Later Han
   3. Early Han policies
      a) Seeking a middle way between Zhou decentralization and Qin over-centralization
      b) Royal relatives were not reliable, returned to centralized rule
   4. The Martial Emperor (reigned 141-87 B.C.E.)
      a) Han Wudi, the "Martial Emperor," ruled for 54 years with vision and vigor
      b) Pursued two policies: centralization and expansion
   5. Han centralization
      a) Adopted Legalist policies
         (1) Built an enormous bureaucracy to rule the empire
         (2) Continued to build roads and canals
         (3) Levied taxes on agriculture, trade, and craft industries
         (4) Imperial monopolies on production of iron and salt
      b) Established Confucian educational system for training bureaucrats
         (1) Confucianism as the basis of the curriculum in imperial university
         (2) Thirty thousand students enrolled in the university in Later Han
   6. Han imperial expansion
      a) Invaded and colonized northern Vietnam and Korea
      b) Extended China into central Asia
         (1) Han organized vast armies to invade Xiongnu territory
         (2) Han enjoyed uncontested hegemony in east and central Asia

III. From Economic Prosperity to Social Disorder

A. Productivity and Prosperity during the Former Han
   1. Social structure
      a) Patriarchal households averaged five inhabitants
      b) Large compound families also developed
      c) Women's subordination as seen in Ban Zhao's *Admonitions for Women*
      d) Cultivators were the majority of the population
   2. Iron metallurgy: Farming tools, utensils, and weapons
   3. Silk textiles
      a) Sericulture spread all over China during the Han
      b) High quality Chinese silk became a prized commodity in India, Persia, Mesopotamia, and Rome

4. Paper production
   a) Invented probably before 100 C.E.
   b) Began to replace silk and bamboo as writing materials
5. Population growth
   a) Increased from twenty to sixty million from 220 B.C.E. to 9 C.E.
   b) Despite light taxation, state revenue was large

B. Economic and Social Difficulties
1. Expeditions consumed the empire's surplus
   a) Raised taxes and confiscated land of some wealthy individuals
   b) Taxes and land confiscations discouraged investment in manufacture and trade
2. Social tensions, caused by stratification between the poor and rich
3. Problems of land distribution
   a) Economic difficulties forced some small landowners to sell property
   b) Some sold themselves or their families into slavery
   c) Lands accumulated in the hands of a few
   d) No land reform, because Han needed cooperation of large landowners
4. The reign of Wang Mang
   a) A powerful Han minister
   b) Dethroned the baby emperor, claimed imperial title himself, 9 C.E.
   c) Land reforms—the "socialist emperor"
   d) Overthrown by revolts, 23 C.E.

C. The Later Han Dynasty (25-220 C.E.)
1. The Yellow Turban Uprising
   a) Rulers restored order but did not address problem of landholding
   b) Yellow Turban uprising inflicted serious damage on the Han
2. Collapse of the Han
   a) Factions at court paralyzed the central government
   b) Han empire dissolved, China was divided into regional kingdoms

Significant Individuals

Ban Zhao (p. 170) — Well-educated woman from a prominent Han family; wrote a widely read treatise entitled *Admonitions for Women* that emphasized humility, obedience, subservience, and devotion to their husbands as the virtues most appropriate for women.

Confucius (551-479 B.C.E.) (pp. 154-55) — Most influential thinker of classical China, honored as a sage by later generations. The founder of Confucianism.

Han Feizi (ca. 280-233) (p. 161) — Most influential spokesman for Legalism who synthesized Legalist ideas in a collection of powerful and well argued essays on statecraft.

Han Wudi (141-87 B.C.E.) (p. 167) — "Martial Emperor," greatest and most energetic emperor of the Han dynasty. During his rule, the centralization of imperial rule was strengthened and the territory of China extended to Vietnam, Korea, and central Asia.

Laozi (p. 158) — Founder of Daoism; lived during the sixth century B.C.E. He was believed to be the author of the first Daoist work, the *Daodejing* (Classic of the Way and of Virtue), but the book was certainly a contribution of many hands over several centuries after him.

Liu Bang (p. 166) — Founder of the Han dynasty, overthrew the Qin dynasty and proclaimed himself the emperor of China in 206 B.C.E.

Maodun (reigned 210-174 B.C.E.) (p. 169) — Most successful ruler of the Xiongnu; ruled a vast federation of nomadic peoples that stretched from the Aral Sea to the Yellow Sea. The well-disciplined army of Maodun was a serious threat to the Han empire.

Mencius (372-289 B.C.E.) (pp. 156-57) — Principal spokesman for the Confucian school; firmly believed in the goodness of human nature and advocated government by benevolence and humanity. His ideas deeply influenced the Confucian tradition.

Qin Shihuangdi (reigned 221-210 B.C.E.) (pp. 163-66) — Literally, "the First Emperor of Qin," a title that the king of Qin granted to himself after he unified China in 221 B.C.E. Under his rule, the Qin dynasty established a tradition of centralized imperial rule that would continue throughout the history of imperial China. Because of his massive public works and cruel punishments, however, he has been viewed as the most infamous tyrant in Chinese history.

Shang Yang (ca. 390-338 B.C.E.) (pp. 160-61) — Chief minister of the Qin state; one of the foremost exponents of Legalist doctrine, whose implementation of Legalist policies made the Qin a strong state.

Sima Qian (p. 153) — Historian of the Han dynasty, known as the father of Chinese historians; suffered from punitive castration when his evaluation of a dishonored general contradicted the emperor's judgment.

Wang Mang (pp. 172-73) — Usurper of the Han dynasty; seized the throne in 9 C.E. and introduced a series of wide-ranging reforms, prompting some modern historians to call him a "socialist emperor." Resistance from disgruntled landlords, coupled with poor harvests and famine, sparked wide-spread revolts, ending his dynasty and life in 23 C.E.

Xunzi (298-238 B.C.E.) (pp. 157-58) — Influential Confucian scholar, with a tendency toward Legalism in his ideas; believed that human nature was basically bad and selfish, so that strong social discipline was necessary to bring order to society; advocated clear, well-publicized standards of conduct; shared Confucian views of social optimism, political activism, and moral education.

Zhuangzi (369-286 B.C.E.) (p. 158) — Chinese philosopher, the second founder of Daoism, whose work, the *Zhuangzi*, provided a well-reasoned compendium of Daoist views.

Chapter Glossary

The Book of Lord Shang (p. 161) — Legalist work, contributed by Shang Yang and other Qin ministers; contained Legalist ideas and policies of the Qin state.

Confucianism (pp. 154-57) — School of thought founded by Confucius; advocated political activism and moral education as the way to save China from the chaos of the Warring States period. Politically, it was a doctrine of elitism which emphasized enlightened leadership of *junzi* ("superior individuals").

dao (pp. 158-59) — Central concept of Daoism, meaning "the way," "the way of nature," or "the way of the cosmos." To be more specific, it figured as the original force of the cosmos, an eternal and unchanging principle that governs all the workings of the world. In Daoist writings, it appears as a supremely passive force which does nothing but accomplishes everything.

Daodejing (p. 158) — First and most influential Daoist work, allegedly written by Laozi, but actually completed by many hands over several subsequent centuries.

Daoism (pp. 158-60) — School of thought during the Warring States period, appearing as a critique to Confucian activism; represented an effort to understand the fundamental character of nature in order to learn how to live in harmony with it. By encouraging the development of a reflective and introspective consciousness, Daoism served as a counterbalance to the activism and extroversion of the Confucian tradition.

eunuchs (pp. 153, 173) — Personal servants of imperial households. Men went through voluntary castration in order to work in the harem of the emperor or king. Sometimes they seized enormous power because of their close relationships with the rulers or various factions at court.

The Great Wall (p. 163) — Massive defensive barriers built to protect China proper from raids of nomadic peoples from the northwest. The Qin dynasty enrolled a huge amount of human labor to link existing sections of barriers into an enormous wall, which was further extended and strengthened by later dynasties.

Legalism (pp. 161-62) — School of thought in classical China that promoted a practical and ruthlessly efficient approach to statecraft. Legalists believed that a strong and well-regulated government was of foremost importance to bring peace and order to society, and the foundations of a state's strength were agriculture and armed forces. They advocated clear and strict laws of rewards and punishments to harness selfish desire and energy of individuals for the interests of the state.

paper (p. 171) — First invented during the Han dynasty, probably before 100 C.E. Chinese craftsmen began to fashion hemp, bark, and textile fibers into sheets of paper, which was less expensive than silk and easier to write on than bamboo.

Qin (pp. 162-66) — One of the warring states located in west China; conquered other states and unified China in 221 B.C.E. The Qin empire was short-lived but its centralized imperial rule left a permanent mark on the history of imperial China thereafter.

terra cotta army (p. 165) — More than 15 thousand life-sized pottery figures buried in the tomb of the First Emperor to guard him in death. The terra cotta soldiers, horses, and weapons were made individually, with great details. The tomb has been under excavation since 1974.

wuwei (p. 159) — Chief moral virtue of Daoism, which can be understood as disengagement from the affairs of the world, such as advanced education or personal striving. *Wuwei* calls for individuals to live simple and unpretentious lives and keep in harmony with nature. By this moral virtue, Daoism encouraged less government, small and simple community life, and individual freedom from humanly-constructed standards of behavior.

Xiongnu (p. 169) — Turkish speaking nomadic people from the steppes of central Asia, frequently raiding the northwest borders of China; pacified by Han Wudi's army.

The Yellow Turban Uprising (p. 173) — Peasant revolt against the Han dynasty during the 2nd century C.E. So called because the rebels wore yellow turbans on their heads. The uprising was put down, but it severely undermined the imperial rule of Han.

Map Exercises

1. On the following map, label the natural barriers that restricted expansion of Chinese empires and contributed to the relative isolation of China (see Map 7.1, p. 162, of your textbook):

   - East: Yellow Sea, East China Sea
   - South: South China Sea
   - North: Gobi Desert

(Note also that on the west there were the Tibetan Plateau and the Himalayan Mountains contributing to China's restrictions and relative isolation. On this point, see Map 7.2, p. 168, of your textbook.)

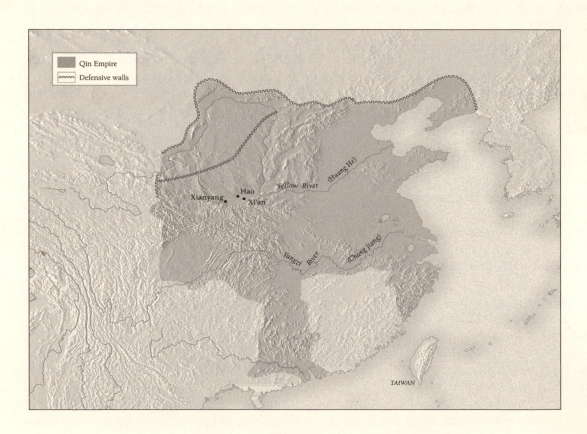

2. Compare Map 7.1 with Map 7.2 (pp. 162 and 168 in your textbook) and describe the territorial expansion of China during the Han dynasty.

3. What was the nature of the relationships between the Xiongnu and the Chinese during Qin and Han times? Give a geographical explanation of their relationships.

Self Test/Student Quiz

1. In 99 B.C.E. the great historian of China, Sima Qian, suffered from castration because

   a. he was blamed for distorting history.
   b. he inflicted this pain on himself in order to be a eunuch.
   c. his view contradicted the emperor's judgment.

2. Confucius left an enduring mark on Chinese society as

   a. an educator and political advisor.
   b. a man involved in the practice of statecraft as an ambitious official.
   c. a great traveler and writer of deep philosophical treatises.

3. By *junzi*, or "superior individuals," Confucius meant

   a. highly talented men readily available for filling government posts.
   b. men of moral integrity capable of making wise and fair judgments.
   c. individuals who displayed their sense of superiority over others.

4. Which of the following key Confucian concepts is incorrectly described?

   a. *Ren*: Filial piety, or unconditional obligation to respect parents and grandparents.
   b. *Li*: A sense of propriety.
   c. *Xiao*: respecting and taking care of parents and grandparents when they were still alive, and worshipping them after they died.

5. Mencius, the principal spokesman for the Confucian school, advocated that

   a. the evil nature of human beings could be improved by moral education.
   b. government should be organized through benevolence and humane action.
   c. government should be run by laws.

6. The concept *dao* means

   a. natural laws such as those defined by modern physics.
   b. the original force of the cosmos, an eternal and unchanging principle that governs all the workings of the world.
   c. passive and yielding forces that exist only in water and empty spaces.

7. An individual who practiced the Daoist virtue of *wuwei* would

    a. motivate him/herself to change the world.
    b. follow high ethical standards and strive for success.
    c. go with the flow of the cosmos and live in harmony with nature.

8. Individuals in traditional China could live as Confucians by day and Daoists by night. This refers to the fact that

    a. the difference between Confucianism and Daoism was as clear-cut as day and night.
    b. Confucianism and Daoism were not mutually exclusive, but in many people's eyes, complemented each other.
    c. the Chinese, like other peoples, were active in daytime and became passive at night.

9. To make a strong and powerful state, Legalist ministers

    a. encouraged commerce, entrepreneurial activity, and education.
    b. won the people's support by providing them with legal rights.
    c. encouraged agricultural cultivation and military service.

10. After the unification of Qin, the First Emperor ordered

    a. the burying alive of Confucian scholars and the burning of most books.
    b. all the people to speak the same dialect, which was Mandarin.
    c. the castration of the great historian Sima Qian.

11. The excavation site of the First Emperor's tomb nearby Xi'an is a great tourist attraction. When you visit the tomb, you can certainly see

    a. a great army of Qin soldiers and cavalry, buried alive.
    b. sacrificed slaves, concubines, and craftsmen who designed and built the tomb.
    c. the emperor's skeleton in the suit of jade plaques sewn together with gold threads.

12. The great Qin empire only lasted a few years. It was ended by

    a. a military coup.
    b. waves of revolts.
    c. violence of court factions.

13. When Liu Bang restored order and established the Han dynasty, he

    a. relied exclusively on his relatives for support of his rule.
    b. relied exclusively on bureaucrats to exercise effective control of China.
    c. relied on both his relatives and bureaucratic officials.

14. Han Wudi, the greatest and most energetic emperor of the Han dynasty, was remembered by later generations

    a. as a "Martial Emperor."
    b. as a "socialist emperor."
    c. for his successful conquest of central Asia.

15. In preparing for governmental officials, the imperial university of the Later Han enrolled more than three thousand students, with its curriculum primarily based on

    a. the statecraft policies of Legalism.
    b. political science and the study of law.
    c. Confucianism.

16. Han Wudi, or the "Martial Emperor," decided to go on the offensive against the Xiongnu primarily because

    a. he intended to invade the Persian empire from central Asia.
    b. other methods were not effective to pacify the Xiongnu and stop their raids.
    c. the powerful Xiongnu leader, Maodun, killed his father.

17. Which of the following is not true with regard to Chinese silk?

    a. Sericulture was first discovered by the Chinese during the Han dynasty.
    b. Chinese silk was especially fine because of advanced sericulture techniques.
    c. During Han times, Chinese silk became a prized commodity in India, Persia, Mesopotamia, and even the distant Roman empire.

18. The monumental work of Sima Qian was most likely written on

    a. bamboo strips.
    b. silk.
    c. paper.

19. After Wang Mang usurped the throne of the Han, he attempted

    a. to be a socialist emperor.
    b. to solve the problem of court factions.
    c. to solve the problem of landholding.

20. The principal events leading to the collapse of the Han dynasty occurred during

    a. the Yellow Turban Uprising.
    b. the violence precipitated by court factions.
    c. both a and b.

Textual Questions for Analysis

1. Compare and contrast Confucianism and Daoism and explain why the combination of the two could constitute a "good life" for individuals as well as for the state.

2. Legalism made the Qin one of the most powerful empires of the world, but it also made the Qin the most vulnerable dynasty in Chinese history. Explain.

3. Based on variety of items excavated from the tomb of the First Emperor, what can you say about the emperor's personality, daily life, and politics?

4. When Liu Bang established the Han dynasty in 206 B.C.E., what governmental models did he use for making imperial policies? What made him give up one model for another?

5. Discuss Wang Mang's reforms in historical context. What sociopolitical problems was he facing at the time? What might have been his motives in launching reforms? Why did his reforms fail?

6. Through the policies of centralization during the Qin and Han dynasties, what problems were solved? What problems remained unsolved? What new problems were created by centralized rule?

Documentary Evidence

Memorial on the Burning of Books

The First Emperor was aided in his efforts toward unification by a group of astute and ruthless statesmen identified with Legalist doctrines, the most important of whom was Li Si (died 208 B.C.E.), who became prime minister of the new empire. At Li's urging the First Emperor carried out a series of sweeping changes and innovations that, in the course of a few years, radically affected the entire structure of Chinese life and society. When criticisms and opposition against the new regime arose, prime minister Li met them with typically Legalist measures, as we can see from the following memorial submitted by him to the First Emperor. (From W. Theodore de Bary, et al., *Sources of Chinese Tradition*. Vol. 1, New York: Columbia University Press, 1960, pp. 140-41).

> In earlier times the empire disintegrated and fell into disorder, and no one was capable of unifying it…. Everyone cherished his own favorite school of learning and criticized what had been instituted by the authorities. But at present Your Majesty possesses a unified empire, has regulated the distinctions of black and white, and has firmly established for yourself a position of sole supremacy. And yet these independent schools, joining with each other, criticize the codes of laws and instructions. Hearing of the promulgation of a decree, they criticize it, each from the standpoint of his own school. At home they disapprove of it in their hearts; going out they criticize it in the thoroughfare. They seek a reputation by discrediting their sovereign; they appear superior by expressing contrary views, and they lead the lowly multitude in the spreading of slander. If such license is not prohibited, the sovereign power will decline above and partisan factions will form below....

Your servant suggests that all books in the imperial archives, save the memoirs of Qin, be burned. All persons in the empire, except members of the Academy of Learned Scholars, in possession of the *Book of Odes*, the *Book of History*, and discourses of the hundred philosophers should take them to the local governors and have them indiscriminately burned. Those who dare to talk to each other about the *Book of Odes* and the *Book of History* should be executed and their bodies exposed in the market place. Anyone referring to the past to criticize the present should, together with all members of his family, be put to death.… Books not to be destroyed will be those on medicine and pharmacy, divination by the tortoise and milfoil, and agriculture and arboriculture. People wishing to pursue learning should take the officials as their teachers.

QUESTIONS TO CONSIDER

1. According to Li Si, could the unification of the empire sustain itself without the unification of thought? What roles should scholars play in society?

2. Write a memorial to the First Emperor criticizing prime minister Li's above suggestions. Try your best to persuade the emperor that the Legalists' harsh policies would not make a long-lasting dynasty, but would doom the empire instead. Be careful with your tongue for the emperor had a short temper and a sharp sword.

Chapter 8

State, Society, and the Quest for Salvation in India

Introduction and Learning Objectives

This chapter deals with classical India, its two empires—Mauryas and Guptas, two permanent social institutions—caste and *jati*, and three influential religions—Jainism, Buddhism, and Hinduism. It opens with the description of a Greek ambassador who lived in India during the turn of the 5th and 4th centuries B.C.E. The ambassador had little to say about the glory of imperial rule in India, but portrayed India as a distinctive society with well-established cultural traditions. The accounts of the foreign ambassador reveal the central theme of the chapter—that centralized imperial government did not succeed nearly as well in India as it did in Persia and China, but cultural cohesion was maintained through many centuries nonetheless in the politically-divided subcontinent. Why did the Indian subcontinent not produce powerful states and long-lasting empires? Why did political disunity not lead to formations of different cultural traditions within the subcontinent? The authors' discussions in this chapter lead us to make connections among such factors as the relative weakness of central governments, the central roles played by castes and *jati*, and the triumphal quest for salvation by a number of religions in classical India.

For the most part, classical India fell under the sway of regional kingdoms rather than the rule of centralized empires. The Mauryan and the Gupta dynasties, the two exceptions to this rule, founded centralized, imperial states that embraced much of India, but neither empire survived long enough to make centralized rule a lasting feature of Indian political life. Even foreign invasions did not promote the desire of unification for self-defense. In fact, the Mauryan empire was founded in the political vacuum left by the withdrawal of Alexander's army, while the repeated invasions of the White Huns left the rule of the Gupta empire an empty name. The Indian rulers in both empires never attempted to expand their territories beyond the subcontinent. Despite the infrequence of military campaigns and few public works, the governments of both dynasties nevertheless suffered from severe financial problems that gave them no means to support big armies and maintain large bureaucratic systems. This being the case, classical India did not suffer from repressive military regimes and aggressive bureaucracies endured by many other peoples.

The social institutions of caste and *jati*, and religions of personal salvation, were the two dominant features of classical Indian life. The weakness of the political regimes was well compensated by the creation of the systems of caste and *jati* that served many functions performed by governments in other societies. The growth of trade and the proliferation of industries encouraged further development of the caste system. As a result, numerous *jati* began to function as subcastes, assuming much of the responsibility for maintaining social order in India. Along with emerging towns, growing trade, increasing wealth, and a developing social structure, classical India also saw the appearance of new religions that addressed the needs of changing times. Jainism and Buddhism appeared as a challenge to the established cultural and social order because both sought to escape the cycle of incarnation without depending on the services of the *brahmins*, and neither recognized social distinctions based on caste or *jati*. As a result, their message had a strong appeal to members of lower castes. Hinduism developed as a theoretical foundation of the caste system, but during the classical period, it also underwent an evolution that transformed it into a popular religion of salvation. As a departure from the asceticism and detachment taught by the old teachings of the Upanishads, Hinduism during the classical era offered salvation to masses of people who had to lead active lives in the world. Because Hinduism addressed the interests and needs of ordinary people better than Jainism and Buddhism did, it became the most popular religion in classical India. Neither the development of the caste system nor the emergence of new religions helped India to develop strong states and powerful empires, but weak political regimes helped India to consolidate its cultural tradition by sponsoring the popular religions.

After studying this chapter, students should understand and be able to discuss the following issues:

- the rise and fall of the two Indian empires

- economic development and corresponding changes in the caste and *jati* systems

- the teachings of Jainism, Buddhism, and Hinduism during the classical era

- differences and similarities among classical India, China, and Persia in terms of imperial rule, social structure, and cultural tradition

Chapter Outline

I. The Fortunes of Empire in Classical India

   A. The Mauryan Dynasty and the Temporary Unification of India
      1. Magadha Kingdom
         a) Intrusions of Cyrus (520 B.C.E.) and Alexander (327 B.C.E.)
         a) A political vacuum left by Alexander's withdrawal
         c) Magadha kingdom filled the vacuum
      2. Chandragupta Maurya
         a) The founder of the Mauryan empire
         b) Overthrew the Magadha kingdom in 321 B.C.E.
         c) Conquered the Greek state in Bactria
         d) Chandragupta's empire embraced all of northern India
      3. Chandragupta's government
         a) Government procedures devised by Kautalya, the advisor of the empire
         b) The political handbook, *Arthashastra*, outlined administrative methods
      4. Ashoka Maurya (reigned 268-232 B.C.E.)
         a) Chandragupta's grandson, the high point of the Mauryan empire
         b) Conquered the kingdom of Kalinga, 260 B.C.E.
         c) Ruled through tightly organized bureaucracy
         d) Established capital at Pataliputra
         e) Policies of encouraging agriculture and trade

5. Decline of the Mauryan Empire
   a) Ashoka died in 232 B.C.E.
   b) Suffered from acute financial and economic difficulties
      (1) High cost for maintaining army and bureaucrats
      (2) Debasing the currency, not a effective resolution
   c) The empire collapsed by 185 B.C.E.
B. The Revival of Empire under the Guptas
   1. The Gupta Dynasty
      a) After the Mauryan empire, India was controlled by regional kingdoms
      b) The Gupta state rose to power in Magadha
      c) Chandra Gupta (not related to Chandragupta) founded the new dynasty
      d) Gupta dynasty was relatively decentralized
   2. Gupta decline
      a) Invasion of White Huns weakened the empire
      b) After the 5th century C.E., Gupta dynasty continued in name only
      c) Large regional kingdoms dominated political life in India

II. Economic Development and Social Distinctions

A. Towns and Trade
   1. Towns and manufacturing
      a) Towns dotted the India countryside after 600 B.C.E.
      b) Towns provided manufactured products and luxury goods
      c) Large scale business: the example of Saddalaputta
   2. Long-distance trade
      a) Invasions by Persian empires helped to build extensive trade networks
      b) Trade with China through the silk roads of central Asia
      c) Trade in the Indian Ocean basin boomed
      d) Trade with Indonesia, southeast Asia, Mediterranean basin
B. Family Life and the Caste System
   1. Social and gender relations
      a) Strong patriarchal families
      b) Subordination of women to men as seen in literary works
      c) Child marriage placed women under control of old men
   2. Development of caste system
      a) New social groups of artisans, craftsmen, and merchants appeared
      b) Individuals of same trade or craft formed a guild
      c) Functions of guilds: social security and welfare systems
      d) Guilds functioned as subcastes, or *jati*
   3. Wealth and social order
      a) Trade and industry brought prosperity to many *vaishyas* and *shudras*
      b) Old beliefs and values of early Aryan society became increasingly irrelevant

III. Religions of Salvation in Classical India

A. Jainism and the Challenge to the Established Cultural Order
   1. Vardhamana Mahavira
      a) Born in north India, 540 B.C.E.
      b) Left family, searching for salvation from cycle of incarnation
      c) Gained enlightenment, taught an ascetic doctrine

     d) His disciples began to lead a monastic life

     e) Mahavira became *Jina*, the "conqueror," and followers, *Jains*

  2. Jainist doctrine and ethics

     a) Inspired by the Upanishads

     b) Everything in the universe possessed a soul

     c) Striving to purify one's selfish behavior to attain a state of bliss

     d) The principle of *ahimsa*, nonviolence toward all living things

     e) Believed that almost all occupations entailed violence of some kind

     f) Too demanding, not a practical alternative to the cult of the *brahmins*

  3. Appeal of Jainism

     a) Social implication: Individual souls equally participated in ultimate reality

     b) The Jains did not recognize social hierarchies of caste and *jati*

     c) Became attractive to members of lower castes

     d) The ascetic tradition continues to today

B. Early Buddhism

  1. Siddhartha Gautama (563-483 B.C.E.)

     a) Born in 563 B.C.E. in a small tribal state governed by his father

     b) Witnessed miseries of the human condition

     c) Gave up his comfortable life and began searching for enlightenment

     d) Intense meditation and extreme asceticism

     e) Received enlightenment under the bo tree and became Buddha

  2. The Buddha and his followers

     a) "Turning of the Wheel of the Law," 528 B.C.E.

     b) Organized followers into a community of monks

     c) Traveled throughout north India, bringing enlightenment to others

  3. Buddhist doctrine: The *dharma*

     a) The Four Noble Truths

        (1) All life involves suffering

        (2) Desire is the cause of suffering

        (3) Elimination of desire brings an end to suffering

        (4) The Noble Eightfold Path brings the elimination of desire

     b) The Noble Eightfold path: Right belief, right resolve, right speech, right behavior, right occupation, right effort, right contemplation, and right meditation

     c) Religious goal: personal salvation, or *nirvana*, a state of perfect spiritual independence

  4. Appeal of Buddhism

     a) Appealed strongly to members of lower castes

        (1) Salvation without services of the brahmins

        (2) Did not recognize social hierarchies of castes and *jati*

     b) Less demanding than Jainism, more popular

     c) Used vernacular tongues, not Sanskrit

     d) Holy sites and pilgrims

     e) The monastic organizations—extremely efficient at spreading the Buddhist message and winning converts to the faith

  5. Ashoka's support

     a) Emperor Ashoka became a devout Buddhist, 206 B.C.E.

     b) Banned animal sacrifices in honor of *ahimsa*

     c) Granted lands to monasteries

     d) Sent missionaries to Bactria and Ceylon

C. Mahayana Buddhism
1. Early Buddhism made heavy demands on individuals
    a) Giving up personal property
    b) Forsaking the search for social standing
    c) Detaching oneself from worldly pleasures
2. Development of Buddhism
    a) Buddha became a god
    a) The notion of *boddhisatva*—"an enlightened being"
    c) Monasteries began to accept gifts from wealthy individuals
    d) Buddhism became more attractive
3. The spread of Mahayana Buddhism
    a) *Mahayana*—"the greater vehicle"
    b) Spread to central and east Asia
    c) Buddhist monasteries were also educational institutions
    d) Nalanda, the best known monastery and school
D. The Emergence of Popular Hinduism
1. The epics
    a) *Mahabharata*, a secular poem revised by brahmin scholars to honor the god Vishnu, the preserver of the world
    b) *Ramayana*, a secular story of Rama and Sita was changed into a Hindu story
2. The *Bhagavad Gita*
    a) A short poetic work
    b) A dialogue between the god Vishnu and a warrior
    c) Illustrated expectations of Hinduism and promise of salvation
3. Hindu ethics
    a) Lower demands for achieving salvation
    b) Individuals should meet their responsibilities in detached fashion
    c) Balance of *dharma, artha, kama* would help an individual to attain *moksha*
4. Popularity of Hinduism
    a) Became more popular than Buddhism
    b) The Guptas and their successors helped Hinduism become the dominant religion in India

Significant Individuals

Ashoka Maurya (p. 180) — Chandragupta's grandson, best known emperor of Mauryan dynasty, reigned 268-232 B.C.E.; conquered the kingdom of Kalinga through a bloody campaign in 260 B.C.E. Converted to Buddhism and sponsored the new religion throughout his empire. His rule represented the highest point of the Mauryan empire in terms of territory and central administration.

Chandra Gupta (p. 182) — Founder of the Gupta empire who rose to power in Magadha about 320 C.E. (Note: He was not related to Chandragupta Maurya, the founder of Mauryan empire)

Chandragupta Maurya (p. 179) — King of the state of Magadha and founder of the Mauryan empire. Rose to power in north India after Alexander's army withdrew from the region. Tradition holds that he abdicated his throne for an existence so ascetic that he starved himself to death.

Faxian (p. 183) — Chinese Buddhist monk who traveled widely in India searching for texts of the Buddhist scriptures during the reign of Chandra Gupta II (reigned 375-415 C.E.). His accounts left valuable records for the reconstruction of Indian history.

Kautalya (p. 179) — Advisor or minister of Chandragupta's government who devised administrative procedures and diplomatic strategies for the Mauryan empire. Some of his advice and ideas survived in the political handbook known as the *Arthashastra*.

Megasthenes (p. 177) — Greek ambassador who lived in India during late 4th and early 3rd centuries B.C.E. Wrote a book, *Indika*, which portrayed India as a wealthy land that supported a distinctive society with well-established cultural traditions.

Siddhartha Gautama (p. 189) — Founder of Buddhism; born to a *kshatriya* family about 563 B.C.E.; sought enlightenment through intense meditation and extreme asceticism, and received enlightenment under a bo tree; taught that enlightenment could be achieved only by abandoning desires for all earthly things.

Vardhamana Mahavira (p. 187) — The great teacher of Jainism, born in northern India about 540 B.C.E. to a prominent *kshatriya* family; taught an ascetic doctrine of detachment from the world and formed a monastic order to perpetuate and spread his message. His disciples referred to him as *Jina*, "the conqueror," and referred to themselves as *Jains*.

Chapter Glossary

ahimsa (p. 188) — Jainist principle, meaning nonviolence toward other living things or their souls. To observe this principle, devout Jainist monks went to extremes to avoid harming the millions of souls they encountered each day.

Arthashastra (p. 179) — Political handbook containing Kautalya's and others' advice to the Gupta dynasty regarding principles of government. It outlined methods of administering the empire, overseeing trade and agriculture, collecting taxes, maintaining order, conducting foreign relations, waging war, and obtaining information through spies.

Bhagavad Gita (p. 194) — "Song of the Lord," a short poetic work of India, also an episode of the *Mahabharata*. The work contained a dialogue between a warrior and the god Vishnu, which clearly illustrated both the expectations and promise of Hinduism for its believers.

boddhisatva (p. 192) — "The enlightened being," a Buddhist concept referring to individuals who had reached spiritual perfection and merited the reward of *nirvana* but who intentionally delayed their entry into *nirvana* in order to help others who were still struggling; a notion articulated by Mahayana Buddhist theologians between the 3rd and 1st century C.E.

Bodh Gaya (p. 191) — One of the holy sites of Buddhism, a place where Gautama received enlightenment under a bo tree.

Buddha (p. 189) — "The enlightened one," a title referring to Siddhartha Gautama, the creator of Buddhism.

Buddhism (p. 190) — One of the world religions originating in India during the 6th century B.C.E.; founded by Siddhartha Gautama, the Buddha. Its fundamental doctrine was based on the Four Noble Truths taught by the Buddha. The religious goal was to achieve personal salvation called *nirvana*, a state of perfect spiritual independence. To achieve this goal, Buddhism stressed reducing desires for material goods and other worldly attractions.

Charvaka (p. 187) — Anti-religious sect of classical India which believed in atheistic materialism: The gods were figments of the imagination, *brahmins* were charlatans who enriched themselves by hoodwinking others, and human beings came from dust and returned to dust like any other animal in the natural world. This sect did not achieve long-lasting popularity.

Deer Park of Sarnath (p. 191) — One of the Buddhist holy sites where Buddha preached his first sermon in 528 B.C.E.

dharma (p. 190) — Basic doctrine shared by Buddhists of all sects, including the teachings of the Four Noble Truths and the Noble Eightfold Path.

Gupta empire (pp. 182-83) — The second Indian empire, founded by the Gupta family during the 4th century C.E. Extended to all but the southern regions of the Indian subcontinent. Less centralized than Mauryan empire.

Hinayana (p. 193) — Pejorative term for Theravada Buddhism; literally meant "the lesser vehicle," so called because of its strict adherence to the original Buddha's teachings and monastic life, which, by the later Mahayana standard, could only carry a few monks to salvation. In later centuries, Theravada Buddhism became popular in Ceylon, Burma, Thailand, and other parts of southeast Asia.

Hinduism (pp. 194-96) — Most popular religion of salvation in India, drawing inspiration from the Vedas and Upanishads. Basic teachings included the four principal aims of human life: obedience to religious and moral laws (*dharma*); the pursuit of economic well-being and honest prosperity (*artha*); the enjoyment of social, physical, and sexual pleasure (*kama*); and the salvation of the soul (*moksha*).

Jainism (pp. 187-88) — One of the most influential Indian religions; became popular beginning in the late 5th century B.C. Taught that everything possessed a soul and the practice of nonviolence toward other living things or their souls. Represented an alternative to the traditional cults of *brahmins*.

Kalinga (p. 180) — Indian kingdom located in the east-central part of the subcontinent (modern Orissa). Maintained hostility toward the Mauryan empire while controlling several principal trade routes of India. Lost its independence to emperor Ashoka Maurya after a bloody war in 260 B.C.E.

Magadha (pp. 178-79) — Regional kingdom of India, located in the central portion of the Ganges plain. It developed into the Mauryan empire in 321 B.C.E.

Mahabharata and *Ramayana* (p. 194) — Two great Indian epics. Originally these were secular tales transmitted orally during the late years of the Vedic age (1500-500 B.C.E.). The *Mahabharata* dealt with a massive war over control of northern India between two groups of cousins; the *Ramayana* was originally a love and adventure story involving the trials faced by the legendary Prince Rama and his loyal wife Sita. Revised later by *brahmin* scholars to bear Hindu values.

Mahayana (pp. 191-93) — one of two major subdividing trends in Buddhist belief. Believers in the Mahayana tradition shared with other Buddhists certain basic concepts in Buddhist doctrine, but articulated the notion of the *boddhisatva*, individuals who intentionally delayed their entry into nirvana to help others struggling to get there. Theologians in this tradition began to teach that *boddhisatvas* could perform good deeds on behalf of others, thus opening up the possibility of salvation to the masses.

Mahayana literally meant "the greater vehicle," so called because it could carry more people to salvation. In later centuries, Mahayana Buddhism also became established in central Asia, China, Korea, and Japan.

The Mauryan empire (pp. 178-82) — First Indian empire, representing a temporary unification of India, lasting from 321 to 185 B.C.E.; unified almost the entire Indian subcontinent except the southernmost region.

Nalanda (p. 193) — Famous Buddhist monastery, founded during the Gupta dynasty in the Ganges River valley near Pataliputra. The monastery was an educational center which attracted many pilgrims and students from foreign lands to study with the most renowned masters of Buddhist doctrine.

nirvana (p. 190) — Religious goal of Buddhism, a state of perfect spiritual independence, an escape from the cycle of incarnation.

Pataliputra (pp. 177, 180-81) — Capital for both Mauryan and Gupta empires, the fortified city near modern Patina.

stupas (p. 191) — Shrines housing relics of the Buddha and his first disciples; became the objects of pilgrim worship of Buddhists.

"Turning of the Wheel of the Law" (p. 190) — A term used by early Buddhists to refer to the first sermon by the Buddha at the Deer Park of Sarnath about 528 B.C.E., so called because the sermon represented the beginning of the Buddha's quest to promulgate the law of righteousness.

White Huns (p. 183) — Nomadic people from central Asia, a branch of the Xiongnu; occupied Bactria during the fourth century C.E. and crossed the Hindu Kush mountains into India. Their invasions of India seriously weakened the Gupta empire.

Map Exercises

1. Fill in the following information on the map below (based on Map 8.1, p. 179, of your textbook):

   - Regions: Magadha, Kalin, Deccan Plateau, Gandhara, Punjab, Bactria, Burma, Ceylon
   - Cities: Pataliputra, Sarnath, Bodh Gaya, Taxila
   - Mountains: Himalayas, Hindu Kush
   - Rivers: Ganges River, Hindus River

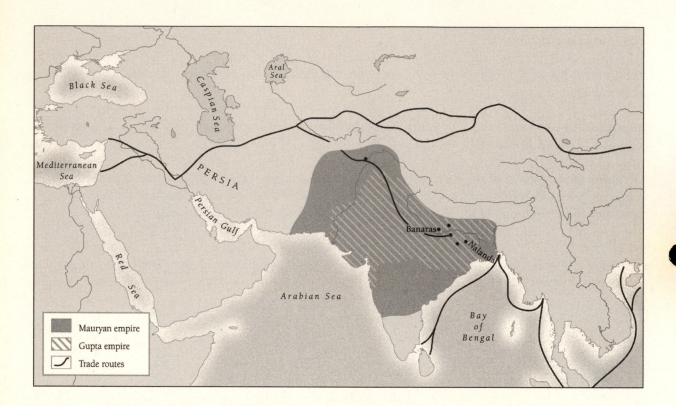

2. For India, the Hindu Kush mountains were never a formidable geographical barrier to foreign immigrations and invasions. Explain.

Self-Test/Student Quiz

1. Which of the following was NOT conveyed by the author of the *Indika*:

   a. Indian ants were as big as foxes and could mine gold from the earth.
   b. Large Indian armies used elephants as war animals.
   c. The Indians were suffering from poverty and all kinds of miseries.

2. In contrast to Persia and China, classical India

    a. was isolated from the outside world by formidable geographical barriers.
    b. lacked a strong and continuing imperial tradition.
    c. was a backward country in terms of economy and culture.

3. The invasions of Cyrus and Alexander played an important role in Indian politics and history because

    a. the conquests brought India, Persia, and Mesopotamia together as one country.
    b. foreign religions began to take root in Indian society.
    c. the intrusions destroyed many petty kingdoms and created a political vacuum.

4. The man who founded the first Indian empire was

    a. Chandragupta Maurya
    b. Chandra Gupta
    c. Ashoka Maurya

5. In the political handbook *Arthashastra*, Kautalya advised emperor Chandragupta to

    a. adopt the statecraft practices of the Chinese Legalists.
    b. use spies, including prostitutes, to gather information.
    c. avoid wars by all means, for the sake of Jainism and Buddhism.

6. Ashoka, the great emperor of the Mauryan empire,

    a. was the only emperor who extended India beyond the subcontinent.
    b. converted to Buddhism after his bloody war against Kalinga.
    c. abdicated his throne and led a life so ascetic that he starved himself to death.

7. Which of the following caused the Mauryan empire to decline and collapse?

    a. financial difficulties caused by maintaining the army and bureaucracy.
    b. peasant rebellions and factional violence among members of the imperial court.
    c. foreign invasion from Bactria.

8. Compared with the Mauryan empire, the Gupta empire was

    a. much bigger in size.
    b. more powerful and stable.
    c. less centralized.

9. The White Huns occupied Bactria and prepared to cross the Hindu Kush into India during the 4th and 5th centuries. Their invasions

    a. reduced the Gupta empire into an empty name.
    b. galvanized local kingdoms to unify themselves for self-defense.
    c. met fierce resistance from the Gupta empire.

10. The relatively high level of economic development of classical India can be best seen from its

    a. big cities.
    b. towns and trade.
    c. agricultural villages and cotton production.

11. Archaeologists working in southern India have unearthed hoards of Roman coins. These coins might have belonged to

    a. Indian merchants who exported ant-mined Indian gold to Rome.
    b. Alexander of Macedon.
    c. Roman merchants who came to India to collect Indian pepper.

12. Which of the following is NOT true with respect to marriage in classical India?

    a. Child marriage was common.
    b. Inter-caste marriage was forbidden by law but became common in reality.
    c. An ideal wife was the one who was weak-willed, faithful, and loyal to her husband.

13. In classical India, *jati*

    a. were economically self-sufficient and politically autonomous.
    b. had their own courts to control crimes and solve disputes.
    c. were not much different from guilds of other societies.

14. "Economic development and social change in classical India had profound implications for the established cultural as well as social order" (p. 187 of your textbook). By this the authors mean

    a. social distinctions based on castes and *jati* were practically out of date.
    b. asceticism became unnecessary when more and more people became wealthy.
    c. new religions emerged to meet the needs of changing times.

15. Among the principles of Jainist ethics, the most important was

    a. *ahimsa*.
    b. *Jina*.
    c. *kama*.

16. According to legend, Siddhartha Gautama, the first Buddha, abandoned his family and comfortable life to lead the existence of a holy man because of his concern with

    a. suffering.
    b. the souls of everything in the universe.
    c. social responsibility associated with his caste.

17. The religious goal of early Buddhism was

    a. "Turning of the Wheel of the Law."
    b. Four Noble Truths and Noble Eightfold path
    c. *nirvana.*

18. According to the authors of the textbook, Jainism and Buddhism appealed especially to members of lower castes because both religions

    a. practiced asceticism, which poor people could afford to do.
    b. did not recognize social distinctions based on caste or *jati.*
    c. organized monastic orders that provided the poor with shelters and a meaningful lifestyle as monks.

19. As for Ashoka's support of Buddhism, which of the following statements do NOT apply?

    a. He banned animal sacrifices and hunting, and became a vegetarian.
    b. He built monasteries and stupas, made pilgrimages to Buddhist holy sites, and sent Buddhist missionaries to foreign countries.
    c. He abdicated his throne, abandoned his imperial family, lived in a Buddhist monastery, and finally attained *nirvana.*

20. One of the differences between early Buddhism and Mahayana Buddhism was that

    a. Mahayana theologians invented the notion of the *boddhisatva.*
    b. Mahayana theologians revised the Four Noble Truths.
    c. Mahayana Buddhists did not honor the Buddha as a god.

21. Buddhism gradually lost its popularity in India because

    a. it did not promise to make life easy for its adherents.
    b. *brahmins*, the dominant class of classical India, no longer tolerated Buddhism.
    c. Buddhist monks were very much spoiled by the comforts of monasteries richly endowed by wealthy patrons.

22. All but one of the following is true with regard to Hinduism:

    a. It restricted sexual activities.
    b. It became the most popular religion of classical India.
    c. It did not have a single founder like Siddhartha Gautama for Buddhism.

Textual Questions for Analysis

1. What were the main characteristics of the Mauryan and Gupta empires?

2. Trace the development of the caste system from the early Aryan period to classical India, explaining how the caste system evolved as both a religious and social institution.

3. How did economic development and social change stimulate the emergence of new religions in classical India?

4. In what sense were Jainism and Buddhism a challenge to the established cultural and social order? Both new religions accepted some and rejected other concepts of the Upanishads' teachings. What elements were accepted and rejected?

5. In the competition between Buddhism and Hinduism, what changes occurred that made both religions popular during the classical period in India? Why did Buddhism eventually lose its popularity to Hinduism?

Documentary Evidence

The *Arthashastra*

The *Arthashastra* is the ancient Indian political handbook ascribed to Kautilya, the advisor of emperor Chandragupta Maurya. The original version of the manual was lost, and what follows is from a much later version which still bears Kautilya's name. Most parts of the manual advised how a king should conduct public affairs diligently. To manage his time as efficiently as possible, a king should divide the day and the night into sixteen equal parts, and during his waking time, he should be energetically active in administering his empire, including such matters as overseeing trade and agriculture, collecting taxes, maintaining order, and obtaining information from spies. After assigning the tight daily schedule for the king, the author then offered the following advice (From William Theodore de Bary, ed., *Sources of Indian Tradition*. New York: Columbia University Press, 1958, pp. 248, 254).

> A king should attend to all urgent business, he should not put it off. For what has been thus put off becomes either difficult or altogether impossible to accomplish....

> In the happiness of the subjects lies the happiness of the king; in their welfare, his own welfare. The welfare of the king does not lie in the fulfillment of what is dear to him; whatever is dear to the subjects constitutes his welfare....

> When one king is weaker than the other, he should make peace with him. When he is stronger than the other, he should make war with him. When he thinks: "The other is not capable of putting me down nor am I capable of putting him down," he should mark time [apparent indifference means marking time]. When he possesses an excess of the necessary means, he should attack. When he is devoid of strength, he should seek refuge with another. When his end can be achieved only through the help of an ally, he should practice duplicity [keeping oneself engaged simultaneously in peace and war with the same state means duplicity].

QUESTIONS TO CONSIDER

1. There seem to be two themes running through the above passage. One is the concern for the happiness of the subject and the hard work of the king in this regard, which resembles markedly the Chinese ideas of Confucian activism and government by humanity. The other is "the law of the fishes," i.e., the big fish eat the little ones in foreign relations, which is remarkably close to Chinese Legalist statecraft. Write a short essay to compare the *Arthashastra* of Mauryan times with Confucianism and Legalism of the Qin and Han dynasties.

2. By reading the above advice, we can identify the influence of Hindu belief on Kautilya. Explain.

Chapter 9

Mediterranean Society: The Greek Phase

Introduction and Learning Objectives

This chapter deals with the formation of Greek cultural tradition and its remarkable expansion to the larger world. The making of classical Greece began with the ancient Minoan and Mycenaean societies, which, during the 3rd and 2nd millennia B.C.E., drew their cultural inspirations from Mesopotamians, Egyptians, Phoenicians, and other peoples active in the Mediterranean region. By the 8th century B.C.E., the characteristic institution of Greek life, the polis or city-state, had emerged. Classical Greece began to flourish and reached its height during the 5th century B.C.E., which has come to be closely identified with the achievements of Athenian democracy in politics and secular rational thinking in philosophy. Although the Greeks had reason to be proud of their successful resistance to the invasions of vast Persian armies, the independent Greek city-states could neither form a coherent empire nor stop fratricidal warfare among themselves. The struggle for hegemony between Athens and Sparta left the Greek peninsula vulnerable to the new Macedonian king Philip II, who came to unify a weakened and divided Greece during the mid-4th century B.C.E.

When Alexander succeeded to the Macedonian throne after Philip II, he inherited not only a kingdom but brilliant Greek culture as well. Through his spectacular conquest of the Persian empire, Alexander brought the East and West together under his control and opened the door to the spread of Greek culture throughout the Middle East. In so doing, Alexander and his successors created a new period of Greek history called the Hellenistic era. During the centuries between Alexander's death and the expansion of the Roman empire in the eastern Mediterranean, the Hellenistic empires governed cosmopolitan societies and sponsored interactions between peoples from Greece to India. The Hellenistic world was the world of Greeks and non-Greeks, whose economic exchanges and cultural contacts prepared the way for Rome.

Within the big picture which covers almost two millennia of Greek history, the authors' discussions focus on the development of the Greek poleis, the differences in lifestyle and political philosophy between Athens and Sparta, and the triumph of Greek rational philosophy over popular religions which apparently lacked a spiritual dimension and concern for the after-life. At various points, the authors urge students to compare classical Greece with classical Persia, China, and India in terms of politics, economies, religions, and philosophies.

After reading this chapter, students should understand and be able to discuss the following issues:

- Greek poleis as cultural, economic, and political units

- differences between Athens and Sparta in terms of lifestyle and political philosophy

- cultural tradition and identity of the Greeks

- characteristics of classical Greek philosophy

- Greek influence during the Hellenistic age

Chapter Outline

I. **Early Development of Greek Society**

   A. Minoan and Mycenaean Societies
      1. Knosses
         a) Minoan society arose on the island of Crete, late 3rd millennium B.C.E.
         b) Lavish palaces at Knossos, between 2000 and 1700 B.C.E.
         c) Linear A, a kind of written language, is found
      2. The Island of Crete
         a) Between 2200 and 1450 B.C.E., the center of Mediterranean commerce
         b) Received early influences from Phoenicia and Egypt
         c) Established colonies on Cyprus and many islands in the Aegean Sea
      3. Decline of Minoan Society
         a) After 1700 B.C.E., a series of earthquakes, volcanic eruptions, and tidal waves
         b) After 1450 B.C.E., wealth attracted a number of invaders
         c) By 1100 B.C.E., Crete fell under foreign domination
      4. Mycenaean society
         a) Indo-European immigrants settled in Greek, 2000 B.C.E.
         b) Adapted Minoan Linear A into their script Linear B
         c) Stone fortresses in the Peloponnesus (southern Greece) protected agricultural settlements
         d) Most important settlement was Mycenae, hence, Mycenaen society
         e) Overpowered Minoan society and expanded to Anatolia, Sicily, and Italy
      5. Chaos in the eastern Mediterranean
         a) The Mycenaeans engaged in Trojan war, about 1200 B.C.E.
         b) Foreign invasions to Mycenaen homeland
         c) From 1100 to 800 B.C.E., chaos reigned in the eastern Mediterranean
   B. The World of the Polis
      1. The Polis
         a) In the absence of a centralized state, the polis emerged
         b) As city-states, poleis took various political forms
         c) Sparta and Athens were the most important poleis
      2. Sparta
         a) Situated in a fertile region of the Peloponnesus
         b) Began to extend their control during the 8th and 7th centuries B.C.E.
         c) Reduced the neighboring peoples to the status of *helots*, or servants
         d) By the 6th century B.C.E., *helots* outnumbered Spartans by 10 to 1
         e) Maintained domination by a powerful military machine
      3. Spartan society
         a) Discouraged social distinction, observed austere lifestyle
         b) Distinction was drawn by prowess, discipline, and military talent
         c) Commitment to military values was strong

4. Athens
    a) Population growth and economic development caused political strain
    b) Sought to negotiate order by democratic principles
    c) Citizenship was open to free adult males, not to foreigners, slaves, and women
5. Athenian society
    a) Maritime trade brought about prosperity to Attica, the region of Athens
    b) Aristocratic landowners were principal beneficiaries
    c) Owners of small plots began to sell lands, some became slaves
    d) Class tension became intensified, the 6th century B.C.E.
6. Solon and Athenian democracy
    a) Solon forged a compromise between the classes
    b) Opened polis councils for any citizen
7. Pericles (ca. 443-429 B.C.E.)—the most popular democratic leader of Athens
C. Greece and the Larger World
    1. Greeks founded more than 400 colonies
    2. Effects of Greek colonization
        a) Facilitated trade among Mediterranean lands and people
        b) Spread of Greek language and cultural traditions
        c) Stimulated development of surrounding areas
D. Conflict with Persia and Its Results
    1. The Persian War (500-479 B.C.E.)
        a) Cyrus and Darius controlled Anatolia
        b) Greek cities on Ionian coast revolted, 500 B.C.E.
        c) The battle of Marathon, 490 B.C.E.
        d) Xerxes seized Athens, but his navy lost in the battle of Salamis, 480 B.C.E.
        e) Persian army retreated back to Anatolia, 479 B.C.E.
    2. The Delian League
        a) The alliance among Greek poleis against Persian threat
        b) Military force from Athens, finance from other poleis
        c) Persian threat subsided, poleis no longer wanted to make contributions
    3. The Peloponnesian War (431-404 B.C.E.)
        a) Tensions led to two armed camps, under leadership of Athens and Sparta
        b) Unconditional surrender of Athens, 404 B.C.E.
E. The Macedonians and the Coming of Empire
    1. The kingdom of Macedon, a frontier state north of peninsular Greece
    2. Philip of Macedon (re. 359-336 B.C.E.)
        a) Built a powerful army, overcame the power of clan leaders
        b) Began to offend Greece from 350 B.C.E.
        c) Brought Greece under control by 338 B.C.E.
    3. Alexander of Macedon and his conquests
        a) At age 20, Alexander succeeded Philip
        b) Began to invade Persia, controlled Ionia and Anatolia, 333 B.C.E.
        c) By 331 B.C.E., controlled Syria, Egypt, Mesopotamia
        d) Invaded Persian homeland and burned Persepolis
        e) Crossed Indus River by 327 B.C.E.
        f) Died in 323 B.C.E. at age of 33
F. The Hellenistic Empires
    1. Alexander's realm was divided into three states: Antigonid, Ptolemaic, Seleucid
    2. The Hellenistic Era: the age of Alexander and his successors

3. The Antigonid empire
   a) Continuous tension between the Antigonid rulers and Greek cities
   b) The economy of Athens flourished again through trade
   c) Overpopulation, many moved to the Seleucid empire
4. The Ptolemaic empire
   a) The wealthiest of the Hellenistic empires
   b) The rulers did not interfere in Egyptian society
   c) Efficient organization of agriculture, industry, and taxation
   d) Royal monopolies over textiles, salt, and beer
5. Alexandria
   a) The capital of Ptolemaic empire, at the mouth of the Nile
   b) Cultural center: the famous Alexandria Museum and Alexandria Library
6. The Seleucid empire
   a) More Greek influence than in Egypt
   b) Greek and Macedonian colonists flocked to Greek cities of the former Persia
   c) Colonists created a Mediterranean-style urban society
7. The legacy of the Hellenistic age

II. The Fruits of Trade: Greek Economy and Society

A. Trade and the Integration of the Mediterranean Basin
   1. Trade
      a) Production of olive oil and wine, in exchange for grain and other items
      b) Trade brought about prosperity, population growth, and colonization
      c) Merchant ships with 400 tons capacity were common
      d) Some cities relied more on commerce than on agriculture
   2. Complex commercial and Economic organizations
   3. Panhellenic festivals
      a) A sense of a larger Greek community prevailed among all Greeks
      b) Colonists shared the same religion and language
      c) Periodic panhellenic festivals reinforced their common bonds
   4. The Olympic games, the best known panhellenic festival
B. Family and Society
   1. Greek society in Homer's works
      a) Heroic warriors and outspoken wives in Homer's world
      b) Strong-willed human beings clashed constantly
   2. Patriarchal society
      a) Male family heads ruled households, could abandon newborns
      b) Upper-class women often wore veils outside homes, accompanied by servants
      c) Women could not own landed property but could operate small business
      d) Priestess was the only public position for women
      e) Spartan women enjoyed higher status than women of other poleis
   3. Sappho
      a) Female poet, earned reputation for literary talent
      b) Instructed young women in music and literature at home
      c) Critics charged her with homosexual activity

4. Slavery
   a) By law, slaves were private chattel property of their owners
   b) Worked as cultivators, domestic servants
   c) Educated or skilled slaves worked as craftsmen and business managers

III. The Cultural Life of Classical Greece

A. Rational Thought and Philosophy
   1. The formation of Greek cultural traditions
      a) From the 8th century, drew inspirations from Mesopotamia and Egypt
      b) About 800 B.C.E., adapted the Phoenicians' alphabet to their own language
      c) During the 5th century, began to shape their own cultural tradition
      d) The Greek cultural feature: a philosophy based on human reason
   2. Socrates (470-399 B.C.E.)
      a) An Athenian philosopher, determined to understand human beings
      b) Encouraged reflection on ethics and morality
         (1) Integrity was more important than wealth and fame
         (2) "The unexamined life is not worth living"
      c) Critical scrutiny to traditional ethical teachings
      d) Was condemned to death on charge of corrupting Athenian youths
   3. Plato (430-347 B.C.E.)
      a) A zealous disciple of Socrates
      b) The theory of Forms or Ideas
      c) His *Republic* expressed the ideal of philosophical kings
   4. Aristotle (384-322 B.C.E.)
      a) Plato's disciple, but distrusted theory of Forms or Ideas
      b) Devised rules of logic to construct powerful arguments
      c) His works provided a coherent and comprehensive vision of the world
   5. Legacy of Greek philosophy
      a) Intellectual authorities for European philosophers until 17th century
      b) Intellectual inspiration for Christian and Islamic theologians.
      c) Provided a powerful intellectual framework for future generations
B. Popular Religion and Greek Drama
   1. Greek deities: Zeus and scores of subordinate deities
   2. Various types of religious cults
   3. Tragic drama
      a) Dramas performed at annual theatrical festivals
      b) Great tragedians explored the possibilities and limitations of human action
   4. Comic drama took savage delight in lampooning the public and political figures
C. Hellenistic Philosophy and Religion
   1. The Hellenistic philosophers
      a) Epicureans: identified pleasure as the greatest good
      b) Skeptics: doubted certainty of knowledge, sought equanimity
      c) Stoics: Taught individuals duty to aid others and lead virtuous lives
   2. Religions of salvation
      a) Mystery religions promised eternal bliss for true believers
      b) The Egyptian cult of Osiris became very popular
      c) Speculation about a single, universal god emerged

Significant Individuals

Aeschylus, Sophocles, and Euripides (p. 221) — Great tragedians of classical Greece, lived in the 5th century B.C.E.

Alexander of Macedon (pp. 210-11) — Successor of Philip II; successfully conquered Egypt, Persia, and north India; died in 323 B.C.E. at age of thirty-three.

Aristophanes (p. 221) — Famous comic dramatist of classical Greece.

Aristotle (p. 220) — Greek philosopher; Plato's pupil and teacher of Alexander of Macedon; believed that philosophers could rely on their senses to provide accurate information about the world and then depend on reason to sort out its mysteries; devised rigorous rules of logic as means of constructing compelling arguments.

Homer (p. 199) — The *Iliad* and the *Odyssey* are ascribed to him. Scholars now know that the two epic poems had been recited for generations before Homer lived. Some experts believe that Homer was not a real man so much as a convenient name for several otherwise anonymous scribes who committed the two epics to writing. Others believe that a man named Homer had a part in preparing a written version of the two epics, but that others also contributed significantly to his work.

Pasion (pp. 216-7) — A Greek slave of the late 5th and early 4th centuries B.C.E.; worked first as a porter and then a bank clerk. With his owners' trust and rewards, Pasion gained his freedom and became the owner of the bank. He outfitted five warships from his own pocket, and won a grant of Athenian citizenship.

Pericles (ca. 443-429 B.C.E.) (p. 205) — Statesman of Athens, popular democratic leader. Under his leadership, Athens became the most sophisticated and democratic of the Greek poleis.

Philip II (p. 210) — Ruled Macedon from 359 to 336 B.C.E.; built a powerful military machine and gained centralized control over clans in Macedon. Later he entered into Greece, and by 338 B.C.E. he had overcome all organized resistance and brought Greece under his control. He was assassinated in 336 B.C.E.

Plato (p. 218) — Greek philosopher, great pupil of Socrates; lived from 430 to 347 B.C.E.; believed that human reason or knowledge could arrive at an understanding of what he called Forms or Ideas—the ultimate perfect reality he thought underlay nature; suggested the ideal form of government ruled by a philosopher-king.

Sappho (p. 216) — Female poet of Greece, active during the years around 600 B.C.E. Taught young women music and literature and was charged with homosexual activity.

Socrates (p. 217) — Athenian philosopher who lived from 470 to 399 B.C.E.; tutor of Plato; encouraged rational reflection on moral and ethical issues; sought to reason through means of skeptical questioning of traditional ethical teachings. A jury of Athenian citizens condemned him to death for corrupting the minds of Athenian youths.

Solon (p. 205) — Athenian aristocrat of the 6th century B.C.E., a democratic reformer who eased class tension by compromise. His reforms forbade enslavement for debt and opened the councils of the poleis to any citizen wealthy enough to devote time to public affairs.

Chapter Glossary

Alexandria, Egypt (p. 213) — Capital of the Ptolemaic empire, founded by Alexander at the mouth of the Nile as one of many cities named to honor him; a commercial and cultural center, especially known for the sites of the famous Alexandrian Museum and Alexandria Library.

Antigonid empire (pp. 212-13) — One of the three Hellenistic empires, founded in Greece and Macedon; lasted until the Romans established their authority in the eastern Mediterranean during the 2nd century B.C.E.

Athens (p. 205) — One of the most important poleis (city-states) of classical Greece, known for its democratic politics, commercial agriculture, and skills of foreign trade.

The Battle of Marathon (p. 208) — One of the two important battles of the Persian war fought between Persians and Athenians at Marathon in 490 B.C.E. The Athenians succeeded in defending themselves and defeating the Persian army and fleet.

The Battle of Salamis (p. 208) — One of the important battles of the Persian war. The battle took place in the narrow strait between Athens and the island of Salamis and resulted in the Persian navy being shattered by the Greek fleet.

Delian League (p. 209) — Alliance formed by several Greek poleis after the Persian war; Athens became the leader of the alliance, and other poleis contributed financial support, which went largely to the Athenian treasury.

Dionysus (p. 221) — The god of wine in popular religion of classical Greece, also known as Bacchus. Religious ritual in honor of Dionysus was celebrated primarily by women during the spring of the year.

Epicureans (p. 222) — Greek philosophical school of the Hellenistic era, founded by Epicurus (341-270 B.C.E.); identified pleasure as the greatest good, which meant a state of quiet satisfaction or freedom from emotional turmoil and pressure of the Hellenistic world.

Hellenistic empires (p. 212) — Three Greek empires formed from the Macedonian empire after Alexander's death: the three empires were the Antigonids, Ptolemies, and Seleucids.

Hellenistic Era (p. 212) — Historians refer to the age of Alexander and his successors as the Hellenistic era—an age when Greek cultural traditions expanded their influence beyond Greece itself (*Hellas*) to a much larger world.

helots (p. 204) — Servants of the Spartan state; served as agricultural labor to keep Sparta supplied with food. By the 6th century B.C.E., the helots probably outnumbered the Spartan citizens by more than ten to one. The helots were not slaves, but they could not leave the land.

Iliad **and** *Odyssey* (p. 199) — The great epic poems of ancient Greece, attributed to Homer; possibly the work of many authors. The *Iliad* offered a Greek perspective on a war waged by a band of Greek warriors against the city of Troy in Anatolia during the 12th century B.C.E. The *Odyssey* recounted the experiences of the Greek hero Odysseus as he sailed home after the Trojan war.

The kingdom of Macedon (pp. 209-10) — Frontier state north of peninsular Greece which rose to prominence after the 4th century B.C.E. Population consisted partly of cultivators and partly of sheep herders. The state was loosely organized, with the king and semiautonomous clans controlling political affairs; became centralized under Philip II and served as the basis for unification of Greece and the later Macedonian empire.

Knossos (p. 200) — An important site of ancient Crete society, where an enormous complex of lavish palaces were built decorated with vivid frescos depicting Minoans at work and play.

Linear A (p. 200) — The script of Minoan society which used written symbols to stand for syllables rather than words, ideas, vowels, or consonants. So far linguists have not yet been able to decipher this script.

Linear B (p. 202) — The syllabic script used in Mycenaean society. It was an adoption of Minoan Linear A to the early form of Greek.

Minoan society (pp. 200-201) — The sophisticated society of ancient Crete, lasting from 2200 to 1100 B.C.E.; received early influences from Phoenicia and Egypt and built lavish palaces at Knossos; also devised a script known as Linear A.

Mycenaean society (pp. 201-202) — The ancient society of the Greek peninsula, established by Indo-European immigrants; lasted from 1600 to 1100 B.C.E. Named after Mycenae, one of the most important settlements. Learned about writing and large-scale construction from the Cretans.

Olympic games (p. 215) — The best known of the panhellenic festivals, held once every four years beginning in 776 B.C.E. The games were observed by all Greek city-states and involved athletic contests. Winners of events received olive wreaths and became celebrated heroes in their home poleis.

panhellenic festivals (p. 215) — The festivals of the Greek world. Greeks from all parts gathered periodically to participate in the festivals that featured athletic, literary, and musical contests in which individuals sought to win glory for their poleis.

Peloponnesian War (p. 209) — Civil war of the Greek world, fought between 431 and 404 B.C.E. Poleis were divided into two armed camps under the leadership of Athens and Sparta. Resulted in Athens' unconditional surrender to Sparta, but the latter failed to achieve political unification of Greece.

Peloponnesus (p. 202) — The southern part of the Greek peninsula where massive stone fortresses and palaces were built to offer protection for small agricultural communities. Sparta became one of the most powerful poleis in the Peloponnesus.

Persian War (500-479 B.C.E.) (p. 208) — Fought between the Persian empire and Greek city-states. The Greeks successfully resisted the military assaults of Persian armies and maintained their independence from Persian control.

polis (p. 203) — City-states of classical Greece. The term *polis* originally referred to a citadel or fortified site that offered refuge for local communities during times of war or other emergencies. By about 800 B.C.E. these sites developed into urban centers and extended their authority over surrounding regions. Poleis (the plural of polis) functioned as the principal centers of Greek society between 800 and 338 B.C.E.

Ptolemaic empire (pp. 212-13) One of the three Hellenistic empires, founded in Egypt, which the Ptolemaic dynasty ruled until the Roman conquest of Egypt in 31 B.C.E.

The Republic (pp. 218-19) — Written by Plato; held that the ideal state was one where either philosophers ruled as kings or kings were themselves philosophers.

Seleucid empire (pp. 212-13) — One of the three Hellenistic empires, founded in the former Achaemenid empire, which was displaced by the Parthians during the 2nd century B.C.E. In this empire, Greek influence reached its greatest extent over a wide-ranging territory stretching from the eastern Mediterranean region of Anatolia to the region of Bactria in central Asia.

skeptics (p. 222) — Greek philosophical school of the Hellenistic era; doubted the possibility of certain knowledge, and sought equanimity.

Sparta (p. 204) — One of the most important poleis in classical Greece, located in the fertile southeastern region of the Peloponnesus; known for its oligarchic regime, austere lifestyle, and commitment to military values.

stoics (p. 222) — Group of Greek philosophers of the Hellenistic era; emphasized inner moral independence and tranquillity cultivated by strict discipline of the body and mind.

Trojan war (p. 202) — Legendary war between the Mycenaeans and the city of Troy in Anatolia about 1200 B.C.E.

Zeus (p. 220) — The grandson of the earth and sky gods and the paramount ruler of the divine realm in the popular religion of classical Greece. Zeus's heavenly court included scores of subordinate deities who had various responsibilities.

Map Exercises

1. Fill in the following information on the map below (based on Map 9.1, p. 202, of your textbook):

   - Seas: Black Sea, Mediterranean Sea, Aegean Sea, Ionian Sea
   - Islands: Cyprus, Crete, Sicily, Sardinia, Rhodes
   - Greek cities: Sparta, Olympia, Athens, Thebes
   - Greek colonies: Phasis, Massalia, Neapolis, Byzantium

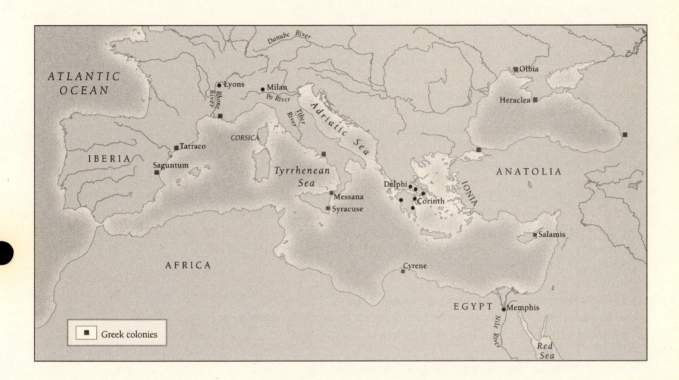

2. Explain the commercial economy and colonization of classical Greece from a geographical point of view.

3. Study Map 9.4, p. 212 of your textbook, and connect each empire with its cities:

<u>Empire</u>	<u>Cities</u>
Antigonid empire	Susa
	Babylon
Ptolemaic empire	Memphis
	Sparta
Seleucid empire	Persepolis
	Alexandria

4. When an Athenian merchant decided to ship commodities on land from Ionia to the Punjab, which major cities he might he have gone though? What means of transportation were available to him? What kind of commodities would he have wanted to sell to make a profit?

Self-Test/Student Quiz

1. In Homer's *Iliad* and *Odyssey*, the ancient Greeks were portrayed as

    a. expert and fearless seafarers.
    b. professional pirates.
    c. warriors with human heads and horse bodies.

2. Which of the following is not true with regard to Minoan and Mycenaean societies?

    a. Both societies developed written languages.
    b. Both built palaces.
    c. Both societies were established by Indo-European immigrants.

3. Choose the correct chronological order for the following persons and events:

    a. Sappho, Socrates, Philip II
    b. The Trojan War, the Peloponnesian War, the Persian war
    c. Mycenaean society, the Antigonid empire, Sparta

4. By "tyrants" the Greeks meant

    a. oppressive despots with no popular support.
    b. ambitious politicians who gained power by irregular means.
    c. extremely popular leaders of poleis.

5. Which of the following were not part of Spartan life?

    a. Boys were taken away from their mothers for military training.
    b. The helots were slaves, owned by the state.
    c. Vigorous physical exercise for girls was encouraged, in hopes that they would bear strong children.

6. All of the following were Athenian political leaders except

    a. Sophocles
    b. Solon
    c. Pericles

7. How democratic was the Athenian democracy? Choose the best description.

    a.   Citizenship was open to all residents.
    b.   Slavery was abolished through Solon's reform.
    c.   All citizens were qualified to join the city councils.

8. Between the mid-8th and the late 6th centuries B.C.E., the Greeks founded more than four hundred colonies along the shores of the Mediterranean and the Black Sea. The driving force behind such a movement was primarily

    a.   population pressure.
    b.   earthquakes and volcanic eruptions on the Greek peninsula.
    c.   a sense of pride associated with military conquests of other peoples.

9. One of the following was NOT a consequence of Greek colonization:

    a.   It quickened the social development of the peoples living in Western Mediterranean and Black Sea regions.
    b.   It led to direct conflict between the Greeks and the Persians.
    c.   It made Greeks weak and isolated from one another.

10. The Delian League was created to

    a.   conduct democratic reforms in Athens.
    b.   discourage further Persian invasions.
    c.   maintain peace within the Greek world.

11. The Peloponnesian War was fought between

    a.   two groups of Greek adversaries under the leadership of Athens and Sparta.
    b.   Thebes and Corinth.
    c.   Anatolian Greeks and peninsular Greeks.

12. The freedom and independence of the Greek poleis finally fell under control of

    a.   Xerxes by 480 B.C.E.
    b.   Philip II by 338 B.C.E.
    c.   Alexander by 336 B.C.E.

13. By 327 B.C.E. Alexander's troops refused to proceed any further from home after they reached

    a.   Bactria.
    b.   India.
    c.   China.

14. Historians refer to the age of Alexander and his successors as the Hellenistic age because

    a. Greece was finally unified under a single government.
    b. Greece was also called *Hellas*, so that the Greek age is called the Hellenistic age.
    c. this was an age in which the Greek cultural traditions expanded their influence beyond Greece itself to a much larger world.

15. All but one of the following is true with regard to Alexandria of Egypt:

    a. It was the capital of the Hellenistic world.
    b. It was the commercial center of the Mediterranean.
    c. It was the cultural capital of the Hellenistic world.

16. The Greek peninsula was

    a. known for its fertile valleys and copious rainfall.
    b. especially good for travel and communication.
    c. ideal for cultivating olives and grapes.

17. In classical Greece, the people who participated the Olympic games included

    a. athletes from all poleis.
    b. both men and women.
    c. peoples from throughout the Mediterranean region.

18. Choose one from the following scenes which was most UNLIKELY to have been witnessed in classical Greece:

    a. A woman accused her husband of abandoning her newborn baby, but the court rejected her petition.
    b. After her husband's death, a woman managed her large farm alone.
    c. After a woman's homosexuality was exposed, even the homosexual men of her community condemned her.

19. Greek philosophy is often characterized as "rational" because

    a. it was based purely on human reason.
    b. its reasoning was based purely on experiment.
    c. it transformed the Greek myths into philosophical speculation.

20. All of the following were Plato's ideas except

    a. the belief that our display of virtue or other qualities in the world was merely an imperfect reflection of the true reality or ideal qualities he called Forms.
    b. the ideal state was the one that was ruled by a philosophical elite.
    c. the belief that only democracy could make the philosopher-king possible.

21. The most important Greek deity was

    a. Apollo.
    b. Zeus.
    c. Bacchus.

22. The most respected and influential of the Hellenistic philosophers were

    a. the Skeptics.
    b. the Epicureans.
    c. the Stoics.

Textual Questions for Analysis

1. How did legacies of the Minoan and Mycenaean societies contribute to the cultural traditions of classical Greece?

2. Describe the differences between Athens and Sparta in terms of lifestyle and political philosophy.

3. Without a central government, how did the Greeks in different poleis reinforce their common bond and retain their cultural identity?

4. Use what you know about Socrates, Plato, and Aristotle to explain why classical Greek philosophy was rational.

5. Trace the expansion of Macedonia from Philip II to Alexander. What was the main reason for Philip's success? What was the consequence of Alexander's conquests?

6. What happened to Alexander's realm after his death? How did the rule of Hellenistic empires impact the societies of the Greek peninsula, Egypt, and Persia?

Documentary Evidence

Plato on the Equality of Women

The following selection is from Plato's *The Republic*, in which Socrates was the main speaker. Students should pay close attention not only to the author's argument, but also to how the argument was made (From Plato, *The Republic, A New Translation,* by Richard W. Sterling and William C. Scott, New York: W.W. Norton, 1985, pp. 201-211).

It is time to speak of women.... Let us assume that the birth and education of women will be governed by the same guidelines we prescribed for the man. We can decide later whether or not this procedure seems appropriate.

What do you mean?

This. Do we separate off male and female dogs from one another, or do we expect both to share equally in standing guard and in going out to hunt? Should all activities be shared, or so we expect the females to remain indoors on the ground that bearing and nursing the pups incapacitate them for anything else, leaving to the males the exclusive care and guarding of the flocks?

There should be no such differentiation. The only distinction between them is that we consider males to be stronger and females weaker.

Now then, can one get any animal to perform the same functions as another without giving both the same guidance and training?

No.

Then if women are to do the same things as men, we must also teach them the same things?

Yes.

The men were taught music and gymnastics, were they not?

Yes.

It follows that we must teach the women the same two arts, as well as learning and practice in the art of war.

From what you said I suppose it does follow.

Perhaps conventional wisdom would ridicule some of these proposals if we tried to put them into practice.

It surely would....

Yet we have vowed to speak our minds. Therefore we must not be daunted by all the wisecracks that will greet such innovations. Nor must we mind what the resident wits say about women studying music and gymnastics, about women bearing arms, nor, above all, what they say about women riding astride horses.

You are right....

The basic question concerns the nature of women: can a woman perform all or none of the tasks a man performs? Can she manage some but not others? Is she really capable of waging war?...

We can clarify our meaning by observing, for example, that a man and a woman who both have the qualifications to be physician have the same nature. Do you agree?

Yes.

But two men, one a physician and one a carpenter, have different nature?

Oh, entirely different.

So, then, those men and women who display distinct aptitudes for any given kind of work will be assigned to do that work. If a critic can do no more than bring up the one distinction between man and woman—that the one begets and the other bears children—we shall say that for our purposes he has offered no proof of difference at all...

And we shall be right in doing so....

Then we must conclude that sex cannot be the criterion in appointments to government positions. No office should be reserved for a man just because he is a man or for a woman just because she is a woman. All the capabilities with which nature endows us are distributed among men and women alike. Hence women will have the rightful opportunity to share in every task, and so will men, even though women are the weaker of the sexes.

COMPLETE THE FOLLOWING SENTENCES WITH THE BEST ANSWER (see the Answer Key for Documentary Evidence at the end of this Study Guide for the best answers):

1. In making his argument, Plato relied on

    a. religious authorities.
    b. political authorities.
    c. commonsense reasoning.
    d. the Greek feminist movement.

2. According to Plato's reasoning, women in the ideal state

    a. must learn how to ride horses.
    b. were capable of being political leaders.
    c. were the weaker sex.
    d. were no different from men.

Chapter 10

Mediterranean Society: The Roman Phase

Introduction and Learning Objectives

Imperial rule did not take root in Mediterranean society during the Greek phase, as we learned in the last chapter. Classical Greece was severely weakened by civil strife among the independent poleis by the 4th century B.C.E., while its Hellenistic world was divided into three dynasties and then began to fade completely about two centuries later. This chapter deals with the Roman phase of classical Mediterranean society, a phase in which the Roman empire extended many features of the Greek cultural tradition, but also eventually brought Mediterranean lands under the control of a single imperial government, which achieved long-term political stability in the Mediterranean.

The chapter traces the evolution of Rome from the Etruscans in the 8th century B.C.E. to the golden age of the Roman empire from the 3rd to the 1st century B.C.E. It tells how a combination of internal struggle and external expansion shaped the transition of Rome from republic to empire. It also details how the rise of Rome brought about economic integration of the Mediterranean region, spread the capacities of its republican constitution, and led to a centralized imperial form of government centered on the city of Rome during the last decades of the 1st century B.C.E.

The rapid expansion of Roman influence and the imposition of Roman imperial rule not only brought economic and social changes to the peoples throughout the Mediterranean basin, but also created a cosmopolitan atmosphere in which Roman cultural and religious traditions began to take shape. From economic organizations to philosophy, Rome borrowed much from the Greek traditions, but a number of new religions of salvation spread quickly via the Roman roads, especially Mithraism and Christianity. Originally a small and persecuted Jewish sect, Christianity eventually became the official religion of the Roman empire and an essential part of Western cultural traditions.

After studying this chapter, students should understand and be able to discuss the following issues:

- expansion of the Roman empire

- the transition from republic to empire

- the effect of Roman expansion on the development of Europe

- the nature of the *pax romana*

- Judaism and early Christianity

Chapter Outline

I. From Kingdom to Republic

   A. The Etruscans and Rome
      1. Romulus and Remus
         a) According to legend, these twins rescued by a she-wolf and founded Rome in 753 B.C.E.
         b) Indo-European migrants settled in Italy from 2000 B.C.E.
      2. The Etruscans
         a) Probably migrated from Anatolia
         b) Dominated Italy from the 8th to 5th centuries B.C.E.
         c) Declined, attacked by Gaul and defeated by Greek fleets
      3. The kingdom of Rome
         a) A small kingdom on the Tiber River, ruled by monarchies
         b) Easy access to the Mediterranean
         c) Trade routes converged on Rome
   B. The Roman Republic and Its Constitution
      1. Establishment of the Republic
         a) Rome nobility deposed the last Etruscan king in 509 B.C.E.
         b) Republican constitution included two consuls: civil and military
         c) Consuls were elected by an assembly dominated by the patricians
         d) The Senate advised the consuls and ratified major decisions
         e) Both Senate and consuls represented the interests of the patricians
      2. Conflicts between patricians and plebeians
         a) Plebeians' threat to secede from Rome
         b) Patricians granted plebeians the tribunes
         c) Tribunes' power to intervene and veto decisions
         d) Plebeians' tribunes dominated Roman politics, early 3rd century B.C.E.
         e) In times of crisis, ruled by short-term dictatorship
   C. The Expansion of the Republic
         a) Rome consolidated its position in Italy, 5th and 4th centuries B.C.E.
         b) Conflict with Carthage and Hellenistic realms
         c) The Punic Wars (264-146 B.C.E.), defeated Carthaginians
         d) Conflicts with Antigonids and Seleucids, 5 major wars
         e) Rome became a preeminent power in the Mediterranean

II. From Republic to Empire

   A. Imperial Expansion and Domestic Problems
      1. The Gracchi brothers
         a) Tiberius Gracchus represented interests of Rome's lower classes
         b) Served as a tribune, passed a law that set limits for landholding
         c) Assassinated in 132 B.C.E.
         d) The younger brother, Gaius Gracchus, continued the reform
         e) Was branded as a outlaw, killed by mercenaries
         f) The Republican government could no longer maintain power balance

    2. Marius and Sulla
       a) Gaius Marius recruited a private army from landless residents
       b) Became the most prominent general, the late 2nd century B.C.E.
       c) Conservative aristocratic class supported general Lucius Cornelius Sulla
    3. Civil War
       a) Marius seized Rome in 87 B.C.E.
       b) Sulla seized Rome in 83 B.C.E. after Marius died
       c) Sulla's five years of terror in Rome

B. The Foundation of Empire
    1. Julius Caesar
       a) Marius's nephew, favored liberal policies and social reform
       b) Gained fame by sponsoring public spectacles
       c) Conquered Gaul, became more popular
       d) Seized Rome in 49 B.C.E.
       e) Claimed the title "dictator for life," 46 B.C.E.
       f) Social reforms and centralized control
       g) Assassinated in 44 B.C.E.
    2. Augustus
       a) Octavian, the nephew of Caesar, brought the civil conflict to an end
       b) The Senate bestowed upon him the title Augustus, 27 B.C.E.
    3. Augustus's administration
       a) A monarchy disguised as a republic
          (1) preserved traditional republican forms of government
          (2) took all the power into his own hands
       b) Created a new standing army under his control
       c) The imperial institutions began to take root

C. Continuing Expansion and Integration of the Empire
    1. Roman expansion had decisive effects in Gaul, Germany, Britain, and Spain
       a) Romans sought access to resources
       b) Local elite began to build states and control resources
       c) Cities emerged: Paris, Lyons, Cologne, Mainz, London, Toledo, Segovia
    2. The *pax romana*
       a) Meant "Roman peace," lasted for two and half centuries
       b) Facilitated trade and communication from Mesopotamia to Atlantic Ocean
    3. Roman roads
       a) Roman engineers as outstanding road builders
       b) Roads and postal system linked all parts of the empire
    4. Roman law
       a) Tradition: Twelve Tables enacted in 450 B.C.E.
       b) Principle: innocent until proven guilty
       c) Judges enjoyed great discretion

III. Economy and society in the Roman Mediterranean

A. Trade and Urbanization
    1. Commercial agriculture
       a) Owners of *latifundia* focused on production for export
       b) Commercial agriculture stimulated economic specialization and integration

2. Mediterranean trade
   a) Sea-lanes linked ports of the Mediterranean
   b) Roman navy kept the seas largely free of pirates
   c) The Mediterranean became a Roman lake
3. The city of Rome
   a) Wealth of the city fueled its urban development
   b) Statues, pools, fountains, arches, temples, stadiums
   c) First use of concrete as construction material
   d) Rome attracted numerous immigrants
4. City attractions
   a) Public baths, swimming pools, gymnasia
   b) Enormous circuses, stadiums, and amphitheaters

B. Family and Society in Roman Times
1. The *pater familias*
   a) A Roman family consisted of all household members living together
   b) *Pater familias*, or "father of the family," ruled
   c) Women wielded considerable influence within their families
   d) Many women supervised family business and wealthy estates
2. Wealth and social change
   a) Newly rich classes built palatial houses and threw lavish banquets
   b) Cultivators and urban masses lived at subsistence level
   c) Poor classes became a serious problem in Rome and other cities
   d) No urban policy developed, only "bread and circuses"
3. Slavery
   a) Slaves—1/3 of Roman population
   b) Chained together in teams, worked on *latifundia*
   c) Spartacus's uprising in 73 B.C.E.
   d) Working conditions for city slaves were better
   e) Epictetus, an Anatolian slave, became a prominent Stoic philosopher
   f) Urban slaves could hope for manumission

IV. The Cosmopolitan Mediterranean

A. Greek Philosophy and Religions of Salvation
1. Roman deities
   a) Early deities: Jupiter, Mars, Ceres, Janus, Vesta
   b) Newly adapted deities: Juno, Minerva
2. Greek influence
   a) Stoicism appealed to Roman intellectuals
   b) Cicero (106-43 B.C.E.) established Stoicism in Rome
3. Religions of salvation
   a) Flourished in Rome and the Mediterranean basin
   b) Roman roads served as highways for religious spread
4. Mithraism
   a) Mithras, a god of sun and light in Zoroastrian mythology
   b) Roman soldiers adapted it, associated it with military value
   c) Moral teaching of Mithraism, only for men
   d) Goddess Cybele and goddess Isis were also popular

B. Judaism and Early Christianity
1. The Jews and the empire
    a) Monotheistic Jews considered state cults to be blasphemy
    b) The Jewish War (66-70 C.E.), Roman forces defeated the Jewish rebels
2. The Essenes
    a) A new sect of Judaism, founded in Palestine during the 1st century B.C.E.
    b) Strict moral code, baptism, and ritual community meals
3. Jesus of Nazareth
    a) Charismatic Jewish teacher, taught devotion to God and love for human beings
    b) Attracted large crowds through his wisdom and miraculous powers
    c) The teaching "the kingdom of God is at hand" alarmed the Romans
    d) Crucifixion in early 30s C.E.
    e) Became "Christ," or "the anointed one"
    f) The New Testament and the Old Testament became the holy book of Christianity
4. Paul of Tarsus
    a) A Jew from Anatolia, zealously preached his faith beyond Jewish communities
    b) Traveled widely in search of converts
    c) Was finally executed by Roman officials
5. The growth of early Christianity
    a) Against Roman repression, Christianity grew rapidly in the empire
    b) Strong appeal to lower classes, urban population, and women
        (1) Accorded honor and dignity to lower standing individuals
        (2) Provided a sense of spiritual freedom
        (3) Taught the spiritual equality of the sexes
        (4) Promised future glory for true believers
    c) Became the most influential faith in the Mediterranean by the 3rd century C.E.

Significant Individuals

Augustus (pp.233-34) — Title given to Octavian after his defeat of the navy of Mark Antony in 31 B.C.E.; the creator and first emperor of the Roman empire.

Epictetus (p. 241) — Anatolian slave who became a prominent Stoic philosopher. Lectured to large audiences that included high Roman officials and perhaps even emperors; 1st century C.E.

Gaius Marius (p. 232) — Prominent Roman general at the turn of the 2nd and 1st centuries B.C.E.; introduced the concept of a private army recruited from paid volunteers, mostly landless rural residents and urban workers, rather than citizen conscripts from among the small farmers; the innovation created a military force with personal loyalties to the military commander instead of to civilian authorities.

Gracchi brothers (pp. 231-32) — Tiberius and Gaius Gracchus, tribunes who represented the interests of Rome's lower classes; zealously promoted land reform and proposed to extend full Roman citizenship to peoples in most of the Italian peninsula; both killed on the command of the Roman elite, Tiberius in 132 B.C.E. and Gaius in 121 B.C.E.

Jesus of Nazareth (pp. 244-45) — Charismatic Jewish teacher, founder of Christianity; taught devotion to God and love for fellow human beings; viewed as a threat by Roman authorities and was executed in the early 30s C.E. After death, his followers called him "Christ," meaning "the anointed one," the savior who would bring individuals into the kingdom of God.

Julius Caesar (p. 233) — Nephew of the general Marius, and himself a reform-minded general of Rome, responsible for conquest of Gaul in the 50s of the 1st century B.C.E.; brought his army back to Rome and overthrew the republic in 49 B.C.E.; claimed himself a life-time dictator in 46 B.C.E., but was assassinated by the wealthy elite class in 44 B.C.E.

Lucius Cornelius Sulla (p. 232) — Conservative Roman general during the last century B.C.E.; imposed an extremely conservative legislative program that undid the influence of Marius and strengthened the hand of the wealthy in Roman politics.

Marcus Tullius Cicero (p. 242) — Roman philosopher, who helped to establish Stoicism as the most prominent school of moral philosophy in Rome.

Octavian (pp. 233-34) — Grandnephew and adopted son of Julius Caesar; defeated his principle rival, Mark Antony (who had joined forces with Cleopatra, last of the Ptolemaic rulers of Egypt) in 31 B.C.E.; the Senate bestowed upon him the title Augustus in 27 B.C.E.; became the first Roman emperor and ruled Rome for 45 years.

Paul of Tarsus (p. 245) — Jew from Anatolia who zealously preached Christianity throughout the Roman empire; called for individuals to observe high moral standards and to place their faith ahead of personal and family interests; promised a glorious future existence for those who conscientiously observed the faith. He was executed by Roman authorities.

Spartacus (p. 241) — Roman slave, escaped and assembled an army of seventy thousand rebellious slaves in 73 B.C.E.

Chapter Glossary

Carthage (p. 230) — A city-state originally established as a Phoenician colony in north Africa, located near modern Tunis; became the dominant political and commercial power in the western Mediterranean; Fought the Punic War with Rome for hegemony over the western Mediterranean regions.

The Etruscans (p. 227) — A band of Indo-European people who migrated to the Italian peninsula probably from Anatolia; established a powerful kingdom that dominated much of Italy from the 8th to the 6th centuries B.C.E.

The Essenes (p. 244) — Sect of Judaism; observed a strict moral code and participated in rituals designed to reinforce a sense of community; shared many concerns with early Christianity, especially the notion that a savior would deliver them from Roman rule.

The Gauls (pp. 229, 233) — A powerful Celtic people who lived in Gaul (modern France); invaded Italy on several occasions during the 5th century B.C.E. In the 50s of the first century B.C.E., Caesar conquered Gaul and brought it into the Roman empire.

Jupiter (p. 242) — Principal god of Rome, believed to be lord of the heavens.

latifundia (p.231) — Large plantations owned by the wealthy elite and operated by slave labor in Rome.

Mithraism (p. 243) — Cult dedicated to Mithras; originally a Zoroastrian god closely identified with the sun and light. Roman soldiers serving in the Hellenistic world adapted it and associated Mithras with military values such as strength, courage, and discipline.

pater familias (pp. 239-40) — "Father of the family," who by Roman law had the authority to arrange marriages for his children, determine the work or duties of all family members, and punish them for offenses as he saw fit. He also had the right to sell family members into slavery and even to execute them.

patricians (p. 228) — Hereditary aristocrats and wealthy classes of the Roman republic who dominated Roman political and economic life, electing an assembly who selected two consuls and serving as members of the Senate, an advisory body to the consuls.

pax romana (p. 236) — "Roman peace," an era of peace inaugurated by Augustus's rule that persisted for two and a half centuries.

plebeians (p. 228) — Common people or ordinary citizens of Rome, whose tribunes gained political power in struggle against the patricians.

The Punic Wars (p. 230) — Three devastating conflicts between Romans and Carthaginians over political and commercial supremacy in the western Mediterranean regions fought between 264 and 146 B.C.E. The rivalry ended after Roman forces razed the city of Carthage, salted the surrounding earth to render it unfit for agriculture and settlement, and forced many of the survivors into slavery.

Romulus and Remus (p. 226) — Twin brothers in the ancient Roman legends, who were raised by a kindly she-wolf and grew up as strong and courageous men. According to the legends, Romulus founded the city of Rome and became its first king in 753 B.C.E.

Senate (p. 228) — A political body of Roman aristocrats; the members included Rome's most prominent political and military leaders; advised the consuls and ratified all major decisions. Together with the consuls, the Senate largely controlled public affairs in early years of Roman republic.

tribunes (p. 228) — Official representatives of plebeians in the Roman government; had the power to intervene in all political matters and possessed the right to veto measures that they judged unfair.

Map Exercises

1. Compare Map 10.1 (p. 229) with Map 10.2 (p. 235) in your textbook and discuss the territorial expansion of the Roman empire using concrete information.

2. Suppose a Christian missionary preached his faith along one of the Roman roads. He started from the Nile and his destiny was Neapolis. How many regions and major cities did he have to go through? Use Christianity as an example to explain how the Roman roads and the integration of the Mediterranean lands under the Roman empire helped the spread of religions.

Self-Test/Student Quiz

1. About 55 C.E., Paul of Tarsus traveled from a port in Palestine to Rome to

    a. seek converts.
    b. appeal his case.
    c. apply for Roman citizenship.

2. According to the ancient legends, the kingdom of Rome was established in 753 B.C.E. by

    a. Romulus.
    b. a she-wolf.
    c. Aeneas.

3. The society of the Etruscans was ruled by

    a. city-states.
    b. a republican government.
    c. powerful kings.

4. The Roman republic was dominated by

    a. the patricians.
    b. the plebeians.
    c. democratic leaders.

5. Which of the following was NOT done by the Romans after they defeated the Carthaginians in the Punic Wars?

    a. Spreading salt on Carthaginian lands and forcing many survivors into slavery.
    b. Confiscating Carthaginian possessions in north Africa and Iberia.
    c. Exempting Carthaginians from taxation and allowing them to govern their own affairs.

6. The Gracchi brothers were known as

    a. owners of *latifundia*.
    b. reformers.
    c. powerful generals.

7. The rise of private armies directly threatened the existence of the Roman republic. The concept of a private army was first introduced by

    a. Gaius Marius.
    b. Lucius Cornelius Sulla.
    c. Julius Caesar.

8. All but one of the following was NOT done by Caesar after he seized power in 49 B.C.E.

    a. The confiscation of property from conservatives.
    b. The abolition of slavery in Rome.
    c. The institution of a life-time dictatorship by Caesar.

9. Augustus's government was

    a. a republic disguised as a monarchy.
    b. a monarchy disguised as a republic.
    c. an oligarchy disguised as democracy.

10. All the following cities trace their origins to Roman times except

    a. Neapolis.
    b. London.
    c. Paris.

11. By Roman law, when a court held a trial,

    a. a defendant was assumed guilty until proven innocent.
    b. a jury must attend the trial and decide the facts of the case.
    c. the judge enjoyed great discretion in applying laws.

12. All of the following were attractions of the city of Rome except

    a. public baths, swimming pools, and gymnasia.
    b. enormous stadiums for games of baseball, football, and golf.
    c. numerous statues, monumental arches, temples, aqueducts.

13. In Rome, a family meant

    a. an entire household, including slaves, servants, and close relatives who lived together.
    b. the *pater familias*.
    c. "bread and circuses."

14. All but one of the following describe the true status of Roman slaves:

    a. They were often chained together to work on *latifundia*.
    b. In cities, they were often freed when they reached thirty years of age.
    c. They had the right to elect their own tribunes.

15. Romans adopted some deities or cults of OTHER peoples, which included

    a. Jupiter, Mars, and Ceres.
    b. Juno, Cybele, and Isis.
    c. Janus, Vesta, and Cicero.

16. Mithraism was especially popular among

    a. soldiers.
    b. women.
    c. slaves.

17. The Jewish people could not get along well with a number of imperial regimes because

    a. they declined to pay taxes.
    b. they did not respect any secular authorities.
    c. they had difficulty recognizing emperors as divine.

18. The Essenes were

    a. an early Christian sect.
    b. a sect of Judaism.
    c. another term for the Dead Sea scrolls.

19. After Jesus's crucifixion, his followers called him "Christ," meaning

    a. "the anointed one."
    b. "the son of God."
    c. "the enlightened one."

20. The remarkable growth of early Christianity reflected the new faith's appeal particularly to

    a. Roman emperors and high-ranking officials.
    b. Roman soldiers and military officers.
    c. the lower classes, urban populations, and women.

Textual Questions for Analysis

1. Compare and contrast the Roman and Greek phases of Mediterranean society. (Your answer should focus on political forms, cultural traditions, and social structures.)

2. How did the republican constitution of Rome work? Did it work well most of the time?

3. What were the similarities and differences between the Roman republic and Athenian democracy?

4. The imperial expansion of the Roman republic caused serious social and political changes. Explain.

5. Describe the transition from the Roman republic to imperial rule. Was the power balance between the patricians and plebeians better maintained in Caesar's and Augustus's governments than in the republican period?

6. How did the expansion of the Roman empire affect the development of some European countries?

7. What contributed to the spread of Christianity in the Roman empire?

Documentary Evidence

Tacitus, The Great Fire

The Roman treatment of Christians showed a general tolerance with sporadic persecutions. Most persecutions took place in the provinces. However, in late summer of 64 C.E., a great fire devastated the heart of the city of Rome, and the rumors went that the emperor Nero started the fire in order to renovate the city. To stop the rumors, Nero made Christians the scapegoats. Nero's persecution of Christians was reported by Tacitus in *The Annals*, and the following was part of his report (From Harry J. Leon, trans., "Selections from Tacitus," in Paul MacKendrick and Herbert M. Howe, eds., *Classics in Translation*, Vol. II: *Latin Literature*. Madison: The University of Wisconsin Press, 1952, p. 392):

> ...But no amount of human effort, no acts of generosity on the part of the emperor or appeasement of the gods could save Nero's reputation from the general belief that the fire had been set at his command.
>
> In order to put an end to these rumors Nero provided scapegoats and visited most fearful punishments on those popularly called Christians, a group hated because of their outrageous practices. The founder of this sect, Christus, was executed in the reign of Tiberius by the procurator Pontius Pilatus. Thus the pernicious superstition was suppressed for the while, but it broke out again not only in Judaea, where this evil had its origin, but even in Rome, to which all obnoxious and disgraced elements flow from everywhere in the world and receive a large following. The first ones to be seized were those who confessed; then on their information a vast multitude was convicted, not so much on the charge of incendiarism as because of their hatred of humanity. Their executions were made into a sport in that they were covered with skins of wild beasts and torn to pieces by dogs, or they were fastened to crosses or wrapped with flammable materials, so that when the daylight waned, they could be burned to serve as torches in the night. Nero, who had offered his own gardens for this spectacle, gave a chariot-racing exhibition in which he mingled with the crowd dressed as a charioteer or drove a chariot. The result was that despite the fact that these people were criminals worthy of the worst kind of punishment, a feeling of sympathy arose for them, since they were being destroyed not for the public good but to satisfy the cruelty of one man.

COMPLETE THE FOLLOWING SENTENCES WITH THE BEST ANSWER (see the Answer Key for Documentary Evidence at the end of this Study Guide for the best answers):

1. Based on the report by Tacitus, one may say that during the first century C.E., Christianity in the city of Rome was

   a. a very popular religion.
   b. hated by the ruling elite but welcomed by the general public.
   c. drawing a large crowd of followers from the lower classes.

2. Tacitus disapproved of Nero's actions because he thought

   a. Nero was wrong to punish Christians.
   b. Nero did the right thing for the wrong reason.
   c. Nero's punishments were too cruel and inhuman.

Chapter 11

Cross-Cultural Exchanges
on the Silk Roads

Introduction and Learning Objectives

This chapter contributes a unique account of the last phase of the classical world. Instead of dealing with each empire individually through separate chapters, the authors put the silk roads at the center of the discussion, thus treating various societies and empires of Eurasia and north Africa within the vast trading network as a single unit. Indeed, as soon as various regional trading networks of different empires were joined together into one zone of communication and exchange through the silk roads, the pace of cross-cultural exchange quickened as seen from the rising volume of trade and the spread of world religions and technological innovations. The silk roads not only contributed to economic expansion and cultural flourishing of the societies involved, but also facilitated movements of troops and epidemic diseases, which in turn, put a temporary halt on cross-cultural development. From the 3rd century C.E. to about 500, classical societies in Persia, China, India, and the Mediterranean basin had either collapsed or declined. Yet each of these classical societies also experienced cultural change in their last phases, leaving rich legacies that continued to shape political institutions, social orders, and cultural traditions for centuries to come.

The authors' discussion focuses on the fall of the two great empires, Rome and Han. Although each empire had its own causes of decline, both suffered from shrinking population and state revenues, and the localization of regional self-sufficient economies, all of which occurred as a partial result of the devastating epidemic diseases that spread via the silk roads. The authors warn against any theory that attributes the fall of these great empires to a single, simple cause. Instead, they discuss multiple internal problems that weakened the Han and Roman empires, contributing to their inability to deal with foreign threats from without.

In the end, the authors point out that although the silk roads declined, the cultures they helped to spawn were spared complete destruction. Over the centuries following the fall of the Han dynasty, nomadic peoples who entered north China were sinicized. Confucianism temporarily lost its dominant position in China and other eastern traditions grew and flourished, with Daoism and Buddhism becoming popular religions. In the last phase of the Roman empire, Christianity also experienced a great transformation from a repressed faith to a prominent official religion with a well-organized institutional hierarchy and imperial sponsorship. Despite the decline and fall of the great empires, the cultural traditions of the classical world did not simply disappear but profoundly influenced new societies in following centuries.

After studying this chapter, students should understand and be able to discuss the following issues:

- the scope of the silk roads

- the spread of Buddhism, Hinduism, Christianity, and Manichaeism

- social, economic, and political implications of epidemic diseases

- the fall of the Han dynasty and the western Roman empire

- cultural changes in the late Roman empire and post-Han China

Chapter Outline

I. **Long-Distance Trade and the Silk Roads Network**

    A. Trade Networks of the Hellenistic era
        1. The monsoon system
           a) Hellenistic mariners learned monsoon rhythms from Arab and Indian seamen
           b) The monsoon system linked India/Arabia and Egypt/Mediterranean basin
        2. Trade in the Hellenistic world
           a) Exchanges between India/Bactria in east and Mediterranean basin in west
           b) Besides various commodities, also slave trade
    B. The Silk Roads
        1. Trade routes
           a) Overland trade routes linked China to Roman empire
           b) Sea-lanes joined Asia and Mediterranean basin into one network
        2. Trade goods
           a) Silk and spices traveled west
           b) Central Asia produced large horses and jade, sold in China
           c) Roman empire provided glassware, jewelry, art works, perfumes, textiles
        3. The organization of long-distance trade
           a) Merchants of different regions handled long-distance trade in stages
           b) On the seas, long-distance trade was dominated by different empires

II. **Cultural and Biological Exchanges along the Silk Roads**

    A. The Spread of Buddhism and Hinduism
        1. Buddhism in central Asia
           a) First presented in oasis towns of central Asia along silk roads
           b) Further spread to steppelands
         2. Buddhism in China
           a) Foreign merchants as Buddhists in China, 1st century B.C.E.
           b) Popularity of monasteries and missionaries, 5th century C.E.
        3. Buddhism and Hinduism in Southeast Asia
           a) Merchants on silk roads (sea-lanes) were the agents
           b) Rulers referred to themselves as *rajas* ("kings")
           c) Adopted Sanskrit as written language
           d) Many rulers converted to Buddhism, others promoted Hindu cults
           e) Buddhist or Hindu advisors in government

B. The Spread of Christianity
    1. Christianity in the Mediterranean basin
        a) Countless missionaries took Paul of Tarsus as their example
        b) Gregory the Wonderworker popularized Christianity in Anatolia
        c) Christian communities flourished in the Mediterranean basin
    2. Christianity in Southwest Asia
        a) Sizable communities in Mesopotamia and Iran, 2nd century C.E.
        b) Sizable number of converts in southwest Asia until the 7th century C.E.
        c) Their ascetic practices influenced Christian practices in the Roman empire
    3. The Nestorians
        a) A Christian sect developed in southwest Asia
        b) Nestorius emphasized the human nature of Jesus, 5th century C.E.
        c) Nestorian communities in central Asia, India, and China, 7th century C.E.
C. The spread of Manichaeism
    1. Mani and Manichaeism
        a) Prophet Mani, a Zoroastrian, drew influence from Christianity and Buddhism
        b) Perceived a cosmic struggle between light and darkness, good and evil
        c) Offered means to achieve personal salvation
        d) Ascetic lifestyle and high ethical standards
        e) Differentiation between "the elect" and the "hearers"
    2. Spread of Manichaeism
        a) Attracted converts first in Mesopotamia and east Mediterranean region
        b) Special appeal to merchants as hearers
        c) Appeared in all large cities of Roman empire, 3rd century C.E.
    3. Persecutions
        a) The Sasanid rulers suppressed Mani's movement
        b) Roman authorities also persecuted Manichaeans
        c) Manichaeism survived in central Asia
D. The Spread of Epidemic Disease
    1. Epidemic diseases
        a) Common epidemics in Rome and China: smallpox, measles, bubonic plague
        b) Roman empire: population dropped by a quarter from the 1st to 10th century C.E.
        c) China: population dropped by a quarter from the 1st to 7th century C.E.
    2. Effects of epidemic diseases
        a) Both Chinese and Roman economies contracted
        b) Small regional economies emerged
        c) Epidemics weakened Han and Roman empires

III. The Fall of the Han Dynasty

A. Internal decay of the Han state
    1. Problems of factions and land distribution
    2. The Yellow Turban rebellion, 184 C.E.
    3. Collapse of the Han dynasty
        a) Generals usurped political authority, the emperor became a puppet
        b) By 220, generals abolished the Han and divided the empire into three kingdoms
        c) Nomadic peoples came in, China became even more divided

B. Cultural Change in Post-Han China
  1. Sinicization of nomadic peoples
  2. Withering of Confucianism
     a) Confucianism failed to maintain order, became irrelevant
     b) More individuals turned to Daoism and Buddhism
     c) Daoism changed to a religion of salvation
  3. Popularity of Buddhism
     a) Buddhism received strong support from nomadic rulers
     b) Between the 4th and 6th centuries C.E., Buddhism became well established

IV. The Fall of the Roman Empire

A. Internal Decay in the Roman Empire
  1. The barracks emperors
     a) Between 235 and 284 C.E., generals frequently seized the throne
     b) Most barracks emperors died violently
     c) The sheer size of the empire became a problem of control
  2. The emperor Diocletian (284-305 C.E.)
     a) Divided the empire into two administrative districts
     b) A coemperor ruled each district with the aid of a powerful lieutenant
  3. The emperor Constantine
     a) Constantine seized power, claimed to be sole emperor
     b) Established a new capital city: Constantinople
B. Germanic Invasions and the Fall of the Western Roman Empire
  1. Germanic migrations
     a) Migrated from northern Europe, lived in the eastern and northern parts of the empire
     b) Most notable were the Visigoths
        (1) Settled as agriculturalists
        (2) Adopted Roman law and Christianity
        (3) Contributed soldiers to the Roman armies
     c) Roman authorities kept Germanic peoples on the borders as a buffer
  2. The Huns
     a) Under Attila, the Huns began expeditions from the mid-5th century C.E.
     b) Soon disappeared after the death of Attila in 453 C.E.
  3. The collapse of the western Roman empire
     a) Under the Huns' pressure, Germanic peoples streamed into the Roman empire
     b) Established settlements in Italy, Gaul, Spain, Britain, and north Africa
     c) Under Laric, the Visigoths sacked Rome in 410 C.E.
     d) Germanic general Odovacer deposed the Roman emperor, 476 C.E.
     e) Imperial authority survived in the eastern half of the empire
     f) Nomadic states in Spain, Gaul, Britain, and Italy
C. Cultural Change in the Late Roman Empire
  1. Prominence of Christianity
     a) Constantine's edict of Milan, Christianity became a legitimate religion, 313 C.E.
     b) Emperor Theodosius proclaimed Christianity the official religion, 380 C.E.
     c) St. Augustine harmonized Christianity with Platonic thought
  2. The institutional church
     a) Conflicting doctrines and practices among early Christians
     b) Established standardized hierarchy of church officials

c) The bishop of Rome, known as the pope, became spiritual leader

d) Roman empire collapsed, Christianity served as a cultural foundation

Significant Individuals

Attila (p. 268) —Warrior king of the Huns. From the mid-5th century C.E., under his leadership the Huns invaded Hungary, probed Roman frontiers in the Balkan region, menaced Gaul and northern Italy, and attacked Germanic peoples living on the borders of the Roman empire.

Alaric (p. 268) — The leader of the Visigoths; under his command, the Visigoths sacked the city of Rome in 410 C.E.

Constantine (p. 266) — Roman emperor, known for his unification of the Roman empire after it was divided by Diocletian into two administrative districts; established Constantinople as the new capital city; also known as the first Christian emperor of the Roman empire, whose Edict of Milan in 313 C. E. allowed Christians to practice their faith openly.

Diocletian (284-305 C.E.) (p. 266) — Roman emperor, known for his division of the empire into two administrative districts, each ruled by a coemperor with the aid of a powerful lieutenant.

Gregory the Wonderworker (p. 259) — Tireless Christian missionary with a reputation for performing miracles; popularized Christianity in central Anatolia during the mid-third century C.E.

Mani (p. 260) — Founder of Manichaeism; a devout Zoroastrian prophet from Babylon in Mesopotamia who drew religious inspiration from Christianity and Buddhism; lived from 216 to 272 C.E.

Odovacer (p. 268) — Germanic general; in 476 C.E., deposed Romulus Augustus, the last Roman emperor in the western half of the empire.

St. Augustine (354-430 C.E.) (pp. 269-70) — Bishop of Hippo in north Africa; well educated in philosophy; harmonized Christianity with Platonic thought so that Christianity could be easily appreciated by intellectuals and the educated classes.

Theodosius (pp. 268-69) — Emperor of the Byzantine empire, known for his proclamation that made Christianity the official religion of the empire in 380 C.E.

Zhang Qian (pp. 249-50) — A courtier of the Han dynasty who was sent by the emperor to central Asia to arrange for allies against the Xiongnu in 139 B.C.E; twice captured by the Xiongnu but finally managed to escape and return to China twelve years later; became a hero known for his unwavering loyalty to the emperor. His travels contributed to the opening of the silk roads.

Chapter Glossary

barracks emperors (p. 266) — Claimants to the imperial throne of the Roman empire, mostly generals, who frequently replaced one another in a violent manner during the half century from 235 to 284 C.E.

Byzantine empire (p. 268) — The eastern half of the Roman empire which survived invasions of Germanic peoples in the 5th century C.E. and lasted for about one millennium thereafter. The capital city was Constantinople.

church councils (p. 270) — Assemblies of religious authorities of Christianity, held to resolve theological disputes among Christians and determine official doctrines.

The City of God (p. 270) — The famous work of St. Augustine which sought to explain the meaning of history and the world from a Christian point of view.

dioceses (p. 270) — Christian districts presided over by bishops; present in all the prominent cities of the Roman empire from the fourth century C.E. onward

Edict of Milan (p. 268) — Issued by emperor Constantine in 313 C.E., a proclamation that made Christianity a legitimate religion in the Roman empire.

Germanic peoples (p. 267) — Originally the nomadic peoples of northern Europe, including Visigoths, Vandals, Franks, Ostrogoths, Angles and Saxons, and Lombards. Migrated to the eastern and northern borders of the Roman empire from the second century C.E.; beginning in the mid-5th century, invaded the western Roman empire and deposed the emperor there in 476; settled in Italy, Gaul, Spain, Britain, and north Africa.

Manichaeism (p. 260) — Religious sect founded by Mani in the 3rd century C.E.; doctrine sought to blend Zoroastrian, Christian, and Buddhist elements into one religious faith; viewed the world as the site of a cosmic struggle between the forces of light and darkness, good and evil. Taught followers to reject worldly pleasure as a way to achieve personal salvation and eternal association with the forces of light and good. Devout Manichaeans were called "the elect" while the less zealous ones were "hearers." This doctrine attracted converts in Mesopotamia and the Roman empire but survived only in central Asia after the 6th century C.E.

monsoon system (p. 252) — Trading network of the Indian basin linking India and Arabia in the east and Egypt and the Mediterranean basin in the west by the way of the Red Sea; so called because merchant seamen relied on the monsoon winds to govern their sailing and shipping in the Indian Ocean.

The Nestorians (pp. 259-60) — Sect of Christianity founded by the Greek theologian Nestorius during the early 5th century C.E.; doctrine emphasized the human as opposed to the divine nature of Jesus; rejected by Mediterranean church authorities but found large following in southwest Asia. Via the silk roads the Nestorians established communities in central Asia, India, and China.

The pope (p. 270) — From the Latin word *papa* ("father"); bishop of Rome who emerged as a spiritual leader of Christian communities after the collapse of western Roman empire.

silk roads (pp. 250, 252-55) — Network of trade routes that linked much of Eurasia and north Africa through land routes and sea lanes; so called because high-quality silk from China was one of the principal commodities exchanged over the roads.

tetrarchs (p. 266) — The four top co-rulers of the Roman empire, including two coemperors and two powerful lieutenants; ruled the Mediterranean lands after Diocletian divided the empire into two administrative districts. After Diocletian's death in 305 C.E., power struggle among the co-rulers and their generals led to bitter civil war.

Map Exercises

1. Study Map 11.1 on p. 253 of your textbook and answer the following questions:

   A) Identify the routes on the right as land routes or sea lanes of the silk roads:

Land routes	from Luoyang to Kashgar
	from Barbarikon to Berenice
	from Arikamedu to Barygaza
	from Merv to Antioch
Sea routes	from Guangzhou to Arikamedu
	from Tyre to Chang'an
	from Muziris to Pondicherry
	from Bukhara to Taxila

   B) Match each region on the left with native goods traded via the silk roads (see p. 254 of your textbook and <u>note</u> that some of the native goods may have come from more than one region):

Region	Native goods
China	horses, jade
India	ginger
Central Asia	silk
Roman empire	glassware, art works, textiles
Southeast Asia	pepper, sesame oil, cotton textiles
	cinnamon

2. Buddhism, Hinduism, and Christianity were important religions that spread from their original homelands to many other regions by the early centuries C.E. On the map below, mark the original homeland of each of these three religions and use arrows to chart their outward flow. Make sure that you use color markings, or some other method, to differentiate which religion spread to which regions. Be as precise as possible. (You should be familiar with Map 11.2, p. 257 of your textbook, to complete this exercise).

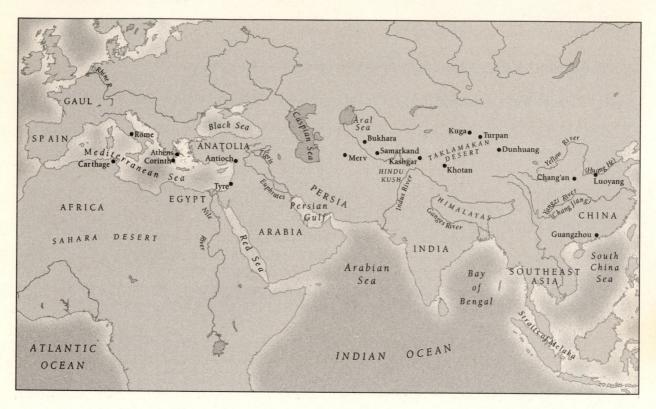

3. Study Map 11.4 on p. 269 of your textbook and complete the following questions (for the best answers, see the Answer Key for Map Exercises at the end of this Study Guide).

   A) Which ONE of the following statements is true?

      a. The Huns invaded both the eastern and western Roman empires.
      b. Vandals and then Visigoths took over Spain.
      c. Franks ruled Gaul and then invaded Italy.
      d. Angles and Saxons settled in Britain.

   B) Which of the following is incorrect?

      a. The Huns were from Hungary.
      b. The Visigoths were from Scandinavia and Russia.
      c. Germanic peoples were all from northern Europe.

Self-Test/Student Quiz

1. In 139 B.C.E., the Chinese emperor dispatched Zhang Qian to central Asia to

    a. open the silk roads.
    b. seek allies against the Xiongnu.
    c. buy large and strong horses.

2. All of the following were favorable conditions for developing long-distance trade during the classical era except that

    a. empires ruled vast areas and maintained good social order.
    b. under imperial rule many roads and bridges were constructed.
    c. emperors encouraged trade in slaves, especially foreign female slaves.

3. The monsoon winds in the Indian Ocean

    a. created tremendous difficulty for traders.
    b. enabled traders to sail safely and reliably to all parts of the Indian Ocean basin.
    c. were actually first discovered and harnessed by merchants of Ptolemaic Egypt.

4. All the following were true with regard to the silk roads except that

    a. the silk roads actually had nothing to do with silk.
    b. because of the silk roads, silk garments became popular among wealthy Romans.
    c. the silk roads linked much of Eurasia and north Africa.

5. When a merchant ship departed from the port of Alexandria to the east along the silk roads, most likely it would bring back

    a. pepper and cinnamon from India.
    b. silk from Bactria.
    c. horses from central Asia.

6. The principal agents for the spread of Buddhism over the silk roads were

    a. the emperor Ashoka and his missionaries.
    b. Indian merchants.
    c. Indian monks.

7. As for the Indian influence in southeast Asia, which of the following is NOT true?

    a. Rulers shaved their heads and called themselves *raja* ("kings").
    b. Rulers adopted Indian Sanskrit as their written language.
    c. Rulers appointed Buddhist or Hindu advisors in their governments.

8. By the third century C.E., Christian communities in Mesopotamia and Iran deeply influenced Christian practices in the Roman empire through their

    a. Nestorian beliefs.
    b. Confucian traditions.
    c. ascetic values.

9. Mani, the founder of Manichaeism, promoted a syncretic blend of

    a. Christianity, Buddhism, and Hinduism.
    b. Zoroastrianism, Christianity, and Buddhism.
    c. Nestorianism, Daoism, and Buddhism.

10. To be a Manichaean, one had to

    a. abstain from marriage, sex, meat, fine clothing, and other personal comforts.
    b. follow a strict moral code in order to achieve eternal association with the forces of light and good.
    c. abstain from pursuing commercial profit.

11. With regard to epidemic diseases on the silk roads, all of the following were true except that

    a. the most devastating diseases were smallpox, measles, and bubonic plague.
    b. the diseases seriously weakened the Han and Roman empires.
    c. the diseases caused steep population loss in India.

12. Immediately after the dissolution of the Han empire in 220 C.E., China was

    a. taken over by nomadic peoples.
    b. divided into three large kingdoms.
    c. replaced by the Sui dynasty.

13. Which of the following did NOT contribute to the popularity of Buddhism in post-Han China?

    a. The threats of epidemic diseases turned the Chinese to Buddhism for personal salvation.
    b. After the collapse of the Han dynasty, Confucianism lost its dominant position.
    c. The nomadic peoples who migrated into north China brought their Buddhist faith to the Chinese.

14. According to the authors of the textbook, the fall of the western Roman empire can be explained by

    a. population decline caused by epidemic disease.
    b. problems caused by the rise of Christianity.
    c. internal problems and external pressures.

15. By dividing the Roman empire into two administrative districts, the emperor Diocletian attempted to

    a.   establish more effective control of the empire.
    b.   share imperial power with the "barracks emperors."
    c.   give up the east half of the empire to Christians.

16. All the following are true with regard to the Visigoths before they invaded the Roman empire, except that

    a.   they adopted Roman law and converted to Christianity.
    b.   they adopted official Roman language and social customs.
    c.   they contributed large numbers of soldiers to the Roman armies.

17. The invasions of the Huns contributed to the fall of the western Roman empire by

    a.   deposing the last emperor of the western Roman empire.
    b.   sacking the city of Rome in 410 C.E.
    c.   pressing the Germanic peoples into the western Roman empire.

18. The emperor who allowed Christians to practice their faith openly for the first time in the Roman empire was

    a.   Constantine.
    b.   Theodosius.
    c.   St. Augustine.

19. In the institutional hierarchy of Christian church, the highest authority was

    a.   the patriarch of Jerusalem.
    b.   the bishop of Rome.
    c.   Jesus Christ.

20. When theological disputes arose among Christians, controversial issues would be brought to

    a.   the pope.
    b.   the patriarchs.
    c.   the church councils.

Textual Questions for Analysis

1. Why were the silk roads important in world history?

2. How did Buddhism and Hinduism spread in Asia?

3. What factors contributed to the prominence of Christianity in the late Roman empire?

4. How did epidemic diseases impact the Roman and Chinese empires?

5. Compare and contrast the fall of the western Roman empire with the fall of the Han empire.

6. What were the reasons for Buddhism gaining popularity in post-Han China?

Documentary Evidence

St. Augustine, *The City of God*

Was the Roman empire doing better under its old gods than under its Christian rulers? Could people of a different religion prevail against orthodox Christian rulers? Although Christianity became the prominent religion of the empire from the early 4th century C.E. and emperors converted to Christianity, questions of the above sort were still a challenge to religious leaders of Church circles, especially when the Visigothic armies led by Alaric sacked Rome in 410 C.E. St. Augustine of Hippo (354-430 C.E.), the most influential theologian of Christianity in the 5th century C.E., began to stress the legitimacy of Christianity as an official religion and to explain the debacle of Rome in his famous work *The City of God* (From Philip F. Riley, et al., *The Global Experience: Readings in World History to 1500*. Vol. 1, 3rd ed., New Jersey: Prentice-Hall, pp. 157-58.)

On Emperor Constantine...God bestowed such an abundance of earthly favors as no man would dare wish for. He permitted him to found a city to share in the imperial rule of Rome, a daughter, so to speak, of Rome herself but without any temples or images of the demons. He reigned for a long time, maintaining the whole Roman world as sole emperor. He was most victorious in directing and waging wars, and he was always successful in putting down usurpers. He was very old when he died of sickness and age, and he left sons to rule after him.

Theodosius...put down the usurper Eugenius, who had illegally installed himself in that emperor's place, prevailing against his very powerful army more by prayer than by the sword. Some soldiers who were there have told me that all the spears they were throwing were snatched from their hands by a very strong wind, which blew away from Theodosius' side in the enemy's direction, and that it not only gave greater force to whatever they threw against them but even turned back the spears which the enemy soldiers were throwing into their own bodies....

All the destruction, killing, looting, burning, and suffering which took place in the recent sack of Rome happened in accordance with the customs of waging war. What was altogether new and previously unheard of, however, was that the barbarian brutality was so tamed that they picked the largest of the basilicas and allowed them to remain sanctuaries, where no one could be struck down and from which no one could be dragged away. Many people were led there to freedom and safety by soldiers showing sympathy for them.... Anyone who does not see fit to credit this to the name of Christ—yes, to Christian times—is blind. Anyone who sees this new turn of events but fails to praise it is most ungrateful.

QUESTIONS TO CONSIDER

1. According to St. Augustine's examples, what were the personal benefits or advantages for emperors to believe in Christianity?

2. How did St. Augustine justify Christianity against the awkward situation created by the Visigoths' sack of Rome? Supposing that what he reported was true, do you think he made a strong case? Why or why not?

Chapter 12

A Survivor Society: Byzantium

Introduction and Learning Objectives

As a political heir to Rome and a survivor of the classical era, the Byzantine empire inherited Greco-Roman cultural and political traditions. In the course of over a millennium of development, however, the empire inevitably took on distinctive characteristics of its own. This chapter deals with the vicissitudes of the Byzantine empire, its tense relationship with western Europe, as well as its cultural influence on the Slavic peoples of eastern Europe and Russia. More than a mere survivor, Byzantium had its glorious days in the post-classical world, and its cultural influence can be seen even today among some Slavic peoples.

Initially part of the greater Roman empire, the Byzantine empire withstood problems that brought down the Western Roman empire in the 5th century C.E. and survived for another millennium, until 1453. From the reign of the emperor Justinian, Byzantium began to take on a life of its own and became a political and economic powerhouse of the postclassical era. Its attempt to restore the greater Roman empire was not a success, however, and from the 7th century C.E., Islamic states came to claim a large portion of Byzantine territory in the eastern and southern Mediterranean; at the same time, Slavic peoples dominated lands to the north, and western Europeans organized increasingly powerful states in lands to the west. Under the pressure of external threats, the Byzantine empire drew its strength from a free peasantry through the *theme* system. Until the 12th century, Byzantium dominated the wealthy and productive eastern Mediterranean region, with its manufactured goods enjoying a reputation for high quality in markets from the Mediterranean basin to India. Its long process of decline started from within: alliances of generals and local aristocrats substantially undermined the free peasantry, reduced military recruits, and the income of the central government, resulting in the empire's inability to face outside challenges.

Throughout its history, the Byzantine empire also drew heavily on the rich cultural traditions of classical Mediterranean society and the Roman empire. The Greco-Roman legacy was especially noticeable in the Byzantine imperial system, the bureaucracy, the church, and education. The legacy, however, was drawn upon only selectively. Byzantium's tightly centralized rule and caesaropapism had little to do with Athenian democracy, but instead was a continuation of the imperial tradition of the late Roman empire. Greek cultural influence was strong in the areas of language, religion, and education. Much of the tension between Byzantium and western Europe can be traced to their different, selective borrowings from the classical legacy. The split of Christianity between east and west was just one obvious example, resulting in the creation of the Eastern Orthodox church and the Roman Catholic church beginning in 1054.

The importance of the Byzantine empire in world history rests ultimately in its decisive influence on cultural developments among the Slavic peoples in eastern Europe and in Russia. From Byzantium, these peoples received the Cyrillic alphabet, methods of statecraft, commercial skills, and Eastern Orthodox Christianity. Although Byzantium did not leave a political heir of its own, its cultural tradition lived on in several Slavic societies.

After studying this chapter, students should understand and be able to discuss the following issues:

- political development in the Byzantine empire

- Greco-Roman influence on Byzantium

- the importance of the *theme* system

- theological differences between the Eastern Orthodox church and the Roman Catholic church

- the influence of Byzantium on the development of eastern Europe and Russia

Chapter Outline

I. **The Early Byzantine Empire**

   A. The Later Roman Empire and Byzantium
      1. The later Roman empire
         a) Western half crumbled, eastern half remained intact
         b) The Byzantine emperors faced different challenges
            (1) Conflict with Sasanid dynasty (226-641 C.E.) in Persia
            (2) Invasions of migratory peoples from the north and east
      2. The early Byzantine State
         a) Tightly centralized rule of a highly exalted emperor
         b) Caesaropapism: Emperors' important roles in ecclesiastical affairs
         c) Emperors also stood above the law
         d) Dress and court etiquette designed to enhance rulers' status
   B. Justinian (527-565 C.E.) and His Legacy
      1. Justinian and Theodora
         a) The imperial couple came from obscure origins
         b) Justinian seized power when in imperial bureaucracy
         c) Theodora was a sagacious advisor
      2. Justinian Code
         a) Issued the *Corpus iuris civilis* (*The Body of the Civil Law*)
         b) The code influenced civil law codes of western Europe
      3. Belisarius and Byzantine conquests
         a) Belisarius reconquered part of the western Roman empire from 533 C.E.
         b) Threats from Sasanids and Slavic peoples
   C. Islamic Conquests and Byzantine Revival
      1. The emergence of the Islamic state
         a) Arab peoples conquered the Sasanid empire and part of Byzantium
         b) Prolonged sieges of Constantinople by Islamic armies
         c) Byzantine survived partly because of "Greek fire"

2. Imperial organization
   a) The *theme* system strengthened Byzantine society
   b) The revival of the empire
      (1) reconquered Syria from Arab Muslims, the 10th century
      (2) "Basil the Bulgar Slayer," crushed the Bulgars in the Balkans
D. Byzantium and Western Europe
   1. Tensions between them
      a) Ecclesiastical tensions
         (1) Constantinople: conducted affairs in Greek, caesaropapist emperors
         (2) Rome: conducted affairs in Latin, autonomy from imperial authorities
      b) Churches in the east and west looked down upon each other
   2. Political grievances
      a) Some upstart states of western Europe claimed imperial authority
         (1) Charlemagne received imperial crown from the pope in 800
         (2) Otto of Saxony claimed himself an emperor in 962
      b) The insults from Liudprand of Cremona, the ambassador of Otto

II. Byzantine Economy and Society

A. The Agricultural Economy
   1. The peasantry
      a) The backbone of the Byzantine army and economy
      b) Landless peasants worked under share-cropping arrangements
      c) Invasions of the 6th and 7th century led to the *theme* system
      d) Since the 11th century, free peasants declined
   2. Consequences of the peasantry's decline
      a) Large landowners shifted tax burden to peasants
      b) Large landowners raised forces on their own estates
      c) The pool of military recruits shrank
B. Industry and Trade
   1. Manufacturing enterprises
      a) Byzantine craftsmen enjoyed a high reputation in various industries
      b) High-quality silk became an important industry from the late 6th century
   2. Trade
      a) Constantinople, an important center for Eurasian trade
      b) The *bezant* was the standard currency of the Mediterranean basin
      c) Byzantium drew enormous wealth from foreign trade
   3. Banks and partnerships supported commercial economy
C. Urban Life
   1. Housing in Constantinople
      a) Enormous palaces owned by aristocrats
      b) Less splendid dwellings owned by the less privileged classes
   2. Attractions of Constantinople
      a) A city of baths, taverns, restaurants, theaters, the Hippodrome
      b) The most popular game—chariot races
   3. Greens and Blues
      a) The two factions of fans for chariot races
      b) Frequent fights in the street between them

c) Joined together in a popular uprising, 532
d) The riot left Constantinople in shambles

III. Classical Heritage and Orthodox Christianity

A. The Legacy of Classical Greece
1. Byzantine education
   a) State-organized school system, training bureaucrats
   b) Private education of aristocratic families
   c) Basic literacy was widespread even among the lower classes
2. Scholarship
   a) Emphasized more on humanities than on natural science
   b) The educated considered themselves direct heirs of classical Greece
B. The Byzantine Church
1. Church and state
   a) Church's close relationship with the imperial government
   b) Constantine actively participated in religious debate
   c) Under caesaropapist emperors, church was a department of the state
2. Iconoclasm
   a) Inaugurated by Emperor Leo III in 726 C.E.
   b) The unpopular policy sparked protests and riots throughout the empire
   c) The iconoclasts abandoned their effort in 843 C.E.
3. Greek Philosophy and Byzantine theology
   a) Examining philosophical issues from a philosophical point of view
   b) Debate about Jesus's nature, a philosophical issue
C. Monasticism and Popular Piety
1. Asceticism
   a) Extreme asceticism and self-denial by some Christians
   b) "Pillar saints"
2. Byzantine monasticism and St. Basil
   a) The earliest monasteries of dedicated hermits, ascetics
   b) Reforms of monasteries urged by St. Basil, the 4th century C.E.
   c) Monasteries also provided social services to local communities
   d) Not centers of learning as monasteries of western Europe
D. Tensions between Eastern and Western Christianity
1. Constantinople and Rome
   a) The iconoclastic movement in the east was criticized by the west
   b) Ritual and doctrinal differences—source of conflict
2. Schism
   a) Power struggle led to mutual excommunication, 1504
   b) Origins of Eastern Orthodox church and Roman Catholic church

IV. The Influence of Byzantium in Eastern Europe

A. Domestic Problems and Foreign Pressures
1. Social problems
   a) Generals and local aristocrats allied, a challenge to imperial power
   b) Free peasants were declining in number and prosperity
   c) Imperial government suffered from fewer recruits and fiscal problems

2. Challenges from the west
    a) Norman army expelled Byzantine authorities in southern Italy
    b) Normans and other western Europeans mounted a series of crusades
    c) The fourth crusade seized Constantinople
    d) Byzantine forces recaptured the capital in 1261
3. Challenges from the east
    a) The Muslim Saljuqs invaded Anatolia, defeated Byzantine army, 1071
    b) The loss of Anatolia sealed the fate of the Byzantine empire
    c) Ottoman Turks captured Constantinople in 1453, the end of the empire
B. Early Relations between Byzantium and Slavic Peoples
1. Eastern Europe and Russia
    a) Maintained close contact with Byzantium from the 6th century
    b) The peoples included Serbs, Croats, and Bulgars
    c) Began to influence Bulgarian politics and culture after the 8th century
2. Missions to the Slavs
    a) Byzantium sent missionaries to Balkan lands and Bulgar
    b) The mission of Saints Cyril and Methodius, mid-9th century
    c) Cyrillic writing stimulated conversion to Orthodox Christianity
C. Byzantium and Russia
1. Beginning in the mid-9th century, Russians started to organize a large state
2. The conversion of Prince Vladimir, 989
    a) Kiev served as a conduit for spread of Byzantine culture and religion
    b) Byzantine art and architecture dominated Kiev
3. The growth of Kiev
    a) The princes established caesaropapist control of Russian Orthodox church
    b) Russians later claimed to inherit the imperial mantle of Byzantium

Significant Individuals

Basil II (976-1025 C.E.) (p. 286) — Byzantine emperor, known as "Basil the Bulgar Slayer" for his successful campaign against the neighboring Bulgars. After his victory at the battle of Kleidion in 1014 C.E., Basil reportedly commanded his forces to blind fourteen thousand Bulgarian survivors.

Belisarius (p. 284) — Brilliant general of the Justinian reign; launched military campaigns to reconquer western Europe in 533 and brought Italy, Sicily, northwestern Africa, and southern Spain under control of the Byzantine empire.

Charlemagne (p. 286) — Frankish ruler, received an imperial crown from the pope in Rome in 800, and thus directly challenged Byzantine claims to imperial authority over the western lands of the former Roman empire.

Justinian, 527-565 C.E. (p. 283) — Byzantine emperor, known for his campaign of rebuilding Constantinople, his codification of Roman law, and his military campaigns that succeeded in control of Italy, Sicily, Northwestern Africa, and southern Spain.

Liudprand of Cremona (p. 287) — Ambassador dispatched by Otto of Saxony to Constantinople in 968. His contempt toward Byzantium revealed tense relations between western Europe and the Byzantine empire.

Prince Vladimir (p. 300) — Ruler of Russian kingdom of Kiev; converted himself and his kingdom to Orthodox Christianity in 989.

St. Basil (329-379 C.E.) (p. 294) — Patriarch of Constantinople whose effort to reform and regulate Byzantine monasteries contributed to the spread of Basilian monasticism throughout the empire.

Sts. Cyril and Methodius (p. 299) — Two brothers from Thessaloniki in Greece who were sent as missionaries by Byzantine government to Bulgaria and Moravia (which included much of the modern Czech, Slovakian, and Hungarian territories) during the mid-9th century; responsible for creating an alphabet, known as the Cyrillic alphabet, for previously illiterate Slavic peoples.

Theodora (p. 283) —Wife of emperor Justinian; offered advice on sensitive political, diplomatic, and theological issues.

Chapter Glossary

Bulgaria (pp. 286, 299) — Powerful kingdom in northern portions of Balkan peninsula; exerted constant pressure on borders of the Byzantine empire; defeated by emperor Basil II at the battle of Kleidion in 1014 C.E.; development strongly influenced by Byzantium.

Byzantine empire (p. 280) — Eastern half of the Roman empire, named after Byzantion—latinized as Byzantium—a modest market town and fishing village. The emperor Constantine designated Byzantion as the site of a new imperial capital, Constantinople. Beginning in the 7th century, it lost Palestine, Syria, and Egypt to Islam. Collapsed in 1453 under the attack of Ottoman Turks.

Caesaropapism (p. 282) — Refers to the domination of imperial rule over Christianity in the Byzantine empire; emperors not only ruled as secular lords but also played an active and prominent role in ecclesiastical affairs.

Constantinople (p. 280) — Literally, "city of Constantine." Capital of the Byzantine empire built under the Roman emperor Constantine. In 1453, fell to the Ottoman Turks who renamed it Istanbul.

Corpus iuris civilis (p. 283) — *"Body of the Civil Law,"* codified under emperor Justinian; influenced civil law codes throughout much of western Europe.

Eastern Orthodox church (pp. 295-96) — Christian church of the Byzantine empire after the schism of Christianity in 1054 C.E. Its theology reflected the strong and continuing influence of classical Greek philosophy.

The fourth crusade (1202-1204) (p. 297) — Expedition originally intended to recapture Jerusalem and other sites holy to Christians from Muslims, but diverted by Venetian merchants to the sacking of Constantinople in 1204. Byzantine forces recaptured the capital in 1261.

Greek fire (pp. 285-86) — A devastating incendiary weapon consisting of a mixture of sulphur, lime, and petroleum; utilized effectively by Byzantine forces against Islamic invaders during the late 7th and early 8th centuries.

Greens and Blues (p. 290) — Two factions of fans for chariot races in Constantinople before the 7th century. Often fought in the streets against each other, but in 532 the two factions united to protest against high taxes. The rioters seized the Hippodrome (the large stadium for chariot racing) and proclaimed a new emperor. The uprising was quelled and thousands of rioters were killed by the government army.

Hagia Sophia (p. 283) — Magnificent church constructed in Constantinople during the reign of Justinian. Later became a mosque and a museum, which ranks as one of the world's most important examples of Christian architecture.

iconoclasm (p. 293) — Byzantine imperial policy inaugurated by emperor Leo III (re. 717-741 C.E.) to destroy religious images and prohibit their use in churches. Debates about iconoclasm raged in Byzantium for more than a century.

Kiev (p. 300) — Trading center in southern Russia, situated on the Dnieper River along the main trade route linking Scandinavia and Byzantium. Through Kiev, the Russian kingdom dominated much of the territory between the Volga and the Dnieper from the 10th to the 13th century.

Normans (p. 296) — A Scandinavian people who seized Normandy (in northern France) during the early 11th century and settled there. Within a few decades, Norman armies led by Robert Guiscard took over southern Italy and expelled Byzantine authorities there.

Ottoman Turks (p. 297) — MuslimTurks who captured Constantinople in 1453 and absorbed Byzantium into their expanding Ottoman empire.

Roman Catholic church (p. 295) — Christian church of western Europe after 1054 C.E., presenting opposing doctrinal positions to those of the Eastern Orthodox church of the Byzantine empire.

Saljuqs (p. 297) — One of the nomadic Turkish peoples who invaded the Byzantine empire in the 11th century. In 1071, they defeated the Byzantine army at the battle of Manzikert and took over much of Anatolia.

theme (p. 285) — Administrative organization of the Byzantine empire devised to strengthen the free peasantry. Each province (*theme*) was under the control of a general who assumed responsibility for both military defense and civil administration. Generals recruited armies from free peasants who received allotments of land in exchange for military service.

Map Exercises

1. Study Map 12. 1 on p. 281 of your textbook and identify TWO of the following cities which did not belong to the Byzantine empire:

   Carthage   Alexandra   Rome   Jerusalem   Babylon   Antioch   Ctsiphon

2. Make connections between regions, on the left, and their peoples, on the right:

Regions	Peoples
Spain	Avars
North Africa	Slavs
Italy	Franks
Persia	Vandals
France	Ostrogoths
The Balkans	Sasanids
Eastern Europe	Visigoths

3. Study Map 12.2 on p. 297 of your textbook and explain which parts of the Byzantine empire were lost to Normans and Muslim Saljuqs.

Self-Test/Student Quiz

1. According to the Byzantine historian Procopius's account, high-quality silk production was

    a. developed by Byzantine craftsmen by improving the cocoons of wild silkworms.
    b. introduced by two Christian monks from China to the Byzantine empire.
    c. introduced to the Byzantine empire through several routes.

2. By convention, the Byzantine empire is also called

    a. Byzantion.
    b. Constantinople.
    c. Byzantium.

3. The term caesaropapism refers to the fact that the Byzantine emperors

    a. claimed divine favor.
    b. claimed divine status.
    c. claimed half human and half divine status.

4. Should you have visited the Byzantine imperial court, you could NOT have seen

    a. the emperor wearing heavily bejeweled crowns and dressed in yellow silk robes.
    b. high officials prostrating themselves on the floor, kissing the emperor's feet, and calling themselves slaves.
    c. artificial birds singing and mechanical lions roaring and swishing their tails.

5. Which of the following was NOT true of Theodora?

    a. She was emperor Justinian's wife, advisor, and aid.
    b. She was the daughter of a bear keeper in the circus and a stripper.
    c. She was the dominant political figure of her age, controlling the empire from behind the scenes.

6. Emperor Justinian is best remembered for his

    a. plan to destroy Constantinople in order to rebuild it.
    b. codification of Roman law, known as *Body of the Civil law*.
    c. complete reconstitution of the classical Roman empire.

7. Under the *theme* system,

    a. Byzantine generals used "Greek fire" to defend their provinces (*themes*).
    b. free peasants received allotments of land in exchange for military service.
    c. generals cooperated with governors in civil administration of provinces (*themes*).

8. The battle of Kleikion in 1014 C.E. was fought between

    a. Byzantium and the Bulgars.
    b. the Byzantine army and European crusaders.
    c. Byzantine forces and the Muslim Saljuqs.

9. All of the following were economic policies of the Byzantine government except

    a. preventing land accumulation by wealthy classes in order to protect free peasants.
    b. preventing wealthy and powerful entrepreneurs from monopolizing the silk industry.
    c. issuing the *bezant* (Byzantine gold coin) to monopolize trade in the Mediterranean basin.

10. Which of the following were NOT part of mass entertainment in Constantinople?

    a. celibacy, fasting, and perching atop tall pillars.
    b. athletic matches and chariot races.
    c. contests between wild animals, circuses featuring clowns, jugglers, and dwarfs.

11. In Constantinople, the Greens and the Blues were

    a. two armies of the Byzantine empire.
    b. two factions of chariot racing fans.
    c. two groups of underground gangsters.

12. From the 6th century, well educated Byzantines

    a. considered themselves the direct heirs of classical Greece.
    b. spoke both Latin and Greek.
    c. placed more emphasis on the natural sciences than on the humanities.

13. Emperor Leo III (reigned 717-741) launched the campaign of iconoclasm because

    a. by destroying paintings and images of Jesus and the saints, he wanted to give the ecclesiastical authorities a lesson.
    b. he was convinced that the veneration of religious images was sinful, tantamount to the worship of physical idols.
    c. he suffered from severe mental illness, and the religious images drove him crazy.

14. All but one of the following was true in describing monasteries of the Byzantine church:

    a. they grew out of the efforts of devout individuals to lead especially holy lives.
    b. they provided social services to their communities.
    c. they were centers of thought and learning.

15. In 1054 C.E., the Byzantine patriarch and the pope of Rome mutually excommunicated each other because of their disagreements over matters of

    a. rituals such as whether priests should shave their beards.
    b. the doctrinal dispute about Jesus's relationship to God and the Holy Spirit.
    c. rituals, doctrine, and the authority of church.

16. From the early eleventh century, the most serious domestic problem of the Byzantine empire was

    a. intermarriages between generals' children and local aristocrats.
    b. the decline of the free peasantry in both number and prosperity.
    c. frequent fights between the Greens and the Blues.

17. During the 12th and 13th centuries, countries of western Europe mounted a series of crusades in order to

    a. recapture Jerusalem and other sites holy to Christians from Muslim control.
    b. change Eastern Orthodox Christianity to Roman Catholic Christianity.
    c. destroy Constantinople and control the trade of the Mediterranean basin.

18. The people who finally brought down the Byzantine empire were

    a. crusaders of western Europe.
    b. Muslim Saljuqs.
    c. Ottoman Turks.

19. All but one of the following was NOT a consequence of the missions of Saints Cyril and Methodius to the Slavic peoples:

    a. The Cyrillic alphabet became the writing system of the Slavic peoples.
    b. The Byzantine empire and Slavic peoples united to fight against the Islamic armies.
    c. Eastern Orthodox Christianity was adopted by the Slavic peoples.

20. By converting Russia to Orthodox Christianity in 989, Prince Vladimir of Kiev

    a. became a devout Christian.
    b. claimed that Kiev was the world's third Rome.
    c. helped to spread Byzantine influence in Russia.

Textual Questions for Analysis

1. What did Byzantium inherit from the Greco-Roman legacy?

2. How did the *theme* system emerge? Why was it important to the Byzantine economy and politics?

3. How did Eastern Orthodox Christianity differ from Roman Catholic Christianity? What factors contributed to the schism between them?

4. Compare and contrast the decline of the Byzantine empire with that of the Chinese Han empire.

5. What were the roles of Byzantium in shaping the development of the Slavic peoples?

Documentary Evidence

Procopius, "The Unsavory Life of Theodora"

The Byzantine historian, Procopius of Caesarea, was also the private secretary to general Belisarius. Besides the works he wrote for the public, which detailed various wars and significant events, he also wrote and kept for himself a small book called *The Secret History*, in which he wrote a vitriolic description of the vices and scandals of Justinian, Theodora, general Belisarius, and his wife Antonina. The following section is about the early life of Theodora before she met and married emperor Justinian. From his vitriolic critique of Theodora, we can learn something about the daily lives of the lower classes of the Byzantine empire. (From Procopius, *The Secret History*, Vol. 6, translated by H.B. Dewing. Cambridge, Mass.: Harvard University Press, 1935/1960, pp. 107-111).

There was in Byzantium a certain Acacius, keeper of the animals used in the circus, an adherent of the Green Faction, a man whom they called Master of the Bears. This man had died a natural death during the reign of Anastasius, leaving three girls, Comito, Theodora and Anastasia, the eldest of whom was not yet seven years of age. And the woman, now reduced to utter distress, entered into marriage with another husband, who, she thought, would later on assist her in both the care of the household and in her first husband's occupation.... And when these children came of age, the mother immediately put them on the [circus] stage there—since they were fair to look upon—not all three at the same time, but as each one seemed to her to be ripe for this calling. Now Comito, the first one, had already scored a brilliant success among the harlots of her age; and Theodora, the next in order, clothed in a little sleeved frock suitable to a slave girl..., being immature, was quite unable to sleep with a man or to have a woman's kind of intercourse with one, yet she did engage in intercourse of a masculine type of lewdness with the wretches, slaves though they were, who, following their masters to the theatre, incidentally took advantage of the opportunity afforded them to carry on this monstrous business, and she spent much time in the brothel in this unnatural traffic of the body. But as soon as she came of age and was at last mature, she joined the women of the stage and straightway became a courtesan.... Later on she was associated with the actors in all the work of the theatre, and she shared their performances with them, playing up to their buffoonish acts intended to raise a laugh. For she was unusually clever and full of gibes, and she immediately became admired for this sort of thing....

And as she wantoned with her lovers, she always kept bantering them, and by toying with new devices in intercourse, she always succeeded in winning the hearts of the licentious to her;

for she did not even expect that the approach should be made by the man she was with, but on the contrary she herself, with wanton jests and with clownish posturing with hips, would tempt all who came along, especially if they were beardless youths. Indeed, there was never anyone such a slave to pleasure in all forms; for many a time she would go to a community dinner with ten youths or even more, all of exceptional bodily vigour who had made a business of fornication, and she would lie with all her banquet companions the whole night long, and when they all were too exhausted to go on, she would go to their attendants, thirty perhaps in number, and pair off with each one of them; yet even so she could not get enough of this wantonness.

On one occasion she entered the house of one of the notables during the drinking, and they say that in the sight of all the banqueters she mounted to the projecting part of the banqueting couch where their feet lay, and there drew up her clothing in a shameless way, not hesitating to display her licentiousness. And though she made use of three openings, she used to take Nature to task, complaining that it had not pierced her breasts with larger holes so that it might be possible for her to contrive another method of copulation there. And though she was pregnant many times, yet practically always she was able to contrive to bring about an abortion immediately.

And often even in the theatre, before the eyes of the whole people, she stripped off her clothing and moved about naked through their midst, having only a girdle about her private parts and her groins, not, however, that she was ashamed to display these too to the populace, but because no person is permitted to enter there entirely naked, but must have at least a girdle about the groins. Clothed in this manner, she sprawled out and lay on her back on the ground. And some slaves, whose duty this was, sprinkled grains of barley over her private parts, and geese, which happened to have been provided for this very purpose, picked them off with their beaks, one by one, and ate them. And when she got up, she not only did not blush, but even acted as if she took pride in this strange performance. For she was not merely shameless herself, but also a contriver of shameless deeds above all others....

QUESTIONS TO CONSIDER

1. From Procopius's account, what do we learn about the circus, slaves, and coutesans in Byzantium?

2. Why do you think Procopius was so critical of the behavior of someone like Theodora, who advanced from the lower classes to the role of empress? What might this tell you about social hierarchy and its role in Byzantium? What else would you need to know about Procopius to be fully convinced of the truthfulness of his account?

Chapter 13

A New Society: The Realm of Islam

Introduction and Learning Objectives

Until the 7th century C.E., Arabia was a nomadic backwater on the periphery of cultural centers of the eastern Mediterranean. In the year 570, however, a child name Muhammad was born, and his life not only represented a new force that would blossom in the Arabian peninsula, but also bear the name of a new faith that would change world history. Muhammad did not plan to found a new religion or imagine the *dar al-Islam* ("house of Islam," or all the lands under the Islamic empire). Instead, his intention was to express his faith in Allah and to perfect the teachings of earlier Jewish and Christian prophets by announcing a revelation more comprehensive than those Allah had entrusted to other prophets. His message soon attracted a circle of devout and committed disciples, and by the time of his death in 632, most of Arabia had accepted Islam, the faith founded on an individual's submission to Allah. Within decades following the prophet's death, Arab armies marched into Mesopotamia and Persia, imposing their authority and creating a new empire that stretched from the Iberian peninsula to the Indus valley. In succeeding centuries, Islam was spread widely by merchants, holy men, and warriors far beyond the conquered lands.

The rapid expansion of Islam eventually provided a political framework over a vast portion of the eastern hemisphere and encouraged the development of a massive trade and communication network. Merchants, diplomats, and other travelers moved easily throughout the Islamic world. Straddling Africa and Asia, the Islamic empire provided key links and channels for exchange between east and west. Muslim traders and conquerors became the prime agents for the transfer of crops, technology, and ideas among the many cultural centers of the post-classical world. Examples of this transfer included the spread of a number of important food and industrial crops, Indian numerals, and Chinese paper making technology.

Arising from nomadic and mercantile society, the Arab Muslims drew deep inspiration from cultural traditions of the complex societies of the post-classical world. After toppling the Sasanid dynasty, Muslim conquerors adopted Persian statecraft to administer their lands. Persian literature, science, and religious values also found a place in Islamic society. During later centuries, Muslims drew inspiration from Greek and Indian traditions as well. Thus Muslims did not invent a new Islamic society, but rather fashioned it by blending elements from Arab, Persian, Greek, and Indian societies. While drawing influence from other societies, however, the Islamic faith thoroughly transformed the cultural traditions that it absorbed. Muslim scholars studied, preserved, and improved on the learning of a few highly developed classical societies. For several centuries, many Muslim works in philosophy, literature, mathematics, and sciences reachedremarkable heights. Despite the constant internal frictions and external pressures that gradually weakened Islamic rule long before it was conquered by the Mongols in 1258, the *dar al-Islam* represented the most prosperous and cosmopolitan society of the postclassical world.

The chapter concludes with an account of the formation of the Islamic cultural tradition, emphasizing the central importance of the Quran, the roles played by *ulama*, *qadis*, and *sufis*, as well as the function of *hajj* in establishing cultural unity for the vastly different lands of the Islamic world.

After studying this chapter, students should understand and be able to discuss the following issues:

- the nature of pre-Islamic Arabian society

- the origins and basic teachings of Islam

- contrasts between the Umayyad and Abbasid dynasties

- causes for the decline of the Abbasid dynasty

- social and cultural changes in the *dar al-Islam*

- formation of the Islamic cultural tradition

Chapter Outline

I. **A Prophet and His World**

    A. Muhammad and His Message
        1. The Arabian peninsula
            a) Nomadic Bedouin lived in the desert-covered peninsula for millennia
                (1) Kept herds of sheep, goats, and camels
                (2) Organized in family and clan groups
                (3) Importance of kinship and loyalty to the clan
            b) Post-classical Arabia, active in long-distance trade
            c) An important link between India/China and Persia/Byzantium
        2. Muhammad's early life
            a) Muhammad ibn Abdullah born in a Mecca merchant family, 570 C.E.
            b) Difficult early life, married a wealthy widow, Khadija, in 595
            c) Became a merchant at age 30, exposed to various faiths
        3. Muhammad's spiritual transformation
            a) At age 40, he experienced visions
                (1) There was only one true god, Allah ("the god")
                (2) Allah would soon bring judgment on the world
                (3) The archangel Gabriel delivered these revelations to Muhammad
            b) Did not intend to found a new religion, but his message became appealing
        4. The Quran
            a) Followers compiled Muhammad's revelations
            b) Quran ("recitation"), became the holy book of Islam
            c) A work of magnificent poetry

B. Muhammad's Migration to Medina
   1. Conflict at Mecca
      a) His teachings offended other believers, especially the ruling elite of Mecca
      b) Attacks on greed offended wealthy merchants
      c) Attacks on idolatry threatened shrines, especially the black rock at Ka'ba
   2. The *hijra*
      a) Under persecution, Muhammad and followers fled to Medina, 622 C.E.
      b) The move, known as *hijra*, was the starting point of the Islamic calendar
   3. The *umma*
      a) Organized a cohesive community called *umma* in Medina
      b) Led commercial adventure, sometimes launched raids against Mecca caravans
      c) Helped the poor and needy
   4. The "seal of the prophets"
      a) Referred himself as the "seal of the prophets,"—the final prophet of Allah
      b) Held Hebrew scriptures and New Testament in high esteem
      c) Determined to spread Allah's wish to all humankind
C. The Establishment of Islam in Arabia
   1. Muhammad's return to Mecca
      a) He and his followers conquered Mecca, 630
      b) Imposed a government dedicated to Allah
      c) Destroyed pagan shrines and built mosques
   2. The Ka'ba
      a) The Ka'ba shrine was not destroyed
      b) In 632, Muhammad led the first Islamic pilgrimage to the Ka'ba
   3. The Five Pillars of Islam
      a) Obligations taught by Muhammad, known as the Five Pillars
      b) The Five Pillars bound the *umma* into a cohesive community of faith
   4. Islamic law: the *sharia*
      a) Emerged during the centuries after Muhammad
      b) Detailed guidance on proper behavior in almost every aspect of life
      c) Drew inspiration especially from the Quran
      d) Through the *sharia*, Islam became more than a religion, but also a way of life

II. The Expansion of Islam

A. The Early Caliphs and the Umayyad Dynasty
   1. The *caliph*
      a) Upon Muhammad's death, Abu Bakr served as *caliph* ("deputy")
      b) Became head of the state, chief judge, religious leader, military commander
   2. The expansion of Islam
      a) Between 633-637, seized Byzantine Syria, Palestine, and most of Mesopotamia
      b) By 640's, conquered Egypt and north Africa
      c) In 651, toppled Sasanid dynasty
      d) In 711, conquered the Hindu kingdom of Sind
      e) Between 711-718, conquered northwest Africa, most of Iberian peninsula
   3. The Shia and Sunnis
      a) The Shia sect, originally supported Ali, served as a refuge
      b) The Sunnis ("traditionalists"), accepted legitimacy of early caliphs
      c) Two sects struggled over succession

4. The Umayyad dynasty (661-750 C.E.)
    a) The dynasty temporarily solved problem of succession
    b) Established capital city at Damascus in Syria
    c) Ruled the *dar al-Islam* for the interests of Arabian military aristocracy
5. Policy toward conquered peoples
    a) Levied *jizya* (head tax) on those who did not convert to Islam
    b) Even the converts did not enjoy wealth and position of authority
6. Umayyad decline
    a) Caliphs became alienated even from other Arabs from the early 8th century
    b) By the mid-century, faced strong resistance of the Shia faction
    c) The discontent of conquered peoples also increased

B. The Abbasid Dynasty
    1. Abu al-Abbas
        a) A descendant of Muhammad's uncle
        b) Allied with Shias and non-Arab Muslims
        c) Seized control of Persia and Mesopotamia during 740's
        d) Shattered Umayyad forces at a battle in 750
        e) Soon after, trapped and annihilated the Umayyad clan
    2. The Abbasid dynasty (750-1258 C.E.)
        a) Showed no special favor to Arab military aristocracy
        b) No longer a conquering empire
        c) Empire still growing, but not initiated by the central government
    3. Abbasid administration
        a) Relied heavily on Persian techniques of statecraft
        b) Central authority ruled from the court at Baghdad
        c) Appointed governors to rule provinces
        d) *Ulama* and *qadis* ruled local communities
    4. Harun al-Rashid (786-809 C.E.)
        a) Represented the high point of the dynasty
        b) Baghdad became metropolis, center for commerce, industry, and culture
    5. Abbasid decline
        a) Struggle for succession between Harun's sons led to civil war
        b) Governors built their own power bases
        c) Popular uprisings and peasant rebellions weakened the dynasty
        d) A Persian noble seized control of Baghdad in 945
        e) Later, the Saljuq Turks controlled the imperial family

III. Economy and Society of the Early Islamic World

A. New Crops, Agricultural Experimentation, and Urban Growth
    1. The spread of food and industrial crops
        a) Indian plants traveled to other lands of the empire
        b) Staple crops: sugarcane, rice, new varieties of sorghum and wheat
        c) Vegetables: spinach, artichokes, eggplants
        d) Fruits: oranges, lemons, limes, bananas, coconuts, watermelons, mangoes
        e) Industrial crops: cotton, indigo, henna
    2. Effects of new crops
        a) Increased varieties and quantities of food
        b) Industrial crops became the basis for a thriving textile industry

3. Agricultural experimentation
   a) Numerous agricultural manuals
   b) Agricultural methods and techniques improved
4. Urban Growth
   a) Increasing agricultural production contributed to the rapid growth of cities
   b) A new industry: paper manufacture
B. The Formation of a Hemispheric Trading Zone
   1. Camels and caravans
      a) Overland trade traveled mostly by camel caravan
      b) Caravanserais in Islamic cities
   2. Maritime trade
      a) Arab and Persian mariners borrowed the compass from the Chinese
      b) Borrowed the lateen sail from southeast Asian and Indian mariners
      c) Borrowed astrolabe from the Hellenistic mariners
      d) The story of Ramisht, a wealthy Persian merchant of the 12th century
   3. Banks
      a) Operated on large scale and provided extensive services
      b) Letters of credit, or *sakk*, functioned as bank checks
   4. The organization of trade
      a) Entrepreneurs often pooled their resources in group investments
      b) Different kinds of joint endeavors
      c) Traders even went to West Africa, Russia, Scandinavia
   5. Al-Andalus
      a) Referring to Islamic Spain, conquered by Muslim Berbers
      b) Claimed independence from the Abbasid dynasty
      c) Participated actively in the commercial life of the larger Islamic world
      d) The example of the merchant-scholar al-Marwani
      e) Products of al-Andalus enjoyed a reputation for excellence
      f) The prosperity of the capital city, Cordoba
C. The Changing Status of Women
   1. The Quran and women
      a) The Quran enhanced security of women
      b) The Quran and *sharia* also reinforced male domination
   2. Veiling of women
      a) Adopted veiling of women from Mesopotamia and Persia
      b) Women's rights provided by the Quran were often reduced

IV. Islamic Values and Cultural Exchanges

A. The Formation of an Islamic Cultural Tradition
   1. The Quran and *sharia* were main sources to formulate moral guidelines
   2. Promotion of Islamic values
      a) *Ulama, qadis*, and missionaries were main agents
      b) Education also promoted Islamic values
   3. *Sufis*
      a) Islamic mystics, also most effective missionaries
      b) Encouraged devotion to Allah by passionate singing or dancing
      c) Al-Ghazali: Human reason was too frail and confusing
      d) Sufis led ascetic and holy lives, won respect of the people

   e) Encouraged followers to revere Allah in their own ways

   f) Tolerated those who associated Allah with other beliefs

  4. The hajj

   a) The Ka'ba became the symbol of Islamic cultural unity

   b) Pilgrims helped to spread Islamic beliefs and values

 B. Islam and the Cultural Traditions of Persia, India, and Greece

  1. Persian influence on Islam

   a) Most notable in literary works

   b) The verses of Omar Khayyam and *The Arabian Nights* were widely known

  2. Indian Influences—adopted "Hindi numerals," which Europeans later called "Arabic numerals"

  3. Greek Influences

   a) Muslims philosophers especially liked Plato and Aristotle

   b) Effort of harmonizing the two traditions met resistance from Sufis

Significant Individuals

Abu al-Abbas (p. 312) — Descendant of Muhammad's uncle; allied with Shias and with non-Arab Muslims to launch rebellion against the Umayyad dynasty; founded the Abbasid dynasty that lasted from 750 to 1258 C.E.

Abu Bakr (p. 309) — The prophet Muhammad's close friend and devoted disciple; after Muhammad's death, became the first caliph of the Islamic community.

al-Ghazali (p. 324) — Persian theologian and famous Islamic Sufi (1058-1111); argued that Greek philosophy and human reasoning were vain pursuits that would inevitably lead to confusion rather than understanding, and only through devotion to Allah and guidance from the Quran could human beings begin to appreciate the uniqueness and power of Allah.

Harun al-Rashid (p. 313) — One of the famous caliphs whose reign (786-808 C.E.) brought the Abbasid dynasty to its high point; known for his support of artists and writers, lavish living, and luxurious gifts; his death led to civil war over succession between his sons seriously damaging Abbasid authority.

Ibn Rushd (p. 324) — Twelfth century Muslim philosopher (1126-1198), known in the west as Averroes; followed Aristotle and sought to articulate a purely rational understanding of the world; had profound influence on the development of European scholasticism during the 13th century.

Khadija (p. 305) — First wife of Muhammad, a wealthy widow in Mecca.

Muhammad (p. 305) — Muhammad ibn Abdullah (570-632 C.E.), founder and prophet of Islam; born in Mecca; received revelations from Allah about 610 C.E. and by his own understanding and account, became the last prophet of Allah.

Chapter Glossary

Abbasid (p. 312) — Islamic dynasty founded by Abu al-Abbas after the Umayyad dynasty; ruled the *dar al-Islam* from Baghdad from 750 to 1258 C.E.

al-Andalus (p. 319) — Islamic Spain; established by Muslim Berber conquerors from north Africa during the early 8th century; refused to recognize the Abbasid dynasty and styled themselves caliphs in their own right from the 10th century.

Allah (p. 305) — "The god"; supreme god who ruled the universe in the strictly monotheistic religion of Islam.

The Arabian Nights (p. 322) — Also known as *The Thousand and One Nights*; collection of popular tales of adventure and romance set in the Abbasid empire and the court of Harun al-Rashid.

Arabic numerals (p. 323) – The numerical system of India by Arabs westward; included a symbol for zero and contributed to the development of mathematical thought.

Baghdad (p. 312) — Capital of the Abbasid dynasty (also capital of modern Iraq); a magnificent city that the early Abbasid caliphs built near the Sasanid capital of Ctesiphon; protected by three round walls.

Bedouin (p. 304) — Nomadic people of the Arabian peninsula; society based on herding of sheep, goats, and camels; organized themselves through kinship networks such as family and clan; became the earliest converts to Islam.

caliph (p. 309) – Literally means "deputy"; head of the state, religious leader, chief judge, and military commander of the Islamic world.

dar al-Islam (p. 304) — Arabic term for "house of Islam," referring to the many lands of varied cultural background under Islamic rule.

Five Pillars (pp. 308-309) — Religious duties obligatory for all Muslims, including monotheistic belief in Allah, daily prayer, fasting during the month of Ramadan, alms contributions, and *hajj*, or pilgrimage.

hajj (pp. 303, 308, 322) — Holy pilgrimage to Mecca to worship at the Ka'ba. In 632, Muhammad's visit to the Ka'ba changed the pagan shrine into an Islamic holy site and the *hajj* into an Islamic tradition. One of the Five Pillars of Islam required that each Muslim with physical and financial capability must undertake the *hajj* and make at least one pilgrimage to Mecca.

hijra (p.307) — "Migration"; refers to the flight of Muhammad and his followers from Mecca to Yathrib (Medina) in 622 C.E.; recognized as the beginning of the official Islamic calendar.

Hindi numerals (p. 323) — Indian numerical system known in the west as Arabic numerals because European peoples learned the Indian symbols through Arab Muslims.

Islam (p. 303) — "Submission"; major world religion founded by Muhammad ibn Abdullah in the Arabian peninsula; required obedience to the rule and will of Allah, the only god recognized by the believers.

jizya (p. 311) — Special head tax levied by Arab conquerors on those who did not convert to Islam during the Umayyad dynasty.

madrasas (p. 321) — Institutions of higher education of Islamic world; appeared in the 10th century and became common in major Islamic cities during the 12th century.

Mecca (pp. 303, 307) — Arabian city located on the west coast of the Red Sea; original home of Muhammad; holy site of the Ka'ba, and became chief religious pilgrimage point in the Islamic world beginning with Muhammad's visit in 632.

Muslim (p. 303) — "One who has submitted"; a Muslim is a believer in Islam.

qadis (p. 312) — "Judges" and moral authorities of Islamic communities; heard legal cases and rendered decisions based on the Quran and *sharia*.

Quran (p. 306) — "Recitation"; holy book of Islam; revelations received by Muhammad from Allah; compiled in the early 650s by devout Muslims; served as the definitive authority for Islamic religious doctrine and social organization.

sakk (p. 317) — Letters of credit in the banking system of the Islamic world; enabled merchants to draw letters of credit in one city and cash them in another; the root of the modern word for "check."

"seal of the prophets" (p. 308) — Title used by Muhammad to refer to himself, meaning that he was the final prophet through whom Allah revealed his divine message to humankind.

sharia (p. 309) — Islamic holy law; reflected social and ethical values derived from Islamic religious principles.

Shia (p. 310) — "Party"; political and theological sect within Islam; originally the sect was formed to support Ali and his descendants as caliphs; served as a refuge and a source of support for opponents of the dominant Sunni sect.

Sufis (p. 321) — Mystics of Islamic faith; sought an emotional and mystical union with Allah rather than an intellectual understanding of Islam; especially effective as missionaries because of their kindness, holiness, tolerance, and charismatic appeal.

Suljuq Turks (p. 313) — Nomadic people from central Asia; invaded the Byzantine empire and ruled the Islamic empire in the name of Abbasid caliphs from the mid-11th century.

Sunnis (p. 310) — "Traditionalists"; political and theological sect within Islam; supported the legitimacy of the Umayyad caliphs.

ulama (p. 312) — "People with religious knowledge"; learned officials and moral authorities of Islamic communities; pious scholars who sought to develop public policy in accordance with the Quran and *sharia*.

Umayyad (pp. 310-11) — Most prominent Meccan merchant clan; dominated politics and economy of Mecca; established dynasty and built capital city at Damascus; dynasty lasted from 661 to 750 C.E.

umma (p. 308) — "Community of the faithful"; communities originally organized by Muhammad and his followers in Medina, which soon became the model of Islamic social organization.

Map Exercises

1. Study Map 13. 1 on p. 310 of your textbook and circle the cities which were NOT under Islamic rule in 733 C.E.:

Mecca	Alexandria	Paris	Merv	Tunis	Baghdad
Siraf	Rome	Bukhara	Constantinople	Medina	

2. Complete the following sentence: The Islamic world during the 8th century included Arabia, Persia, Northern Africa, _____, _____, and _____.

3. How far did Muslim merchants travel? What kinds of commodities did they obtain from the regions they visited?

Self-Test/Student Quiz

1. The *hajj*, or pilgrimage to Mecca,

   a. drew Muslim men by hundreds of thousands from all over the world to Mecca.
   b. started in 632 C.E.
   c. was a special occasion for solemn observation, joy, and celebration.

2. The word *Islam* means

   a. submission.
   b. one who has submitted.
   c. the god.

3. The nature of the society into which the prophet Muhammad was born is that it was

   a. a society of nomadic herders and merchants.
   b. a desert society with many camels.
   c. an agricultural society dominated by warriors.

4. Beginning in 610, Muhammad experienced profound spiritual revelations which led him to believe that

   a. he was chosen by Allah to create a new religion.
   b. he was the last prophet of Allah.
   c. Judaism and Christianity were major offenses to Allah.

5. The Quran is to Islam as

    a. the New Testament is to Christianity.
    b. the Avesta is to Zoroastrianism
    c. Yahweh is to Judaism.

6. Under pressure from authorities in Mecca, Muhammad and his followers fled to Medina in 622. Muslims called this move

    a. the *hijra*.
    b. the *umma*.
    c. Yathrib.

7. The Five Pillars are to Muslims as

    a. the Ten Commandments are to Moses.
    b. the Noble Eightfold Path is to Buddhists.
    c. the four Vedas are to the Aryans.

8. All but one of the following is true with regard to the *sharia:*

    a. It offered detailed guidance on proper behavior in almost every aspect of life.
    b. It was created by the prophet Muhammad.
    c. It drew inspiration especially from the Quran.

9. One of the differences between a Muslim caliph and an Egyptian pharaoh was that

    a. the caliph was more powerful than the pharaoh.
    b. the caliph was a successor of the prophet while the pharaoh was a king.
    c. the caliph was a religious leader while the pharaoh was a god-king.

10. The Umayyad dynasty was founded by

    a. the Shias.
    b. the Sunnis.
    c. Abu al-Abbas.

11. All of the following were done by the Umayyad caliphs except that

    a. they maintained their simple lifestyle even in their capital city Damascus.
    b. they levied a special head tax called *jizya* on non-Muslims.
    c. they showed great favor to the Arab military aristocracy.

12. Differing from the Umayyad caliphs, the Abbasid rulers

    a. were from the Shia sect.
    b. did not allow the Arabs to play a large role in government.
    c. paid more attention to administration rather than expansion of the empire.

13. *Ulama* and *qadis* were important in Islamic society because they

    a.   developed public policies and heard cases in accordance with the Quran and the *sharia*.
    b.   were learned priests in the roles of magistrates and judges.
    c.   were effective missionaries encouraging the people's obedience and devotion to Allah.

14. All but one of the following was true with regard to the Saljuq Turks:

    a.   they invaded the Byzantine empire and seized much of Anatolia.
    b.   they converted to Islam about the mid-10th century.
    c.   they usurped the Abbasid caliphate and claimed the title of caliph for themselves.

15. During Abbasid times, the Arabs learned from China the technique of making

    a.   fine silk.
    b.   paper.
    c.   gunpowder and cannons.

16. Islamic Spain, known as al-Andalus, was

    a.   controlled by Muslim Berber conquerors.
    b.   part of the Abbasid empire.
    c.   almost ruined by the nomadic Berbers from north Africa.

17. All the following were rights of Islamic women except that

    a.   they could legally inherit property, divorce husbands, and engage in business ventures.
    b.   they were equal to men before Allah, not the property of their menfolk.
    c.   a woman could take up to four husbands, just as a man could take up to four wives.

18. The veiling of women as a social custom of the Islamic world was

    a.   forbidden by the Quran.
    b.   practiced long before Muhammad was born.
    c.   adopted from Persia and the eastern Mediterranean.

19. Sufis were especially effective as missionaries because of their

    a.   kindness and holiness.
    b.   tolerance and charismatic appeal.
    c.   all of the above.

20. All but one of the following is correct in describing cultural influences on Islam:

    a.   Persian literature deeply influenced Islamic literary works.
    b.   Indian numerals had a profound influence on the development of mathematical thinking among Muslims.
    c.   Greek rational reasoning had a long-lasting influence on the theological development of Islam.

Textual Questions for Analysis

1. What was the essential nature of Bedouin society prior to Muhammad's revelation? How did Islam substantially change Bedouin society?

2. Why did struggle over succession became a recurrent theme of Islamic political history? Did the constant competition between Shias and Sunnis weaken or strengthen Islamic rule over the vast empire? Why?

3. What made the Abbasid dynasty more cosmopolitan and long-lasting than the Umayyad dynasty?

4. What were the causes of weakness of the later Abbasid dynasty? Compare the decline of the Abbasid empire with similar phenomena of another empire with which you are familiar.

5. According to the Quran and the *sharia*, what rights did Muslim women have? How did imperial expansion affect Muslim women's position?

6. Use concrete examples to describe the economic progress and cultural achievements of the Muslims.

Documentary Evidence

Women's Position in the Quran

Arab women enjoyed rights not accorded to women in many other societies. They could legally inherit property, divorce husbands on their own initiative, and engage in business ventures. In some respects the Quran enhanced the security of Muslim women, but for the most part, it also reinforced male domination. The following two excerpts are from the Quran (*Holy Qur'an*, trans. M. H. Shakir, Elmhurst, N.Y.: Tahrike Tarsile Qur'an, 1985, 4: 34 and 24: 31).

4: 34. Men are the maintainers of women because Allah has made some of them to excel over others and because they spend out of their property; the good women are therefore obedient, guarding the unseen as Allah has guarded; and (as to) those on whose part you fear desertion, admonish them, and leave them alone in the sleeping-places and beat them; then if they obey you, do not seek a way against them; surely Allah is High, Great.

24: 31. And say to the believing women that they cast down their looks and guard their private parts and do not display their ornaments except what appears thereof, and let them wear their head-coverings over their bosoms, and not display their ornaments except to their husbands or their fathers, or the fathers of their husbands, or their sons, or the sons of their husbands, or their brothers, or their brothers' sons, or their sisters' sons, or their women, or those whom their right hands possess, or the male servants not having need (of women), or the children who have not attained knowledge of what is hidden of women; and let them not strike their feet so that what they hide of their ornaments may be known; and turn to Allah all of you, O believer! So that you may be successful.

QUESTIONS TO CONSIDER

1. According to the passage 4:34, what were the characteristics of a good Muslim woman? If a man feared desertion by his wife, what was he supposed to do to her?

2. One of the possible purposes of the veiling of women in the Islamic world (as discussed in passage 24:31) is to emphasize the subservient position of women with respect to men. Can you see any parallels between this dictum for Muslim women and the very different ways that contemporary American women are encouraged to think about aspects of their physical appearance? It might be useful to consider the high emphasis put upon "sex appeal" in terms of women's personal appearance in the contemporary west, and what may be behind that emphasis.

Chapter 14

The Resurgence of Empire in East Asia

Introduction and Learning Objectives

In the Sui, Tang, and Song, three vigorous dynasties of postclassical China, we see the remarkable ability and determination of the Chinese in restoring political unity and innovating on the basis of Chinese tradition. Following the collapse of the Han dynasty in the 3rd century C.E., China suffered from political division, civil strife, and repeated foreign invasions for three and a half centuries. After the short-lived Sui dynasty, however, China during the Tang-Song era became the most advanced economy the world had yet seen. It certainly surpassed the Han in material splendor, productivity, international influence, urbanization, volume of trade, and technological innovations. This was a period in which Chinese products such as porcelain and silk were widely consumed by the peoples of Eurasia, and in which the Chinese developed a taste for foreign products. Scores of the world's most populous cities emerged in China, and, as an indicator of the level of commercialization, the Chinese began to use letters of credit ("flying cash") and paper money for commercial transactions.

What accounted for the unparalleled prosperity and stability of post-classical China? The authors point out that among governmental measures of great significance were the construction of the Grand Canal, which integrated south and north China as a coherent economy; the implementation of the equal-field system, which strengthened the small peasant economy and thus ensured the financial and military resources of the central government; and the development of the civil service examination system, which successfully diverted the energy and passion of millions of young men into study of the Confucian classics and service to the state. Indeed, the civil service examination system not only enabled the central government to recruit a large number of talented and loyal men as bureaucrats, but also contributed to the revival of interest in Confucianism, which soon evolved into a more intricate body of learning called Neo-Confucianism during the Song.

The emergence of Neo-Confucianism had great significance for east Asia. The authors argue that Buddhism contributed a great deal to the theoretical innovations of Neo-Confucianism. Buddhism had taken root in China during the earlier period of disunity, but during the Tang-Song era it grew to maturity. In competition with Confucianism and Daoism for material resources and popularity, Buddhism emerged victorious, but its key concepts had to be cast in Daoist philosophical terms. Buddhist metaphysical themes and its speculative aspects enriched the moral and political concerns of Confucianism and as well as Chinese culture as a whole.

Understandably, Tang-Song China furnished a set of institutions and a way of life for neighboring countries to emulate, an issue that is explored in the last section of the chapter, with focus on Korea, Vietnam, and Japan. The authors argue that the Chinese pursuit of cultural domination through unequal tributary relations actually served the interests of these less developed and smaller neighbors. By making Chinese emperors overlords of other lands, the tributary network facilitated trade relations and cultural borrowing. As a result, Chinese Neo-Confucianism, Buddhism, and political institutions all found their way to Korea, Vietnam, and Japan. China's heavy influence, however, did not eradicate the cultural identities of the satellite countries. All three borrowed Chinese culture to suit their own needs and retained their own cultural traditions.

171

After studying this chapter, students should understand and be able to discuss the following issues:

- comparison between the Sui, Tang, and Song dynasties in terms of centralized imperial rule

- measures that brought about Tang-Song prosperity

- the mutual influences among Buddhism, Confucianism, and Daoism

- Chinese influence on Korea, Vietnam, and Japan

- comparisons between the *dar al-Islam* and the Chinese empire

Chapter Outline

I. **The Restoration of Centralized Imperial Rule in China**

    A. The Sui Dynasty (589-618 C.E.)
1. After the Han dynasty, turmoil lasted for more than 350 years
2. Reunification by Yang Jian in 589
3. The rule of the Sui
   a) Constructions of palaces and granaries, repairing the Great Wall
   b) Military expeditions in central Asia and Korea
   c) High taxes and compulsory labor services
4. The Grand Canal
   a) One of the world's largest waterworks before modern times
   b) Purpose: to bring abundant food supplies of the south to the north
   c) The canal integrated the economies of the south and north
5. The fall of the Sui
   a) High taxes and forced labor generated hostility among the people
   b) Military reverses in Korea
   c) Rebellions broke out in north China beginning in 610
   d) Sui Yangdi was assassinated in 618, the end of the dynasty

    B. The Tang Dynasty (618-907 C.E.)
1. Tang Taizong (627-649)
   a) A rebel leader seized Chang'an, proclaimed a new dynasty, the Tang
   b) Tang Taizong, the second Tang emperor, a ruthless but extremely competent ruler
   c) China enjoyed an era of unusual stability and prosperity
2. Extensive networks of transportation and communications
3. Adopted the equal-field system
4. Bureaucracy of merit
   a) Recruited government officials through civil service examinations
   b) Career bureaucrats relied on the central government, loyal to the dynasty

     5. Foreign relations
        a) Political theory: China was the Middle Kingdom, or the center of civilization
        b) Tributary system became diplomatic policy
     6. Tang decline
        a) Casual and careless leadership led to dynastic crisis
        b) Rebellion of An Lushan in 755, weakened the dynasty
        c) The Uighurs became de facto rulers
        d) The equal-field system deteriorated
        e) A large scale peasant rebellion led by Huang Chao lasted from 875 to 884
        f) Regional military commanders gained power, beyond control of the emperor
        g) The last Tang emperor abdicated his throne in 907

C. The Song Dynasty (960-1279 C.E.)
     1. Song Taizu (reigned 960-976 C.E.), the founder of the Song dynasty
     2. Song weaknesses
        a) Financial problems: Enormous bureaucracy and high salary devoured surplus
        b) Military problems: Civil bureaucrats in charge of military forces
        c) External pressures: Seminomadic Khitan and nomadic Jurchen
        d) The Song moved to the south, ruled south China until 1279

II. The Economic Development of Tang and Song China

A. Agricultural Development
     1. Fast-ripening rice increased food supplies
     2. New agricultural techniques increased production
     3. Population growth: 45 to 115 million between 600 and 1200 C.E.
     4. Urbanization
        a) Chang'an had about 2 million residents
        b) Hangzhou had about 1 million residents
        c) Scores of cities boasted population of one hundred thousand or more
     5. Commercialized agriculture, some regions depended on other regions for food
     6. Patriarchal social structure
        a) Tightening of patriarchal structure for preserving family fortunes
        b) Ancestor worship became more elaborate than before
     7. Foot binding gained popularity during the Song

B. Technological and Industrial Development
     1. Porcelain
        a) High quality porcelain since the Tang, known as *chinaware*
        b) Technology diffused to other societies, especially to Abbasid Arabia
        c) Exported vast quantities to southeast Asia, India, Persia, and Africa
     2. Metallurgy
        a) Improvement: used coke instead of coal in furnaces to make iron and steel
        b) Iron production increased tenfold between the early 9th and 12th century
     3. Gunpowder
        a) Discovered by Daoist alchemists during the Tang
        b) Bamboo "fire lances," a kind of flame thrower, and primitive bombs
        c) Gunpowder chemistry diffused throughout Eurasia

4. Printing
   a) Became common during the Tang
   b) From block-printing to movable type
   c) Books became widespread
5. Naval technology: "South-pointing needle"—the magnetic compass
C. The Emergence of a Market Economy
   1. Financial instruments: "flying cash" (letters of credit) and paper money
   2. A cosmopolitan society: Communities of foreign merchants in large cities of China
   3. Economic surge in China promoted economic growth in the eastern hemisphere

III. Cultural Change in Tang and Song China

A. Establishment of Mahayana Buddhism
   1. Foreign religions in China: Nestorian and Muslim communities
   2. Dunhuang, an oases on the silk road, became a location for Buddhist settlement and transmission of Mahayana Buddhism to China
   3. Buddhism in China
      a) Attraction: moral standards, intellectual sophistication, and salvation
      b) Monasteries became large landowners, helped the poor and needy
      c) Also posed a challenge to Chinese cultural tradition
   4. Buddhism and Daoism
      a) Chinese monks explained Buddhist concepts in Daoist vocabulary
      b) *Dharma* as *dao*, and *nirvana* as *wuwei*
      c) Teaching: one son in monastery would benefit whole family for 10 generations
   5. Chan Buddhism
      a) A syncretic faith: Buddhism with Chinese characteristics
      b) Chan (or Zen in Japanese) was a popular Buddhist sect
         (1) emphasized intuition and sudden flashes of insight
         (2) mediation techniques resembled Daoist practice
      c) Monasteries appeared in all major cities
   6. Hostility to Buddhism
      a) Resistance from Daoists and Confucians
      b) Criticism focused on celibacy, alien origin, and unproductive landholding
   7. Persecution
      a) Critics of Buddhism found allies in the imperial court
      b) Tang emperor ordered closure of monasteries in 840s
      c) Buddhism survived because of popular support
B. Neo-Confucianism
   1. Buddhist influence on Confucianism
      a) Early Confucianism focused on practical issues of politics and morality
      b) Confucians began to draw inspiration from Buddhism
         (1) Logical thought and argumentation of Buddhism
         (2) Metaphysical issues: nature of soul, man's relation with cosmos
   2. Zhu Xi (1130-1200 C.E.), the most prominent Neo-Confucian scholar
   3. Neo-Confucian influence
      a) Adapted Buddhist themes and reasoning to Confucian interests and values
      b) Influenced east Asian thought
         (1) In China, it was an officially recognized creed
         (2) Influenced Korea, Vietnam, and Japan for half a millennium

IV. China and East Asia

A. Korea and Vietnam
1. The Silla Dynasty of Korea (669-935 C.E.)
   a) Tang armies conquered much of Korea, the Silla dynasty organized resistance
   b) Korea entered into a tributary relationship with China
2. China's influence in Korea
   a) Tributary embassies included Korean royal officials and scholars
   b) The Silla kings built a new capital at Kumsong modeled on the Tang capital
   c) Korean elite turned to Neo-Confucianism, peasants turned to Chan Buddhism
3. Difference from China: aristocracy and royal houses dominated Korea
4. China and Vietnam
   a) Viet people adopted Chinese agriculture, schools, and thought
   b) Tributary relationship with China
   c) When Tang fell, Vietnam gained independence
5. Difference from China
   a) Many Vietnamese retained their religious traditions
   b) Women played more prominent roles in Vietnam than in China
6. Chinese influence in Vietnam: bureaucracy and Buddhism

B. Early Japan
1. Nara Japan (710-794 C.E.)
   a) The earliest inhabitants of Japan were nomadic peoples from northeast Asia
   b) Ruled by several dozen states by the middle of the 1st millennium C.E.
   c) Inspired by the Tang example, one clan claimed imperial authority over others
   d) The imperial court modeled on that of the Tang
   e) Built a new capital (Nara) in 710 C.E., modeled on Chang'an
   f) Adopted Confucianism and Buddhism, but maintained their Shinto rites
2. Heian Japan (794-1185 C.E.)
   a) Moved to new capital Heian (modern Kyoto) in 794
   b) Japanese emperors as ceremonial figureheads and symbols of authority
   c) Effective power in the hands of the Fujiwara family
   d) Emperor did not rule, which explains the longevity of the imperial house
   e) Chinese learning dominated Japanese education and political thought
3. *The Tale of Genji*: women contributed most to Japanese literature and writing
4. Decline of Heian Japan
   a) The equal-field system began to fail
   b) Aristocratic clans accumulated most lands
   c) Taira and Minamoto, the two most powerful clans, engaged in wars
   d) The clan leader of the victorious Minamoto claimed the title of *shogun*, military governor, and ruled in Kamakura

C. Medieval Japan
1. Japanese feudalism
   a) Feudal Japan: Kamakura (1185-1333 C.E.) and Muromachi (1336-1573 C.E.) periods
   b) Provincial lords controlled Japan, vied for power against each other

2. The samurai
    a) Professional warriors of provincial lords
    b) Valued loyalty, military talent, and discipline
    c) Observed samurai code called *bushido*
    d) To preserve their honor, engaged in ritual suicide called *seppuku*

Significant Individuals

An Lushan (p. 332) — Military commander of Tang dynasty; launched rebellion in 755 and seized the Tang capital at Chang'an. Revolt was suppressed two years later, but the dynasty was severely weakened.

Huang Chao (pp. 332-33) — Leader of a large-scale uprising during the Tang, lasted from 875 to 884. Rebels caused tumult in much of eastern China.

Song Taizu (p. 333) — Title for the first Song emperor (reigned 960-976 C.E.); pacified warlords after the collapse of the Tang dynasty and founded the Song dynasty. Policies emphasized civil administration over military affairs.

Sui Yangdi (pp. 329-30) — Second and last emperor of the Sui dynasty, reigned from 604 to 618; responsible for construction of the Grand Canal; assassinated in 618.

Tang Taizong (p. 330) — Second emperor of Tang dynasty, reigned from 627 to 649; murdered his two brothers and pushed his father aside to gain throne; built a splendid capital at Chang'an; sought to reinforce interests of small peasants by light taxes and the equal-field system; strengthened bureaucracy by using civil service examination system; competent ruler who brought unusual stability and prosperity to China.

Yang Jian (pp. 328-29) — Founder of the Sui dynasty; claimed the title of emperor for himself in 581 and reunified China in 589.

Xuanzang (pp. 327-28, 344) — Buddhist monk of the Tang dynasty; traveled to India and spent 12 years there studying Buddhism beginning in 630 C.E. His pilgrimage became a legend that helped to popularize Buddhism in China.

Zhu Xi (p. 345) — Most prominent philosopher of Neo-Confucianism during the Song dynasty; wrote extensively on metaphysical themes such as the nature of reality; stressed importance of philosophical investigations to practical affairs.

Chapter Glossary

block-printing (p. 338) — Technique of printing which was popular during the early Song; involved carving a reverse image of an entire page onto a wooden block, inking of the block, and pressing a sheet of paper on top. By the mid-11th century, Chinese printers also invented reusable and movable type.

bushido (p. 350) — "The way of the warrior"; behavior code widely observed by samurai in feudal Japan; emphasized virtues of absolute loyalty, courage, physical strength, and a spirit of aggression.

Chan Buddhism (p. 344) — Popular Buddhist sect in China (also known by its Japanese name, Zen); had little interest in written texts but instead emphasized intuition and sudden flashes of insight in search of spiritual enlightenment.

Chang'an (pp. 330, 336) — Capital of Tang Dynasty built under Tang Taizong; the world's most populous city with as many as two million residents; a cosmopolitan, cultural mecca.

civil service examinations (pp. 331-32) — Examinations periodically given by governments for recruiting government officials; tests were based on classic works of Chinese literature and philosophy; originating from the Han dynasty, and became completely institutionalized during the Tang and Song dynasties.

Dunhuang (p. 342) — Oasis city in western China on the silk road; site of hundreds of Buddhist cave temples, and known for its leading role in spreading Mahayana Buddhism in China.

equal-field system (p. 331) — System of landholding during the early Tang dynasty. To ensure equitable land distribution, government allocated land to individuals and their families according to the land's fertility and the recipients' needs. A family could keep one-fifth of the land as hereditary property while the rest would be subject to periodic redistribution to adjust for changing circumstances of the recipients.

fast-ripening rice (p. 335) — Strain of rice originally cultivated by Vietnamese which enabled farmers to harvest twice a year; introduced to south China via military ventures during the Tang dynasty.

flying cash (p. 339) — Chinese letter of credit or early form of currency issued by banks to facilitate trade between different locations; popularly used during the early Tang dynasty to alleviate the shortage of copper coins.

foot binding (p. 337) — Chinese custom since the Song dynasty; involved tight wrapping of young girls' feet with strips of cloth that prevented natural growth of the bones and resulted in tiny, malformed, curved feet. Practiced to enhance women's attractiveness, display their high social standing, and gain better control of their behavior.

Grand Canal (p. 329) — Artificial waterway constructed under emperor Sui Yangdi which extended about 1,240 miles from south to north; served as the principal conduit for internal trade and transportation.

gunpowder (p. 338) — Explosive powder discovered by Daoist alchemists while seeking elixirs during the Tang dynasty; popularly used in China to make fire crackers and weapons; quickly diffused throughout Eurasia.

Hangzhou (p. 336) — Capital city of the later Song dynasty; had more than one million residents during the late 13th century; known for its scenic beauty and economic prosperity.

Heian Japan (pp. 348-49) — Period of Japanese history between 794 and 1185 C.E.; characterized by new developments in politics and culture; imperial house became a symbol of national authority while effective power was in the hands of the Fujiwara family; lifestyle of aristocrats, as depicted in *The Tale of Genji*, was uniquely Japanese.

Jurchen (p. 335) — Nomadic people from Manchuria; conquered the Khitan empire, overran northern China and captured the Song capital in the early 12th century; ruled north China until 1279 while south China continued under the rule of the Song dynasty.

Kamakura and **Muromachi** (pp. 349-50) — Two periods of Japanese medieval history, lasting from 1185 to 1573 C.E.); characterized by the development of feudalism.

Khitan (pp. 334-35) — Seminomadic people from Manchuria; ruled a vast empire stretching from northern Korea to Mongolia from the 10th century; forced the Song court to present large tribute payments of silk and silver in exchange for peace; conquered by the Jurchen in the early 12th century.

li and *qi* (p. 345) — Two elements in Zhu Xi's theory that accounted for all physical being. *Li* referred to principles that define the essence of all beings, and *qi* defined material forms or shapes of various beings.

Nam Viet (p. 347) — Chinese term for Vietnam, meaning "the southern Viet"; became a tributary state of Tang China; gained independence after the fall of the Tang dynasty during the early 10th century.

Nara Japan (p. 348) — Period of Japanese history lasting from 710 to 794 C.E. Inspired by the Tang example, Japanese authorities established a court modeled on that of the Tang, instituted a Chinese style bureaucracy, implemented an equal-field system, provided official support for Confucianism and Buddhism, and built a capital city at Nara that was a replica of the Tang capital at Chang'an.

Neo-Confucianism (p. 345) — Represents new development of Confucianism during the Song dynasty as Chinese intellectuals were increasingly influenced by Buddhist thought. Retained Confucian tradition but became more speculative and philosophical than the early Confucianism; became the basis of the Confucian civil service examination system.

paper money (p. 340) — Printed notes issued by Chinese private banks as currency to facilitate commercial transactions beginning in the late 9th century; by the 11th century, issuing paper money became an exclusive right of the Chinese government.

samurai (p. 350) — Professional warriors of feudal Japan; served provincial lords with their fighting skills; emphasized virtues of loyalty, strength, courage, and a spirit of aggression.

seppuku or *hara-kiri* (p. 350) — Ritual suicide of disembowelment practiced by Japanese samurai to avoid dishonor and humiliation.

shogun (pp. 349-50) — The most powerful regional lord in Japan who assumed leadership under the symbolic authority of the emperor. The title *shogun* was first used in the Kamakura period (1185-1333 C.E.).

Silla (pp. 332, 346-47) — Korean dynasty, ruling from 669 to 935 C.E.; rallied forces to resist invasion of the Chinese Tang armies during the 7th century; but entered into a tributary relationship with China thereafter and was deeply influenced by the Chinese political and cultural tradition.

south-pointing needle (p. 338) — Chinese term for magnetic compass; invented and used for naval purposes during the Song dynasty.

tributary relationship (p. 332) — Unequal relationships between China and surrounding countries; peoples of the neighboring lands would recognize Chinese emperors as their overlords. Envoys from subordinate states would regularly present gifts to Chinese court and perform the kowtow ritual as tokens of their subordination. In return, tributary states received confirmation of their authority as well as lavish gifts from the Chinese court. The system facilitated trade and cultural exchange between China and other countries.

Uighurs (p. 332) — Nomadic Turkish people; invited by the Tang authorities to suppress An Lushan's revolt in 757; became de facto rulers of the Tang imperial court after the revolt was pacified.

Map Exercises

1. Study Map 14.1 on p. 329 of your textbook, and answer the following questions:

    A) Where was Dunhuang? Why was it important for Chinese religious life?

    B) Describe the Grand Canal and discuss its economic significance.

2. Compare the size of the Tang empire (Map 14.1) with that of the Song empire (Map 14.2, p. 334), and explain how the Song lost its territory.

Self-Test/Student Quiz

1. Xuanzang became a well-known monk of the Tang dynasty because

    a. he was the only Chinese who made the pilgrimage to Mecca.
    b. his travels and study in India helped to popularize Buddhism in China.
    c. he was persecuted by the emperor for his violation of the ban on traveling abroad.

2. All of the following describe the Sui dynasty except:

    a. It reunified China and launched military campaigns in central Asia and Korea.
    b. It imposed high taxes and compulsory labor services for construction of the Grand Canal.
    c. It brought about great prosperity in China and long-lived imperial rule.

3. The Tang maintained an efficient communication network, which can be seen by the fact that

    a. the Tang court could communicate with the most distant cities of the empire in about three months.
    b. emperors at Chang'an could have fresh seafood delivered from Ningbo, a city 620 miles away.
    c. the Grand Canal was initiated under Tang rule.

4. Under the equal-field system, the Tang government

    a. allotted land according to the land's fertility and the recipients' needs.
    b. eliminated the possibility of concentrated landholdings among the wealthy.
    c. was able to levy heavy taxes on the recipients.

5. The Tang government was run primarily by

    a. hereditary aristocratic families.
    b. royal kinsmen and relatives.
    c. bureaucrats of intellectual merit.

6. "There was always something of a fictional quality to the [tributary] system." By this the authors mean that

    a. envoys from subordinate lands were not sincere in performing the ritual kowtow to Chinese emperors.
    b. Chinese authorities had little real influence in the supposedly subordinate lands.
    c. Chinese courts also gave lavish gifts to foreign envoys.

7. One cause for Tang decline during the mid-8th century was that

    a. the emperors neglected public affairs in favor of music and mistresses.
    b. military campaigns in central Asia, Korea, and Vietnam drained Tang finances.
    c. the central government abolished the equal-field system.

8. Compared with the Tang dynasty, the Song dynasty was

    a. less militarized.
    b. less centralized.
    c. equal in size.

9. The Song government moved from north to south in the early 12th century because of the invasion of

    a. the Khitan.
    b. the Jurchen.
    c. the Uighurs.

10. Fast-ripening rice

    a. was introduced to China from Japan.
    b. enabled cultivators to harvest three times a year.
    c. increased food supply and supported a large population.

11. Song China experienced a tightening of patriarchal social structure, which can be seen from

    a. the veneration of family ancestors, a practice that became much more elaborate than before.
    b. the popularity of food binding among elite families.
    c. both a and b.

12. All but one of the following were not major technological innovations of Tang and Song China:

    a. Gunpowder and the magnetic compass.
    b. Printing and making of fine porcelain.
    c. Paper making the production of salt from wells.

13. The Chinese term "flying cash" meant

    a. paper money printed by the government as a substitute for heavy copper currency.
    b. letters of credit used by merchants.
    c. that money changed hands so quickly it seemed as though it could fly.

14. During Tang times several foreign religions came to China. The foreign faiths that did NOT arrive in China included

    a. Nestorian Christianity and Manichaeanism.
    b. Hinduism and Jainism.
    c. Zoroastrianism and Islam.

15. In order for Buddhism to be accepted in China, Chinese Buddhists

    a. changed the Buddha and the *boddhisatvas* into Daoist deities.
    b. accommodated Buddhism to Chinese values such as filial piety.
    c. paid high taxes from their monasteries to the Chinese government.

16. The most important representative of Song Neo-Confucianism was

    a. Zhu Xi.
    b. Xuanzang.
    c. Song Taizu.

17. Despite cultural borrowing and imitation, Korea was still different from China in that

    a. aristocrats dominated Korean society while bureaucrats dominated Chinese life.
    b. Koreans accepted Neo-Confucianism but rejected Buddhism.
    c. the Silla capital at Kumsong did not resemble the Chinese capital at Chang'an.

18. All of the following are true of Vietnam during Tang and Song times except that

    a. many Vietnamese retained their indigenous traditions in preference to Chinese cultural traditions.
    b. Vietnamese authorities established an administrative system and bureaucracy modeled on that of China.
    c. Vietnamese women also practiced foot binding in imitation of their Chinese sisters.

19. The earliest phases of Japanese history included

    a. the Kamakura and Muromachi periods.
    b. the Nara and Heian periods.
    c. the Taira and Minamoto periods.

20. In medieval Japan, professional warriors were called

    a. *samurai.*
    b. *bushido.*
    c. *shogun.*

181

Textual Questions for Analysis

1. Through the Sui, Tang, and Song dynasties, what did Chinese authorities do to reinforce centralized imperial rule?

2. What accounts for the decline and fall of the Tang dynasty?

3. How did Song imperial policies differ from those of the Tang? What were the major problems faced by Song emperors?

4. How can you describe the economic prosperity of the Tang-Song era? What factors contributed to this economic prosperity?

5. What were the major cultural changes during the Tang-Song era?

6. The Tang-Song era was an innovative period in terms of technology and commercial practice. Explain.

7. What were the similarities and differences among Korea, Vietnam, and Japan in terms of receiving Chinese cultural influence?

Documentary Evidence

Bushido

Professional warriors of medieval Japan were called *samurai* or *bushi*. By the 12th century, they emerged from various domains as a dominant social class, and their values permeated the lives of all other social classes. *Bushido*, or the way of warriors, was not a written code of conduct for the ruling *samurai* class but was a widely-observed set of norms consisting of a few maxims. Drawing from Zen Buddhism, Shintoism, and Confucian moral precepts, the principles of *bushido* placed high value on justice, honor, duty, loyalty, courage, and self-control. The following excerpt is from the teachings of Tsunetomo Yamamoto (1659-1719) on *bushido*. The author was a *samurai* turned Zen monk. (From Tsunetomo Yamamoto, *Hagakure: The Book of the Samurai*, translated by William Scott Wilson, Tokyo and New York: Kodansha International, Ltd., 1979, pp. 17, 33, 66-67).

The Way of the Samurai is found in death. When it comes to either/or, there is only the quick choice of death. It is not particularly difficult. Be determined and advance. To say that dying without reaching one's aim is to die a dog's death is the frivolous way of sophisticates. When pressed with the choice of life or death, it is not necessary to gain one's aim....

Every morning, the samurai of fifty or sixty years ago would bathe, shave their foreheads, put lotion in their hair, cut their fingernails and toenails rubbing them with pumice and then with wood sorrel, and without fail pay attention to their personal appearance. It goes without saying that their armor in general was kept free from rust, that it was dusted, shined, and arranged.

Although it seems that taking special care of one's appearance is similar to showiness, it is nothing akin to elegance. Even if you are aware that you may be stuck down today and are firmly resolved to an inevitable death, if you are slain with an unseemly appearance, you will show your lack of previous resolve, will be despised by your enemy, and will appear unclean. For this reason it is said that both old and young should take care of their appearance....

If one were to say in a word what the condition of being a samurai is, its basis lies first in seriously devoting one's body and soul to his master. And if one is asked what to do beyond this, it would be to fit oneself inwardly with intelligence, humanity and courage. The combining of these three virtues may seem unobtainable to the ordinary person, but it is easy. Intelligence is nothing more than discussing things with others. Limitless wisdom comes from this. Humanity is something done for the sake of others, simply comparing oneself with them and putting them in the fore. Courage is gritting one's teeth; it is simply doing that and pushing ahead, paying no attention to the circumstances. Anything that seems above these three is not necessary to be known.

As for outward aspects, there are personal appearance, one's way of speaking and calligraphy. And as all of these are daily matters, they improve by constant practice. Basically, one should perceive their nature to be one of quiet strength. If one has accomplished all these things, then he should have a knowledge of our area's history and customs. After that he may study the various arts as recreation. If you think it over, being a retainer [i.e., samurai] is simple....

BASED ON YOUR READING, COMPLETE THE FOLLOWING SENTENCES:

1. "The Way of the Samurai is found in death." By this the author meant
_____.

2. The primary reason for a samurai to maintain good appearance was
_____.

3. The basis of being a samurai lies first in _____ to his master.

4. The three inward virtues of a samurai were _____, _____ and _____. The three outward virtues included _____, _____, and
_____.

Chapter 15

India and the Indian Ocean Basin

Introduction and Learning Objectives

While the vast Arab empire emerged in the west and the Chinese empire resurfaced in the east during the postclassical era, the Indian subcontinent was dominated by regional kingdoms. The political weakness of India left it vulnerable to foreign invasions. Already in the classical period, the politically divided subcontinent had suffered from frequent raids and incursions of a number of northern nomadic peoples. None of the nomads, however, could pose a serious challenge to the Indian cultural tradition. The situation changed during the postclassical era when foreign invaders and merchants brought one more world religion—Islam—to the religiously rich subcontinent. Could the Indians, who alone produced two world religions, absorb another world religion radically different from their own?

The authors' discussion reveals clearly the profound differences between foreign Islam and native Hinduism (the predominant religion of India at the time). The Hindu pantheon made places for numerous gods and spirits, and it was open, tolerant, and inclusive, whereas Islamic theology was doctrinaire, proselytizing, exclusive, and stood on the foundation of a firm and uncompromising monotheism. Strong egalitarianism could be found in Islamic doctrines, while Hindu beliefs made caste hierarchy an ideal. Gradually, however, Islamic faith made its way among Indians. By 1500 C.E., about one-quarter of the subcontinent's population had converted to the foreign faith, mostly in northern India. How could this happen?

The authors' discussion includes a number of factors that helped Islam to spread in India. First, the Muslim invaders in the north cruelly suppressed Hinduism and Buddhism and strongly encouraged conversion to Islam. Second, Islam had strong appeal to members of lower castes, who converted to the new faith in hopes of improving their social status or escaping discrimination. Third, besides merchants from the Islamic world, the most effective agents of Islam were Sufi mystics who encouraged a personal, emotional, and devotional approach. Apparently rigid Islamic doctrines could be quite flexible in practice when Sufis permitted their Indian followers to observe rituals and deities not recognized by the Islamic faith. Finally, the gap between Hinduism and Islam was further narrowed when Hindu *bhakti* leaders and Islamic Sufis emphasized piety, devotion, and emotional involvement with their gods. Originally a movement of piety and devotion to Hindu values, the *bhakti* movement increasingly encountered Muslims in the north and became deeply attractive to certain Islamic values, especially monotheism and the notion of the spiritual equality of all believers. The movement went so far that a guru named Kabir even taught that the Hindu deities, Shiva and Vishnu, and the Islamic god Allah, were all manifestations of a single, universal deity, whom all devout believers could find within their own hearts.

Another important point discussed by the authors is that despite political disunion, India actively participated in cross-cultural trade and played a major role in integrating the economies of the entire Indian Ocean basin. With its economic prosperity and cultural richness, India served well as an important source of political and cultural inspiration throughout south and southeast Asia. The adoption of Indian culture was peaceful and voluntary, as Indian merchants and missionaries introduced Hinduism, Buddhism, Sanskrit writing, and Indian forms of political organization to southeast Asia. Beginning about the 12th century, Muslim Indian merchants also brought Islam to these lands where the new faith attracted a sizable following.

After studying this chapter, students should understand and be able to discuss the following issues:

- Islamic incursions in the north and Hindu kingdoms in the south

- the coming of Islam and its interaction with Hinduism

- the economic growth of India and its role in the Indian Ocean basin

- the cultural influence of India on developments in southeast Asian states

Chapter Outline

I. **Islamic and Hindu Kingdoms**

  A. The Quest for Centralized Imperial Rule
    1. North India
      a) After fall of the Gupta empire, north and south followed different trajectories
      b) The turbulent north
        (1) tension and intermittent wars among regional kingdoms
        (2) invasion of nomadic Turkish-speaking peoples
    2. Harsha (reigned 606-648 C.E.)
      a) King Harsha temporarily restored unified rule in most of north India
      b) Harsha also a man of piety, liberality, and scholarship
    3. Collapse of Harsha's kingdom
      a) Not able to overcome autonomy of regional authorities
      b) Fell victim to an assassin, the unified kingdom fell apart
  B. Introduction of Islam to northern India
    1. The conquest of Sind
      a) Arab exploratory military ventures in Sind since the mid-7th century
      b) Formal conquest of Sind (northwestern India, Indus River valley) in 711
      c) Passed to the Abbasid caliphs from the mid-8th century
      d) The fringe of the Islamic world, no effective authority
    2. Merchants and Islam
      a) Muslim merchants formed small communities in all major cities of coastal India
      b) Large Muslim population found in Gujarat region before 1000 C.E.
    3. Turkish migrants and Islam
      a) Several Turkish groups converted to Islam, the 10th century
      b) Some moved to Afghanistan and established an Islamic state
    4. Mahmud of Ghazni
      a) Leader of the Turks in Afghanistan, mounted expeditions in north India
      b) Demolished Hindu and Buddhist sites and established mosques
    5. The Sultanate of Delhi (1206-1526 C.E.)
      a) Mahmud's successors conquered north India, 1206
      b) Established an Islamic state known as the sultanate of Delhi

6. The rule of the sultanate of Delhi
    a) Sultans' authorities did not extend far beyond the capital at Delhi
    b) Depended on goodwill of Hindu kings to carry out policies
    c) 19 out of 35 sultans perished at the hands of assassins
    d) Islam began to have a place in India
C. The Hindu Kingdoms of Southern India
    1. The south: politically divided but relatively peaceful
    2. The Chola kingdom (850-1267 C.E.)
        a) A larger kingdom, ruled Coromandel coast
        b) At its high point, conquered Ceylon and parts of southeast Asia
        c) Navy dominated waters from South China Sea to Arabian Sea
        d) Not a tightly centralized state, local autonomy was strong
        e) Began to decline by the 12th century
D. The kingdom of Vijayanagar (1336-1565 C.E.)
    1. Established by two Indian brothers
    2. Renounced Islam in 1336, returned to their Hindu faith

II. Production and Trade in the Indian Ocean Basin

A. Agriculture in the Monsoon World
    1. The monsoons
        a) Indian agriculture depended on monsoon rains in spring and summer
        b) Supplemented by irrigation during dry months.
    2. Irrigation systems
        a) No big river in south India, waterworks included dams, reservoirs, canals, wells
        b) Stored rain water in large reservoirs, connected to canals
        c) One reservoir constructed during the 11th century covered 250 sq. miles
    3. Population growth: 53 million in 600 C.E. to 105 million in 1500 C.E.
    4. Urbanization
        a) Delhi became the second largest Muslim city
        b) A number of other cities had one hundred thousand residents
B. Trade and Economic Development of Southern India
    1. Internal trade
        a) Self-sufficient in staple food
        b) Metals, spices, special crops found only in certain regions.
        c) Through trade, south India and Ceylon experienced rapid economic growth
    2. Temples and society in south India
        a) Hindu temples served as economic and social centers
        b) Possessed large tracts of land, hundreds of employees
        c) Temple administrators were to maintain order, deliver taxes
        d) Served as banks, engaged in business ventures
C. Cross-cultural Trade in Indian Ocean Basin
    1. Dhows and junks
        a) Dhows averaged 100 tons in 1000 and 400 tons in 1500
        b) Larger ships plied Indian Ocean, no longer followed coastal lines
        c) Large Chinese and southeast Asian junks also sailed the Ocean
    2. Emporia and warehouses
        a) India, the natural site for emporia and warehouses
        b) Merchants also built emporia outside India
        c) Indian port cities became clearing houses of trade and cosmopolitan centers

3. Trade goods
   a) Silk and porcelain from China
   b) Spices from southeast Asia
   c) Pepper, gems, pearls, and cotton from India
   d) Incense and horses from Arabia and southwest Asia
   e) Gold, ivory, and slaves from east Africa
4. Specialized production
   a) Production of high-quality cotton textiles thrived
   b) Stimulated specialization and growth of other industries
   c) Other specialized industries: sugar, leather, stone, carpets, iron and steel

D. Caste and society
   1. Caste and migration
      a) Caste helped to integrate immigrants into Indian society
      b) Some Turkish peoples and Muslim merchants were absorbed
   2. Caste and social change: guilds and subcastes
   3. Expansion of caste system
      a) During the classical era, castes extended to the south
      b) Merchant and craft guilds emerged as subcastes in the south

III. The Meeting of Hindu and Islamic Traditions

A. The Development of Hinduism
   1. Hinduism predominated in southern India, Islam in the north
   2. Vishnu and Shiva
      a) Decline of Buddhism benefited Hinduism
      b) The growth of Vishnu and Shiva cults
      c) Hindus associated many gods and goddesses with the above two cults
   3. Devotional cults: to achieve mystic union with gods as a way of salvation
   4. Shankara: preferred disciplined logical reasoning
   5. Ramanuja: understanding of ultimate reality was less important than devotion

B. Islam and its Appeal
   1. Conversion to Islam
      a) Conversion was slow and gradual
      b) Some converted for improving their lower social statuses
      c) Often an entire caste or subcaste adopted Islam en masse
      d) By 1500, about 25 million Indian Muslims
   2. Sufis
      a) The most effective missionaries, a devotional approach to Islam
      b) Permitted followers to observe old rituals and venerate old spirits
      c) Emphasized piety and devotion
   3. The *bhakti* movement
      a) Sought to erase distinction between Hinduism and Islam
      b) *Bhakti* leaders became attracted to certain Islamic values
      c) Guru Kabir (1440-1518) — important *bhakti* teacher, taught that Shiva, Vishnu, and Allah were one deity
      d) Neither Sufis nor *bhakti* leaders succeeded in completely harmonizing the two faiths

IV. The Influence of Indian Society in Southeast Asia

    A. The Indianized States of Southeast Asia
       1. Indian influence in southeast Asia
         a) Indian merchants brought their faiths to southeast Asia
         b) Ruling elite of southeast Asia became acquainted with Indian traditions
         c) The states sponsored Hinduism and Buddhism
         d) Showed no interest in Indian caste system
       2. Funan (1st to 6th century C.E.)
         a) Located at lower reaches of Mekong River (parts of Cambodia and Vietnam)
         b) The first Indianized state, capital city at the port of Oc Eo
         c) Drew enormous wealth by controlling trade
         d) Adopted Sanskrit as official language
       3. Decline of Funan
         a) Bitter power struggle weakened Funan, the 6th century
         b) Migrants from the south overwhelmed Funan
         c) Chams and Khmers dominated Funan
       4. Srivijaya (670-1025 C.E.)
         a) Established after the fall of Funan on Sumatra
         b) Maintained sea-trade between China and India by navy
         c) Chola kingdom of south India eclipsed Srivijaya in the 11th century
       5. Angkor (889-1431 C.E.)
         a) Kingdom built by Khmers at Angkor Thom
         b) The city was a microcosmic reflection of Hindu world order
         c) Turned to Buddhism during the 12th and 13th centuries
         d) Thais invaded the capital in 1431, and Khmers abandoned it
         e) Rediscovered by French missionaries in the mid-19th century in jungle
       6. Other states
         a) Singosari (1222-1292 C.E.) and Majapahit (1293-1520 C.E.)
         b) Each Indianized state had its own characteristics
    B. The Arrival of Islam in Southeast Asia
       1. Conversion to Islam
         a) Conversion was slow and quiet
         b) Ruling elite converted in cities while rural residents retained their traditions
         c) Islam was not an exclusive faith in southeast Asia
         d) Sufis appealed to a large public in these countries
       2. Melaka
         a) The powerful state of Melaka sponsored Islam during the 15th century
         b) Controlled maritime trade
         c) Originally a Hindu state, Melaka became predominantly Islamic

Significant Individuals

Harihara and **Bukka** (p. 360) — Co-founders of Vijayanagar kingdom; official delegates of the sultan in Delhi; renounced Islam, returned to their Hindu faith, and claimed independence in south India in 1336 C.E.

Harsha (p. 357) — King of the Harsha kingdom; reigned from 606 to 648 C.E.; maintained a powerful army and temporarily unified most of north India; enjoyed a reputation for piety, liberal attitude, and scholarship.

Mahmud of Ghazni (p. 358) — Leader of Muslim Turks in Afghanistan; frequently raided north India at the beginning of the 11th century C.E.; destroyed many Buddhist sites and established mosques or Islamic shrines at the sites of Hindu and Buddhist structures.

Kabir (p. 370) — Spiritual leader of the *bhakti* movement; active at the turn of the 15th and 16th centuries C.E.; taught that Shiva, Vishnu, and Allah were all manifestations of a single, universal deity, whom all devout believers could find within their own hearts.

Paramesvara (p. 374) — Prince of Sumatra and founder of the Melaka state.

Ramanuja (p. 369) — Brahmin philosopher of south India; active during the 11th and early 12th centuries C.E..; taught intensive devotion to Vishnu for personal salvation, and challenged Shankara's intellectual system of thought.

Shankara (p. 369) — *Brahmin* philosopher of south India; active during the early 9th century C.E.; mistrusted emotional services and ceremonies; believed that only through disciplined logical reasoning man could understand ultimate reality.

Chapter Glossary

Angkor (p. 373) — Kingdom of southeast Asia; lasted from 889 to 1431 C.E.; known for its capital city at Angkor Thom, designed as a microcosmic reflection of the Hindu world order.

bhakti (p. 370) — Religious movement that emerged in southern India during the 12th century C.E.; originally encouraged traditional piety and devotion to Hindu values, but as the movement spread to the north, it began to incorporate certain Islamic values, especially monotheism and the notion of spiritual equality of all believers.

Chola (p. 359) — Large kingdom of southern India; ruled the Coromandel coast from 850 to 1267 C.E.; conquered Ceylon and parts of southeast Asia during the 11th century C.E.

dhow (p. 364) — Large commercial ships favored by Indian, Persian, and Arab sailors.

Funan (pp. 371-72) — First Indianized kingdom of southeast Asia; dominated the lower reaches of the Mekong River from the 1st through the 6th centuries C.E.

Majapahit (p. 373) — Small kingdom on Java, ruled between 1293 and 1520 C.E.

Melaka (p. 374) — Powerful kingdom of southeast Asia, based on Malay peninsula; founded during the late 14th century; changed from a Hindu state to an Islamic state during the mid-15th century.

Sind (pp. 357-58) — Region of the Indus River valley in northwestern India; conquered by the army of the Ummayad caliphate in 711 C.E. and later became part of the Abbasid empire.

Singosari (p. 373) — Small kingdom on Java, ruled between 1222 and 1292 C.E.

Srivijaya (p. 373) — Kingdom of southeast Asia, based on the island of Sumatra; lasted from the 7th century to the 11th century C.E.; received strong Indian influence.

sultanate of Delhi (p. 358) — State founded by Muslim Turks who conquered northern India at the beginning of the 13th century C.E. and established their rule, at least in name, for more than three centuries.

Vijayanagar (p. 360) — Large kingdom of south India, based in northern Deccan; lasted from 1336 to 1565 C.E.

Map Exercises

1. Locate the four states listed below on the map (consult Map 15.1, p. 357, in your textbook). Also, link up the characteristics, listed on the right, with the **correct** state names, on the left.

States	Characteristics
Harsha's kingdom	Situated in the deep south, ruled the Coromandel coast from 850 to 1267 C.E.
Vijayanagar	Conquered most Hindu kingdoms in the north, established an Islamic state in the 13th century
Chola kingdom	Based in the northern Deccan, claimed independence from the Sultanate of Delhi in 1336
Sultanate of Delhi	Unified most of north India, its rule lasted for about half a century beginning in the 7th century

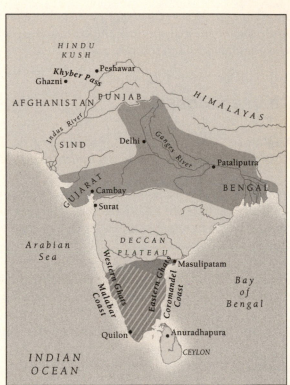

2. Study Map 15.2 on p. 365 of your textbook, and use the information about major trade routes to discuss the important role played by India in the trade network of the Indian Ocean basin.

3. Explain how monsoon patterns affected cross-cultural trade in the Indian Ocean basin.

Self-Test/Student Quiz

1. The *Book of the Wonders of India* was

   a. a truthful account of Indian history during the 10th century C.E.
   b. a collection of tall tales about foreign lands.
   c. written by an Indian shipmaster.

2. Differing from the south, northern India during the postclassical era was

   a. turbulent and chaotic.
   b. peaceful and stable.
   c. wealthy and prosperous.

3. All but one of the following does not describe Harsha's kingdom:

   a. It was the first Indian state to be Islamicized.
   b. It restored unified rule in most of northern India through military force.
   c. It collapsed upon Marsha's death.

4. The correct chronological order for Islamic incursions in northern India was

   a. sultanate of Delhi, conquest of Sind, raids by Mahmud of Ghazni.
   b. raids by Mahmud of Ghazni, conquest of Sind, sultanate of Delhi.
   c. conquest of Sind, raids by Mahmud of Ghazni, sultanate of Delhi.

5. Besides the influence of invading soldiers and immigrants, Islam also entered India through

   a. the presence of merchants from the Islamic world.
   b. the rhythms of monsoons.
   c. the presence of Muslim slaves shipped to India.

6. The Chola kingdom and the kingdom of Vijayanagar

   a. were Indianized states of southeast Asia.
   b. imposed centralized, imperial rules in southern India.
   c. were two of the larger states to form in southern India.

7. Agriculture of the Indian subcontinent relied on

   a. monsoon rains.
   b. irrigation systems.
   c. both a and b.

8. According to the account of Cosmas Indicopleustes, southern India and Ceylon during the 6th century were

   a. the world's most urbanized lands.
   b. great markets for imports and exports.
   c. famous for their dhows, junks, and emporia.

9. Besides their religious purpose, Hindu temples also served as

    a. large land owners, educational institutions, and banks.
    b. peace makers, tax deliverers, and organizers of irrigation.
    c. economic and social centers.

10. In terms of foreign trade and specialized industry, silk was to China as

    a. cotton was to India.
    b. spices were to southeast Asia.
    c. slaves were to east Africa.

11. All of the following were true with regard to the development of the caste system during the postclassical era except that

    a. it helped to integrate immigrants into Indian society.
    b. guilds of merchants and manufacturers became the most powerful castes of India.
    c. it extended to southern India.

12. Invasions of India by Turkish Muslims hastened the decline of Buddhism because

    a. Buddhists were convinced that Buddha was not helpful for personal salvation.
    b. Muslim rulers banned Buddhism.
    c. the invaders looted and destroyed Buddhist stupas and shrines.

13. Shankara and Ramanuja were

    a. two Hindu philosophers with very different ideas about personal salvation.
    b. two *brahmin* philosophers who worshipped the same Hindu deity.
    c. equally important to the development of devotional cults in popular Hinduism.

14. Islam in India had a strong appeal to members of lower castes because

    a. conversion to Islam made them equal with other caste members.
    b. Islam promised the spiritual equality of all believers.
    c. Allah was more competent than Shiva and Vishnu in terms of salvation.

15. The *bhakti* movement was

    a. launched by guru Kabir in southern India.
    b. a campaign designed to expel Islam from India.
    c. a religious movement that sought to erase the distinction between Hinduism and Islam.

16. All of the following were adopted by ruling elites of southeast Asia except

    a. the Indian caste system.
    b. the model of Indian states.
    c. Hinduism and Buddhism.

17. Funan was

    a. the first southeast Asian state known to have become Indianized.
    b. the only Islamic state in southeast Asia.
    c. the only state which was not Indianized in southeast Asia.

18. The capital of the Angkor state was

    a. a microcosmic reflection of the Buddhist world order.
    b. famous for its Islamic architecture.
    c. rediscovered in the jungle by Europeans in the mid-19th century.

19. In southeast Asian lands, Islam had strong appeal to

    a. members of lower social classes.
    b. ruling elites and urban dwellers.
    c. rural residents in the countryside and hills.

20. Differing from other southeast Asian states, Melaka was predominantly a

    a. Buddhist state.
    b. Confucian state.
    c. Islamic state.

Textual Questions for Analysis

1. Discuss the different pathways through which Islam entered India.

2. Once Islam had arrived in India, how did it spread? What were the difficulties it met and what was its appeal to some Indians?

3. Compare and contrast the Indians' adoption of Islam with that of the Melakans.

4. Discuss the multiple functions of Hindu temples in southern India.

5. What was the role of India in the economic development of the Indian Ocean basin?

6. What are some differences and similarities between India's influence in southeast Asia and China's influence in east Asia?

Documentary Evidence

Bhakti Poetry

    Bhakti, the devotional religion that flourished from the 12th to the 18th century throughout India, found expression in *bhakti* poetry. It was an expression of intense and passionate devotion to one of the two great Hindu gods, Shiva or Vishnu. It was also an expression of disregard for social conventions, including family life, religious rituals, and normal economic and political values. As such, it provided an outlet for economic and social discontent as well as for religious aspirations, as we will see in the following three poems by three *bhakti* "poet-saints" of different periods. (The first two poems are from Ainslie T. Embree, ed., *Sources of Indian Tradition*, vol. 1, 2nd ed., New York: Columbia University Press, 1988, pp. 347-50; the third one (abridged) is from Wm. Theodore de Bary, et al., *Sources of Indian Tradition*, New York: Columbia University Press, 1958, pp. 360-62. Footnotes are based on Ainslie T. Embree, as above, pp. 342-43, 347-49, 373).

I. Basavanna (c. 1106-1168)[1]

The lamb brought to the slaughterhouse eats the leaf garland with which it is decorated.... The frog caught in the mouth of the snake desires to swallow the fly flying near its mouth. So is our life. The man condemned to die drinks milk and ghee....

He who knows only the *Gita* is not wise; nor is he who knows only the sacred books. He only is wise who trusts in God.

When they see a serpent carved in stone, they pour milk on it; if a real serpent comes, they say, "Kill, kill." To the servant of God, who could eat if served, they say, "Go away, go away"; but to the image of God which cannot eat, they offer dishes of food.

Sweet words are equal to all prayers. Sweet words are equal to all penances. Good behavior is what pleases God.... Kindness is the root of all righteousness.

Those who have riches build temples for Thee; what shall I build? I am poor. My legs are the pillars; this body of mine is the temple.

II. Mahadevi (the 12th century)[2]

I love the Handsome One: he has no death, decay, nor form; no place or side; no end nor birthmarks. I love him, O mother, listen.

I love the Beautiful One, with no bond nor fear, no clan, no land, no landmarks for his beauty.

So my lord, white as jasmine, is my husband.

Take these husbands who die, decay, and feed them to your kitchen fires!

Better than meeting and mating all the time is the pleasure of mating once after being far apart.

When he's away, I cannot wait to get a glimpse of him.

Friend, when will I have it both ways, be with Him yet not with Him, my lord white as jasmine?

---

[1] Basavanna, the great poet-saint of the South Indians, was a passionate devotee of Shiva. He disregarded the restrictions of caste and preached egalitarianism.

[2] Many of the poet-saints were women, who, even more than men, risked the censure of society by their unconventional lives. According to the legends, Mahadevi was married to the king, but she gave all her love to Shiva, not to her husband. In this poem, she simply called Shiva her husband!

III. Kabir (the 15th century)[3]

O servant, where dost thou seek Me?

Lo! I am beside thee. I am neither in temple nor in mosque: I am neither in Kaaba nor in Kailash [abode of Shiva]: Neither am I in rites and ceremonies, nor in Yoga and renunciation. If thou art a true seeker, thou shalt at once see Me: thou shalt meet Me in a moment of time. Kabir says: "O Sadhu! God is the breath of all breath."

It is needless to ask of a saint the caste to which he belongs, for the priest, the warrior, the tradesman, and all the thirty-six castes alike are seeking for God....

If God be within the mosque, then to whom does this world belong? If Rama be within the image which you find upon your pilgrimage, then who is there to know what happens without?

Hari is in the East: Allah is in the West. Look within your heart, for there you will find both Karim and Rama; all the men and women of the world are His living forms.

Kabir is the child of Allah and of Rama: He is my Guru, He is my Pir [Sufi saint].

QUESTIONS TO CONSIDER

1. How did the three saint-poets view written sacred texts, religious rites, ceremony, and conventional social values, especially the caste system? How did they see their relationships with the gods?

2. In terms of religious aspiration and social function, what differences were there among the three *bhakti* saint-poets?

3. Compare the *bhakti* movement with Islamic Sufism in postclassical India. Specifically, how did the leaders of the two religious movements view inner devotion and outward observances by individual believers?

---

[3] Kabir was one of the most influential Hindi poets of north India. As a member of a very low caste of weavers, his verses reflect the folk wisdom of the common people, and Hindus and Muslims both claim him and revere his poetry for its intense devotionalism. In this poem, Kabir referred to God as "Rama," "Hari," or "Karim," which were names of Vishnu.

Chapter 16

The Foundations of Christian Society in Western Europe

Introduction and Learning Objectives

When the western Roman empire crumbled in the Mediterranean basin, different groups of Germanic peoples began to form their own states in northern and western Europe. These peoples were not Roman descendants with classical Greco-Roman knowledge, but were newly transformed nomads who received little Roman influence. When their commercial link with the Mediterranean basin was severed by Muslim invasions, western Europe was reduced to a rural society, with its rudimentary agriculture unable to produce much surplus or support a large centralized state. The great Roman power that once provided considerable cultural unity, social stability, and commercial life now gave way to constant fighting among the Germanic peoples themselves and frequent invasions by other peoples, notably Muslims, Magyars, and Vikings. Surely enough, western Europe had a tough and rough beginning during the postclassical era.

The central theme of this chapter is the making of feudal Europe during the early medieval era (500 to 1000 C.E.). It consisted of developments in three areas—political decentralization, a self-sufficient rural economy, and Christianity as a cultural foundation. The authors begin their discussion with a number of Germanic successor states seeking political order in the midst of the violence that haunted Europe. Among them the most impressive were the Franks, who, especially under the leadership of Charlemagne, extended their kingdom into an empire with some measure of centralization. The quick collapse of Charlemagne's empire, however, proved that Europe was not yet ready for the formation of large centralized states. Therefore, like other Germanic peoples in England and Germany, the Franks also built decentralized but more effective regional kingdoms to cope with external pressures. At this conjuncture, the authors' discussion leads student to see the interplay of two processes in the formation of feudal Europe. One was the development of a complicated and multitiered network of lord-vassal relationships for the provision of self-defense during a period of weak central authority and invasions. The other was the merging of slaves and free peasants into a new category called serfs who pledged their labor and obedience to a lord in exchange for security, enabling lords to organize large estates into self-sufficient manors. Economic activity on manors was slow and inefficient, but it was able to support a decentralized feudal order, and by the 10th century, political stability began to serve as a foundation for economic recovery.

The formation of feudal Europe also involved the rise of Christianity as a spiritual authority and cultural foundation. Here we witness the political alliance between state authorities and the Roman church, evidenced in such important events as the conversion of Clovis, the coronation of Charlemagne and Otto I, and English kings' adoption of Roman Christianity. Such alliances not only strengthened the spiritual authority of the papacy, but also provided secular authorities with access to educated and literate individuals for political service. Meanwhile, the politics of conversion from above was well supported and reinforced by the development of monasteries from below. Not only did monasteries provide a great variety of services to meet the needs of rural populations, they also kept alive the intellectual life of western Europe. The conversion of western Europe to Roman Christianity proved that Greco-Roman traditions were not completely forgotten, as western Christianity preserved elements from the classical traditions of the Mediterranean and served as the foundation for a new cultural unity in western Europe.

After reading and studying this chapter, students should understand and be able to discuss the following:

- the emergence of Germanic successor states and their struggle for political order

- the political institutions and economic system that comprised feudal Europe

- the conversion of western Europe to Roman Christianity

- comparisons between western Europe and other postclassical societies

Chapter Outline

I. **The Quest for Political Order**

  A. Germanic Successor States
    1. Germanic kingdoms
      a) Visigoths dominated Spain, from 470's to early 8th century
      b) Ostrogoths dominated Italy, the 5th century to 530's
      c) Lombards ruled Italy, 550's to the mid-8th century
      d) Burgundians and Franks controlled Gaul
      e) Angles, Saxons, and other Germanic peoples established kingdoms in Britain
    2. The Franks
      a) Only Franks built an impressive imperial state
      b) Relied on agricultural resources instead of maritime trade
    3. Center of gravity shifted from Italy to northern lands
  B. The Franks and the Temporary Revival of Empire
    1. The rise of the Franks
      a) Developed group identity during the 3rd century C.E.
      b) Politically inexperienced and little exposure to Roman society
    2. Clovis
      a) A strong military and political leader
      b) Led the Franks and wiped out the last vestiges of Roman authority in Gaul
      c) Military campaigns against other Germanic peoples
      d) Built the most powerful and dynamic state in western Europe
    3. Clovis's conversion
      a) Many other Germanic peoples converted to Arian Christianity
      b) The Franks converted to Roman Christianity
      c) Alliance with the Roman church greatly strengthened the Franks
    4. The Carolingians
      a) Leaders lost effective control after Clovis's death
      b) Carolingians, an aristocratic clan, asserted authority, the early 8th century
      c) Charles Martel's son claimed the throne for himself, 751
    5. Charlemagne (reigned 768-814 C.E.)
      a) Charles Martel's grandson, founder of Carolingian empire
      b) Control extended to northeast Spain, Bavaria, north Italy
      c) Rulers of eastern Europe and southern Italy paid tribute to him

6. Administration
    a) Capital city at Aachen (in modern Germany)
    b) Relied on aristocratic deputies, known as counts
    c) Used *missi dominici* to oversee local authorities
7. Charlemagne as emperor
    a) Pope Leo III proclaimed Charlemagne emperor, 800
    b) The coronation strained relations with Byzantine emperors

C. Decline and Dissolution of the Carolingian Empire
    1. Louis the Pious (re. 814-840)
        a) Charlemagne's only surviving son, lost control of the counts
        b) His three sons divided the empire into three kingdoms, 843
    2. Invasions
        a) Muslims raided south, seized Sicily, parts of northern Italy and southern France
        b) Magyars invaded from the east
        c) Vikings invaded from the north
    3. The Vikings
        a) Their Scandinavian homelands—Norway, Denmark, and Sweden
        b) Mounted raids in many European regions from Russia to Spain
        c) Outstanding seafarers, even established a colony in Canada about 1000
        d) Fleets could go to interior regions via rivers, attacking towns and villages

D. The Establishment of Regional Authorities
    1. England
        a) Small kingdoms merged into larger realm against Scandinavian raids
        b) King Alfred (reigned 871-899) expanded to the north
        c) Alfred's successors controlled all England about the mid-10th century
    2. Germany
        a) After Carolingian empire, local lords took matters into their own hands
        b) King Otto I (reigned 936-73) defeated Magyars in 955
        c) Imposed authority in Germany, led armies to support the papacy in Italy
        d) Otto's coronation by the pope in 962
    3. France
        a) Counts and other local authorities became local lords
        b) Vikings settled in northern France and established some small states

II. Feudal Society

A. The Feudal System
    1. Lords and vassals
        a) Lord provided vassal a grant known as a benefice, usually grants of land often called fiefs
            (1) enabled the vassal to devote time and energy to serve the lord
            (2) provided resources to maintain horses and military equipment
        b) Vassals owed lord loyalty, obedience, respect, counsel, and military service
        c) The lord-vassal relationship was not entirely new, but became dominant now
    2. Feudal politics
        a) Multitiered network of lord-vassal relationships
        b) Political stability depended on discipline and control of vassals

B. Serfs and Manors in Feudal Europe
   1. Serfs
      a) Slaves and peasants took agricultural tasks, frequently intermarried
      b) Free peasants often turned over themselves and their lands to a lord for protection
      c) Serfs as an intermediate category emerged about the mid-7th century
   2. Serfs' obligations
      a) Labor service and rents in kind
      b) Could not move to other lands without permission
      c) Obligations fulfilled, serfs had right to work on land and pass it to heirs
   3. Manors
      a) Principal form of agricultural organization
      b) A manor was a large estate, controlled by the lord and his deputies
      c) Many lords had the authority to execute serfs for serious misconduct
      d) Manors were largely self-sufficient communities
C. The Economy of Feudal Europe
   1. Agriculture
      a) Agricultural production suffered from repeated invasions
      b) Small wooden plows of Mediterranean farmers did not work well in the north
   2. Heavy plows
      a) Heavy plows appeared in the 6th century, could turn soils
      b) Became common from the 8th century, production increased
      c) Cultivation of new lands, watermills, and rotating crops
   3. A rural society
      a) Agricultural surplus not enough to support large cities
      b) Towns were few and sparsely populated
   4. Trade
      a) Trade and urban centers began to develop by the 10th century
      b) Trade took place in Mediterranean, North Sea, and Black Sea
   5. Population
      a) In 200 C.E., European population stood at 36 million
      b) In 400 C.E., 31 million
      c) In 600 C.E., 26 million
      d) In 800 C.E., edged up to 29 million
      e) In 900 C.E., 30 million
      f) By 1000 C.E., back to 36 million

III. The Formation of Christian Europe

A. The Politics of Conversion
   1. The Franks and the Church
      a) Frankish rulers viewed themselves as protectors of the papacy
      b) Charlemagne also worked to spread Christianity in northern lands
   2. The spread of Christianity
      a) Charlemagne's military campaigns, forced the Saxons to accept Christianity
      b) Pagan ways did not disappear immediately
      c) By 1000 C.E., all western Europe had adopted Roman Christianity

B. The Papacy
    1. Pope Gregory I (590-604 C.E.)
        a) Organized defense of Rome against Lombards' menace
        b) Reasserted papal primacy over other bishops
        c) Strongly emphasized the sacrament of penance
    2. The conversion of England
        a) Gregory's missionary campaigns in western Europe
        b) First converted English kings
        c) By 800 C.E., England was securely in the fold of the Roman church
C. Monasticism
    1. Origin
        a) Devout Christians practiced asceticism in deserts of Egypt, 2nd and 3rd century
        b) Monastic lifestyle became popular when Christianity became legal, 4th century
    2. Monastic rules
        a) St. Benedict (480-547 C.E.) provided a set of regulations
        b) Virtues of Benedictine monks: poverty, chastity, and obedience
    3. St. Scholastica (482-543 C.E.)
        a) St. Benedict's sister, a nun
        b) Adapted the *Rule,* and provided guidance for religious life of women
    4. The roles of monasteries
        a) Became dominant feature in social and cultural life of western Europe
        b) Accumulated large landholdings
        c) Organized much of the rural labor force for agricultural production
        d) Provided a variety of social services
            (1) Inns and shelters for travelers and refugees
            (2) Orphanages, medical centers
            (3) Schools
            (4) Libraries and scriptoria
        e) Monks patiently and persistently served the needs of the rural population

Significant Individuals

Alfred (p. 389) — Early king of Angles and Saxons in England; expanded from his base in southern England to territories further north held by Danish invaders; built a navy to challenge the Vikings at sea and constructed fortresses on land to secure the conquered areas; reigned from 871 to 899.

Charlemagne (pp. 383-85, 395-96) — Grandson of Charles Martel, reigned from 768 to 814; established a substantial empire which covered France, Germany, northeastern Spain, Bavaria, and northern Italy, and introduced some centralized institutions; received coronation in 800 by the pope.

Charles Martel (p. 383) — Founder of Carolingian dynasty; did not claim the title of Frankish king himself, but ruled as deputy to the last of Clovis's descendants.

Clovis (pp. 381-83) — Early Frankish king; ruled the Franks from 481 to 511; converted to Roman Christianity; built a powerful kingdom in Gaul that laid down the foundation for Charlemagne's empire.

Louis the Pious (p. 386) — Charlemagne's only surviving son, reigned from 814 to 840; weak monarch who lost control of the counts and other local authorities of the Carolingian dynasty. After his death, his three sons divided Carolingian dynasty into three kingdoms.

200

Otto I (pp. 389-90) — Early king of Saxony in Germany (reigned 936-973); defeated a Magyar army and ended the Magyar threat in 955; imposed authority throughout Germany; twice led armies into Italy to support the papacy against Lombard magnates; received coronation from the pope in 962.

Pope Gregory I (pp. 396-97) — Also known as Gregory the Great, was pope from 590 and 604; organized defense of Rome and reasserted papal primacy over other bishops; theologically emphasized the sacrament of penance; helped to extend Roman Christianity to western Europe through missionary activity.

Pope Leo III (pp. 385) — 9th century pope who proclaimed Charlemagne emperor and placed an imperial crown on his head on Christmas Day of 800.

St. Benedict of Nursia (pp. 397-98) — Strengthened the early monastic movement by providing it with a set of rules in medieval western Europe during the 6th century.

St. Scholastica (p. 398) — St. Benedict's sister; a nun who adapted St. Benedict's rules and provided guidance for the religious life of women living in convents.

Chapter Glossary

benefice (pp. 390-91) — A grant provided by a lord to his vassals with which the vassal supported himself and his family. Benefices usually were grants of land, often called fiefs, but they sometimes took other forms, such as the right to income from mills, village rents, and money; see also **fief** below.

Carolingians (p. 383) — Frankish royal family who replaced Clovis's line in 751 and ruled France until the 10th century.

counts (p. 385) — Title for aristocratic deputies in Charlemagne's empire; held political, military, and legal authority in local jurisdictions.

fief (pp. 390-91) — Land granted by a lord to his vassal in exchange for his loyalty, obedience, counsel, and military service during the medieval period of European history; see also **benefice** above.

manor (pp. 392-93) — Self-sufficient, large estate of a feudal lord consisting of fields, meadows, forests, agricultural tools, domestic animals, and sometime lakes or rivers, as well as serfs bound to the land; the principal form of agricultural organization in medieval western Europe.

Magyars (p. 387) — Descendants of nomadic peoples from central Asia who had settled in Hungary; raided settlements in Germany, Italy, and southern France from the late 9th to the mid-10th century.

middle ages (p. 379) — Medieval period of European history from about 500 to 1500; so called because it falls between the classical era and modern times.

missi dominici (p. 385) — "Envoys of the lord ruler"; Charlemagne's imperial officials who traveled every year to all local jurisdictions and reviewed the accounts of local authorities.

serfs (p. 392) — Social class of feudal Europe; formed through merging of slaves and free peasants into an intermediate, semi-free category of individuals; owed obligations to the lord whose lands they cultivated.

Vikings (pp. 388-90) — Outstanding Scandinavian seafarers and most feared invaders who mounted raids in Russia, Germany, England, Ireland, France, Spain, and the Balearic Islands during the period from the 8th through the 11th centuries; some of them colonized Iceland and Greenland, some settled in northern France, and a small group even established a colony in Newfoundland in modern Canada.

Map Exercises

1. Study Map 16.1 on page 382 of your textbook and match the Germanic peoples on left with their regions on the right:

Germanic peoples	Region
Visigoths	France
Burgundians	England
Franks	Italy
Angles and Saxons	Spain
Lombards	southern France and northern Italy

2. Study Map 16.2 on p. 386 of your textbook and circle the cities and regions under the Carolingian empire (regions are in all capital letters; cities are not):

Paris	Toledo	Aachen	BAVARIA	London
SAXONY	Monte Cassino	DANISH MARCH	BURGUNDY	Cordoba
Marseilles	SICILY	BRITAIN	LOMBARDY	Rome

3. Study Map 16. 3 on p. 388 of your textbook and answer the following questions: Who were the invaders during the early medieval period? Where were they from? What major regions did they invade?

Self Test/Student Quiz

1. Abu al-Abbas became well-known in the court of Charlemagne as a

    a. distinguished diplomat from the Islamic world.
    b. beloved pet from an Indian king.
    c. gift from the Abbasid court.

2. Historians use the term "middle ages" to refer to

    a. the fact that Europe became mature from 500 to 1500 C.E.
    b. the era from about 500 to 1500 C.E., the medieval era of European history.
    c. the crisis of western Europe.

3. One reason for the Franks' rapid rise in western Europe had to do with Clovis's

    a. conversion to Roman Christianity.
    b. conversion to Arian Christianity.
    c. alliance with the Islamic world.

4. Which of the following was one thing done by Charlemagne?

    a. He built an impressive, if relatively short-lived, empire in western Europe.
    b. He rejected coronation by the pope.
    c. He established a large bureaucracy to rule his empire.

5. The Carolingian empire dissolved primarily because

    A. Charlemagne's descendants were politically weak and disunited.
    B. imperial authority was unable to organize effective defense against invasions.
    C. both a and b.

6. All but one of the following is a correct description of invaders of early medieval Europe:

    a. Muslim invaders seized Sicily, several territories in southern Italy, and southern France.
    b. Magyars were descendants of central Asian nomads who had settled in Hungary.
    c. Vikings were the most feared of all the invaders because they were outstanding horsemen.

7. In England, 9th-century Scandinavian invasions

    a. promoted various small kingdoms to merge into a larger realm.
    b. led to disintegration of a large realm into smaller kingdoms.
    c. gave way to colonization by the Vikings.

8. The term *feudalism* refers to

    a. feuds between aristocratic families that had become a social norm.
    b. a political and social order that decentralized public authority and responsibility.
    c. the king's power being completely overthrown by the feudal lords.

9. The relationship between lord and vassal was

    a. reciprocal.
    b. exploitative.
    c. antagonistic.

10. Serfs were

    a. semifree individuals who owed obligations to the lord whose lands they cultivated.
    b. servants of the lord, who provided the lord with domestic and military services.
    c. agricultural slaves who had no rights on the lord's manor.

11. The rights of serfs included

    a. the right to work on certain land and pass the lands to their heirs.
    b. the right to move from one manor to another.
    c. the right to marry whomever they wanted to marry.

12. All but one of the following describes a manor:

    a. It was a large plantation operated by free peasants with heavy plows.
    b. It was a large estate supervised by a lord and operated with serf labor.
    c. It was a self-sufficient rural community controlled by the lord and his deputies.

13. In the early middle ages, the economic activity of western Europe was

    a. efficient and fast.
    b. agricultural.
    c. commercial and urban.

14. By "politics of conversion," the authors mean

    a. that conversion was a pure political decision, which had nothing to do with religion.
    b. that there were political controversies among Frankish aristocratic clans about conversion.
    c. that a deep commitment to Roman Christianity became a hallmark of Frankish policy.

15. An important pope of the late 6th and early 7th centuries was

    a. Leo III.
    b. Gregory I.
    c. Otto I.

16. The conversion of England was accomplished through

    a. the military threat of Charlemagne.
    b. marriage of Charlemagne's daughter to the English king.
    c. missionary campaigns of Gregory I.

17. According to St. Benedict's *Rule*, monks in monasteries should

    a. live communal, celibate lives.
    b. work hard for personal wealth.
    c. live like hermits, isolated from the outside world.

18. St. Scholastica

    a. established a convent and began to accept nuns for the first time in the history of Christianity.
    b. devised an entirely new set of regulations as guidance for the religious life of women in convents.
    c. adapted her brother's *Rule* as guidance for nuns.

19. As for social services provided by monasteries, all of the following were included except

    a.   inns, refuges, orphanages.
    b.   banks, shops, factories.
    c.   schools, medical care, libraries.

20. One of the major differences between India and western Europe during the postclassical era is that

    a.   India generated an imperial form of government while western Europe did not.
    b.   India actively participated in a larger economic and commercial life while western Europe was largely a rural and self-sufficient society.
    c.   India did not suffer from foreign invasions while western Europe had to fight against foreign invaders.

Textual Questions for Analysis

1. Compared with the society of the Roman empire, what were the major changes or differences in early medieval Europe?

2. How important were foreign invasions to the formation of feudalism in western Europe? Without these invasions, would western Europe have had a centralized imperial government? Why or why not?

3. Describe the essential features of a manor, with emphasis on obligations and rights of serfs to lords.

4. Under what conditions did the economy of western Europe begin to recover during the 9th and 10th centuries?

5. What roles were played by the Frankish rulers and the popes in converting western Europe to Roman Christianity?

6. Why were monasteries important to the society of western Europe during the medieval era?

Documentary Evidence

Making Peace with the Vikings

       After the division of the Carolingian empire in 843, the western portion of the empire became the kingdom of the West Franks (eventually France) under Charles the Bald (see Map. 16.3 on p. 388 of your textbook). Unable to make war against the powerful Viking raiders, the Franks decided to make peace with Rollo, the Viking leader. An anonymous medieval chronicler told the story of how the agreement between Charles and Rollo in 911 led to the creation of Normandy, the land held by Norsemen (the Vikings) in northern France. (From Brian Tierney, ed., *The Middle Ages*, vol. 1, *Sources of Medieval History*, 5th ed., New York: McGraw-Hill, 1992, pp. 129-30).

The Franks, not having the strength to resist the pagans and seeing all France brought to nothing, came to the king and said unanimously, "Why do you not aid the kingdom which you are bound by your scepter to care for and rule? Why is peace not made by negotiation since we cannot achieve it either by giving battle or by defensive fortifications? Royal honor and power is cast down; the insolence of the pagans is raised up. The land of France is almost a desert for its people are dying by famine or by the sword or are taken captive. Care for the kingdom, if not by arms then by taking counsel...."

Immediately Charles, having consulted with them, sent Franco, Archbishop of Rouen, to Rollo, Duke of the Pagans. Coming to him he began to speak with mild words. "Most exalted and distinguished of dukes, will you quarrel with the Franks so long as you live? Will you always wage war on them? What will become of you when you are seized by death? Whose creature are you? Do you think you are God? Are you not a man formed from filth? Are you not dust and ashes and food for worms? Remember what you are and will be and by whose judgment you will be condemned. You will experience Hell I think, and no longer injure anyone by your wars. If you are willing to become a Christian you will be able to enjoy peace in the present and the future and to dwell in this world with great riches. Charles, a long-suffering king, persuaded by the counsel of his men, is willing to give this coastal province that you and Halstigno have grievously ravaged. He will also give you his daughter, Gisela, for a wife in order that peace and concord and a firm, stable and continuous friendship may endure for all time between you and him...."

At the agreed time Charles and Rollo came together at the place that had been decided on.... Looking on Rollo, the invader of France, the Franks said to one another, "This duke who has fought such battles against the warriors of this realm is a man of great power and great courage and prowess and good counsel and of great energy too." Then, persuaded by the words of the Franks, Rollo put his hands between the hands of the king, a thing which his father and grandfather and great-grandfather had never done; and so the king gave his daughter Gisela in marriage to the duke and conferred on him the agreed lands from the River Epte to the sea as his property in hereditary right, together with all Brittany from which he could live.

Rollo was not willing to kiss the foot of the king. The bishops said, "Anyone who receives such a gift ought to be eager to kiss the king's foot." He replied, "I have never bent my knees at anyone's knees, nor will I kiss anyone's foot." But, urged by the entreaties of the Franks, he commanded one of his warriors to kiss the foot of the king. The warrior promptly seized the king's foot, carried it to his mouth and kissed it standing up while the king was thrown flat on his back. At that there was a great outburst of laughter and great excitement among the people. Nevertheless King Charles, Duke Robert, the counts and nobles, the bishops and abbots swore by the Catholic faith and by their lives, limbs and the honor of the whole kingdom to the noble Rollo that he should hold and possess the land described above and pass it on to his heirs.

QUESTIONS TO CONSIDER

1. Under what circumstances did the Franks decide to make peace with the Vikings? How did the Franks persuade the Vikings to accept the terms? What did the Franks have to offer in order to get Rollo's agreement?

2. Why was the kissing-foot protocol so important to the Franks? How did the Vikings behave themselves in the meeting? What kind of attitude did they display toward the Franks?

3. On the Frankish side, who took initiatives in the decision to make peace? Who spoke at the meeting and why?

Chapter 17

Nomadic Empires and Eurasian Integration

Introduction and Learning Objectives

Between the 11th and 15th centuries, two nomadic peoples, Turks and Mongols, came to center stage in world history and mounted a stunning challenge to the sedentary peoples of Eurasia. Their sweeping conquests brought to an end or interrupted a number of empires of the postclassical world, while also constructing vast transregional empires. Turkish people built the most durable of the nomadic empires, but the spectacular conquests of the Mongols most clearly demonstrated the potential of nomadic peoples to project their formidable military might on settled agricultural societies. Despite their massive destruction and savage assaults on ancient and developed centers of various societies, the nomadic empires also laid the foundation for increasing communication, exchange, and interaction among peoples of Eurasia, fostering the integration of the eastern hemisphere. The age of nomadic empires from 1000 to 1500 C.E. foreshadowed the integrated world of modern times.

This chapter begins with a description of Turkish migrations and imperial expansion. After a brief discussion of nomadic economy and society which provided the drive to build vast empires, the authors describe the specific course of Turkish expansion. Though undertaken by different groups for different reasons and by different means, the Turkish conquests of Persia, Anatolia, and India represented part of a larger expansive movement by nomadic peoples. In all three cases the formidable military prowess of Turkish peoples enabled them to move beyond the steppelands of central Asia and dominate settled societies. Yet the Turkish conquests were only a prelude to an astonishing round of empire building launched by the Mongols during the 13th and 14th centuries.

Among these next events were the career and campaigns of Chinggis Khan and the Mongol conquests of China, Persia, and Russia. Beginning with Chinggis Khan in the 13th century, the Mongols turned themselves into a vast war machine on the central Asian steppes, and then turned on settled societies in China, Persia, Russia, and eastern Europe. By the early 14th century, the Mongols had built the largest empire the world had ever seen, stretching from Korea and China in the east to Russia and Hungary in the West. Despite the cruelty associated with the conquests, the Mongols displayed special interest in protecting cross-cultural trade and remarkable cultural tolerance. Several factors caused the decline of the Mongols in China and Persia during the 14th century, including administrative problems, internal factions, and the devastating effects of the bubonic plague.

The decline of the Mongols, however, did not signal the end of nomadic expansion. Rather, the Turkish peoples resumed their expansive campaigns that had been interrupted by the Mongols. During the late 14th century and early 15th century, the Turkish conqueror Tamerlane built a central Asian empire rivaling that of Chinggis Khan himself. Although the empire was short-lived, it deeply influenced three surviving Turkish Muslim states—the Mughal empire in India, the Safavid empire in Persia, and the Ottoman empire based in Anatolia.

After studying this chapter, students should understand and be able to discuss the following issues:

- long-standing patterns of interaction between nomads and settled peoples in Eurasia

- sources of the nomadic drive for building vast empires in Eurasia

- the Turkish and Mongol expansions

- administration of nomadic empires and their impact on the conquered societies

- growth of cross-cultural interaction brought about by nomadic empires

Chapter Outline

I. **Turkish Migrations and Imperial Expansion**

A. Nomadic Economy and Society
   1. Turkish peoples
      a) Organized through clans, spoke related languages
      b) Identities emerged after the Xiongnu confederation broke up
      c) All were nomads or descendants of nomads
   2. Ecology of central Asia
      a) Steppelands, good for grazing animals
      b) Not enough rainfall, no large rivers, agriculture only in oases
   3. Nomads and their animals
      a) Nomads drove their herds in migratory cycles
      b) Lived mostly on animal products
      c) Settlements were few and small
      d) Also produced limited amounts of millet, pottery, leather goods, iron
      e) Migratory habits and climate limited the development of society
   4. Nomads and settled peoples
      a) Avidly sought trade opportunities with settled peoples
      b) Suitable for organizing and participating in long-distance trade
      c) Turkish peoples were prominent on the caravan routes of central Asia
   5. Nomadic society
      a) Two social classes: Nobles and commoners
      b) Autonomous clans and tribes
      c) Great fluidity of social classes
   6. Religions: Shamans, Buddhism, Nestorian Christianity; by 10th century, Islam
   7. Military organization
      a) Khan ("ruler") organized vast confederation for expansion
      b) Confederation consisted of individual tribes
      c) Outstanding cavalry forces, formidable military power
B. Turkish Empires in Persia, Anatolia, and India
   1. Suljuq Turks and the Abbasid empire
      a) Lived on borders of the Abbasid realm, mid-8th to mid-10th centuries
      b) Moved in and served in Abbasid armies thereafter

c) Overshadowed the Abbasid caliphs by the mid-11th century
d) Extended Turkish rule to Syria, Palestine, and other parts of the realm
2. Saljuq Turks and the Byzantine empire
a) Migrated in large numbers to Anatolia, early 11th century
b) Defeated Byzantine army at Manzikert in 1071
c) Anatolian peasants looked up to the Saljuqs as liberators
d) Transformed Anatolia into an Islamic society
3. Ghaznavid Turks dominated northern India

II. The Mongol Empires

A. Chinggis Khan and the Making of the Mongol Empire
1. Chinggis Khan's rise to power
a) Temüjin, born in a noble family, but lived in danger and poverty as a youth
b) Learned art of steppe diplomacy and made alliances
c) Unified Mongol tribes through alliance and conquests
d) Leaders claimed him Chinggis Khan ("universal ruler"), 1206
2. Mongol political organization
a) Organized new military units and broke up tribal affiliations
b) Chose high officials based on talent and loyalty
c) Established capital at Karakorum
d) The Mongol state was much stronger than earlier nomadic confederation
3. Mongol arms
a) Relied on outstanding horsemanship
b) Short bows could shoot from horseback for 200 meters
c) Most mobile forces of premodern world
d) Also used psychological warfare against enemies
4. Mongol conquest of northern China
a) Led by Chinggis Khan, Mongols raided the Jurchen in north China beginning in 1211
b) Captured the Jurchen capital by 1215
c) Controlled north China by 1220
d) South China was still ruled by the Song dynasty
5. Mongol conquest of Persia
a) Chinggis Khan sought to open trade and diplomatic relations with the Saljuq leader, Khwarazm shah, the ruler of Persia, 1218
b) Upon being rejected, Chinggis Khan led force to pursue the Khwarazm
c) Mongol forces destroyed Persian cities and *qanat*
d) Chinggis died in 1227, laid foundation for a mighty empire
B. The Mongol Empires after Chinggis Khan
1. Division of the Mongol empires
a) Chinggis Khan's heirs fought for power and control
b) The empire was divided into four regional empires
2. Khubilai Khan
a) Chinggis Khan's grandson, consolidated Mongol rule in China
b) Promoted Buddhism, supported Daoists, Muslims, and Christians
3. Conquest of southern China
a) Khubilai extended Mongol rule to all of China
b) The Song capital at Hangzhou fell in 1276

       c) Established Yuan dynasty in 1279
       d) Unsuccessful conquests of Vietnam, Burma, Java, and Japan
    4. The Golden Horde
       a) Group of Mongols, led by Chinggis Khan's cousins and brothers, overran Russia between 1237 and 1241
       b) Further overran Poland, Hungary, and eastern Germany, 1241-1242
       c) Maintained hegemony in Russia until the mid-15th century
    5. The ilkhanate of Persia
       a) Khubilai's brother, Hülegü, captured Baghdad in 1258
       b) After great massacre, established the Mongol ilkhanate in Persia
       c) Further ventured into Syria
    6. Mongol rule in Persia
       a) Persians served as ministers, governors, and local officials
       b) Mongols only cared about taxes and order
       c) Ilkhan Ghazan converted to Islam, 1295
       d) The conversion sparked large-scale massacres of Christians and Jews
    7. Mongol rule in China
       a) Outlawed intermarriage between Mongols and Chinese
       b) Forbade Chinese from learning the Mongol language
       c) Brought foreign administrators into China and put them in charge
       d) Dismissed Confucian scholars, dismantled civil service examination
       e) Tolerated all cultural and religious traditions in China
    8. The Mongols and Buddhism
       a) Ruling elite became enchanted with the Lamaist Buddhism of Tibet
       b) Attractions of Lamaist Buddhism:
          (1) magic and supernatural power resembled shamanism of Mongols
          (2) Lamaist leaders tried hard to court the Mongols' favor
C. The Mongols and Eurasian Integration
    1. The Mongols and trade
       a) Mongols worked to secure trade routes and ensure safety of merchants
       b) Maintained good order for traveling merchants, ambassadors, and missionaries
       c) Great increase of long-distance trade in Eurasia
    2. Diplomatic missions
       a) The four Mongol empires maintained close diplomatic communications
       b) Established diplomatic relations with Korea, Vietnam, India, Europe
    3. Resettlement
       a) Mongols needed skilled artisans and educated individuals from other peoples
       b) Often resettled them in different locations to provide services
       c) Uighur Turks served as clerks, secretaries, and administrators
       d) Arab and Persian Muslims also served Mongols far from their homelands
       e) Skilled artisans were often sent to Karakorum, became permanent residents
D. Decline of the Mongols in Persia and China
    1. Collapse of the ilkhanate
       a) In Persia, excessive spending and overexploitation led to reduced revenues
       b) The failure of the ilkhan's paper money
       c) Factional struggle plagued the Mongol leadership
       d) The last ruler died without an heir, the ilkhanate collapsed

2. Decline of the Yuan dynasty
   a) Paper money issued by the Mongol rulers lost value
   b) Factional fighting hastened process of decline
   c) Power struggles, assassinations, and civil war weakened Mongol rule from the 1320s
3. Bubonic plague
   a) Trade and communication expedited spread of bubonic plague
   b) First erupted in southwestern China in 1330s
   c) By the late 1340s it spread to all China, central Asia, southwest Asia, Europe
   d) Depopulation and labor shortage undermined the Mongol regime
   e) Mongols also faced a rebellious population in China
   f) By 1368, the Chinese drove the Mongols back to the steppes.
4. Surviving Mongol Khanates
   a) The khanate of Chaghatai continued in central Asia
   b) The Golden Horde survived until the mid-16th century

III. After the Mongols

A. Tamerlane the Whirlwind (1336-1404)
   1. Expansion of Turkish peoples
      a) After Mongols, Turks resumed their conquest campaigns
      b) Tamerlane built a central Asian empire
      c) The short-lived empire influenced three surviving Turkish Muslim states
   2. The lame conqueror
      a) Timur, a self-made Turkish conqueror
      b) Nicknamed Timur-i-lang, "Timur the Lame," became Tamerlane in English
      c) Rose to power in 1360s and built an imperial capital in Samarkand in 1370
   3. Tamerlane's conquests
      a) First conquered Persia and Afghanistan
      b) Next attacked the Golden Horde
      c) At the end of the 14th century, invaded northern India
      d) Opened the new century with campaigns in southeast Asia and Anatolia
      e) Ruled the empire through tribal leaders
      f) Tribal leaders as overlords relied on existing bureaucrats to collect taxes
   4. Tamerlane's heirs
      a) Bitter struggle among Tamerlane's sons and grandsons
      b) The empire was divided into four main regions
B. The Foundation of the Ottoman Empire
   1. Osman
      a) Large numbers of nomadic Turks migrated to Persia and Anatolia
      b) Osman, a charismatic leader, carved out a small state in N.W. Anatolia
      c) Claimed independence from the Saljuq sultan, 1299
   2. Ottoman conquests
      a) Successful campaigns attracted more followers, known as Ottomans
      b) Established a foothold in Balkan peninsula, 1350s
      c) Temporarily captured Constantinople at the end of the 14th century
      d) Tamerlane's campaigns delayed Ottoman expansion
      e) After Tamerlane's death, Ottomans reestablished their rule

3. The capture of Constantinople
   a) Sultan Mehmed II sacked Constantinople in 1453
   b) Made it his own capital, renamed it Istanbul
   c) Absorbed the remainder of the Byzantine empire
   d) During the 16th century, extended to southwest Asia, southeast Europe, and north Africa

Significant Individuals

Chabi (p. 419) — One of Khubilai Khan's four wives, a Nestorian Christian.

Chinggis Khan (pp. 413-16) — Title for Temüjin, meaning "universal ruler"; born in 1167; united all the Mongol tribes into a single confederation in 1206; established Mongol supremacy in central Asia, and extended Mongol control to Northern China in the east and Persia in the west; died in 1227.

Hülegü (p. 418) — Chinggis Khan's grandson and Khubilai Khan's brother; established the Mongol ilkhanate in Persia; responsible for toppling the Abbasid empire and sacking Baghdad in 1258.

Ilkhan Ghazan (p. 418) — Ruler of the Mongol ilkhanate of Persia; publicly converted to Islam in 1295.

Khubilai Khan (pp. 417-18) — Chinggis Khan's grandson, one of the great khans who ruled China; extended Mongol rule to all China by toppling the southern Song dynasty and establishing the Yuan dynasty in 1279. His conquests of other east Asian regions beyond China were not successful; died in 1294.

Khwarazm shah (p. 416) — Leader of Saljuq Turks in Persia; rejected Chinggis Khan's demand for opening diplomatic and commercial relations in 1218; chastised by Mongol army, fled to an island in the Caspian Sea and died there.

Marco Polo (pp. 415, 417, 419) — Venetian merchant who traveled extensively through central Asia and China in the late 13th century, when Mongol empires dominated Asia; likely served as an administrator in the city of Yangzhou in southern China during the reign of Khubilai Khan. His book of travel is an especially valuable source of information about the Mongol age.

Mehmed II (p. 424) — Also known as Mehmed the Conqueror; sultan of the Ottomans; responsible for capture of Constantinople in 1453 and changing its name to Istanbul.

Osman (p. 424) — Turkish leader in Anatolia; declared independence from the Saljuq sultan in 1299; led his followers, known as Osmanlis or Ottomans, to extend control in the Balkan peninsula.

Ottomans (p. 424) — Followers of Osman, also known as Osmanlis; expansion from the Balkans to Byzantine empire was halted by Tamerlane's army; after dissolution of Tamerlane's empire, resumed their expansion into the Byzantine empire; captured Byzantine capital at Constantinople in 1453 and changed its name to Istanbul. Controlled all of Greece and the Balkan region by 1480; continued to extend their rule to southwest Asia, southeastern Europe, Egypt, and north Africa during the 16th century.

Tamerlane (pp. 422-24) — Turkish conqueror; born in 1336 and came to power in the 1360s in central Asia; launched series of attacks on Persia, Afghanistan, the Golden Horde in southern Russia, and northern India; empire disintegrated after his death in 1405.

Tughril Beg (p. 411) — Leader of Saljuq Turks; controlled the Abbasid capital at Baghdad and was recognized as *sultan* ("chieftain") by the Abbasid caliph in 1055; extended Turkish rule to Syria, Palestine, and other parts of the Abbasid empire.

Chapter Glossary

Battle of Manzikert (p. 411) — Fought between Saljuq Turks and the Byzantine empire in eastern Anatolia in 1071; victorious Saljuqs took the Byzantine emperor captive.

bubonic plague (p. 421) — Devastating epidemic that first erupted in the 1330s in southwestern China; spread throughout China and central Asia and by the late 1340s reached southwest Asia and Europe, where it became known as the Black Death.

Ghaznavids (p. 412) — Group of Turkish people in Afghanistan; in the early 11th century, led by Mahmud of Ghazni to raid northern India; by the late 12th century, the Ghaznavid sultanate of Delhi claimed authority over all of northern India.

The Golden Horde (pp. 418) — Group of Mongols who overran Russia between 1237 and 1241; also mounted expeditions into Poland, Hungary, and eastern Germany; maintained Mongol hegemony in Russia until the mid-15th century.

The great khans (pp. 417) — Title for Mongol khans who ruled China after Chinggis Khan's death; nominally superior to the khans of the other three Mongol empires, but rarely able to enforce their claims to superiority.

ilkhanate (pp. 418-19) — One of the four Mongol regional empires after Chinggis Khan's death; established in Persia in 1258.

kamikaze (p. 418) — Japanese term meaning "divine winds"; used by the Japanese to describe typhoons in 1274 and 1281 that helped them hold off Khubilai Khan's attempted invasions.

Karakorum (pp. 407, 414) — Capital of the Mongol empire under Chinggis Khan; present-day Har Horin, located about 186 miles west of the modern Mongolian capital of Ulaanbaatar; symbolized a source of Mongol authority superior to the clan or tribe.

Khanate of Chaghatai (p. 417) — One of the four Mongol regional empires after Chinggis Khan's death; territory covered much of central Asia.

khanates (p. 417) — Four regional Mongol empires that arose following the death of Chinggis Khan.

Lamaist Buddhism (pp. 419-20) — Sect of Buddhism developed in Tibet; emphasized magic and supernatural powers; became attractive to Mongol rulers in China.

Yuan dynasty (p. 417) — Sinicized Mongol dynasty in China established by Khubilai Khan in 1279; collapsed in 1368.

Map Exercise

1. Study Maps 17.1, Map 17.2, and Map 17.3 (pp. 412, 416, and 423 in your textbook) and complete the following exercise, matching the nomadic groups on the left with the **correct** description on the right:

Nomads	Description
Suljuq Turks led by Tughril Beg	replaced Chaghatai khanate in 1370, built a magnificent capital in Samarkand
Turks who migrated to Anatolia	established Yuan dynasty in China, but campaigns of conquering southeast Asia and Japan failed
Ghaznavid Turks	overran Russia, mounted expeditions into Poland, Hungary, and eastern Germany
Mongols of the great khans	controlled Abbasid caliphs, extended Turkish rule to Syria, Palestine, and other parts of Abbasid realm
Mongols of Chaghatai khanate	toppled Abbasid empire, sacked Baghdad, executed caliph, massacred 200,000 residents
Mongols of the ilkhanate	established a foothold in Balkan peninsula during 1350s, captured Constantinople in 1453
The Golden Horde	established khanate in central Asia, replaced by Tamerlane's empire
Turks led by Tamerlane	established Turkish sultanate in Delhi, claimed authority over all of northern India
Ottomans	defeated Byzantine army at Manzikert in eastern Anatolia, and took Byzantine emperor captive

1. Study Map 17.2 on p. 416 of your textbook, and describe the territories of the four Mongol empires.

Self-Test/Student Quiz

1. By alluding to the story of Guillaume Boucher, the authors of the textbook intend to show that

    a. the goldsmith of Paris was talented in creating a spectacular silver fountain.
    b. the Mongol capital, Karakorum, was magnificent and luxurious.
    c. many roads led to Karakorum during the 13th century.

2. All of the following were prominent nomadic peoples from the 11th to the 15th centuries except

    a. the Huns.
    b. the Turks.
    c. the Mongols.

3. Nomadic peoples of central Asia

    a. lived in *kumiss* and drank *yurts*.
    b. liked to trade with settled peoples.
    c. did not have any religious beliefs.

4. In nomadic society,

    a. there were only two social classes, nobles and commoners.
    b. clans and tribes were autonomous, and tended not to obey orders from nobles of other clans.
    c. the statuses of nobles and commoners were hereditary and unchanging.

5. Nomadic peoples of central Asia could wield massive military power primarily because of their

    a. outstanding cavalry forces.
    b. overwhelming numbers.
    c. superior weaponry.

6. Saljuq Turks who lived in Abbasid Persia and took over Byzantine Anatolia during the early 11th century were

    a. equal co-rulers with the Abbasid caliphs.
    b. led by Tughril Beg as *sultan*.
    c. resented by the peasants of Anatolia.

7. During the 11th and 12th centuries, Ghaznavid Turks

    a. invaded Afghanistan.
    b. converted to Buddhism and Hinduism.
    c. invaded northern India.

8. The man who united all the Mongol tribes into a single confederation in 1206 was

    a. Khubilai Khan.
    b. Hülegü.
    c. Chinggis Khan.

9. Speaking of the Mongols' horsemanship, they could

    a. travel more than 100 kilometers (62 miles) per day to surprise an enemy.
    b. stand on horse back and throw javelins as far as 100 meters (328 feet).
    c. shoot arrows and fell enemies within 400 meters (1312 feet).

10. According to the eye witness account of Marco Polo, all but one of the following was not among the Mongols' military tactics:

    a. avoiding regular medleys, but instead, riding around and shooting into enemies.
    b. pretending to run away, turning backward on horse back, and shooting hard on pursuers.
    c. in case of great urgency, fleeing from one's enemies immediately

11. Chinggis Khan led his army to Persia and wreaked massive destruction on the conquered land. The immediate reason for this havoc was

    a. to eliminate Islam.
    b. to gain revenge against the shah and eliminate the possibility of his survival.
    c. to make Persian lands into Mongol pastureland.

12. After Chinggis Khan's death, the Mongol empire was divided into four regional empires. China, as one of the regional empires, was ruled by

    a. the great khans.
    b. the khans of the Golden Horde.
    c. the ilkhans.

13. All of the following contributed to the failure of Khubilai's ventures in Japan and southeast Asia, except that

    a. the Mongol forces did not adapt well to the environment of southeast Asia.
    b. bubonic plague erupted, and took great tolls among the conquered populations.
    c. the Mongol navies were destroyed by Japanese *kamikaze*.

14. Observing Mongol rule in Persia and China, one can say that the Mongols were

    a. good administrators.
    b. ferocious plunderers.
    c. neither a nor b.

15. As for their rule in China, the Mongols

    a. resisted assimilation to Chinese cultural traditions.
    b. executed Confucian scholars and promoted Buddhism.
    c. encouraged intermarriage between Mongols and Chinese.

16. During the 13th century, long-distance trade in Eurasia increased primarily because

    a. the Mongols worked to secure trade routes and ensure the safety of merchants passing through their vast territories.
    b. Mongol rulers adopted the same paper currency that could be used within all the four regional empires.
    c. Mongol policies encouraged economic growth and specialization of production in various regions.

17. All of the following caused the decline of Mongol rule in China except

    a. peasant rebellions.
    b. bubonic plague.
    c. the mandate of Heaven.

18. The real name of the most famous Turkish leader, known as the lame conqueror, was

    a. Tamerlane.
    b. Timur.
    c. Tamerlane the Whirlwind.

19. Ottomans were

    a. descendants of the Mongols.
    b. Turkish people.
    c. Persians.

20. The man who led the Turkish army and captured Constantinople in 1453 was

    a. Osman.
    b. Tamerlane.
    c. Mehmed II.

Textual Questions for Analysis

1. Use specific examples to demonstrate how nomadic peoples of central Asia interacted with settled peoples through migration, invasion, and control.

2. What accounted for the military might of the Turks and Mongols? How were their armies organized?

3. How did the Mongols rule Persia and China? Overall, were they good administrators? Why or why not?

4. What were the negative and positive aspects of Mongol conquests in Eurasia? Can their conquests be justified on any grounds?

5. Use Mongol rule in Persia and China and Tamerlane's rule in central Asia as examples to explain why most nomadic peoples could not maintain long-lasting empires.

Documentary Evidence

Chinggis Khan in Marco Polo's Words

The Venetian merchant Marco Polo traveled extensively through central Asia and China in the later 13th century, when Mongol empires dominated Asia. After staying in China for about 20 years beginning as a teenager, and serving as an administrator of the Mongol government in China, Marco Polo formed favorable views toward things Chinese and Mongol. The following excerpt is Marco Polo's account of Chinggis Khan, the founder of Mongol empire. The events narrated by Polo occurred about 60 years before he came to China, a time when Chinggis Khan had already become a Mongol legend. (From *The Travels of Marco Polo*, trans. John Masefield, London: J.M. Den & Sons, 1908, pp. 118-20.)

Some time after the migration of the Tartars [Mongols] to this place, and about the year of our Lord 1162, they proceeded to elect for their king a man who was named Chinggis-khan, one of approved integrity, great wisdom, commanding eloquence, and eminent for his valour. He began his reign with so much justice and moderation, that he was beloved and revered as their deity rather than their sovereign; and the fame of his great and good qualities spreading over that part of the world, all the Tartars, however dispersed, placed themselves under his command. Finding himself thus at the head of so many brave men, he became ambitious of emerging from the deserts and wilderness by which he was surrounded, and gave them orders to equip themselves with bows, and such other weapons as they were expert at using, from the habits of their pastoral life. He then proceeded to render himself master of cities and provinces; and such was the effect produced by his character for justice and other virtues, that wherever he went, he found the people disposed to submit to him, and to esteem themselves happy when admitted to his protection and favor.... Upon the subjugation of these places, he appointed governors to them, who were so exemplary in their conduct that the inhabitants did not suffer, either in their persons or their properties.... Seeing how prosperously his enterprises succeeded, he resolved upon attempting still greater things. With this view he sent ambassadors to Prester John,* charged with a specious message, which he knew at the same time would not be listened to by that prince, demanding his daughter in marriage. Upon receiving the application, the monarch indignantly exclaimed: "Whence arises this presumption in Chinggis-khan, who, knowing himself to be my servant, dares to ask for the hand of my child? Depart instantly," he said, "and let him know from me, that upon the repetition of such a demand, I shall put him to an ignominious death." Enraged at this reply, Chinggis-khan collected a very large army, at the head of which he entered the territory of Prester John, and encamping on a great plain called Tenduk, sent a message desiring him [Prester John] to defend himself. The latter advanced likewise to the plain with a vast army, and took his position at the distance of about ten miles from the other. In this conjuncture Chinggis-khan commanded his astrologers and magicians to declare to him which of the armies, in the approaching conflict, should obtain the victory. Upon this they took a green reed, and dividing it lengthways into two parts, they wrote upon one the name of their master, and upon the other the name of Un-khan.... The whole army was assembled to be spectators of this ceremony, and whilst the astrologers were employed in reading their books of necromancy, they perceived

219

the two pieces begin to move and to approach, and after some small interval of time, that inscribed with the name of Chinggis-khan to place itself upon the top of its adversary. Upon witnessing this, the king and his band of Tartars marched with exultation to the attack of the army of Un-khan, broke through its ranks and entirely routed it. Un-khan himself was killed, his kingdom fell to the conqueror, and Chinggis-khan espoused his daughter. After this battle he continued during six years to render himself master of additional kingdoms and cities; until at length, in the siege of a castle named Thaigin, he was struck by an arrow in the knee, and dying of the wound, was buried in the mountains of Altai.

*Prester John was a popular but mythical figure in the imagination of medieval Europeans. According to the legend, a Christian priest name John (hence Prester John) went to the east and created a Christian kingdom there, a defense against Islamic threat. Another name for Prester John was Un-khan.

QUESTIONS TO CONSIDER

1. How did Marco Polo view Mongol rule? In your opinion, what might account for his favorable view of Chinggis Khan in particular and the Mongols in general?

2. In your textbook you have read that after Chinggis Khan consolidated his control in north China he dispatched envoys to the Khwarazm shah (the ruler of Afghanistan and Persia) to pursue trade and diplomatic relations, but that the murder of the envoys by the shah provoked Chinggis Khan's revenge (p. 416). Compare this event with Marco Polo's above account. The identity of a key player in the event is explained differently by Marco Polo. What do you make of such a discrepancy? How would you explain it?

Chapter 18

States and Societies of Sub-Saharan Africa

Introduction and Learning Objectives

The history of sub-Saharan Africa is closely associated with the Bantu migrations and Islamic influence. Beginning about the 2nd millennium B.C.E. and continuing until about 1000 C.E., the long-term process of Bantu migration transformed sub-Saharan Africa from a hunting and gethering society to an agricultural society. After the 10th century, Islam came in with Muslim merchants from north Africa and Arab world, and the commercial involvements of sub-Africa speeded up the state building process. The result was the great diversity of sub-African societies during the postclassical era. In the coastal regions a number of highly commercialized, Islamic states emerged, ranging from large regional empires to small kingdoms and city-states. In certain areas, small hunting and gathering (or fishing) communities survived while the interior regions of sub-Africa were dominated by stateless agricultural societies. By the end of the 1st millennium C.E., 22 million people of sub-Saharan Africa spoke some 800 tongues belonging to the Bantu family of languages. It is such an enormous societal diversity that becomes the central theme of this chapter.

The authors' discussion of Bantu migration illustrates the expansive quality of agricultural society. Agriculture supported a large number of population in a given area, but the increasing population pressure on land forced the people to move beyond the old territories. In sub-Saharan Africa the use of iron tools and introduction of bananas as an important new food crop helped Bantu expansion. When the Bantu approached the limits of their expansion (by about 1000 C.E.), they developed increasingly complex forms of government enabling them to organize their existing societies more efficiently. Hence, a number of chiefdoms and regional kingdoms emerged in west Africa centuries before the coming of Islam. But the process of state and empire building was greatly accelerated by trading with Muslim merchants of north Africa and southeast Asia after the 11th century. The need to control the flow of gold, ivory, and slaves stimulated the formation of formal governments, while the wealth accumulated through trade and taxation enabled rulers to maintain armies and bureaucrats.   In both western and eastern coastal states, it was the ruling elites and merchants who became the first converts to Islam.

The authors' discussion of stateless societies is an important conceptual element in this chapter. In such societies, family and kinship were basic social structures, property was community owned, and gender and age grades largely determined the social position of communal members. Men monopolized public authority, but women enjoyed high status as the source of life. A creator god was honored, and lesser gods and ancestors' spirits were respected. Even in societies with formal governments and Islamic faith, African women still enjoyed higher status and more opportunities than women in other societies. One point that should be kept in mind is that for both stateless societies and societies under states or empires, slaves were an important part of society, either as agricultural labor or as commodities in the thriving slave trade. Moreover, the authors argue that despite its great importance in transforming African social structure, Islam did not replace native African religious beliefs but complemented them. Adding to the great complexity and diversity of sub-Saharan African societies was Christianity. Compared with Islam, however, Christianity was a minor faith, confined primarily to the kingdom of Axum (modern Ethiopia).

After studying this chapter, students should understand and be able to discuss the following issues:

- the dynamics of Bantu migrations

- the nature of stateless societies

- African trade networks with the outside world

- external influences and social changes in the coastal regions of Africa

- the nature of the African slave trade before 1500 C.E.

Chapter Outline

I.   The Bantu Migrations

   A. The Dynamics of Bantu Expansion
      1.   The Bantu peoples
         a)   Originated in the region around modern Nigeria
         b)   Population pressure drove migrations, as early as 2000 B.C.E.
         c)   Spread to south and east
         d)   Languages differentiated into about 500 distinct but related tongues
         e)   Occupied most of sub-Saharan Africa by 1000 C.E.
      2.   Bantu agriculture
         a)   Early migrants relied on agriculture
         b)   Agriculture—population growth—migration
         c)   Conflict with hunting and gathering peoples
         d)   Bantu migrants assimilated hunting and gathering peoples
      3.   Iron metallurgy
         a)   Iron appeared during the 7th and 6th centuries B.C.E.
         b)   Iron tools made agriculture more productive
         c)   Bantu migration accelerated with iron tools
      4.   Bananas
         a)   Between 300 and 500 C.E., Malay seafarers colonized Madagascar and established banana cultivation
         b)   Bananas became well-established in Africa by 500 C.E.
         c)   Introduction of bananas caused another migration surge
      5.   Population growth
         a)   3.5 million people by 400 B.C.E.
         b)   11 million by the beginning of the millennium
         c)   17 million by 800 C.E.
         d)   22 million by 1000 C.E.

B. Bantu Political Organization
    1. "Stateless society"
        a) Early Bantu societies did not depend on elaborate bureaucracy
        b) Societies governed through family and kinship groups
        c) Village council, consisted of male family heads
        d) Chief of a village was from the most prominent family heads
        e) A group of villages constituted a district
        f) Villages chiefs negotiated intervillage affairs
    2. Chiefdoms
        a) Population growth strained resources, increased conflict
        b) Some Bantu communities began to organize military forces, 1000 C.E.
        c) Powerful chiefs overrode kinship networks and imposed authority
        d) Some chiefs conquered their neighbors
    3. Kingdom of Kongo
        a) Villages formed small states along the Congo River, 1000 C.E.
        b) Small states formed several larger principalities, 1200 C.E.
        c) One of the principalities overcame its neighbors and built kingdom of Kongo
        d) Maintained a centralized government with a royal currency system
        e) Provided effective organization until the mid-17th century

II. Islamic Kingdoms and Empires

A. Trans-Saharan Trade and Islamic States in West Africa
    1. Camels
        a) Camels came to north Africa from Arabia, 7th century B.C.E.
        b) After 500 C.E. camels replaced horses and donkeys as transport animals
        c) Camels' arrival quickened pace of communication across the Sahara
        d) Islamic merchants crossed the desert and established relations with sub-Saharan west Africa, by the late 8th century
    2. The kingdom of Ghana
        a) A principal state of west Africa, not related to modern state of Ghana
        b) Became the most important commercial site in west Africa
        c) Provided gold, ivory, and slaves for traders from north Africa
        d) Exchange for horses, cloth, manufactured goods, and salt
    3. Koumbi-Saleh
        a) The capital city of Ghana, a thriving commercial center
        b) Ghana kings maintained a large army of two hundred thousand warriors
    4. Islam in west Africa
        a) Ghana kings converted to Islam by the 10th century
        b) Allowed the people to observe their traditional beliefs
        c) Nomadic raids from the Sahara weakened the kingdom, the early 13th century
    5. Sundiata
        a) After Ghana dissolved, political leadership shifted to Mali empire
        b) The lion prince Sundiata (reigned 1230-55) built the Mali empire
    6. The Mali empire and trade
        a) Controlled and taxed almost all trade passing through west Africa
        b) Enormous caravans linked Mali to north Africa
        c) Besides the capital Niani, many other prosperous cities on caravan routes

7. Mansa Musa
    a) Sundiata's grand nephew, reigned from 1312 to 1337
    b) Made his pilgrimage to Mecca in 1324-1325
        (1) a gargantuan caravan of thousand soldiers and attendants
        (2) gold devalued 25% in Cairo during his visit
8. Mansa Musa and Islam
    a) Upon return to Mali, built mosques
    b) Sent students to study with distinguished Islamic scholars in northern Africa
    c) Established Islamic schools in Mali
9. The decline of Mali
    a) Factions crippled the central government
    b) Military pressures from neighboring kingdoms and desert nomads
    c) The Songhay empire replaced Mali by the late 15th century

B. The Indian Ocean Trade and Islamic States in East Africa
    1. Early visitors to east Africa
        a) Indian and Persian sailors visited the coasts after about 500 B.C.E.
        b) Hellenistic and Roman mariners reached the same coasts
        c) Malay seafarers established colonies on Madagascar
        d) By the 2nd century, Bantu peoples populated much of east Africa
    2. The Swahili
        a) An Arabic term, meaning "coasters"
        b) Dominated east African coast from Mogadishu to Sofala
        c) Spoke Swahili, a Bantu language supplemented with some Arabic words
        d) Trade with Muslim merchants became important by the 10th century
    3. The Swahili city-states
        a) Chiefs gained power through taxing trade on ports
        b) Ports developed into city-states governed by kings, 11th and 12th centuries
    4. Kilwa
        a) One of the busiest city-states on east coast
        b) Multistory stone buildings and copper coins, from the 13th century
        c) By the late 15th century, Kilwa exported about a ton of gold per year
    5. Zimbabwe
        a) A powerful kingdom of east Africa
        b) The 5th and 6th centuries C.E., wooden residences known as zimbabwe
        c) By the 9th century, chiefs began to build stone *zimbabwe*
        d) The magnificent stone complex known as Great Zimbabwe, the 12th century
        e) Eighteen thousand people lived in Great Zimbabwe in the late 15th century
        f) Kings organized flow of gold, ivory, and slaves
    6. Islam in East Africa
        a) Ruling elite and wealthy merchants converted to Islamic faith
        b) Conversion promoted close cooperation with Muslim merchants
        c) Conversion also opened door to political alliances with Muslim rulers

III. Bantu Society and Cultural Development

A. Social Classes
    1. Diversity of African societies
        a) Complex societies developed into kingdoms, empires, and city-states
        b) Coexisted with small states and stateless societies

2. Kinship groups of stateless societies
   a) Extended families and clans as social and economic organizations
   b) Communities claimed rights to land, no private property
   c) Village council allocated land to clan members
3. Sex and gender relations
   a) Men undertook heavy labor
   b) Women were responsible for child rearing, domestic chores
   c) Men monopolized public authority, but women enjoyed high honor as the source of life
   d) Aristocratic women could influence public affairs
   e) Women merchants commonly traded at markets
   f) Sometimes women organized all-female military units
   g) Islam did little to curtail women's opportunities in sub-Saharan Africa
4. Age grades
   a) Publicly recognized "age grades" or "age sets"
   b) Assumed responsibilities and tasks appropriate to their age grades
5. Slavery
   a) Most slaves were captives of war, debtors, criminals
   b) Worked as agricultural labor or sold in slave markets
6. Slave trading
   a) Slave trade increased after the 11th century
   b) Demand for slaves outstripped supply from eastern Europe
   c) Slave raids of large states against small states or stateless societies
   d) In some years, 10 to 12 thousand slaves shipped out of Africa
   e) Ten million slaves were transported by Islamic trade between 750 and 1500

B. African Religion
   1. Creator god
      a) Recognized by almost all African peoples
      b) Created the earth and humankind, source of world order
   2. Lesser gods and spirits
      a) Often associated with natural features
      b) Participated actively in the workings of the world
      c) Believed in ancestors' souls
   3. Diviners
      a) Mediated between humanity and supernatural beings
      b) Interpreted the cause of the people's misfortune
      c) Used medicine or rituals to eliminate problems
      d) African religion was not theological, but practical

C. The Arrival of Christianity and Islam
   1. Early Christianity in north Africa
      a) Christianity reached north Africa during the first century C.E.
      b) It had no influence on sub-Saharan African
   2. The Christian kingdom of Axum
      a) The first Christian kingdom, 4th century C.E., located in modern Ethiopia
      b) In later centuries, it was surrounded by Islamic neighbors
   3. Ethiopian Christianity
      a) Had little contact with Christians of other lands
      b) Shared basic Christian theology and rituals, but developed its own features

4. African Islam
   a) Appealed strongly to ruling elite and merchants of sub-Saharan Africa
   b) Became part of inherited traditions
   c) Accommodated African gender relations
   d) Supplemented rather than replaced traditional religions

Significant Individuals

Mansa Musa (p. 437) — Ruler of Mali empire, grand-nephew of Sundiata; reigned from 1312 to 1337; well known in Islamic world for his grand pilgrimage to Mecca in 1324-1325; policies greatly promoted Islamic faith in his empire.

Sundiata (pp. 429, 436-37) — Founder of the Mali empire, known as the lion prince, reigned 1230-1255 as a Muslim king; hero in the oral tradition of west Africa.

Chapter Glossary

age grades (pp. 443-44) — Age groups of sub-Saharan Africa, also called "age sets;" in communal life, members of different age grades assumed different responsibilities or tasks appropriate their levels of strength, energy, maturity, and experience.

Bantu (pp. 430-33) — Peoples of sub-Saharan Africa; originated in the region around modern Nigeria during the second millennium B.C.E. and spread throughout almost all sub-Saharan Africa by about 1000 C.E.; established divergent societies, but all spoke tongues belonging to the Bantu family of languages.

Great Zimbabwe (p. 440) — Capital city of Zimbabwe; a magnificent stone complex situated between the Zambesi and the Limpopo Rivers; up to eighteen thousand residents lived in the city during the late 15th century.

Kilwa (pp. 439-40) — One of the Swahili city-states that emerged on the east African coast during the 11th or 12th century; actively participated in trade of the Indian Ocean basin and enjoyed tremendous prosperity; suffered a devastating sack by Portuguese mariners in 1505.

kingdom of Axum (p. 446) — Christian kingdom of northeast Africa, located in the highland of modern Ethiopia; converted to Christian faith in mid-4th century C.E.; developed Christianity largely in isolation from the 8th century, and reestablished relations with Christians of other lands from the 16th century.

kingdom of Ghana (p. 435) — Islamic state of west Africa, situated between the Senegal and Niger Rivers in a region straddling the border between the modern states of Mali and Mauritania; emerged probably as early as the 5th or 6th century C.E.; kings converted to Islam by about the 10th century; became the most important commercial site of west Africa, trading gold, ivory, and slaves with Muslim merchants during later centuries; collapsed during the early 13th century.

kingdom of Kongo (p. 433) — Early Bantu kingdom, established during the 14th century in the valley of the Congo River (also known as the Zaire River), which embraced much of modern-day Republic of Congo and Angola; maintained effective authority until the mid-17th century.

Koumbi-Saleh (p. 435) — Capital city of Ghana kingdom, also a thriving commercial center with population of some fifteen thousand to twenty thousand people from the 11th to the early 13th century.

Mali empire (pp. 429, 436-37) — Large Bantu empire of west Africa, established by the lion prince Sundiata on the ruins of the Ghana state during the early 13th century; probably the wealthiest land in sub-Saharan Africa; known for its gold trade; overcome by Songhay empire by the late 15th century.

"stateless societies" (p. 432) — One form of social organization adopted by the Bantu in sub-Saharan Africa; governed mostly through family and kinship groups without elaborate hierarchy of officials or a bureaucracy.

Swahili (pp. 438-39) — Peoples of the east African coast; spoke Swahili, a Bantu language supplemented with words and ideas borrowed from Arabic; established a number of powerful city-states along the coast by the 11th and 12th centuries.

Zimbabwe (p. 440) — Interior kingdom of south-central Africa, emerged from a chiefdom to a state by the early 12th century; actively participated in trade of gold, ivory, and slaves.

Map Exercises

1. Study Map 18.1 on p. 431 of your textbook and answer the following questions: When, where, and how did the Bantu migrations begin? What accounted for the Bantu expansion?

2. What are some similarities and differences between Bantu migrations and Austronesian migrations on the Pacific islands (see Chapter 5)?

3. Study Map 18.2 on p.436 of your textbook and answer the following questions: What were the primary exports of sub-Saharan Africa? What trade routes linked sub-Saharan Africa to markets of the outside world?

4. Match the trade routes on the left with the relevant states on the right:

Trade routes	States
	Malindi
	Sofala
Trans-Saharan trade routes	Ghana
	Kilwa
	Mali
Maritime trade routes	Mogadishu
	Songhay

Self-Test/Student Quiz

1. The remarkable oral tradition of sub-Saharan Africa was preserved primarily by

   a. Muslim African scholars.
   b. professional singers and griots.
   c. village chiefs and diviners.

2. The story of Sundiata was about

   a. the heroic deeds of the lion prince in establishing the Mali empire.
   b. the misery of slaves captured and traded in the Mediterranean basin network.
   c. the coming of Islam as a dominant faith in sub-Saharan societies.

3. Sub-Saharan Africa is defined as

   a. the vast desert in central Africa.
   b. the tropical jungles of south Africa.
   c. central and south Africa south of the Sahara desert.

4. The earliest Bantu migrants were

   a. agriculturalists.
   b. hunting and gathering peoples.
   c. fishing peoples.

5. All of the following stimulated Bantu migrations except

   a. iron metallurgy.
   b. bubonic plague.
   c. bananas.

6. Before the 10th century, the dominant form of social organization in sub-Saharan Africa was the

   a. city-state.
   b. empire.
   c. stateless society.

7. All of the following describe a stateless society except

   a. female chiefs presided over village affairs.
   b. the people were governed through family and kinship groups.
   c. a group of villages constituted a district, but there was no chief or larger government for the district.

8. The kingdom of Kongo

    a. emerged as a powerful state through trading with Muslim merchants of north Africa.
    b. maintained a royal currency system based on cowries from the Indian Ocean.
    c. was a loosely organized government with little authority over officials.

9. The arrival of camels in Africa

    a. made communication across the Sahara possible.
    b. quickened the pace of communication across the Sahara.
    c. replaced elephants as the preferred transport animals throughout the Sahara.

10. Koumbi-Saleh was to the kingdom of Ghana as

    a. Mansa Musa was to the Mali empire.
    b. Niani was to the Mali empire.
    c. Sundiata was to the Mali empire.

11. The conversion to Islam of rulers of the kingdom of Ghana and the Mali empire

    a. stimulated commercial relations with Muslim merchants.
    b. meant that Islamic faith was imposed forcibly on their entire societies.
    c. facilitated the export of Muslim African slaves by these two states to other Islamic countries.

12. Swahili

    a. was an Arabic language.
    b. refers to the peoples of the east African coast.
    c. refers to the city-states of the east African coast.

13. All of the following were Swahili city-states except

    a. Sofala, Mogadishu.
    b. Zimbabwe, Ife.
    c. Malindi, Kilwa.

14. Great Zimbabwe was

    a. a powerful guild of gold merchants of Zimbabwe.
    b. the capital city of Zimbabwe.
    c. an anti-Islamic organization of Zimbabwe.

15. According to João de Barros, the population of Kilwa consisted of

    a. hunters, gatherers, and fishermen.
    b. Bantu and Indonesians.
    c. Arabs and Kaffirs.

16. In stateless societies of the sub-Sahara

    a. slaves did not exist.
    b. private property in land did not exist.
    c. gender differentiation did not exist.

17. After the 11th century, the slave trade became increasingly important in Africa because

    a. demand for slaves in foreign markets outstripped the supply.
    b. many African slaves wanted to be relocated in foreign lands.
    c. both of the above.

18. Unlike many other religions, African religion

    a. did not concern itself with morality and proper behavior.
    b. did not concern itself with matters of theology.
    c. did not concern itself with world order.

19. Compared with Islam, Christianity in sub-Saharan Africa was

    a. a minor faith.
    b. equally important.
    c. more true to original Christian theology than African Islam was to original Islamic theology.

20. Upon adopting Islamic faith, African women

    a. were increasingly confined in their social and economic activities.
    b. did not experience much change in their social status.
    c. enjoyed higher honor than before.

Textual Questions for Analysis

1. What accounted for the dynamics of Bantu migrations before 1000 C.E.?

2. What was the nature of stateless societies in sub-Saharan Africa?

3. Specifically, how was sub-Saharan Africa linked to trade networks of the outside world before 1500 C.E.?

4. Use at least two specific examples to explain how Islam influenced the development of sub-Saharan Africa.

5. Discuss the internal and external factors that contributed to the increasing volume of slave trade in sub-Saharan Africa after the 11th century.

Documentary Evidence

Sundiata's Return to Niani

Griots were highly specialized historians of Africa who, as counselors of kings, were commissioned to memorize the past and transmit it orally from generation to generation. The lengthy epic of Sundiata, the founder of the Mali empire of the 13th century, has been thus preserved. The following excerpt is just a small portion of the epic, which relates that after his great victory over the kingdom of Sosso and the grand celebration at Ka-ba (a small town by the Niger River), Sundiata (also referred to as Djata, Mansa, Maghan Sundiata, the son of Sogolon) led his army to his hometown, the capital city at Niani. (From D.T. Niane, *Sundiata*, trans. G. D. Pickett, Harlow: Longman, 1965. Cited in Oliver A. Johnson, ed., *Sources of World Civilization*, vol. 1, Englewood Cliffs: Prentice Hall, 1994, pp. 430-31.)

Sundiata and his men had to cross the Niger in order to enter old Mali. One might have thought that all the dug-out canoes in the world had arranged to meet at the port of Ka-ba. The fishing tribe of Somona, to whom Djata had given the monopoly of the water, were bent on expressing their thanks to the son of Sogolon. They put all their dug-outs side by side across the Niger so that Sundiata's sofas could cross without wetting their feet.

When the whole army was on the other side of the river, Sundiata ordered great sacrifices. A hundred oxen and a hundred rams were sacrificed. It was thus that Sundiata thanked God on returning to Mali.

The villages of Mali gave Maghan Sundiata an unprecedented welcome.... The road to Mali from the river was flanked by a double human hedge. Flocking from every corner of Mali, all the inhabitants were resolved to see their savior from close up. The women of Mali tried to create a sensation and they did not fail. At the entrance to each village they had carpeted the road with their multi-colored pagnes so that Sundiata's horse would not so much as dirty its feet on entering their village. At the village exits the children, holding leafy branches in their hands, greeted Djata with cries of "Wassa, Wassa, Aye"....

The troops were marching along singing the "Hymn to the Bow," which the crowd took up. New songs flew from mouth to mouth. Young women offered the soldiers cool water and cola nuts. And so the triumphal march across Mali ended outside Niani, Sundiata's city.

It was a ruined town which was beginning to be rebuilt by its inhabitants. A part of the ramparts had been destroyed and the charred walls still bore the marks of the fire. From the top of the hill Djata looked on Niani, which looked like a dead city. He saw the plain of Soundarani, and he also saw the site of the young baobab tree. The survivors of the catastrophe were standing in rows on the Mali road. The children were waving branches, a few young women were singing, but the adults were mute....

With Sundiata peace and happiness entered Niani. Lovingly Sogolon's son had his native city rebuilt. He restored in the ancient style his father's old enclosure where he had grown up. People came from all the villages of Mali to settle in Niani. The walls had to be destroyed to enlarge the town, and new quarters were built for each kin group in the enormous army.

Djata's justice spared nobody. He followed the very word of God. He protected the weak against the strong and people would make journeys lasting several days to come and demand justice of him. Under his sun the upright man was rewarded and the wicked one punished.

In their new-founded peace the villages knew prosperity again, for with Sundiata happiness had come into everyone's home. Vast fields of millet, rice, cotton, indigo, and fonio surrounded the villages. Whoever worked always had something to live on. Each year long caravans carried the taxes in kind to Niani. You could go from village to village without fearing brigands. A thief would have his right hand chopped off and if he stole again he would be put to the sword.

New villages and new towns sprang up in Mali and elsewhere. "Dyulas," or traders, became numerous and during the reign of Sundiata the world knew happiness.

QUESTIONS TO CONSIDER

1. How does the epic depict Sundiata? Is its narrative strategy effective? Should a textbook of world history adopt the griot's narrative method? Why or why not?

2. The epic described an ideal society filled with peace, prosperity, and justice. Does Mali seem like an ideal society to you? Why or why not?

3. By reading the above excerpt, you should glean some useful information regarding social organization, customs, and economic activities of west Africa. Make a list of such information from the above passage and compare it with information about west African society provided in your textbook.

Chapter 19

Western Europe during the High Middle Ages

Introduction and Learning Objectives

After centuries of instability, chaos, and recovery during the early middle ages, western Europe emerged as a vibrant and powerful society during the "high middle ages," the period from about 1000 to 1300 C.E. Refuting an older image of the middle ages as an unfortunate interlude between the glories of the classical Greco-Roman ages and modern times, the authors present the high middle ages as a story of progress and vigorous development full of creative tensions. Dramatic changes in politics, economy, and culture testify to the vitality of feudalism and Christianity which laid down the institutional and cultural foundations for innovations and progress.

The authors' discussion shows the growing dynamism of the high middle ages through four interrelated aspects: the rise of regional states, economic growth, the role of the Roman Catholic church, and European expansion epitomized by the crusades. Although the European dream of an empire did not die, what was accomplished during this period was the creation of powerful regional states based on principles of feudalism. Was the failure to build a European empire a tragedy for European history? Or were competitive regional states a vital source of European strength? While these issues are subject to debate, the authors argue that regional monarchies organized more effective governments and brought about greater regional stability than before, which in turn, encouraged population growth and innovation in agricultural production. Indeed, the high middle ages saw an agricultural revolution that provided abundant food supply for rapid urbanization.

While commercialization and urbanization were common in many other societies, in western Europe these processes were accompanied by the growth of the independent authority of the Roman Catholic church, the revival of interest in classical rational philosophy, the rise of universities, and the prominence of a merchant class in increasingly independent cities. All these had deep implications for the future development of western Europe, and the combination of these elements help to explain the vitality of feudalism during the high middle ages and the rise of modern Europe in the centuries to follow.

The authors also point out that during the high middle ages Europe was no longer the prey of foreign powers, but became a feared military power and a commercial competitor with the Arab world. Beginning about the mid-11th century, Europeans embarked upon a series of expansive ventures in the Atlantic, the Baltic, and the Mediterranean. Although the crusades against Islam in later centuries did not show European military superiority to the Arab world, these military ventures signaled clearly that Europeans were beginning to play a much larger role in the affairs of the eastern hemisphere than they had during the early middle ages. What was the nature of European expansion during the high middle ages? Were the crusades religious wars or commercial ventures? What accounted for the first instance of European expansion since the fall of Rome? The authors' discussion in this chapter leaves ample room for students to form their own opinions.

After studying this chapter, students should understand and be able to discuss the following issues:

- the rise of regional states and their relations with the Roman Catholic church

- the dynamic growth of agriculture and urbanization

- social change within the three estates

- the role of the Roman Catholic church in cultural development

- the nature of European expansion

Chapter Outline

I. **The Establishment of Regional States**

A. The Holy Roman Empire
1. Otto I
   a) Otto of Saxony rose in northern Germany by the mid-10th century
   b) Pope John XII proclaimed him emperor in 962, birth of Holy Roman Empire
2. Investiture Contest
   a) Formerly, important church officials were appointed by imperial authorities
   b) Pope Gregory VII ordered an end to the practice
   c) Emperor Henry IV was excommunicated because of his disobedience
   d) Standing in snow, Henry beseeched Gregory's mercy
3. Frederick Barbarossa
   a) Sought to absorb wealthy Lombardy in north Italy
   b) The papal coalition forced Barbarossa to relinquish his right in Lombardy
   c) Voltaire: Holy Roman Empire was "neither holy, nor Roman, nor an empire"
B. Feudal Monarchies in France and England
1. Capetian France
   a) Hugh Capet, a minor and weak noble, was elected king in 987
   b) In the next three centuries, Capetian kings gained power and wealth gradually
2. The Normans
   a) Descendants of Vikings who carved out a state in Normandy of France
   b) Nominally subject to Carolingian and Capetian rulers, but acted independently
3. Norman England
   a) Duke William of Normandy invaded England in 1066
   b) Introduced Norman style of feudalism to England
C. Regional States in Italy and Iberia
1. Church influence in Italy
   a) The popes ruled a good-sized territory in central Italy
   b) The church also influenced politics of northern Italy
2. Italian states
   a) A series of prosperous city-states emerged by the 12th century
   b) Normans conquered southern Italy, brought it to Roman Catholic Christianity

3. Christian and Muslim states in Iberia
   a) Muslim conquerors ruled most of the peninsula, 8th-11th centuries
   b) Christian kingdoms took the peninsula except Granada by late 13th century

II. Economic Growth and Social Development

A. Growth of the Agricultural Economy
   1. Expansion of arable land
      a) Population pressure by the late 10th century
      b) Serfs and monks began to clear forests and swamps
      c) Lords encouraged such efforts for high taxes
   2. Improved agricultural techniques
      a) Crop rotation methods
      b) Cultivation of beans increased—enriched the land
      c) More domestic animals—also enriched the land
      d) Books and treatises on household economy and agricultural methods
   3. New tools and technology
      a) Extensive use of watermills and heavy plows
      b) Use of horseshoe and horse collar, increased land under cultivation
   4. New food supplies
      a) Before 1000, European diet—grains
      b) After 1000, more meat, dairy products, fish, vegetables, and legumes
   5. Population growth: from 29 to 79 million between 800 C.E. and 1300 C.E.
B. The Revival of Towns and Trade
   1. Urbanization: Peasants and serfs flocked to cities and towns
   2. Textile production
      a) Northern Italian cities and Flanders became centers of wool textiles
      b) Trade in wool products fueled economic development of Europe
   3. Mediterranean trade
      a) Beside Amalfi and Venice, other cities also became important
      b) Italian merchants established colonies in Mediterranean and Black Sea
   4. The Hanseatic League
      a) The Hansa—an association of trading cities, dominated trade of northern Europe
      b) Major European rivers linked Hansa to the Mediterranean
   5. Improved business techniques
      a) Bankers issued letters of credit to merchants
      b) Commercial partnerships for limiting risks of commercial investment
C. Social Changes
   1. The three estates
      a) "Those who pray"—clergy of Roman Catholic church, the spiritual estate
      b) "Those who fight"—feudal nobles, the military estate
      c) "Those who work"—mostly peasants and serfs
   2. Chivalry
      a) Widely-recognized code of ethics and behavior for feudal nobles
      b) Church officials directed chivalry toward Christian faith and piety
   3. Troubadours
      a) Aristocratic women promoted chivalric values by patronizing troubadours
      b) Troubadours drew inspiration from the love poetry of Muslim Spain

4. Eleanor of Aquitaine
   a) Most celebrated woman of her day
   b) Supported troubadours, promoted good manners, refinement, and romantic love
   c) Code of chivalry and romantic poetry softened manners of rough warriors
5. Independent cities
   a) Expansion of cities fit awkwardly in the feudal framework
   b) Urban populations were increasingly able to resist demands of feudal nobles
6. Guilds
   a) Established standards of quality for manufactured goods
   b) Determined prices and regulated entry of new workers
7. Urban women
   a) Towns and cities offered fresh opportunities for women
   b) Women worked in a wide range of occupations
   c) Most guilds admitted women, and women also had their own guilds

III. European Christianity during the High Middle Ages

A. Schools, Universities, and Scholastic Theology
   1. Cathedral schools
      a) Bishops and archbishops in France and northern Italy organized schools
      b) Cathedral schools had formal curricula, concentrated on liberal arts
      c) Some offered advance instruction in law, medicine, and theology
   2. Universities
      a) Student guilds and faculty guilds
      b) Large cathedral schools developed into universities
   3. The influence of Aristotle
      a) Increased communication helped rediscovery of Aristotle
      b) Obtained Aristotle's works from Byzantine and Muslim philosophers
   4. Scholasticism: St. Thomas Aquinas
      a) Aristotle's influence—the emergence of scholastic theology
      b) St. Thomas Aquinas, the most famous scholastic theologian
      c) Sought to harmonize Aristotle's rational power with teachings of Christianity
B. Popular Religion
   1. Sacraments, the most popular was the Eucharist
   2. Devotion to saints for help
   3. The Virgin Mary: the most popular saint
   4. Saints' relics were esteemed
   5. Pilgrimage: to Rome and Compostela, to Jerusalem
C. Reform Movements and Popular Heresies
   1. Dominicans and Franciscans
      a) Organized movements to champion spiritual over materialistic values
      b) Zealously combated heterodox movements
   2. Popular heresy: the movements of Waldensians and Cathars (Albigensians)

IV. The Medieval Expansion of Europe

A. Atlantic and Baltic Colonization
1. Vinland
   a) Scandinavian seafarers turned to North Atlantic Ocean, 9th and 10th centuries
   b) Colonized Iceland and Greenland
   c) Leif Ericsson arrived at modern Newfoundland in Canada which he called Vinland
2. Christianity in Scandinavia
   a) Kings of Denmark and Norway converted to Christianity, 10th century
   b) Norwegian colonies in Iceland, Sweden, Finland also adopted Christianity
B. Crusading Orders and Baltic Expansion
1. Zealous Christians formed military-religious orders against pagan Slavic peoples
2. The Teutonic Knights were most active in the Baltic region
3. Baltic region was absorbed into Christian Europe from the late 13th century
C. The Reconquest (for Christianity) of Sicily and Spain
1. The reconquest of Sicily by Roger Guiscard, 1090
2. The *reconquista* of Spain
   a) The *reconquista* began in 1060s
   b) By 1150, took over half the peninsula
   c) By the 13th century, took almost all the peninsula except Granada
D. The Crusades
1. Pope Urban II
   a) Called for Christian knights to take up arms and seize the holy land, 1095
   b) Peter the Hermit traveled in Europe and organized a ragtag army
   c) The campaign was a disaster for the crusaders
2. The first crusade
   a) French and Norman nobles organized a respectable military expedition, 1096
   b) Jerusalem fell to the crusaders, 1099
   c) Muslims recaptured Jerusalem, 1187
3. Later crusades
   a) By the mid-13th century, launched five major crusades
   b) The fourth crusade (1202-1204) conquered Constantinople
   c) The crusades failed to take over Palestine from the Muslims
4. Economic consequences of the crusades
   a) Crusades encouraged trade between Europeans and Muslims
   b) Demands for silk, cotton textiles, and spices increased
   c) Italian merchants also sought opportunities for direct trade in Asian markets

Significant Individuals

Eleanor of Aquitaine (p. 462) — Most celebrated noblewoman of her day; known for her enthusiastic patronage of troubadours and encouragement of the cultivation of good manners, refinement, and romantic love.

Eric the Red (p. 470) — Leader of Scandinavian seafarers; responsible for discovering and colonizing Greenland in North Atlantic Ocean at the end of the 10th century.

Frederick Barbarossa (reigned 1152 to 1190 C.E.) (p. 454) — Frederick I, emperor of the Holy Roman Empire; policy sought to absorb the wealthy urban region of Lombardy in north Italy; attempt was defeated by a papal coalition with other European states.

Henry IV (1056-1106 C.E.) (p. 454) — Emperor of the Holy Roman Empire; known for his challenge to the pope's policy of appointing church officials by church authorities (the Investiture Contest); upon being excommunicated, Henry IV had great trouble dealing with rebellious German princes; regained imperial control only after beseeching the pope's mercy while standing barefoot in the snow.

Leif Ericsson (p. 470) — Son of Eric the Red; led a group of Scandinavian seafarers and sailed to what they called Vinland (modern Newfoundland in Canada) by about 1000 C.E.; founded a small colony and maintained it for several decades.

Peter the Hermit (p. 473) — Zealous Christian preacher; traveled throughout France, Germany, and the Low Countries to organize crusaders for recapturing Palestine as a response to Pope Urban II' s call; the campaign was a disaster for the crusaders.

Pope Gregory VII (pope from 1073-1085 C.E.) (p. 454) — Active during the 1070s and 1080s; known for his victory over Emperor Henry IV of the Holy Roman Empire during the Investiture Contest.

Roger Guiscard (p. 472) — Norman adventurer; responsible for reconquering Muslim Sicily in 1090 and returning it to Christian hands.

St. Dominic and St. Francis (p. 468) — Founders of orders of mendicants known as the Dominican and Franciscan friars; lived in late 12th and early 13th centuries.

St. Thomas Aquinas (p. 465) — Professor of the University of Paris; most famous scholastic theologian; lived from 1225 to 1274. His teachings combined Aristotle's rational power with Christianity; sought to formulate the most truthful and persuasive system of thought possible.

Urban II (p. 473) — Pope of the 11th century; responsible for launching a crusade; called for Christian knights to take up arms and seize the holy land of Palestine in 1095.

William the Conqueror (p. 455) — Duke William of Normandy; invaded England in 1066 and introduced Norman-style feudalism to England.

Chapter Glossary

Albigensian crusade (p. 469) — Military campaign against the Cathars; called for by Pope Innocent III; feudal warriors from northern France undertook the crusade and ruthlessly crushed Cathar communities in southern France, 13th century.

Capetian France (pp. 454-55) — Term for France during the high middle ages after Hugh Capet, the first Capetian king who reigned beginning in 987; during the following three centuries, Capetian kings gradually gained power and resources to establish centralized authority in France.

Cathars (p. 468) — Also known as Albigensians; adopted the teachings of heretical groups in eastern Europe who viewed the world as a site of an unrelenting, cosmic struggle between the forces of good and evil; followers rejected the Roman Catholic church, sought spiritual perfection, renounced wealth and marriage, and led a strict vegetarian life.

cathedral schools (pp. 464-65) — Schools established by bishops and archbishops in cathedrals of Europe; curricula emphasized the liberal arts; some also offered advanced instruction in law, medicine, and theology; become common during the 11th and 12th centuries.

chivalry (p. 462) — Informal but widely recognized code of ethics and behavior considered appropriate for feudal nobles of Europe; substantially influenced by Christian faith and romantic love cultivated by troubadours.

first crusade (p. 473) — Military expedition organized by French and Norman nobles in 1096; captured Edessa, Antioch, and Jerusalem in the following years; Muslim leader Saladin recaptured Jerusalem in 1187.

fourth crusade (p. 473) — Fourth military expedition attempting to recapture the Holy Land of Palestine; took place between 1202 and 1204; instead of capturing Palestine, crusaders conquered Constantinople and subjected the city to a ruthless sack.

Hanseatic League (p. 461) — Also known as the Hansa; association of trading cities stretching from Novgorod to London and embracing all the significant commercial centers of Poland, northern Germany, and Scandinavia; dominated trade of northern Europe during the high middle ages.

high middle ages (p. 452) — Period of European history from about 1000 to 1300 C.E.

Investiture Contest (p. 454) — Controversy between emperors of the Holy Roman Empire and the popes over appointments of Roman Catholic church officials in the late 11th and early 12th century; the papacy won out over the imperial authorities.

mendicants ("beggars") (p. 468) — Followers of St. Dominic and St. Francis; also known as the Dominican and Franciscan friars; active in towns and cities of Europe during the high middle ages; worked within the Roman Catholic church, but strongly emphasized spiritual over materialistic values.

reconquista (p. 472) — Christians' reconquest of Spain from Muslim control; lasted from the 1060s to 1492.

sacraments (p. 466) — Holy rituals for bringing spiritual blessings to the observants; during the middle ages, the Roman Catholic church recognized seven sacraments, and the most popular one was the Eucharist.

scholasticism (p. 465) — Influential theology of medieval Europe during the 13th century; sought to synthesize the beliefs and values of Christianity with the logical rigor of Greek philosophy.

Teutonic Knights (pp. 470-71) — One of several Christian military-religious orders active in the Baltic region during the 12th and 13th centuries; aided by German missionaries and the Roman Catholic church, became crusaders who fought against the pagan Slavic peoples of Prussia, Livonia, and Lithuania; responsible for bringing the Baltic region into the larger society of Christian Europe.

three estates (p. 461-62) — Conventional classification of European society during the middle ages, referring to "those who pray, those who fight, and those who work."

troubadours (p 462) — Traveling poets, minstrels, and entertainers patronized by aristocratic women; most active in southern France and northern Italy during the 12th and 13th centuries; drew inspiration from the long tradition of love poetry produced in nearby Muslim Spain, and promoted refined behavior and tender, respectful relations between the sexes.

Waldensians (p. 468) — Popular heresy of 12th and 13th-century Europe; protested the increasing materialism of European society; despised the Roman Catholic clergy as immoral and corrupt, and advocated modest and simple lives.

Map Exercises

1. On the following map, fill in the names of the regional states from the list below (based on Map 19.1 on p. 453 of your textbook) and match each state with its description in the following table:

Regional States	Descriptions
France	Established by Otto I in the late 10th century
England	Came into being through the *reconquista*
Holy Roman Empire	Ruled by Capetian Kings
Papal States	Invaded by Normans and ruled by Normal kings
Portugal	Conquered by Teutonic Knights
Sweden	Directly controlled by the popes

2. Study Map 19.2 on p. 471 of your textbook, and answer the following question: Which lands were added to Christian European territory during the high middle ages?

3. Describe the routes of the first and fourth crusades for recapturing Palestine.

Self-Test/Student Quiz

1. In the Investiture Contest, the winner was

    a. Henry IV.
    b. Gregory VII.
    c. Frederick Barbarossa.

2. The Holy Roman Empire was "neither holy, nor Roman, nor an empire" because

    a. the emperors were not crowned by the popes.
    b. the Byzantine emperors did not acknowledge the Holy Roman Empire.
    c. it did not restore imperial unity to western Europe.

3. During the high middle ages, the Capetian Kings gradually centralized power and authority in France by

    a. administrating justice throughout the realm.
    b. introducing Norman-style feudalism.
    c. fighting the Vikings.

4. All of the following contributed to the expansion of arable land in Europe during the high middle ages except

    a. population pressure.
    b. use of the horseshoe and horse collar.
    c. introduction of bananas.

5. According to Pegolotti,

    a. European long-distance trade with China was perfectly safe.
    b. local lords always robbed traveling merchants.
    c. by using paper money in China, Europeans paid higher prices for their goods.

6. The Hanseatic League was

    a. known for its determination to reconquer Spain from Muslim control.
    b. responsible for curbing the expansion of the Holy Roman Empire.
    c. an association of trading cities of northern Europe.

7. In medieval Europe, the three estates meant

    a. England, Scotland, and Ireland.
    b. the three royal estates of the Capetian Kings.
    c. the three social classes.

8. All but one of the following influenced the manners of the European feudal nobility:

    a. long-distance trade.
    b. the Christian faith.
    c. romantic poetry and songs.

9. During the high middle ages, the development of towns and cities "fit awkwardly in the framework of a feudal political order" because

    a. their citizens were not vassals, and their demands for autonomy were not easily quelled.
    b. unlike feudal manors, cities were egalitarian societies.
    c. unlike the organization of the work force on feudal manors, women became part of the working class in cities.

10. Guilds of European cities and towns could do all of the following except

    a. set standards of quality for manufactured goods.
    b. administer justice on behalf of the city government.
    c. determine the prices at which members had to sell their products.

11. Curricula of cathedral schools concentrated on

    a. liberal arts.
    b. Bible reading.
    c. law and medicine.

12. During the high middle ages, European scholars' rediscovery of Aristotle's work led to

    a. the growing dynamism of popular heresies.
    b. the development of scholasticism.
    c. the rise of the Dominicans and Franciscans.

13. The most famous scholastic theologian was

    a. Eucharist.
    b. St. Francis.
    c. St. Thomas Aquinas.

14. Christians' devotion to saints was very much like

    a. the Bantu people's devotion to the creator god.
    b. Buddhists' devotion to Bodhisattvas.
    c. Muslims' devotion to Mecca.

15. All of the following belonged to the popular heresies of medieval Europe except

    a. Waldensians.
    b. Cathars.
    c. mendicants.

16. The Albigensian crusade was

    a. a military campaign against the Muslims.
    b. a military expedition against the Cathars.
    c. a military venture against the pagan Slavic peoples in the Baltic region.

17. Vinland was

    a. conquered by the Teutonic Knights.
    b. reconquered by European crusaders.
    c. colonized by Scandinavian seafarers.

18. The reconquest of Sicily from the Muslims was accomplished by

    a. Eric the Red.
    b. Roger Guiscard.
    c. Robert Guiscard.

19. The term *reconquista* specifically referred to

    a. the reconquest of Spain.
    b. the reconquest of Sicily.
    c. the recapture of Palestine.

20. All but one of the following describes the crusades:

    a. The campaigns showed European military superiority to Muslim armies.
    b. One of the crusades conquered Constantinople instead of recapturing Palestine.
    c. The crusaders traded eagerly with Muslim merchants in the eastern Mediterranean.

Textual Questions for Analysis

1. How did the rulers of the Holy Roman Empire, France, and England consolidate their royal power?

2. Compare and contrast European chivalry with Japanese *bushido* (see Chapter 14).

3. "The expansion of the urban working population promoted the development of towns and cities as jurisdictions that fit awkwardly in the framework of a feudal political order" (p. 463). Explain.

4. Compare and contrast scholasticism and Neo-Confucianism (see Chapter 14). Who were the most influential thinkers in each school of thought? What were their basic ideas? Why did their thought represent new developments in cultural traditions in their own societies?

5. What motives inspired the Crusades? Did the Crusaders achieve their goals? What were the results?

Documentary Evidence

Medieval Student Life

About the mid-12th century, students and teachers of cathedral schools began to organize academic guilds and persuade political authorities to grant charters guaranteeing their rights. These guilds had the effect of transforming cathedral schools into universities. The first universities were those of Bologna, Paris, and Salerno—noted for instruction in law, theology, and medicine, respectively—but by the late 13th century, universities had appeared also in Rome, Naples, Seville, Salamanca, Oxford, Cambridge, and other cities throughout Europe. The following excerpt is not a direct description of medieval student life, but a letter written by a father in 1315 to his two sons studying at the University of Toulouse (Spain) regarding how to live a healthy and productive student life. (From Lynn Thorndike, *University Records and Life in the Middle Ages,* New York: Columbia University Press, 1944, pp. 156-60.)

Beware of eating too much and too often especially during the night. Avoid eating raw onions in the evening except rarely, because they dull the intellect and senses generally.

Avoid all very lacteal foods such as milk and fresh cheese except very rarely. Beware of eating milk and fish, or milk and wine, at the same meal, for milk and fish or milk and wine produce leprosy.

Don't have fresh pork too often. Salt pork is all right.

Don't eat many nuts except rarely and following fish. I say the same of meat and fruit, for they are bad and difficult to digest....

Also, after you have risen from table wash out your mouth with wine. This done, take one spoonful of this powdered confection:

Of meat prepared with vinegar and dried coriander similarly prepared a modicum each; of roast meat, fennel seed, flowers of white eyebright, two ounces each; of candied coriander, candied anise, scraped licorice, each one ounce and a half; of cloves, mast, cubebs, each three drams; of galingale and cardamomum each two drams; of white ginger six drams; of white loaf sugar three drams; made into a powder and put in a paste. And keep this in your room in a secret [or, dry] place, for it will comfort your digestion, head, vision, intellect and memory, and protect from rheum....

Sufficient and natural sleep is to sleep for a fourth part of a natural day or a trifle more or less. To do otherwise is to pervert nature. Too much is a sin, wherefore shun it, unless the case is urgent and necessary....

Don't sleep in winter with cold feet, but first warm them at the fire or by walking about or some other method. And in summer don't sleep with bed slippers on your feet, because they generate vapors which are very bad for the brain and memory.

Don't go straight to bed on a full stomach but an hour after the meal. Also, unless some urgent necessity prevents, walk about for a bit after a meal, at least around the square, so that the food may settle in the stomach and not evaporate in the mouth of the stomach, since the vapors will rise to the head and fill it with rheum and steal away and cut short memory...

If you cannot go outside your lodgings, either because the weather does not permit or it is raining, climb the stairs rapidly three or four times, and have in your room a big heavy stick like a sword and wield it now with one hand, now with the other, as if in a scrimmage, until you are almost winded. This is splendid exercise to warm one up and expel noxious vapors through the pores and consume other superfluities. Jumping is a similar exercise. Singing, too, exercises the chest. And if you will do this, you will have healthy limbs, a sound intellect and memory, and you will avoid rheum. The same way with playing ball. All these were invented not for sport but for exercise. Moreover, too much labor is to be avoided as a continual practice.

Accidents of the soul have the greatest influence, such as anger, sadness, and love of women, fear, excessive anxiety: concerning all which I say nothing more than that you avoid all passions of the soul harmful to you and enjoy yourself happily with friends and good companions, and cultivate honesty and patience which bring the more delights to the soul, and especially if you love God with your whole heart.

QUESTIONS TO CONSIDER

1. According to the author's advice, how should a student maintain good health, sound intellect, sharp memory, and a happy soul? What does the advice suggest about medieval student life?

2. Based on the information provided by the letter, describe the living conditions of medieval students—their diet, daily routine, and pastimes.

3. The author of the letter earned a master's degree in medicine, and his advice reveals some medical knowledge of his time. How would you evaluate this advice?

Chapter 20

Worlds Apart: The Americas and Oceania

Introduction and Learning Objectives

The overall theme of this chapter is that the original inhabitants of the Americas and Oceania went through significant changes as seen from their complex societies and sophisticated cultural and religious traditions during the period from 1000 to 1500 C.E. These changes took place under conditions of isolation, lack of metallurgical technologies, and the absence of wheeled vehicles and transport animals. In the Americas, we see a broad range of societies from small and simple hunting or fishing bands to large empires with distinctive cultural and religious traditions. In Oceania, where isolation was more complete and natural resources were more limited than in the Americas, people established well-organized agricultural societies and chiefly states throughout the Pacific islands.

The authors' discussion of the Americas concentrates on well-documented societies, especially the Aztec and Inca empires. For those who are familiar with the patterns of imperial systems elsewhere, it may seem odd to see the combination of neolithic technology and the great imperial systems in Mesoamerica and Andean America. While a number of similarities can be drawn with other imperial systems, such as the existence of gender hierarchy, social classes, and the military nature of government, both the Aztec and Inca empires were not based on the development of a market economy or the full specialization of production. Nor did these imperial systems encourage the growth of a powerful merchant class. Moreover, without a system of taxation, the development of an extensive bureaucratic system was highly compromised in the Americas.

How to view the rituals of human sacrifice practiced in the Americas has long been a controversial issue. The authors discuss this matter in the larger contexts of American societies and religious traditions. They point out that human sacrifice and bloodletting rituals were an essential part of religious traditions in the Americas, reflecting a desire to keep agricultural society going. Although human sacrifice was common, it was practiced extensively only in the Aztec empire when the warrior class used it as a way of pleasing their war god Huitzilopochtli. In the Inca empire, religious sacrifices often took the alternate forms of agricultural produce or animals such as llamas and guinea pigs instead of humans.

In relative isolation, the development of Oceania was slower. The authors' discussion points to a contrast between the societies of Australia and the Pacific islands. In food-rich but thinly-populated Australia, the hunting and gathering peoples relied on seasonal migration for survival; they maintained their foraging and nomadic life style until the 19th and 20th centuries; and their religious beliefs were concentrated on local geographical features. In the beautiful but resource-poor Pacific islands, the peoples relied on agriculture, domestic animals, and elaborate fishing skills. Population growth and development of limited trade led to the sophistication of chiefly states, especially on large islands. The most hierarchical was probably the society of Hawai'i, where the ruling classes made a variety of *kapu* (taboos) to maintain their wealth and privileges over commoners. Overall, the inhabitants of Australia and the Pacific islands discovered effective means of exploiting their natural environments, and they accomplished much in developing their cultural traditions and political organizations.

After studying this chapter, students should understand and be able to discuss the following issues:

- the nature of the Aztec and Inca empires

- the meanings of bloodletting rituals and human sacrifices

- the nature of chiefly states in the Pacific islands

- comparisons between Australian and Polynesian societies

Chapter Outline

I.   States and Empires in Mesoamerica and North America

    A. The Toltecs and the Mexica
       1. Toltecs
          a) Collapse of Teotihuacan in central Mexico, 9th and early 10th century
          b) Toltecs migrated to central Mexico about the 8th century
          c) Established a large state and powerful army from the mid-10th to the mid-12th century
       2. Tula
          a) Capital city of Toltecs, center of weaving, pottery, and obsidian work
          b) Maintained close relations with societies of the Gulf coast and the Maya
       3. Toltec decline
          a) Civil strife at Tula, beginning in 1125
          b) Nomadic incursion of 1175
          c) By the end of the 12th century, no longer dominating Mesoamerica
       4. The Mexica
          a) Also known as Aztecs, arrived in central Mexico about the mid-13th century
          b) Rough-tough people, wandering and fighting for a century in central Mexico
          c) Settled at Tenochtitlan (modern Mexico City) about 1345
          d) Plentiful food supplies and *chinampas* by Lake Texcoco
       5. The Aztec empire
          a) Military campaigns against neighboring societies, mid-15th century
          b) Conquered and colonized Oaxaco in southwestern Mexico
          c) Made alliance with Texcoco and Tlacopan
          d) Empire ruled 12 million people and most of Mesoamerica
       6. Tribute and trade
          a) Tribute obligations were very oppressive
          b) Empire had no bureaucracy or administration
          c) Allies did not have standing army
          d) Tribute of 489 subject territories flowed into Tenochtitlan

B. Mexica Society
  1. Warriors
     a) Military elite at top of rigid social hierarchy
     b) Mostly from the Mexica aristocracy
     c) Enjoyed great wealth, honor, and privileges
  2. Mexica women
     a) No public role, but enjoyed high honor as mothers of warriors
     b) Honor of bearing children was equal to that of capturing enemies in battle
  3. Priests
     a) Ranked among the Mexica elite
     b) Specialized in calendrical and ritual lore
     c) Advisers to Mexica rulers, occasionally, became supreme rulers themselves
  4. Cultivators and slaves
     a) Cultivators worked on *chinampas* (small plots of reclaimed land) or on aristocrats' land
     b) Paid tribute and provided labor service for public works
     c) Large number of slaves, worked as domestic servants
  5. Craftsmen and merchants
     a) Skilled craftsmen enjoyed some prestige
     b) Tenuous position of merchants:
        (1) supplied exotic goods and military intelligence
        (2) but under suspicion as greedy profiteers
C. Mexica Religion
  1. Mexica gods
     a) Tezcatlipoca: giver and taker of life, patron deity of warriors
     b) Quetzalcóatl: supporter of arts, crafts, and agriculture
  2. Ritual bloodletting: common to all Mesoamericans
  3. Huitzilopochtli: the war god
     a) Human sacrifice was encouraged by devotion to Huitzilopochtli
     b) Honored Huitzilopochtli with a large temple at the center of Tenochtitlan
     c) Hundreds of thousands of skulls in temples sacrificed to this war god
D. Peoples and Societies of the North
  1. Pueblo and Navajo societies
     a) Two large settled societies in the contemporary American southwest
     b) By about 700 C.E., began to build stone and adobe buildings
  2. Iroquois peoples
     a) Agricultural society in the woodlands east of the Mississippi River
     b) Five Iroquois nations emerged from Swasco society, 1400 C.E.
     c) Women were in charge of Iroquois villages and longhouses
  3. Mound-building peoples
     a) Built enormous earthen mounds throughout eastern half of North America
     b) Mounds served as stages of ceremonies and rituals, dwelling, or burial sites
  4. Cahokia
     a) The largest mound at Cahokia, Illinois
     b) Fifteen to 38 thousand people lived in Cahokia society during the 12th century
     c) Burial sites reveal existence of social classes and trade

II. States and Empires in Andean South America

    A. The Coming of the Incas
        1. Chucuito
            a) After Chavín and Moche, several regional states dominated Andean South America
            b) Chucuito dominated highlands around Lake Titicaca
            c) Cultivation of potatoes, herding llamas and alpacas
            d) Traded with lower valleys, chewed coca leaves
        2. Chimu
            a) Powerful kingdom in the lowlands of Peru before the mid-15th century
            b) Irrigation networks, cultivation of maize and sweet potatoes
            c) Capital city at Chanchan, massive brick buildings
        3. The Inca empire
            a) Settled first around Lake Titicaca among other peoples
            b) Ruler Pachacuti launched campaigns against neighbors, 1438
            c) Built a huge empire stretching 4000 kilometers from north to south
            d) Ruled the empire with military and administrative elite
            e) Inca bureaucrats relied on *quipu* (a mnemonic aid made of an array of small cords) to keep track of information
        4. Cuzco: capital of the Inca, might have had 300,000 people in the late 15th century
        5. Inca roads
            a) Two major roads linked the south and north
            b) Paved with stone, shaded by trees
            c) Supported the centralized government, facilitated spread of Quechua language
    B. Inca Society and Religion
        1. Trade
            a) Without a large merchant class, Incas bartered agricultural surplus locally
            b) Not much specialization
        2. The chief ruler
            a) Chief ruler was viewed as descended from the sun
            b) In theory, the god-king owned everything on earth
            c) After death, mummified rulers became intermediaries with gods
        3. Aristocrats and priests
            a) Aristocrats enjoyed fine food, embroidered clothes, and wore ear spools
            b) Priests led celibate and ascetic lives, very influential figures
        4. Peasants
            a) Delivered portion of their products to bureaucrats
            b) Besides supporting ruling classes, revenue also used for famine relief
            c) Provided heavy labor for public works
        5. Inca gods: Inti and Viracocha
            a) Venerated sun god called Inti, considered some other natural forces divine
            b) Also honored the creator god, Viracocha
            c) Sacrifices of animals or agricultural products, not humans
        6. Moral thought
            a) Concept of sin: violation of established order
            b) Concept of after-death punishment and reward
            c) Rituals of absolving sins through confession and penance

III. The Societies of Oceania

    A. The Nomadic Foragers of Australia
       1. Trade
          a) Peoples of Australia maintained nomadic, foraging societies
          b) Exchanged surplus food and small items during their seasonal migrations
          c) Pearly oyster shells were most popular item
          d) Peoples on north coast had limited trade with mariners of New Guinea
       2. Culture and religious traditions
          a) Intense concern with immediate environments
          b) Stories and myths related to geographical features
    B. The Development of Pacific Island Society
       1. Trade between island groups
          a) Clusters of islands formed regional trade networks
          b) Islands far apart from one another were rather isolated
       2. Population growth
          a) Population growth on all larger Pacific islands
          b) Hawai'i had 500 thousand people in the late 18th century
       3. The development of social classes
          a) Workers became more specialized and distinct classes emerged
          b) Social classes: high chiefs, lesser chiefs, priests, commoners
       4. Chiefly states
          a) A chiefly state could rule one or more islands
          b) Chiefs allocated lands, organized men into military forces
          c) Power of high chiefs as seen in commoners' *kapu* (taboos)
       5. Polynesian religion
          a) Priests served as intermediaries between gods and humans
          b) Gods of war and agriculture were common
          c) The *marae* Mahaiatea on Tahiti, a huge step pyramid for religious rituals

Significant Individuals

Itzcóatl (p. 480) — "The Obsidian Serpent," founder of Aztec empire; launched successful campaigns of imperial expansion from 1428 to 1440.

Motecuzoma I (p. 480) — Also known as Moctezuma or Montezuma; successor of Itzcóatl; powerful ruler of the Aztec empire; successful conquests from 1440 to 1469 laid down territorial foundation for the Aztec empire.

Pachacuti (p. 489) — Inca ruler, responsible for military conquests that laid foundation of Inca empire; reigned from 1438 to 1471.

Chapter Glossary

Ali'i nui (p. 496) — High chiefs of Hawai'i; powerful rulers who commanded enormous respect within their societies.

Aztecs (pp. 479-86) — See Mexica.

Cahokia Mound (p. 487) — Enormous earthen mound at Cahokia near East St. Louis, Illinois; built by Iroquois people for ceremonies or ritual performance.

Chanchan (p. 489) — Capital city of Chimu, near the modern city of Trujillo; had 50,000 to 100,000 residents during the late 14th century.

Chimu (pp. 488-89) — Powerful kingdom of Andean South America in the lowlands; dominated the Peruvian coast for about a century before the arrival of the Incas in the mid-15th century.

chinampas (p. 479) — Small plots of land made by the Mexica by dredging the rich and fertile mulch from the bottom of Lake Texcoco.

Chucuito (p. 488) — Kingdom of Andean America, dominated highlands region around Lake Titicaca (the broad region of modern Peru and Bolivia) between the 13th and early 15th centuries.

Cuzco (p. 490) — Capital city of Inca empire, served as administrative, religious, and ceremonial center; population might have reached 300,000 in the late 15th century.

Huitzilopochtli (p. 485) — War god of Aztecs; responsible for Aztecs' growing enthusiasm with human sacrifice.

Inca empire (pp. 489-90) — Largest empire ever built in South America; territory extended 2,500 miles from north to south and embraced almost all of modern Peru, most of Ecuador, much of Bolivia, and parts of Chile and Argentina; maintained effective control from the early 15th century until the coming of Europeans in the early 16th century.

Incas (pp. 489-90) — Most powerful people of Andean America; established Inca empire in the early 15th century that dominated Andean society until the coming of Europeans; spoke Quechua language.

Inti and Viracocha (p. 492) — Inca gods; Inti was the sun god while Viracocha was the creator god; cult of sun or Inti was the most popular among Incas.

Iroquois (pp. 486-87) — Woodlands people east of the Mississippi River; lived in settled communities dominated by women; also known for their buildings of enormous earthen mounds.

kapu (p. 496) — Taboos of Hawaiian people, which included such restrictions on common people as approaching or casting a shadow on the *ali'i nui* (high chiefs), and eating good food or wearing magnificent cloaks preserved for *ali'i nui*.

marae (p. 496) — Ceremonial precinct and temple structure of early Pacific societies; often had several terraced floors with a rock or coral wall designating the boundaries of the sacred space; largest one was *marae* Mahaiatea on Tahiti, which was constructed in the form of a step pyramid.

Mexica (pp. 479-86) — Also known as Aztecs; people of central Mexico; spoke Nahuatl language; built powerful Aztec empire that dominated Mesoamerica during the period from the mid-14th through the early 16th centuries.

Owascos (p. 486) — Woodlands people who lived in what is now up-state New York; five groups of Iroquois peoples emerged from Owasco society by about 1400 C.E.

Pueblo and Navajo (p. 486) — Peoples of southwestern North America; lived in settled societies with large populations.

Quetzalcóatl (pp. 484-85) — A god of Mesoamerica, honored for his support of arts, crafts, and agriculture.

quipu (p. 490) — Mnemonic devise used by Inca bureaucrats to keep track of their responsibilities; consisted of an array of small cords of various colors and lengths, all suspended from one large, thick cord; knots and marks on cords could record statistical information or historical events.

Tenochtitlan (pp. 477, 479) — Capital city of the Aztec empire, sitting on an island in Lake Texcoco; at its high point in the early 16th century, tribute from some 489 subject territories flowed into the city, and its population reached to about two hundred thousand.

Tezcatlipoca (pp. 484-85) — "The Smoking Mirror;" a god of Mesoamericans; honored for his power of giving and taking lives of people.

Toltecs (pp. 478-79) — People of central Mexico; spoke Nahuatl language; became dominant power of the region between 950 and 1150 C.E.

Tula (p. 479) — Capital city of Toltec empire, about thirty miles northwest of modern Mexico City; important center of weaving, pottery, and obsidian work.

Map Exercises

1. Study Map 20.1 on p. 481 and Map 20.2 on p. 489 of your textbook, and match each state on the left with its capital city on the right as follows:

State name	Capital name
Toltec empire	Tenochtitlan
Aztec empire	Chichen Itza
Maya empire	Cuzco
Chimu kingdom	Tula
Inca empire	Chanchan

2. Study Map 20.1, Map 20.2, and Map 20.3 (p. 494) of your textbook, and match each people on the left with a brief description on the right:

People	Description
Toltecs	Spoke Quechua, used *quipu*, dominated Andean America
Aztecs	Nomadic foraging hunters and gathers
Incas	Woodland people of North America, women in charge of society
Pueblo	Agriculturalists of chiefly states
Iroquois	Dominated Mesoamerica before 1150, capital city at Tula
Australians	Spike Nahuatle, developed *chinampas* and human sacrifices
Austronesians	Settled in North America, lived in stone and adobe buildings

Self-Test/Student Quiz

1. In Tenochtitlan, what struck Bernal Díaz (a Spanish army officer) and his fellow soldiers was

    a. the contrast between Tenochtitlan and Venice.
    b. the contrast between the Aztec marketplace and those of Rome and Constantinople.
    c. the contrast between peaceful exchange in the marketplace and the brutality of human sacrifices in temple.

2. The authors point out that by Aztec cultural standards, there was no difficulty reconciling the contrast between peaceful exchange of the marketplace and human sacrifice of temples because

    a. commercial exchange increased societal wealth while human sacrifice reduced the number of consumers—both were essential for the survival of Aztec society.
    b. trade enabled the complex society to function while sacrificial rituals pleased the gods and persuaded them to keep the world going.
    c. trading commodities and victims of human sacrifice were both from the tributary peoples conquered by the Aztecs.

3. After the collapse of Teotihuacan, central Mexico came under unified rule of

    a. the Toltecs.
    b. the Maya.
    c. the Mexica.

4. The term *Aztec* derives from *Aztlan*, meaning

    a. "the place of the seven legendary caves."
    b. "women stealers and land takers."
    c. "the people who eat fly eggs and snakes."

5. In which of the following ways did the marshy land of Lack Texcoco NOT help the Mexica to survive?

    a. The lake harbored plentiful supplies of fish, frogs, and waterfowl.
    b. The lake enabled the Mexica to develop the *chinampa* system of agriculture.
    c. The lake provided great convenience for communication with other peoples.

6. Unlike imperial states in the eastern hemisphere, the Aztec empire

    a. did not have merchants.
    b. had no elaborate bureaucracy.
    c. did not rely on military force.

7. It was the sumptuary law of the Aztecs that commoners should wear

    a. garments made of henequen.
    b. garments made of cotton.
    c. colored capes.

8. In Aztec society, priests

    a. served as rulers.
    b. preached their faith to the general public.
    c. served also as advisers to the rulers.

9. To a large extent, the Mexica enthusiasm for human sacrifice followed from their devotion to the god

    a. Tezcatlipoca.
    b. Huitzilopochtli.
    c. Quetzalcoatl.

10. All of the following describe the Iroquois peoples except

    a. they were woodlands peoples who lived in North America.
    b. women were in charge of villages and longhouses.
    c. they lived in stone and adobe buildings known as pueblo.

11. Before the 16th century, the peoples of Americas who had a script included

    a. the Mexica.
    b. peoples north of Mexico.
    c. the Incas.

12. Before the coming of Europeans, the state which dominated Andean America was

    a. Chucuito.
    b. Chimu.
    c. Inca.

13. The word *Inca* refers to

    a. residents of Cuzco.
    b. the people who spoke Quechua.
    c. a royal residence.

14. For the Incas, advanced education meant

    a. the ability to read and write using their own script.
    b. the ability to record and "read" information using *quipu*.
    c. to learn how to manipulate calendric symbols.

15. The Incas had a magnificent and extensive road system, which

    a. helped in the centralization of imperial power at Cuzco.
    b. encouraged long-distance trade and the rise of a large merchant class.
    c. facilitated cross-cultural communication between the Incas and other peoples.

16. The Inca government had state-owned storehouses, which were maintained for

    a. consumption needs of the royal family.
    b. public relief and social welfare.
    c. payments to governmental officials.

17. Differing from Aztec religion, Inca religion

    a. was monotheistic.
    b. had a moral dimension.
    c. had no rituals of sacrifice.

18. Different groups of aboriginal peoples in Australia

    a. shared the same deities, myths, and stories.
    b. engaged in trade regularly.
    c. settled in different locations suitable for agricultural cultivation.

19. In Hawai'i, the high chiefs were known as

    a. *kapu*.
    b. *heiau*.
    c. *Ali'i nui*.

20. The peoples of Pacific islands did not

    a. possess metallurgical technologies.
    b. build complex societies.
    c. develop any transportation technologies.

Textual questions for Analysis

1. How did the Mexica relate to the Toltecs and Teotihuacan?

2. Describe the political and economic organization of the Aztec empire.

3. Compare the religious beliefs of the Mexica and Incas.

4. How was the Inca empire organized politically and economically?

5. How did the Aztec and Inca societies differ from the societies of Pacific islands?

Documentary Evidence

1. Read the document excerpt on p. 484 of your textbook and answer the following questions: What did home mean to boys and girls of the Mexica? What would boys and girls do when they grew up? Did the different expectations of boys and girls mean that there was gender inequality in Aztec society? Why or why not?

2. Study carefully the two drawings on p. 492 of your textbook, and answer the following question: What do the two drawings tell us about the Incas' society, beliefs, politics, economy, and technology?

Chapter 21

Reaching Out: Cross-Cultural Interactions

Introduction and Learning Objectives

World history is not a mere sum of histories of individual societies, a point that can be illustrated most clearly in this chapter. Based on what has been discussed in previous chapters regarding the period from the 11th to the 15th centuries, this chapter brings together developments across global regions, in which people were not just making histories within their own boundaries, but reaching out to contact other peoples, to make new connections and discoveries and to bring in new technologies, ideas, and crops. Indeed, cross-cultural interaction among the peoples of the eastern hemisphere became more common, regular, and intensive than ever before, making the 11th to the 15th centuries a period that points toward growing global interdependence, a principal characteristic of modern world history.

The chapter begins with a discussion of three major forms of cross-cultural interaction during this period: long-distance trade, political and diplomatic travel, and missionary campaigns. The results were ever-expanding networks of trade that created interlocking connections among the peoples of the eastern hemisphere and made possible the trips of world travelers like Marco Polo and Ibn Battuta. The "Far East" was no longer a mere myth but a potential ally, commercial partner, and a target of religious conversion. The intensified cross-cultural contact not only facilitated agricultural and technological diffusion, but also unwittingly helped disease pathogens to spread. A stunning irony in the midst of the bright side of cross-cultural integration, the devastating bubonic plague broke out in the mid-14th century, with its heavy demographic toll severely disrupting societies and economies throughout Eurasia and north Africa.

But was it all that bad? Could the bubonic plague and horrible demographic disaster hold people back permanently from reaching out? The authors' discussion offers a stimulating evaluation of post-plague history in the 14th and 15th centuries. In China, the ravages of the plague were followed by Chinese resurgence, leading to the downfall of Mongol rule in 1368 and the rise of the Ming dynasty; at the same time, demographic recovery coincided with cultural revival so that the Confucian tradition once again became the dominant Chinese ideology. Soon after, the ambitious and confident Ming emperors began to organize grand naval expeditions that displayed Chinese power at almost all major ports in the Indian Ocean basin. Between 1405 and 1433, seven expeditions led by Zheng He unquestionably showed the world China's hegemony over the seas.

Equally significant was the rise of regional states in western Europe. Out of the chaos of demographic disaster, wars, famines, and revolts, the competitive and insecure kingdoms of Western Europe accelerated the process of state building during the 15th century, largely through means of direct taxation over citizens and maintenance of standing armies. Also, demographic recovery coincided with a cultural flourishing known as the Renaissance. Meanwhile, European mariners ventured from the Mediterranean into the Atlantic Ocean, which served as a highway to sub-Saharan Africa and the sea-lanes of the Indian Ocean basin. By the end of the 15th century, European explorers not only had established sea routes to India but also had made several return voyages to the American continents. Thus, unlike the Chinese reconnaissance of the Indian Ocean basin which suddenly ended in 1433, the European mariners inaugurated a new era in world history, which, in the following centuries, would bring all regions and peoples of the planet into permanent and sustained interaction.

After reading and studying this chapter, students should understand and be able to understand the following issues:

- extensive cross-cultural interactions from 1000 to 1500

- consequences of cross-cultural interactions

- agricultural and technological diffusion–its agents and consequences

- bubonic plague as a catalyst for social changes in China and western Europe

- the comparative and contrasting dimensions of Chinese reconnaissance in the Indian Ocean basin and European exploration in the Atlantic and Indian Oceans

Chapter Outline

I. **Long-distance Trade and Travel**

   A. Patterns of Long-Distance Trade
   1. Trading patterns
      a) Luxury goods of high value traveled overland on the silk roads
      b) Bulkier commodities traveled the sea-lanes of the Indian Ocean
   2. Trading cities
      a) Large trading cities had communities of foreign merchants
      b) Major emporia: strategic locations, good order, reasonable custom fees
      c) Example: Melaka with fifty thousand people and more than 80 languages
      d) Mongol conquests destroyed many cities, but maintained good order thereafter
   3. The Venetian traveler, Marco Polo
      a) The best-known long-distance traveler of Mongol times
      b) Traveled to China with his father and uncle
      c) Back to Venice in 1295 after 17 years in China
      d) Related his travels to fellow prisoners while a prisoner of war
      e) His book-length account of his travels became a best-seller, inspiring numerous European merchants
   B. Political and Diplomatic Travel
   1. Mongol-Christian diplomacy
      a) The 13th century was also a time of active diplomacy
      b) Mongols and Western Europeans, potential allies against Muslims
      c) Pope Innocent IV's envoys to Mongol khans, rejected by Mongols
   2. Rabban Sauma
      a) Dispatched by ilkan of Persia to the pope and European leaders, 1287
      b) Met kings of France and England and the pope, but the mission failed
      c) Ghazan's conversion to Islam in 1295 precluded possibility of alliance

3. Ibn Battuta
   a) Lands newly converted to Islam needed legal scholars
   b) Ibn Battuta, a Moroccan, served as *qadi* to the sultan of Delhi
   c) Later obtained a *qadi* post on Maldive Island
   d) Worked zealously to hear cases and promote Islamic values
   e) Consulted with Muslim rulers and offered advice
C. Missionary Campaigns
   1. Sufi missionaries also ventured to recently conquered or converted lands
   2. Christian missionaries attempted to convert Mongols and Chinese
   3. John of Montecorvino
      a) The first archbishop of Khanbaliq (Beijing) in 1307
      b) Translated the New Treatment, built several churches in China
      c) Baptized some Mongol and Chinese boys
      d) Missions to China continued, but won few converts
D. Agricultural and Technological Diffusion
   1. Spread of crops in sub-Saharan Africa through Muslim travelers
   2. Sugarcane
      a) European crusaders appreciated convenience of refined sugar of Muslims
      b) Sugarcane plantations spread all over the Mediterranean basin
      c) Plantations operated through slave labor
   3. Gunpowder technologies
      a) Mongols helped to spread gunpowder technologies to the West
      b) Gunpowder reached Europe by 1258
      c) Primitive cannons used by Chinese and European armies, early 14th century

II. Crisis and Recovery

A. Bubonic Plague
   1. Plague in China
      a) Mongols helped plague spread from Yunnan to China's interior, early 1300s
      b) In 1331, 90% of population of Hebei province was reportedly killed
      c) 1350s, 2/3 of population was killed in some other provinces
   2. Spread of plague
      a) Plague sparked epidemics in most of western Europe
      b) Frightful effects of the "Black Death"
         (1) Typically killed 60 to 70% of population
         (2) Wiped out entire populations of some small towns and villages
      c) Scandinavia and India escaped the plague's worst effects
      d) Also by-passed sub-Saharan Africa
   3. Population decline
      a) Chinese population dropped by 10 million from 1300 to 1400
      b) European population dropped by about 25% during the same period
      c) Islamic societies also suffered devastating population losses
   4. Social and economic effects
      a) Disrupted societies and economies of Eurasia and northern Africa
      b) In western Europe, rebellious workers demanded higher wages

B. Recovery in China: The Ming Dynasty
  1. Hongwu overthrew Mongol rule and established the Ming dynasty in 1368
  2. Ming centralization
      a) Reestablished Confucian educational and civil service systems
      b) Ruled China directly, without the aid of chief ministers
  3. Mandarins and eunuchs
      a) Relied heavily on mandarins—powerful officials as emissaries of emperors
      b) Also used eunuchs for governmental service
      c) The above two measures enhanced the authority of the central government
  4. Economic recovery
      a) Conscripted labor to repair irrigation systems
      b) Promoted manufacture of porcelain, silk, and cotton textiles
      c) Did not actively encourage trade, but trade flourished due to growth in production
  5. Cultural revival
      a) Actively promoted neo-Confucianism
      b) *Yongle Encyclopedia*, a remarkable anthology
C. Recovery in Western Europe: State Building
  1. Taxes and armies
      a) Demographic recovery and the Hundred Years' War
      b) Regional states were strengthened by the late 15th century
      c) State-building efforts through direct taxes and standing armies
  2. Italian states
      a) Italian city-states flourished from industries and trade
      b) Needed large numbers of officials and armies
      c) Levied direct taxes
  3. France and England
      a) Imposed direct taxes to compensate enormous expenses of Hundred Years' War
      b) Asserted authority of central government over feudal nobility
      c) Unlike France, England did not maintain a standing army
  4. Spain
      a) Marriage of Fernando and Isabel strengthened the state
      b) Sales taxes supported a powerful standing army
      c) Completed the *reconquista* by conquering Granada
      d) Seized southern Italy in 1494
      e) Sponsored Columbus's quest for a western route to China
  5. Competition among European states
      a) Frequent small-scale wars
      b) Encouraged military and naval technology
      c) Technological innovations vastly strengthened European armies
D. Recovery in Western Europe: The Renaissance
  1. Italian renaissance art
      a) City-states sponsored Renaissance innovations in art and architecture
      b) Artists studied human form and emotions
          (1) Masaccio's and Leonard da Vinci's paintings
          (2) Donatello's and Michelangelo Buonarotti's sculptures
  2. Renaissance architecture
      a) Simple and elegant style, inherited from Classical Greek and Rome
      b) Most impressive achievement—domed buildings
      c) Filippo Brunelleschi's cathedral of Florence

3. The humanists
    a) *Humanists*—scholars interested in literature, history and moral philosophy
    b) Preferred elegant and polished language of classical Greek and Rome
    c) Traveled throughout Europe searching for classical works
4. Humanist moral thought
    a) Re-evaluated medieval ethical teachings through classical works
    b) Promoted moral life while participating in the affairs of the world

III. Exploration and Colonization

A. The Chinese Reconnaissance of the Indian Ocean Basin
    1. Zheng He's expeditions
        a) Ming emperor permitted foreigners to trade in Quanzhou and Guangzhou
        b) Refurbished a large navy
        c) Sponsored seven massive naval expeditions in the Indian Ocean basin
        d) Purposes: controlling foreign trade, impressing foreign peoples
        e) Zheng He's ships were the largest marine crafts in the world
        f) Gift exchanges with the peoples visited
    2. Chinese naval power
        a) Zheng had little need to engage in hostilities with other peoples
        b) He ruthlessly suppressed pirates
        c) Intervened in a civil disturbance in Ceylon
        d) Expeditions enhanced Chinese reputation in the Indian Ocean basin
    3. End of the voyages, 1433
        a) Confucian ministers argued to redirect resources to agriculture
        b) Mongols mounted a new threat
        c) Imperial officials destroyed nautical charts
        d) Technology of building large ships was forgotten
B. European Exploration in the Atlantic and Indian Oceans
    1. Portuguese exploration
        a) European goals: to expand Christianity and commercial opportunities
        b) Portuguese mariners emerged as the early leaders
        c) Prince Henrique of Portugal embarked on campaign to spread Christianity
        d) Seized Moroccan city of Ceuta in 1415
    2. Colonization of the Atlantic Islands
        a) Venture into the Atlantic, colonized Madeiras and Azores Islands
        b) Discovered some other islands off the west coast of Africa
        c) Cultivated sugarcane on new islands, collaborated with Italian investors
    3. Slave trade
        a) Portuguese took advantage of established slave trade in Africa
        b) Thousands of slaves were delivered yearly to plantations on Atlantic islands
    4. Indian Ocean trade
        a) Portuguese searched for a sea route to Asian markets
        b) Bartolomeu Dias reached Cape of Good Hope, entered the Indian Ocean, 1488
        c) Vasco da Gama arrived at Calcut in 1498, returned to Lisbon with huge profit
        d) Portuguese mariners dominated trade between Europe and Asia
        e) Armed with cannons, Portuguese ships in Indian Ocean signaled the beginning of European imperialism in Asia

5. Cristóforo Colombo (known in English as Christopher Columbus)
   a) Conceived the idea of sailing west to reach Asian markets
   b) Plan was declined by Portuguese king, but sponsored by kings of Spain
   c) Set sail in 1492, made three voyages to the Caribbean region
   d) Other mariners soon followed Columbus and explored American continents

Significant Individuals

Bartolomeu Dias (p. 525) – Portuguese mariner; sailed around the Cape of Good Hope in 1488; proved to Europeans that it was possible to sail from Europe to the Indian Ocean.

Christopher Columbus (Cristóforo Colombo) (p. 525) – Genoese mariner; crossed the Atlantic Ocean and sailed to the Bahamas in 1492, with his voyage sponsored by the Catholic Kings of Spain.

Desiderius Erasmus of Rotterdam (p. 519) – Famous humanist of Renaissance times; worked diligently to prepare accurate texts and translations of the New Testament and other important Christian writings; responsible for publishing the first edition of the Greek new Testament in 1516.

Donatello (p. 519) – Italian sculptor of Renaissance times; lived from 1386 to 1466.

Filippo Brunelleschi (p. 519) – Famous Italian architect (1377-1446) of Renaissance times; responsible for the construction of a magnificent dome on the cathedral of Florence during the 1420s and 1430s.

Francesco Petrarca (p. 520) – Florentine humanist (1304-1374); worked diligently in searching for classical works of ancient Greek and Roman authors throughout Europe.

Hongwu (p. 515) – Founder of the Ming dynasty in China; an orphaned beggar who rose to power by joining rebellions against Mongol rule in China; toppled Mongol rule and proclaimed himself emperor in 1368; reestablished the Confucian educational and civil service systems.

Ibn Battuta (pp. 501-502, 508) – Muslim scholar of Morocco; world traveler of the 14th century; served as a *qadi* (judge) in north India and the Maldive Islands; lived between 1304 and 1369.

John of Montecorvino (pp. 509-510) – Italian Franciscan, went to China in 1291; became the first archbishop of Khanbaliq (Beijing) in 1307; baptized some six thousand individuals in China; translated the New Testament into Turkish; died in 1328.

Leonardo da Vinci (p. 519) – Italian painter of Renaissance times (1452-1519); relied on the technique of linear perspective to represent the three dimensions of real life on flat, two-dimensional surfaces.

Marco Polo (pp. 506-507) – Venetian merchant (1253-1324) who traveled to China while it was under Mongol rule; met Khubilai Khan and undertook many diplomatic missions for the Mongol government. His stories of travel circulated widely throughout Europe and deeply influenced Europeans' desire for exploring Chinese markets.

Masaccio (p. 519) – Renaissance painter of Italy, lived from 1401-1428.

Michelangelo Buonarotti (p. 519) – Famous Italian sculptor of Renaissance times; lived from 1475 to 1564.

Prince Henrique (p. 524) – Often called Prince Henry the Navigator, prince of Portugal, responsible for seizing the Moroccan city of Ceuta in 1415; adopted policy of encouraging Christian expansion and exploration of commercial opportunities overseas.

Rabban Sauma (p. 507) – Nestorian Christian priest of Turkish ancestry; dispatched in 1287 by the Mongol ilkhan of Persia as an envoy to the pope and European political leaders for seeking support; mission did not succeed.

Vasco da Gama (p. 525) – Portuguese mariner; took the first voyage around the tip of Africa to India in 1497.

Zheng He (p. 521) – Eunuch of the Ming court; led seven grand naval expeditions between 1405 and 1433; presented Chinese naval power to important port cities in the Indian Ocean basin.

Chapter Glossary

Several terms appearing in this chapter have already been defined in previous chapters and will not be repeated here.

Catholic Kings (p. 517) – Refers to Fernando of Aragon and Isabel of Castile, whose marriage in 1469 united the two wealthiest and most important Iberian realms and strengthened the state of Spain. The Catholic kings conquered the Islamic kingdom of Granada, established hegemony throughout most of the Italian peninsula, and sponsored Christopher Columbus's voyages.

Ming dynasty (p. 515) – Chinese dynasty after the Mongols' Yuan dynasty, established by the Hongwu emperor in 1368. Government became even more centralized under the Ming than before and returned to reliance on a Confucian-trained civil service.

Renaissance (pp. 518-20) – Cultural flowering of western Europe from the 14th through the 16th centuries. Arts and scholarly works reflected a revived interest in the classics of ancient Greece and Rome and a growing concern for individualism and secularism.

Yongle Encyclopedia (p. 516) – Enormous anthology compiled by Ming scholars and sponsored by the Yongle emperor. It contained all significant works of Chinese history, philosophy, and literature, and ran to about 23,000 manuscript rolls, each equivalent to a medium-sized book.

Map Exercises

1. Study Map 21.1 on pp. 504-505 in your textbook and answer the following questions:

    A) Suppose Marco Polo and Ibn Battuta were traveling at the same time. At which of the following locations might they have met: the Mali empire, Melaka, Khanbaliq, or Kilwa? Why is only one of these locations possible?

    B) What motivated Marco Polo and Ibn Battuta to undertake their long-distance travels? Why were long-distance travels important to world history?

2. Trace the routes and dates of the spread of the bubonic plague.

3. Study Map 21.2 on pp. 522-23 of your textbook and work on the following questions:

   A) Match the voyages on the left with the places visited on the right in the following table:

Voyages	Places
Zheng He's voyages	San Salvador
	Aden
Dias's voyages	Bay of Bengal
	Cape Verde Islands
Da Gama's voyage	Strait of Melaka
	Cape of Good Hope
Columbus's voyage	Cuba
	Indian Ocean basin

   B) Compare Chinese and European voyages of exploration in terms of purpose (or motivation), sponsorship, mariners, ships, routes, activities, and consequences.

Self-Test/Student Quiz

1. By alluding to the story of Ibn Battuta, the authors intend to illustrate the theme of the chapter –

   a. A Moroccan Muslim scholar could work in any kingdom of the Islamic world.
   b. Newly conquered Islamic lands needed legal scholars as *qadi*.
   c. The peoples of Ibn Battuta's time traveled more regularly than ever before, and cross-cultural interactions were thus intensified.

2. Which of the following was not among the major motives for long-distance travel between 1000 and 1500 C.E.?

   a. diplomatic missions
   b. tourist interests
   c. missionary campaigns

3. Generally speaking, a silk merchant in long-distance trade would prefer to travel

   a. overland.
   b. via sea-lanes.
   c. using camels.

4. A city could serve as a major emporium for long-distance trade networks if it

   a. was under control of a centralized government.
   b. enjoyed a strategic location.
   c. levied excessive customs fees.

5. The primary significance of Marco Polo's travels is the fact that

    a. he was the first foreigner who worked for a Chinese government.
    b. he discovered China, and opened the Chinese market to European merchants.
    c. his story deeply influenced European readers, and encouraged European merchants to participate in the lucrative trade of Eurasia.

6. In response to the envoys of Pope Innocent IV for military alliance against the Muslims in 1240s and 1250s, the Mongol khan

    a. agreed upon a military alliance but refused to convert to Christianity.
    b. demanded submission of Christians to the Mongols or face destruction.
    c. upon conversion to Christianity, agreed to marry the daughter of the king of Spain.

7. In seeking European support of the Mongols' campaigns against Muslim, Rabban Sauma's mission of 1287 was

    a. a failure.
    b. a huge success.
    c. a great embarrassment involving humiliation and the destruction of Rabban Sauma's reputation among the leaders of Europe.

8. Islamic legal scholars often traveled from one country to another and worked as *qadi* because

    a. this was the Islamic tradition established by Muhammad.
    b. recently converted lands needed Islamic scholars to enforce the *sharia*.
    c. working in foreign lands facilitated their undertaking of the *hajj*.

9. Working as a *qadi* in the Maldive Islands, Ibn Battuta

    a. became a famous Sufi mystic.
    b. heard legal cases.
    c. successfully persuaded island women to cover their breasts.

10. According to Franciscan John, a Roman Catholic missionary working in China during the early 14th century,

    a. Christians were treated very well by the Mongols.
    b. no Mongols or Chinese ever converted to Christianity.
    c. he had translated the New Testament into Chinese.

11. All of the following were lands hard hit by the 14th century plague except

    a. China and Europe
    b. north Africa and southwest Asia.
    c. India and sub-Saharan Africa.

12. The man who led rebellious forces and toppled Mongol rule in China was

   a. a eunuch.
   b. from a poor family.
   c. a famous Confucian scholar.

13. The regional states of western Europe were strengthened through

   a. direct taxation on citizens.
   b. reliance on knights as a military force.
   c. the Renaissance.

14. In Spain, the process of state building was accelerated by

   a. sponsoring Christopher Columbus's quest for a western route to China.
   b. making alliances with the Islamic states of northern Africa.
   c. the marriage of Fernando of Aragon and Isabel of Castile.

15. The term Renaissance refers to

   a. a revival of interest in commercial life and overseas exploration during the 15th and 16th centuries in western Europe.
   b. a remarkable cultural flowering that took place from the 14th to the 16th centuries, reflecting the continuing development of a sophisticated urban culture in western Europe.
   c. a remarkable demographic recovery from the devastating population losses caused by the bubonic plague.

16. The term humanist referred primarily to

   a. scholars interested in literature, history, and moral philosophy.
   b. scholars who advocated universal love for all fellow human beings.
   c. scholars interested in antireligious movements.

17. Which of the following was not a goal of Zheng He's expeditions:

   a. to impose control over foreign trade with China.
   b. to explore the possibility of Chinese merchants trading with European countries.
   c. to impress foreign people with the power and might of the Ming dynasty.

18. Which of the following was not a goal of European explorations:

   a. to discover the new lands called "America."
   b. to expand Roman Catholic Christianity.
   c. to search for commercial opportunities.

19. The Portuguese mariner who first sailed to the Cape of Good Hope in 1488 was

   a. Vasco da Gama.
   b. Bartolomeu Dias.
   c. Christopher Columbus.

20. Christopher Columbus's voyages were sponsored by

    a. Prince Henry the Navigator.
    b. the Catholic Kings.
    c. the king of Italy.

Textual Questions for Analysis

1. Discuss cross-cultural interactions from 1000 to 1500, focusing on long-distance trade, political and diplomatic missions, and missionary campaigns.

2. Trace the spread of gunpowder and discuss how gunpowder weapons contributed to state-building efforts in western Europe.

3. How did the bubonic plague spread? What were the social and economic effects of the plague?

4. What were the differences between Chinese and European explorations during the 15th century? What accounts for these differences?

5. Do you think the Mongols' conquests during the 13th century contributed to the rise of the western Europe in the following centuries? Why or why not?

Documentary Evidence

Christopher Columbus's First Voyage to America

Christopher Columbus conceived the idea of sailing west to reach Asian markets. His ambitious plan was rejected by the king of Portugal but was sponsored by the Catholic kings, Fernando and Isabel of Spain. On August 3, 1492, Columbus's fleet of three ships set sail, which crossed the Atlantic Ocean and arrived at San Salvador in the Bahamas in October. The following is part of the record from his first voyage. (From Christopher Columbus, *Journal of First Voyage to America*. New York: A. & C. Boni, 1924, pp. 20-26.)

Wednesday, Oct. 10th. Steered W.S.W. and sailed at time ten miles an hour, at others twelve, and at others, seven; day and night made fifty-nine leagues' progress; reckoned to the crew but forty-four. Here the men lost all patience, and complained of the length of the voyage, but the Admiral [Columbus] encouraged them in the best manner he could, representing the profits they were about to acquire, and adding that it was to no purpose to complain, having come so far, they had nothing to do but continue on to the Indies, till with the help of our Lord, they should arrive there.

Thursday, Oct. 11th. Steered W.S.W.; and encountered a heavier sea than they had met with before in the whole voyage....

After sunset steered their original course W. and sailed twelve miles an hour till two hours after midnight, going ninety miles, which are twenty-two leagues and a half.... At two o'clock in the morning the land was discovered, at two leagues' distance; they took in sail and remained under the squaresail lying to till day, which was Friday, when they found themselves near a small island, one of the Lucayos, called in the Indian language Guanahani. Presently they descried people, naked, and the Admiral landed in the boat, which was armed, along with Martin Alonzo Pinzon, and Vincent Yanez his brother, captain of the Nina. The Admiral bore the royal standard, and the two captains each a banner of the Green Cross, which all the ships had carried; this contained the initials of the names of the King and Queen each side of the cross, and a crown over each letter. Arrived on shore, they saw trees very green, many streams of water, and diverse sorts of fruits. The Admiral called upon the two Captains, and the rest of the crew who landed, and also to Rodrigo de Escovedo, notary of the fleet, and Rodrigo Sanchez, of Segovia, to bear witness that he before all others took possession (as in fact he did) of the island for the King and Queen his sovereigns, making the requisite declarations, which are more at large set down here in writing. Numbers of the people of the island straightway collected together. Here follow the precise words of the Admiral:

"As I saw that they were very friendly to us, and perceived that they could be much more easily converted to our holy faith by gentle means than by force, I presented them with some red caps, and strings of beads to wear up the neck, and many other trifles of small value, wherewith they were much delighted, and became wonderfully attached to us. Afterwards they came swimming to the boats, bringing parrots, balls of cotton threads, javelins and many other things which they exchanged for articles we gave them, such as glass beads, and hawks' bells; which trade was carried on with the utmost good will. But they seemed on the whole to me, to be a very poor people. They all go completely naked, even the women, though I saw but one girl. All whom I saw were young, not above thirty years of age, well made, with fine shapes and faces; their hair short, and course like that of a horse's tail, combed toward the forehead, except a small portion which they suffer to hang down behind, and never cut.... It appears to me, that the people are ingenious, and would be good servants; and I am of opinion that they would very readily become Christians, as they appear to have no religion. They very quickly learn such words as are spoken to them. If it please our Lord, I intend at my return to carry home six of them to your Highness, that they may learn our language. I saw no beasts in the island, nor other sorts of animals except parrots."

These are the words of the Admiral.

QUESTIONS TO CONSIDER

1. How did Columbus persuade his crew when the men were out of patience and began to complain about the seemingly endless voyage?

2. What were the motives of the voyage as revealed by the journal notes? Did the crew share the same motives as the King and Queen of Spain?

3. How did Columbus describe the native people of the island? How did such descriptions serve the purposes of European exploration?

Answer Key, Map Exercises

NOTE: THE PAGE NUMBERS LISTED HERE REFER TO PAGES IN THE TEXTBOOK, NOT THE STUDY GUIDE.

Chapter 11

11-3-A) Answer key: p. 269

a.   Not a good choice. The Huns invaded both parts of the Roman empire.
b.   Not the right choice, because the statement is correct.
c.   The right choice. The Franks ruled Gaul but did not invade Italy where Visigoths, Vandals, and Lombards struggled for control.
d.   Not the right choice. Angles and Saxons DID invade and settle in Britain.

11-3-B) Answer key: p. 269

a.   The right choice. The Huns' homeland was in central Asia.
b.   Not the right choice, because the statement is true.
c.   Not the right choice, because the statement is true.

Answer Key, Self-Test/Student Quiz Questions

NOTE: THE PAGE NUMBERS LISTED HERE REFER TO PAGES IN THE TEXTBOOK, NOT THE STUDY GUIDE.

Chapter 1

1-1. Answer key: p. 8

a. No. This is not the scholarly convention.
b. No. The first human beings of the fully modern type, the Cro-Magnon peoples, appeared on the earth about 40,000 years ago. These paleolithic people certainly belonged to prehistory.
c. Yes. This is just a convention without a scientific criterion. Writing is not an entirely reliable indicator of stages of societal development but provides historians with a convenient way of studying the past.

1-2. Answer key: p. 8

a. Yes. These include DNA, chromosomal patterns, life sustaining proteins, and blood types.
b. Not a good answer. The slight difference in genetic makeup and body chemistry have led to enormous differences in levels of intelligence.
c. Not really. Human brains are much larger and have big frontal regions that enable humans to develop reflective thought.

1-3. Answer key: pp. 7, 9

a. No. She was no longer an ape, despite her short, hairy body and limited intelligence. She walked upright on two legs and she had well-developed hands with opposable thumbs, which enabled her to fashion stone tools.
b. Yes. Literally, the term *Australopithecus* means "the southern ape," but *Australopithecus* was a hominid.
c. No. Although Lucy could walk upright on two legs, she could not talk, she knew nothing about controlling fire, and her brain was much smaller than that of *Homo erectus*.

1-4. Answer key: p. 9

a. Good choice. Apes and monkeys are not human species and do not belong to the hominids.
b. Not a good choice. These prehistoric, humanlike creatures were hominids.
c. Not a good choice. These are human species belonging to the family of hominids.

1-5. Answer key: pp. 9-12

a. Not a good answer. *Homo erectus* means "upright-walking human," but *Australopithecus* already knew how to walk upright on two legs.
b. No. *Homo erectus* themselves did not know how to domesticate animals.
c. The best answer. *Homo erectus* had well-developed language skills, while Australopithecus had at best a limited ability of verbal communication.

1-6. Answer key: p. 12

a. Not true. Each hunting band probably had about 30 to 50 members, and a large band would be not effective in hunting.
b. Not true. *Homo sapiens* were much larger in body size than *Australopithecus*.
c. The best answer. The term *Homo sapiens* means "consciously thinking human," because they had large brains well-developed in frontal regions where conscious and reflective thought takes place.

1-7. Answer key: pp. 14-16

a. No. There was no cultivation yet in the paleolithic era.
b. The best answer. Wild animals and naturally growing plants were the principal food sources.
c. Not really. Men most likely engaged in hunting while women played the major role in gathering.

1-8. Answer key: p. 15

a. No. In hunting and gathering society, individuals have little opportunity to accumulate private property.
b. The best answer. Because men and women were equally important in searching for food, paleolithic society probably did not promote the domination of one sex over the other.
c. No. Hunting and gathering peoples organized themselves through small bands. Without private property, the notion of family and clan had no meaning to them.

1-9. Answer key: pp. 16-17

a. Yes. The sites of Neandertal burials clearly show this point.
b. No. Archaeologists did not find cave paintings of Neandertal peoples.
c. No. We do not know if Neandertal peoples practiced ancestor worship or not.

1-10. Answer key: p. 17

a. No. Cro-Magnon peoples were more intelligent than *Homo sapiens* such as the Neandertal peoples.
b. Yes. Cro-Magnon peoples were the first human beings of the fully modern type indistinguishable from contemporary human beings.
c. No. Cro-Magnon people appeared about 40 thousand years ago, while *Homo erectus* lived between 1.5 million and 200 thousand years ago.

1-11. Answer key: pp. 17-18

a. No. The name "Venus figurines" was given by modern archaeologists after the Roman goddess of love. It does not mean that Cro-Magnon peoples honored Venus.
b. No. The figurines did not display love-making activities.
c. Yes. Although this is no more than educated guesswork, most scholars accept the point.

1-12. Answer key: p. 18-19

a. Not a good choice. Paintings in the living quarters of Cro-Magnon peoples might have been an aesthetic expression.
b. Good choice. No cave paintings indicate this.
c. Not a good choice. Most of the subjects in the paintings were large animals, which might reflect a desire for successful hunting through exercising "sympathetic magic"—to gain control over subjects by capturing their spirits.

1-13. Answer key: pp. 19-20

a. Yes. The era lasted from about 12 to 6 thousand years ago.
b. Not the best answer. Revolution is an event, not an era. Beside, the authors of the textbook believe that the term "agricultural revolution" is misleading.
c. Not a good answer. Paleolithic peoples before them had also used stone tools, but the neolithic peoples applied the use of these tools to agricultural cultivation, a fact that distinguishes them from the paleolithic peoples.

1-14. Answer key: p. 20-21

a. No. Quite to the contrary, agriculture required much more work than hunting and gathering.
b. Yes. This was important because hunting became increasingly difficult as foraging peoples made large animals scarce.
c. Not the best answer. This was not the most compelling reason for human communities to turn from foraging to agriculture although it certainly played a secondary role. The *causative* factor here was most likely the need to produce a more stable food supply for a growing population.

1-15. Answer key: pp. 21-26

a. Not a good choice. Agriculture brought about dramatic population growth.
b. Not a good choice. No longer foraging for food, neolithic peoples tended to settle in villages and towns.
c. Good choice. Invention of writing was not directly associated with agriculture, nor was it, strictly speaking, a social change.

1-16. Answer key: pp. 23-24

a. Yes. It came into existence before 8000 B.C.E.
b. No. The village might have had 2,000 residents, mostly cultivating wheat and barley.
c. No. The village did not have much trade or specialization of production as in cities.

1-17. Answer key: p. 24

a. Not the best answer. These crafts might have been important but did not involve the highest neolithic technologies brought about by specialized labor.
b. Not the best answer. Compared with answer c, these do not represent the greatest potential of specialized labor in neolithic times.
c. The best answer. These three enterprises represent the greatest potential of specialized labor and became essential elements of all neolithic societies of the eastern hemisphere.

1-18. Answer key: pp. 24-26

a. Yes. Differences in wealth and social status are clear from the quality of interior decorations in houses and the value of goods buried with individuals from different social classes.
b. No. The earliest metal with which humans worked systematically was copper, and iron had to wait for many centuries to be discovered after the era of Çatal Hüyük.
c. No. There is no evidence for this.

1-19. Answer key: p. 26

a. No. Neolithic people did not yet have the ability to write.
b. The best answer. These gods and goddesses were associated with the natural rhythms of agricultural society—life bearing, birth, growth, death, and regeneration of life.
c. No. Most agricultural peoples no longer lived in caves.

1-20. Answer key: p. 27

a. Yes. The world's first known cities grew out of agricultural villages and towns in the valleys of these two rivers during the period from roughly 4000 to 3500 B.C.E.
b. No. Cities emerged in Egypt through similar processes to those in the Tigris and Euphrates region, but not until later centuries.
c. No. Cities also emerged in China from agricultural villages and towns, but not until after those of the Tigris and Euphrates region.

Chapter Two

2-1. Answer key: pp. 31, 36

a. Not a good answer. The process itself seems not to have revealed the wealth of an agricultural society, although agricultural surplus made the specialized activity of mummification possible.
b. The best answer. Food offerings, of course, were largely agricultural products, and surviving tomb paintings depict scenes of farmers cultivating their crops.
c. Not a good answer. Pyramids were certainly not part of funerary customs for common Egyptians who were agriculturists, even though the large stone structures indicate the wealth of kings who controlled the enormous food surplus produced by Egyptian farmers.

2-2. Answer key: pp. 32-37, 41, and 46-48

a. Yes. But one should note that this is only a partial explanation for the formation of the two complex societies. Increased food supplies also made cities possible, and enabled government officials to tax the people and maintain military forces.
b. No. Writing systems were probably not invented by scholars. Pictographs, for instance, were first used by government officials, priests, and merchants for particular purposes.
c. A poor answer. Specialization, not food supply, might have encouraged craftsmen to experiment with iron metallurgy, but the technology of iron metallurgy was not indispensable for the formation of complex societies.

2-3. Answer key: p. 33

a. Not an adequate answer. Both the Hebrews and the Phoenicians were sub-groupings of Semitic peoples.
b. No. The Akkadians were a sub-group of Semitic peoples.
c. The best answer. Together, Sumerians and Semites, including speakers of Akkadian, Hebrew, Aramaic, and Phoenician, made up the two major groups of people inhabiting ancient Mesopotamia.

2-4. Answer key: p. 35

a. Not a correct answer. In world history, most government headquarters have been located in cities, but not many of them have been city-states.
b. Yes. Autonomy of the city government was the crucial factor defining a city-state.
c. No. Cities can never be economically self-sufficient since they cannot produce their own food supply.

2-5. Answer key: p. 35

a. No. The process of desiccation of the Sahara, which occurred from 5000 B.C.E., was probably beyond the knowledge of Herodotus, who traveled in Egypt about 450 B.C.E.
b. No. This was not why Herodotus proclaimed Egypt "the gift of the Nile," even though many Egyptians drank the water of the Nile.
c. Yes. This is precisely what Herodotus meant by "the gift of the Nile."

2-6. Answer key: pp. 35-36

a. Wrong. Egypt did not face many external dangers that threatened Mesopotamia: the Red Sea, the Mediterranean Sea, and hostile deserts protected it from foreign invasion.
b. No. The centralized state made the building of monumental pyramids possible, not the other way around.
c. Yes. Menes unified Egypt through conquest in about 3100 B.C.E. and established a centralized state that lasted for about 3000 years.

2-7. Answer key: pp. 31, 36

a. Not the best answer. Mummification and other funeral rituals were also practiced by some common people.
b. Yes. Without such an optimistic belief in an afterlife, mummification and pyramids would have been unnecessary.
c. No. There is no evidence to support such a statement.

2-8. Answer key: p. 36

a. Yes. It was also known as Cheops. It was built with 2,300,000 limestone blocks, some weighing up to 15 tons each, with an average weight of 2.5 tons. It is estimated that the pyramid required the services of some 84,000 laborers working 80 days per year for 20 years.
b. No. We do not know if Menes ever had a pyramid.
c. No. Horus was not a person but the sky god of Egypt.

2-9. Answer key: pp. 38-39

a. No. In the prologue of the laws, Hammurabi proclaimed that the gods had named him "to promote the welfare of the people, ...to cause justice to prevail in the land...."
b. Wrong. Earlier Mesopotamian rulers had promulgated laws perhaps as early as 2500 B.C.E., and Hammurabi borrowed liberally from his predecessors in compiling his laws.
c. Yes. By the laws, offenders suffered punishments resembling their violations.

2-10. Answer key: pp. 41-42

a. Yes. Mesopotamian metal workers invented bronze metallurgy in about 3000 B.C.E., while the same technology became widespread in Egypt only after the 17th century B.C.E. Mesopotamian craftsmen began to experiment with iron metallurgy as early as the 4th millennium B.C.E., and the same technology became known much later in Egypt.
b. Not a good answer. The city walls of Babylon of the 7th and 6th centuries B.C.E. might have been bigger than an Egyptian pyramid in size, but that did not necessarily mean that the technology of building such city walls was more advanced than that used to build a pyramid.
c. Wrong. When Sumerians built their watercraft in Mesopotamia by about 3500 B.C.E., Egyptians began to navigate the Nile.

2-11. Answer key: pp. 43-44

a. Not a good answer. The two sets of terms, although sounding different, were actually very much the same thing. The pharaoh, for instance, was the king of Egypt.
b. Not right. Both the pharaohs of Egypt and the kings of Mesopotamia, one way or another, relied on divine power to legitimize their authorities.
c. Yes. This was a major difference in the political organizations of these two societies.

2-12. Answer key: p. 45

a. Yes. Since the major concern of the laws was with legitimacy of offspring and reputation of the husband, to sell wives and children was not a violation of the law.
b. No. Their partners also deserved death by drowning.
c. No. The laws recognized only men as heads of households.

2-13. Answer key: 45-46

a. Not a good answer. Mesopotamians insisted on the virginity of brides at marriage, so it was LIKELY for a man to divorce his bride should she have lost her virginity to another man.
b. Not a good choice. Although only one woman had become a pharaoh in Egypt, a powerful lady very well may have had such a dream.
c. Yes. This was most unlikely because Mesopotamian women wore veils only after they married.

2-14. Answer key: pp. 46-47, 52

a. Not quite right. Both cuneiform and hieroglyphic writings were more advanced than pure pictographic writing.
b. Best choice. This combination enabled a scribe not only to record common items, but also to convey abstract ideas.
c. Wrong. Alphabetic writing was invented by the Phoenicians in about 1500 B.C.E.

2-15. Answer key: p. 48

a. Not the best answer. How the sciences and religions were related in these two societies is not quite clear to us. The pharaoh himself and many Sumerian kings claimed to be divine powers themselves, not just secular rulers.
b. No. It seemed that priests, scribes, and officials were more noble than these two professions.
c. Best answer. Remember that both Mesopotamia and Egypt were agricultural societies.

2-16. Answer key: p. 48

a. Not the best answer. The book mentioned the building of the city walls but it was not the theme of the book.
b. Best answer. The book explored the themes of human friendship, relations between humans and the gods, and especially the meaning of life and death.
c. Not the best answer. The book contained a religious message but it did not describe religious rituals and practice.

2-17. Answer key: pp.48-49

a. Wrong. The pharaoh was not above the gods. He was a god king.
b. Wrong. For much of Egyptian history, the people honored a number of gods, such as Amon-re and Osiris. A Mesopotamian might have believed in several deities, but each city held one deity in especially high esteem.
c. Yes. The national gods of Egypt were Amon-Re and Osiris. The gods in Mesopotamia were city-gods.

2-18. Answer key: pp. 48-49

a. No. Historians have no knowledge of such a fact.
b. Yes. Egyptians believed that death was inevitable but that it was also a gateway into afterlife. The Mesopotamians believed not only that it was inevitable but that it was the end of existence.
c. Not a good answer. Mesopotamians were probably yearning for immortality as much as the Egyptians were, as may be seen from *The Epic of Gilgamesh*.

2-19. Answer key: pp. 49-50

a. Wrong. The cult demanded observance of high moral standards.
b. Yes. Remember, Osiris weighed the heart of the dead against a feather symbolizing justice, and those with heavy hearts carrying a burden of evil and guilt did not merit immortality (see the illustration on p. 50 of your textbook).
c. No. Osiris was a god responsible for fertility.

2-20. Answer key: pp. 50-51

a. Not the best answer. It was true before 1300 B.C.E. After that, however, the Hebrews began to honor only one supreme god, known as Yahweh.
b. Yes, the best choice. Yahweh, the creator and sustainer of the world, was the only supreme god as taught by Moses and worshipped by the Hebrews after 1300 B.C.E.
c. No. Although Hebrews' monotheism profoundly influenced the development of Christianity and Islam, they were not the founders of the two religions.

2-21. Answer key: p. 52

a. Not the best answer. Although the Phoenicians were especially good at industry and trade (because of their meager land), these were not their best contribution to world history.
b. Not the best answer. Although the Phoenicians adapted some aspects of Mesopotamian cultures, they have become even more famous in world history for the invention of alphabetic writing.
c. Yes. By about 1500 B.C.E. the Phoenician scribes simplified Mesopotamia's cuneiform writing system by devising twenty-two symbols representing consonants. Their alphabetic writing system influenced the writing systems throughout most of the world.

2-22. Answer key: p. 53

a. Yes. The Nubians did not enjoy much in the way of fertile land but developed high skills of metal working. Their ironworking spread to other regions of sub-Saharan Africa where iron was abundant, and because of the Nubians, iron metallurgy became prominent throughout much of the continent.
b. Not a good answer. Even though it was true that Egyptian culture had a great influence on surrounding areas, Nubians were probably not the primary agents of spreading Egyptian culture.
c. Not the best answer. Although the invasion happened, how it altered the development of African history as a whole is hard to say.

Chapter 3

3-1. Answer Key: pp. 58-59

a. Not right. Harappan writing is still indecipherable.
b. Not right. The earliest Harappan physical remains are still inaccessible because they are below the water table.
c. Yes. Archaeologists have discovered sites of about one hundred Harappan cities since the 1920s, and all of them are above the water table.

3-2. Answer key: p. 59

a. Yes. These were the main foodstuffs of the Dravidian peoples.
b. No. These were major foodstuffs of East Asia.
c. No. Dravidians might have loved these Mesoamerican foods if they had been available. There is no evidence to suggest that they were.

3-3. Answer key: p. 60

a. Not a good answer. This speculation is not tenable because Harappa was not a multi-racial society. Moreover, to adopt the same standards of weights and measures was not necessarily an oppressive policy.
b. The best answer. This is the speculation of the authors of the textbook, although some other historians doubt the existence of a strong Harappan state.
c. Not the best answer. One wonders how commercialization would have affected architectural styles and brick sizes.

3-4. Answer key: p. 61

a. Yes. Many people lived in one-room tenements in barracks-like structures, while a few families lived in large houses of two and three stories. Large houses had their own wells and built-in brick ovens.
b. Not the best answer. Social distinctions are not made evident through these items because almost all houses had private bathrooms with showers and toilets that drained into city sewage systems.
c. No. These are not parts of archaeological excavations although they could be good indicators of social distinctions.

3-4. Answer key: p. 62

a. Not a good answer. An answer to this question must be based on what we know of Harappan religions, not what we know about the religions of other societies.
b. No, it does not. The figure of the dancing girl was very lively, but we do not know if it was associated with creation and procreation.
c. Yes. Hinduism, which developed after Harappan society, contained some deities of fertility that were similar to those found in Harappan cities.

3-6. Answer key: p. 62

a. No. Good speculation, but there is no evidence to support it.
b. The best answer, at least according to the textbook. When the Indus valley had been deforested and became a desert, it was impossible to support the large populations of the two major cities (each had about thirty-five to forty thousand people).
c. No. The Aryans did not suddenly conquer Harappan society. Their migration to India was a gradual and relatively peaceful process.

3-7. Answer key: pp. 63-65

a. Not the best answer. In this case, historians have to rely on linguistic and archaeological studies to trace the migration process.
b. The best answer. In the late 18th and 19th centuries, linguists noticed that many languages of Europe, Persia, and India featured remarkable similarities in vocabulary and grammatical structure, which became the key clues for the history of migration.
c. Not the best answer. Without linguistic evidence, physical remains discovered by archaeologists would not automatically reveal the origins of people on the subcontinent.

3-8. Answer key: pp. 64-65

a. Not a well-educated guess. The Indo-European migrations were conducted primarily through integration with other peoples, not through military conquests.
b. Not entirely true. The Indo-Europeans still lived in tribal society, not more advanced than the society of the Dravidians.
c. The best answer. Horse-riding gave them great advantages over hunting-gathering peoples as well as the peoples of settled agriculture. Indo-Europeans also differentiated peoples by color.

3-9. Answer key: pp. 65-66

a. No. Historical periods were devised by historians, not by the Aryans themselves.
b. Yes. Since the four Vedas are important historical sources for understanding early Aryan society in India, scholars refer to this period as the Vedic Age.
c. No. This may have been true, but is an insufficiently precise answer to the question posed.

3-10. Answer key: pp. 67-68

a. Not the best answer. *Jati* referred to subcastes determined largely by occupations. One caste could have as many as one or two thousand *jati.*
b. No. *Brahmins,* or the caste of priests, was merely one of the four main castes.
c. Yes. *Varna* was a Sanskrit word meaning "color," used by the Aryans to distinguish social classes. Later, as the distinction between "wheat-colored" Aryans and darker-skinned Dravidians disappeared, the term *varna* was still used for social classification of the people. *Varna* has close connotations with the Portuguese word *caste.*

3-11. Answer key: pp. 68-69

a. Yes. Remember, Aryan India did not have a central government or powerful state. The caste system played a large role in maintaining social order.
b. Not true. The caste system evolved (as seen in the increasingly complicated *jati*) to accommodate social changes and to reflect new social conditions.
c. Not true. It was not easy for an individual to go beyond what his or her *jati* permitted.

3-12. Answer key: p. 69

a. No. According to the hymn, gods like Indra and Agni were born from Purusha's mouth when he was sacrificed by other gods.
b. No. To be sacrificed was hardly Purusha's intention, nor did he intend to create the four castes.
c. Yes. According to the hymn, the four castes were generated from Purusha's mouth, arms, thighs, and feet, respectively.

3-13. Answer key: p. 70

a. The right choice. The schist carving illustrates the devotion of a mother to her child, not women's subordination to men.
b. Not the best answer. The *Lawbook* subjected women to the guidance of the principal men in their lives.
c. Yes. Compared with answer b, this one is better. According to the custom of *sati*, a widow voluntarily threw herself on the funeral pyre of her deceased husband to join him in death, a sign that women were encouraged to view themselves as subservient to men.

3-14. Answer key: pp. 71-72

a. Yes. Both ritual sacrifices and the god of war were important for the Aryans to cope with the instability and turbulence of early Vedic society.
b. No. Historical records do not indicate the importance of fertility and immortality in Aryan religion.
c. Not a good answer. Only later in the Vedic age, beginning about 800 B.C.E., did Aryan religious thought undergo a shift from ritual sacrifices to spirituality.

3-15. Answer key: pp. 72-74

a. Not the best answer. Without the religious tradition of the Dravidians, Aryan spirituality might have taken a different direction.
b. Not the best answer. The Upanishads incorporated the religious values of both the Dravidians and the Aryans.
c. Yes. The Upanishads drew inspiration both from the Aryan Vedas and from Dravidian concepts of reincarnation and natural spirits.

3-16. Answer key: p. 73

a. No. *Samsara* meant to return to earth in a new incarnation, a painful cycle of birth and rebirth that an individual soul tried to escape.
b. Yes. *Moksha* is the state of a deep, dreamless sleep that came with permanent liberation from physical incarnation, or permanent union with Brahman, the universal soul.
c. No. *Karma* accounted for the specific incarnations which could not be avoided because they were pre-determined by one's behavior and conduct in former lives.

3-17. Answer key: pp. 73-75

a. Not the best answer. The authors argue that, "It would be a mistake to consider these doctrines merely efforts of a hereditary elite to justify its position and maintain its hegemony over other classes of society" (p. 75; underlining added for emphasis).
b. Not the best answer. The authors also assert, "The doctrines of samsara and karma certainly reinforced the Vedic social order" (p. 73).
c. The best answer. In other words, the doctrines of the Upanishads can be viewed as a form of intellectual or philosophical speculation used to justify social inequalities (among other things).

3-18. Answer key: p. 74

a. No. This was just one of the analogies used by the man to explain the nature of reality.
b. Yes. The man used a number of analogies just to explain this single point.
c. Wrong. Quite the opposite, the man explained that each person was not a separate individual, but rather was identical to Brahman and hence a participant in universal reality.

3-19. Answer key: pp. 73, 75

a. Wrong. Quite the contrary, an individual should try not to be attached to the material world, in order to identify oneself with the ultimate reality of Brahman.
b. No. The doctrine of karma can be seen as a doctrine of ethical standards. The individuals who lived virtuous lives and fulfilled all their duties could expect rebirth into a purer and more honorable existence.
c. Right. Those who accumulated a heavy burden of karma by not observing ethical standards would suffer in a future incarnation by being reborn into a miserable existence.

3-20. Answer key: p. 75

a. Not the best answer. Although the statement itself is true, it is not the particular reason a believer should respect animals and insects.
b. The best answer. To be merciful, a devout believer would not wish to cause additional suffering to the miserable souls embodied in animals and insects.
c. No. Actually, both answers are true, but answer b is better than answer a, as explained above.

Chapter 4

4-1. Answer key: pp. 79-80

a. Not the best answer. Too general.
b. Not the best answer. Not specific enough.
c. Right. These were the specific values promoted by the three sage kings.

4-2. Answer key: pp. 80-81

a. Not the best answer, although the river was indeed turbulent in the summer season.
b. Yes. The deposit of silt lifted the bottom of the river, often caused floods, and changed the course of the river.
c. Not a good answer. Loess also provided fertile soil for agriculture.

4-3. Answer key: p. 81

a. Yes. Finely painted pottery and bone tools have been excavated at Banpo, a site of Yangshao society.
b. No. Yangshao society existed in north China, while rice was cultivated in south China.
c. No. Bronze metallurgy was invented in the Shang dynasty which came later.

4-4. Answer key: p. 81-82

a. Not the best answer. Scholars suspect that the site at Erlitou might have been the capital of Xia but there is still insufficient evidence to prove this conjecture.
b. No. This statement is wishful thinking.
c. Yes. The grand effort of controlling the Yellow River demanded large-scale, formal organization.

4-5. Answer key: p. 82

a. Yes. Bronze metallurgy was the most advanced technology of the time, and an army armed with bronze weaponry would have had a great advantage over those without.
b. No. Shang rulers monopolized bronze technology for their own uses.
c. Not a good answer. Weapons could be made from many other materials.

4-6. Answer key: p. 83

a. Incorrect. These items were excavated from this tomb.
b. Incorrect. These items were excavated at this site.
c. Good choice. The Shang people seemed not to have mastered the technique of mummification and no paintings were found in this tomb.

4-7. Answer key: pp. 84-85

a. Yes. In justifying their overthrew of the Shang, the Zhou founders developed the theory of "the mandate of heaven," which influenced Chinese politics thereafter.
b. No. This fact might have been true, but it is not the foundation of a political theory.
c. Not the best answer. By saying this, the Zhou king simply articulated his new theory of "the mandate of heaven."

4-8. Answer key: p. 85

a. Not the best answer. A ruler could be challenged if he did not obey the will of heaven or lost the mandate of heaven.
b. Best answer. The Zhou theory assumed an interrelationship between heaven and earth, and the ruler functioned as a mediator between the two in order to maintain cosmic harmony and balance.
c. Not true. A Chinese king or emperor was a secular ruler, not a god king like an Egyptian pharaoh.

4-9. Answer key: p. 85

a. No. "The son of heaven" did not rely on democratic participation of his subjects.
b. Yes. The entrusted in return owed allegiance, tribute, and military support to the central government.
c. No. This division of powers was a much later creation of modern European states.

4-10. Answer key: p. 85

a. Yes. In addition to the decentralization of Zhou administration, the abundance of inexpensive iron production made its monopolization impossible. As a result, subordinate rulers could arm themselves with iron weapons to resist the central government.
b. No. Iron weapons were not inferior to bronze weapons.
c. No. There is no evidence to support this statement.

4-11. Answer key: pp. 87-90

a. Not the right choice. Note that this question is framed in the negative; all of these groups were social classes in ancient China.
b. Not the right choice. Note that this question is framed in the negative; all of these groups were social classes in ancient China.
c. Right. There were no organized religions, so there was no priestly class. Moreover, the rulers of the first three dynasties were kings, not emperors, and monks appeared much later in Chinese history.

4-12. Answer key: p. 90

a. No. Unlike gods or deities, the spirits of ancestors were believed to have influence only on their own surviving families.
b. Yes. It was such practical goals that made the veneration of ancestors so popular.
c. Not really. Ancestors were always respected by their descendants whether or not they produced efficacious rewards.

4-13. Answer key: p. 91

a. Not true. Female ancestors were also worshipped by family descendants.
b. Not true. Female members also participated in honoring ancestors.
c. Yes. By doing so, the family patriarch became the mediator between the living and the dead.

4-14. Answer key: p. 92

a. Not a good answer. Settled agriculture had already emerged during neolithic times, long before the three dynasties.
b. The best answer. Although we are not sure about the process, the large states might have brought military and political contributions of men into sharp focus, making a matrilineal society no longer appropriate.
c. No. There is no demonstrated connection between bronze technology and the shift from matrilineal society.

4-15. Answer key: p. 93-94

a. The best answer. By predicting events or telling the future, diviners certainly helped kings to make decisions.
b. No. This has nothing to do with the oracle bones at the time they were created. Only in the 1890s, when oracle bones were first discovered were they called "dragon bones," and used as potent medicine to relieve pains.
c. Not the best answer. Although various important events were recorded on the bones, they were used primarily for asking questions about how best to shape the future.

4-16. Answer key: p. 94

a. Yes. It is the writing of ideas, often combining two or more pictographs into one word to convey complex or abstract notions.
b. Not the best answer. Pictographs alone were not enough to represent complex ideas. The majority of Chinese characters are ideographs.
c. No. Phonetic or alphabetic writing never developed in China.

4-17. Answer key: p. 95

a. An incorrect choice. The *Book of Songs* was a collection of poems and the *Book of Changes* was about foretelling the future.
b. An incorrect choice. The *Book of History* was the political history of the Zhou dynasty; the *Book of Etiquette* was about polite behavior and rituals.
c. Right. These were not part of Zhou culture because organized religions did not exist during Zhou times.

4-18. Answer key: pp. 96-97

a. Not the best answer. Language was not a fundamental barrier for cultural assimilation.
b. Yes. The steppelands were inhospitable to cultivating crops, and by herding animals, the nomads could not possibly live in towns and cities.
c. Not a good answer. Nomadic peoples did not always treat the Chinese as their enemies.

4-19. Answer key: p. 98

a. Not the best answer. There is no evidence to indicate organized conquests and colonization.
b. Yes. Many indigenous peoples adopted Chinese ways while others fled.
c. No. The indigenous peoples of the Yangzi region were not different races from the Chinese.

4-20. Answer key: p. 99

a. Yes. It was situated in the central region of the Yangzi, and governed its affairs autonomously.
b. No. The people of Chu accepted developing Chinese traditions and language.
c. No. The society of Chu was very much the same with that of north China.

Chapter 5

5-1. Answer key: pp. 103, 112

a. No. The Maya seemed not to emphasize sexual potency or fertility in their religious rituals.
b. No. There was no goddess to be found in Maya beliefs.
c. Yes. Maya priests taught that the gods had shed their blood to water the earth and nourish crops of maize, and that humans should imitate the sacrifice.

5-2. Answer key: p. 104

a. No. This is precisely when and where migrations took place.
b. Yes. Human groups took advantage of these bridges by migrating to new lands.
c. No. There is no evidence to support this claim.

5-3. Answer key: p. 106

a. Not a good choice, because this statement is true.
b. Good choice. Humans trekked from Siberia to Alaska over the Bering land bridge, which later became the Bering Straits when high water returned about 20,000 years ago.
c. Not a good choice because this statement is true. At the time of the great migrations, settled agriculture was not yet practiced.

5-4. Answer key: p. 105

a. No. Various food crops, such as beans, chili peppers, avocados, squashes, and gourds were native to Mesoamerica.
b. No. Large animals such as horses and oxen were unknown to early Mesoamericans.
c. Yes. Later they also cultivated tomatoes along with a large array of other previously known food crops such as beans, chili peppers, avocados, squashes, and gourds.

5-5. Answer key: p. 105

a.   The best answer. Not only were the Olmecs the originators of the first complex society, but Olmec cultural traditions influenced all complex societies in Mesoamerica until the 16th century.
b.   No. The designation "rubber people" was given to the Olmecs because the region they inhabited was filled with rubber trees.
c.   No. They lived on the coast of the Gulf of Mexico, near the modern Mexican city of Veracruz.

5-6. Answer key: p. 106

a.   No. We have no surviving paintings of the Olmecs.
b.   No. There have been no discoveries of books produced by the Olmecs.
c.   Yes. Olmec ceremonial centers featured a complex of temples, pyramids, altars, stone sculptures, and tombs of rulers. It took a tremendous quantity of human labor to produce such centers.

5-7. Answer key: p. 107

a.   The best answer. The Olmecs deliberately destroyed their capitals, most likely during civil conflicts.
b.   Not a good answer. Human sacrifice was only subjected on war captives, which should not have caused Olmec society itself to decline.
c.   There is no evidence to suggest this.

5-8. Answer key: pp. 105, 108

a.   The best answer. San Lorenzo was one of the Olmec ceremonial centers, just as Tikal was one of the Mayas' ceremonial centers.
b.   No. Chichén Itzá was a state of the Maya, which organized a loose empire in Northern Yucatan.
c.   No. La Venta was another ceremonial center of the Olmecs.

5-9. Answer key: pp. 108-109

a.   Not a good choice. All of these structures were important in Tikal.
b.   Good choice. These two terms did not refer to real animals, but were common names for Mayan kings.
c.   Not a good choice. All these classes were important in the bustling city of Tikal.

5-10. Answer key: pp. 110-11

a.   Yes. The solar year had 365.242 days which governed the agricultural cycle, while the ritual year had 260 days divided into twenty months for ritual purposes.
b.   No. It contained a 52-year cycle; the traditional Chinese calendar contained a 60-year cycle.
c.   No. It was devised by Maya priests with sophisticated mathematical knowledge.

5-11. Answer key: pp. 111-12

a.   Not really. It contained both ideographic elements and symbols for syllables.
b.   No. Maya scribes wrote works of history, poetry, and myth, and kept genealogical, administrative, and astronomical records.
c.   Yes. Maya paper was made from beaten tree bark or vellum made from deerskin. The books were destroyed by Spanish conquerors and missionaries in the 16th century.

5-12. Answer key: pp. 114-16

a. No. Paintings and murals suggest that Teotihuacan was a theocracy of sorts.
b. No. Until about 500 C.E. there was little sign of military organization in Teotihuacan.
c. The best answer. They were both heirs of the Olmecs.

5-13. Answer key: p. 116

a. This is the best answer. Unlike the situation for the Maya, where there is much speculation about their decline but little hard evidence, archeological evidence suggests much more strongly for Teotihuacan that they were defeated and destroyed by military actions against them by surrounding peoples.
b. This is not the best answer. All of these causes are speculated for the decline of the Maya but not for the people of Teotihuacan.
c. No, because scholars are relatively certain, based on archeological evidence, that Teotihuacan was destroyed by military action against it.

5-14. Answer key: p. 116

a. Yes. Because of the geographical barriers in this region, Andean society developed largely in isolation.
b. No. This was the heartland of Olmec society.
c. No. These were the locations of Austronesian societies.

5-15. Answer key: pp. 117-18

a. No. The name of the cult was given by modern scholars after the modern town of Chavín de Huantar, one of the cult's most prominent sites.
b. The best answer. Its popularity can be seen from the extensive temples and carvings throughout the territory occupied by modern Peru.
c. Not a good answer. We simply do not know the precise meaning of the cult. One theory suggests that the cult arose when maize became an important crop in south America.

5-16. Answer key: pp. 118-19

a. Yes. The Mochica state dominated the coasts and valleys of northern Peru during the period 300 to 700 C.E.
b. Not a good answer. Mochica was not simply a ceremonial center but rather a state that oversaw a wide range of activities of the people who lived within its influence.
c. No. See answer a above.

5-17. Answer key: pp. 118-19

a. This is the best answer.
b. There is no evidence to support this point.
c. Not the best answer. Although religious belief was very important to all early peoples in the Americas, the Mochica state was especially successful in marshaling military might against its neighbors to consolidate its power.

5-18. Answer key: p. 119

a. This is the best answer for two reasons. First, these were not typical scenes in Mochican society; rather, they are reminiscent of scenes from early Chinese society. Secondly, Mochican art works were ceramics, not paintings.
b. Not the best answer because these were typical scenes from Mochican society and thus represented in Mochican ceramics.
c. Not the best answer because these were typical scenes from Mochican society and thus represented in Mochican ceramics.

5-19. Answer key: pp. 120-21

a. Not a good answer. There were not many environmental differences between these two islands and before 3000 B.C.E., the peoples of both islands were hunters and gatherers.
b. The best answer. The Austronesians colonized New Guinea but not Australia.
c. Not a good answer. The question of whether or not the peoples of Australia had kangaroos to eat is not sufficient to determine why they did not practice agriculture. If the Austronesians had introduced agriculture to Australia as they had done in New Guinea, the aboriginal peoples there might also have turned to agriculture.

5-20. Answer key: pp. 122-23

a. Not a good choice. Without these skills, their migrations to the Pacific islands would have been impossible.
b. Not a good choice. Population pressure and internal conflicts on one island often worked as a positive force for migration, pushing small groups to search for new opportunities on other islands.
c. The best choice. There is no evidence of a relationship between chiefly political organization and the impetus for migration.

Chapter 6

6-1. Answer key: p. 132

a. Wrong. The Sumerians did not migrate to Persia, although the Sumerian empires ruled Persia for centuries before the 6th century B.C.E.
b. Incorrect. The migration was not from Anatolia, but from central Asia.
c. Yes. The migration to Persia was accomplished during the centuries before 1000 B.C.E.

6-2. Answer key: pp. 132-33

a. Right choice. The Medes and Persians knew little about agriculture and certainly knew nothing about rice cultivation.
b. Not a good choice. The statement well describes the two peoples.
c. Not a good choice. Both of these were characteristics of the two peoples.

6-3. Answer key: p. 133

a. No. He was remembered for his cultural toleration of the peoples he conquered.
b. Not a good answer. The statement is true, but it has nothing to do with his title.
c. Yes. The Persians of Cyrus's time retained their nomadic tradition.

6-4. Answer key: p. 134

a. No. Should Cyrus have lived long enough, he certainly would have mounted a campaign against Egypt. But he was mortally wounded in 530 B.C.E. by nomadic raiders from the north.
b. Yes. He was the son of Cyrus, and conquered Egypt in 525 B.C.E.
c. No. He may have conquered Egypt if Cambyses had not done it several year before him.

6-5. Answer key: pp. 135-36

a. The best answer. Concrete examples include construction of the Royal Persian Road, the new capital at Persepolis, the division into satrapies, and standardization of taxes, coins, and laws.
b. No. The Persian rulers generally displayed a high level of toleration of different cultures and traditions within their empires.
c. No. Imperial spies were conscripted to watch over the regional satraps, not over local people.

6-6. Answer key: p. 136

a. No. It took about ninety days or three months.
b. No. When the road was accomplished, the battle of Marathon (490 B.C.E.) had not occurred yet.
c. Yes. This amazing speed of communication was achieved by keeping fresh horses in 111 postal stations along the Royal Road which could be used by imperial couriers traveling from one station to the next.

6-7. Answer key: pp. 137-38

a. No. These rebellions were successfully repressed, and they were not called the Persian Wars.
b. Yes. The rebellious Greek city states successfully resisted the mighty military forces of the Achaemenid empire.
c. No. Alexander's invasion of the Persian empire occurred about one and half centuries after the Persian Wars.

6-8. Answer key: p. 138

a. No. Quite to the contrary, his army was far smaller than the Persian army.
b. Not a good answer. He proclaimed himself heir to the Achaemenid rulers only after he conquered the Achaemenid empire.
c. Yes. In all these respects, his army was better off than the Persian army.

6-9. Answer key: p. 138

a. Not true. They actually retained the Achaemenid systems.
b. Yes. The Seleucids were from Macedonia, and they were seen as foreigners by the native Persians.
c. No. The Seleucid empire was established at the beginning of the 4th century B.C.E., while the Islamic empire rose from the 7th century C.E. onward.

6-10. Answer key: pp. 138-39

a. Good choice. The Parthians primarily were NOT cultivators.
b. Not a good choice. The statement is true.
c. Not a good choice. The Parthians did have a formidable heavy cavalry, which enabled them to defeat the Seleucids and enlarge their imperial holdings.

6-11. Answer key: pp. 139-40

a. No. Although on three occasions Roman armies captured the Parthian capital at Ctesiphon, the Parthian empire as a whole never was in danger of falling to the Romans.
b. No. Islamic conquests began in the mid-7th century.
c. Yes. The Sasanids overthrew the Parthians in 224 C.E.

6-12. Answer key: p. 141

a. Not a good answer. The rise of bureaucratic stars might have undermined the positions and power of the old warrior class and clan leaders, but the latter were never completely displaced.
b. Yes. Both warriors and bureaucrats were powerful and indispensable.
c. Not the best answer. The kings or emperors reigned and ruled the empires.

6-13. Answer key: p. 142

a. No. The purpose of building underground canals was not to save land. In classic Persian times, availability of land seemed not to be a problem.
b. Not the best answer. Although classic Persia had numerous slaves and some slaves participated in the construction, *qanat* were built primarily by free peasants.
c. Yes. Should water have been plentiful and readily available for irrigation, *qanat* would have been unnecessary.

6-14. Answer key: p. 143

a. Yes. This can be demonstrated by the example of Gimillu, a slave who served the temple community of Eanna in Uruk.
b. No. To marry or not was a decision made by slave owners, not by slaves themselves.
c. No. Slaves worked at tasks set by their owners, not by themselves.

6-15. Answer key: p. 144-45

a. Not really. Although long-distance trade was very important, the empire would have collapsed if there had been insufficient agricultural surplus.
b. No. The peoples under the Persian empires lived in highly complex societies such as those of Mesopotamia, Egypt, and India, very different from societies that subsisted on the nomadic practices of animal herding.
c. Yes. Agriculture was the economic foundation of all complex societies in classical and traditional times.

6-16. Answer key: p. 144

a. Yes. A merchant could conduct his trade in Mesopotamia or Egypt under the same laws and using the same coins. The empires provided good trade routes on land and sea which made up a vast commercial network.
b. Not a good answer. Commercial activities were well-protected by imperial rule, but there seemed to be no commercial laws.
c. No. There is no evidence to indicate the existence of state-owned banks, although private banks were common in large cities.

6-17. Answer key: p. 145

a. The best answer. Zoroastrianism emerged from the teachings of Zarathustra, a man from a Persian aristocratic family. The religious ideas of Zoroastrianism were highly original.
b. Not really. Of course, the formation of Zoroastrianism was influenced by various pre-existing religious beliefs, but it was not a borrowed religion.
c. No. Persian Zoroastrianism was not related to the Indian Upanishads.

6-18. Answer key: pp. 145-46

a. Not the best answer. The holy book, called the Avesta, was a later compilation of the earliest teachings from various Zoroastrian priests, teachings that perished over the centuries. As such, it is not the best source to study the teachings of Zarathustra.
b. Yes. Over the centuries, the Zoroastrian priests (*magi*) took special effort and diligence to preserve Zarathustra's own compositions through oral transmission. The *Gathas* were believed to be Zarathustra's own works.
c. No. The Vedas were sacred books of the early Indians.

6-19. Answer key: p. 146

a. Not a good choice. Zoroastrianism taught about such a cosmic conflict.
b. Not a good choice. This was part of Zoroastrian teachings.
c. Good choice. Asceticism was not part of Zoroastrianism. Quite to the contrary, Zoroastrianism allowed human beings to enjoy wealth, sexual pleasure, and social prestige, as long as they did so in moderation and behaved honestly toward others.

6-20. Answer key: p. 149

a. Yes. Islamic armies toppled the last Persian empire in 651 C.E. Although the conquerors did not outlaw Zoroastrianism altogether, they placed political and financial pressure on the *magi* and Zoroastrian temples, which eventually forced the believers to turn to Islam.
b. Not the best answer. The Sasanid government was a zealous sponsor of Zoroastrianism until it was toppled.
c. Not a good answer. Zoroastrian believers converted more to Islam than to Christianity.

Chapter 7

7-1. Answer key: p. 153

a. Not a good answer. His comprehensive work of Chinese history was well-received by his contemporaries.
b. No. Voluntary castration for a career of eunuch was not rare in imperial China, but Sima Qian's castration was neither voluntary nor with the intention of becoming a eunuch. Rather, it was inflicted on him as a form of punishment.
c. Yes. His open defense of an imperially-dishonored general enraged the emperor, who ordered the historian to undergo this humiliating punishment.

7-2. Answer key: pp. 154-55

a. Yes. He was a successful educator and he gave advice to the rulers of different states. Through teaching and offering advice, his ideas spread and left an enduring mark on Chinese history.
b. Not the best answer. He once was an ambitious petty official but that did not make him a great sage of China.
c. Not the best answer. He traveled from state to state for selling his ideas and recommending himself to high official posts, but he was not remembered for his accomplishments as a traveler. His ideas were the source of great philosophical reflection, but he himself did not write these down. Instead, the master's sayings were recalled and recorded in the *Analects* by his students after his death.

7-3. Answer key: pp. 155

a. Not the best answer. For Confucian moralists, talent alone was never enough to be a *junzi*.
b. Yes. A *junzi* was a man of both superior morality and superior talent.
c. No. A *junzi* was supposed to be courteous, respectful, and even humble before others.

7-4. Answer key: p. 156

a. Right choice. This definition is incorrect. *Ren* meant an attitude of kindness and benevolence or a sense of humanity.
b. Not the right choice, because the definition is correct.
c. Not the right choice, because the definition is correct.

7-5. Answer key: pp. 156-57

a. Not a good answer. Mencius strongly believed that human nature was basically good. Moral education was to restore the goodness of human nature, not to improve evil human nature.
b. Yes. He emphasized the Confucian virtue of *ren,* and government by benevolence and humanity meant that rulers would levy light taxes, avoid wars, support education, and encourage harmony and cooperation.
c. No. Government by strict laws was a Legalist idea. To Mencius and other Confucians, moral education was more important than laws.

7-6. Answer key: pp. 158-59

a. Not the best answer. Differing from natural laws of modern scientists, the *dao* was also believed to govern the workings of human society.
b. Yes. But don't forget that the *dao* governs the workings of the world only in a passive and yielding manner.
c. Not the best answer. *Dao* existed in everything. Things like water penetrating rocks were merely some examples used by Daoists to explain the passive and yielding nature of the *dao*.

7-7. Answer key: p. 159

a. No. That would be Confucian activism, which was precisely counterbalanced by the Daoist doctrine of *wuwei*—disengagement from world affairs.
b. No. Daoism cast profound doubt over the constructed nature of ethical standards or success, which more often than not ran counter to the *dao*. Daoists were skeptical of those who strove too hard for worldly success.
c. Yes. The Daoist way of life was natural, simple, unpretentious, and self-content, and could be achieved only through *wuwei*.

7-8. Answer key: pp. 159-60

a. Not a good answer. The saying meant that individuals could strive for a better society and personal success as Confucianists, but also needed time for reflection and introspection, as Daoism advised.
b. The best answer. For many centuries, it was rather common for Confucian scholar-officials to devote their private hours and retirement to reflection on human nature and the place of humans in the larger world as Daoism taught.
c. No. Good imagination, but who said the Chinese, or any other people, were passive at night?

7-9. Answer key: p. 161

a. No. Quite to the contrary, these lines of work were viewed by Legalists as distracting the people from agricultural production for the state and therefore should be discouraged.
b. No. By promulgating strict laws, the Legalists intended to harness individuals' energy for the interests of the state, not to give the people legal rights. The popularity of the state was not much of a concern for the Legalists.
c. Yes. Agriculture and military might were viewed as the foundations of a state's strength.

7-10. Answer key: p. 164

a. Yes. Some 460 Confucian scholars were buried alive because of their open criticism of Qin policies, and books without utilitarian value were burned.
b. No. The Qin state standardized written script, not spoken dialects.
c. No. Sima Qian lived in the Han dynasty, long after the First Emperor's rule.

7-11. Answer key: p. 165

a. Not the best answer, because the army was made of pottery (or terra cotta), and was not composed of real men.
b. Yes. These were real men and women, not terra cotta.
c. No. The emperor's remains have still not been identified. Jade burial suits have been excavated in Han tombs (see the illustration on p. 172 of your textbook), not in Qin tombs.

7-12. Answer key: pp. 165-66

a. No. There was no military coup against the emperor.
b. Right. Massive public works plus cruel punishments caused massive peasant rebellions which brought down the dynasty.
c. No. Because of the short life of the empire, court factions seemed not to be a devastating problem affecting the survival of the Qin dynasty.

7-13. Answer key: p. 166

a. Not the best answer. He did not rely exclusively on his relatives for support
b. Not the best answer. He did not rely exclusively on bureaucratic officials.
c. The best answer. Liu Bang experimented with a third path between Zhou decentralization and Qin over-centralization. He soon found that his relatives alone were not entirely reliable, and turned for additional assistance to members of a centralized bureaucracy.

7-14. Answer key: pp. 167-68

a. Not an adequate answer. Han Wudi literally meant the "Martial Emperor," but the term itself does not convey the full scope of Han Wudi's accomplishments in expanding the territory of the empire.
b. No. Wang Mang, the usurper of the Han throne, not Han Wudi, is called a "socialist emperor" by some modern historians because of his land reforms.
c. Yes. Han Wudi brought the nomadic Xiongnu into submission, extended China into central Asia, and colonized Vietnam and Korea.

7-15. Answer key: p. 168

a. No. With the downfall of the Qin dynasty, Legalism lost its political favor in China. A Legalist legacy was the reality of the Han dynasty, but no one would openly admit to being a Legalist.
b. No. The imperial university was not a modern school for training bureaucrats. The term "political science" as we understand it did not exist in ancient and traditional China, nor did law schools.
c. Yes. Confucianism was the only Chinese tradition at that time sufficiently developed to provide rigorous intellectual discipline.

7-16. Answer key: p. 169

a. No. Han Wudi did not have territorial ambitions with respect to the Persian empire.
b. The best answer. The Han tried to pay tribute to the Xiongnu, and to arrange marriages between female members of the Han imperial family and Xiongnu leaders, but none of these efforts pacified the Xiongnu or stopped their raids against Chinese villages and towns.

c. No. It was true that in disciplining his forces, Maodun ordered soldiers to shoot their arrows at his favorite horse, his wife, his father's best horse, and finally, his father. But none of these events had anything to do with Han Wudi's decision to advance into central Asia.

7-17. Answer key: p. 171

a. The best answer. The origins of sericulture in China predate the ancient Xia dynasty in the Yellow River valley. During the Han dynasty, knowledge of sericulture and silk production spread to the south as well.
b. Not the best choice, because the statement is correct. Other peoples of Eurasia obtained silk from varieties of silkworms inferior to those used by the Chinese, and the fabrics were of a poor quality.
c. No, this statement is correct.

7-18. Answer key: pp. 153, 171

a. Yes. It was troublesome to write on bamboo strips and to tie them into rolls, but they were commonly used nonetheless to compose books and long essays.
b. Not a good answer. Silk was very expensive and was therefore used only to write imperial edicts or short letters.
c. No. Sima Qian died in 90 B.C.E., long before the invention of paper around 100 C.E.

7-19. Answer key: p. 173

a. No. Wang Mang himself knew nothing of the modern concept of "socialism." Some modern historians have called him a "socialist emperor" because of his desire to redistribute land to the peasantry.
b. Not a good answer. Wang Mang did not do much to solve the problem of court factions.
c. Yes. Wang Mang ordered officials to break up large estates and redistribute the lands to landless farmers. This radical land reform was unsuccessful.

7-20. Answer key: p. 173

a. Not the best answer. The uprising was not the only series of events that lead to the breakdown of the dynasty.
b. Not the best answer. Power struggles among court factions paralyzed the central government, but peasant rebellions also weakened the dynasty.
c. The best choice. Peasant rebellions undermined the legitimacy of the Han dynasty, while internal struggles of different court factions eventually led to the disintegration of the empire.

Chapter 8

8-1. Answer key: p. 177

a. Not a good answer, because Megasthenes, the author, did make this claim in his book.
b. Not a good answer. This information was recorded in the *Indika*.
c. The best answer. The Greek author portrayed India as a wealthy land with well-established cultural traditions.

8-2. Answer key: p. 178

a. Not true. India was much less isolated than China.
b. Yes. For the most part, classical India was dominated by petty kingdoms instead of by powerful empires.
c. Not a good answer. "Backwardness" is hard to define in cross-cultural comparisons.

8-3. Answer key: p. 178

a. Not a good answer. Foreign armies never conquered the entire Indian subcontinent but only the northwestern part of India.
b. Not true. The Indians did not adopt foreign religions during the period of foreign occupation.
c. The best answer. The withdrawal of Alexander from the Punjab (325 B.C.E.) presented the king of Magadha a rare opportunity to unify India.

8-4. Answer key: p. 179

a. Yes. He was the creator of the Mauryan empire, the first state to bring a centralized and unified government to most of the Indian subcontinent.
b. No. Chandra Gupta was the founder of the Gupta empire, which appeared a few centuries later.
c. No. Ashoka Maurya was the grandson of Chandragupta. The Mauryan empire reached its highest point during Ashoka's rule.

8-5. Answer key: pp. 179-80

a. No. It would be interesting to compare Legalist statecraft of China and the measures of the *Arthashastra*, for the two appeared at about the same time and had very much in common. But in terms of their development at the time, the two were unrelated to each other.
b. The best answer. Notice that "imperial spies" in the Persian and Chinese empires were formal government officials, but spies in the Indian empire held no government posts.
c. No. Kautalya's advice included how to wage wars against neighboring kingdoms. There is no historical record to indicate that Kautalya was a believer in Jainism or Buddhism.

8-6. Answer key: pp. 180, 191

a. Not true. No emperors in classical India ever unified the entire subcontinent or extended control beyond the subcontinent.
b. Yes. This he did, immediately after the war which caused about 100,000 deaths of Kalingans by his estimation.
c. No. Tradition holds that Chandragupta did these things, not Ashoka, his grandson.

8-7. Answer key: p. 182

a. The best answer. Because of acute financial and economic difficulties, the rulers could no longer hold the realm together.
b. No. These sound like the problems of Chinese rulers, not those of the emperors of classical India.
c. Not a good answer. Only after financial problems had severely weakened the Indian empire did the Greek-speaking rulers of Bactria begin to encroach upon northwestern India.

8-8. Answer key: pp. 182-83

a. Not true. The Gupta empire was not larger in size than the Mauryan empire.
b. Not really. It's hard to tell.
c. Yes. The Guptas left local governing to their allies in various regions of the empire.

8-9. Answer key: p. 183

a. The best answer. The cost of self-defense drained the financial resources of the Gupta empire and the weakened dynasty could no longer sustain itself.
b. No. This did not happen.
c. Not a good answer. Initially, the Gupta repelled the Huns, but by the end of the 5th century, the Gupta empire was too weak to organize resistance and the Huns moved across the Hindu Kush almost at will, establishing several kingdoms in northern and western India.

8-10. Answer key: pp. 184-85

a. Not a good answer. There is insufficient information to indicate this.
b. The best answer. Flourishing towns in the countryside and growing trade, both domestic and foreign, seemed to be the best indicators of escalating economic development in classical India.
c. Not the best answer. Although agriculture was the economic foundation of India society, towns, manufacturing industries, and trade were better indicators of the rising tide of economic development in classical India.

8-11. Answer key: p. 185

a. Not a good answer. Indian gold was not mined by ants, despite the fact that the Greek ambassador, Megasthenes, wanted people to believe so. Moreover, gold was not an export item of India.
b. No. Alexander left India in 325 B.C.E., too early for him to carry around Roman coins.
c. The best answer. Indian pepper was so popular in the Mediterranean basin that the Romans established direct commercial relations and built several trading settlements in southern India.

8-12. Answer key: p. 186

a. Not the right choice. This statement is true.
b. Good choice. Inter-caste marriage was strictly forbidden by laws and customs.
c. Not a good choice. Such an ideal wife can be found in the two great Indian epics, *Mahabharata* and *Ramayana*.

8-13. Answer key: p. 186

a. No. *Jati* were guilds of various occupations, not independent communities producing everything for their own members. They also had to pay taxes to the state.
b. Yes. Indeed, *jati* assumed much of the responsibility for maintaining social order in India.
c. Not a good answer. *Jati* were guilds, but played much more important roles in Indian society than in other societies.

8-14. Answer key: p. 187

a. Not really. The authors do not imply that castes and *jati* were out of date, but rather, were continuously developed to cope with social and economic change.
b. No. Both Jainism and Buddhism, which practiced asceticism, became popular in classical India.
c. Yes. The authors discussed three religions that emerged alongside economic development and social change.

8-15. Answer key: pp. 187-88, 195

a. Yes. This was a principle of non-violence toward all living things or their souls. By observing this principle, Jainists believed that they could escape the cycle of repeated incarnations and attain a state of bliss.
b. No. *Jina* meant "the conqueror," which was the title given by Jainists to their great teacher, Vardhamana Mahavira.
c. No. *Kama* was an important concept in Hinduism, meaning the enjoyment of social, physical, and sexual pleasure. Jainists certainly could not allow *kama* to spoil their asceticism.

8-16. Answer key: p. 189

a. Yes. He perceived the suffering of human lives and began to search for enlightenment and explanation for suffering.
b. No. This was typically a Jainist concern.
c. No. This was typically a concern of Hinduism.

8-17. Answer key: p. 190

a. No. This phrase referred to the first sermon of the Buddha, which took place at the Deer Park of Sarnath about 528 B.C.E.
b. No. These were the basic doctrines of Buddhism, providing an explanation for human suffering and means to eliminate it. The doctrine itself was not the religious goal of the believers.
c. The best answer. To attain *nirvana* was the fundamental goal of the believers. *Nirvana* meant an escape from the cycle of incarnation and entrance into a state of perfect spiritual independence.

8-18. Answer key: pp. 190-91

a. No. The authors' discussions do not lead to such an implication.
b. Yes. Indeed, both religions taught detachment from the world, which played down the importance of social distinctions based on caste and *jati*.
c. No. The authors do not imply this. The popularity of the two religions does not necessarily mean that many people became monks in Jainist or Buddhist monasteries.

8-19. Answer key: p. 191

a. Not the right choice. This statement is true.
b. Not the right choice. The statement is true.
c. The best choice. He did not abdicate his throne or abandon his family. Did he escape the cycle of incarnation and attain *nirvana*? Only Buddha knows.

8-20. Answer key: pp. 192-93

a. Yes. The notion of *boddhisatva* was not taught by the Buddha. In Mahayana, the *boddhisatvas* intentionally delayed their entry into *nirvana* to help other who were still struggling.

b. Not true. Mahayana theologians did not revise the Four Noble Truths which were shared by all Buddhist sects as the basic doctrine.

c. Not true. In early Buddhism the Buddha was not honored as a god, but as a sage or a holy man. Mahayana Buddhism changed the Buddha into a god.

8-21. Answer key: p. 196

a. Not a good answer. This statement cannot explain the immense popularity Buddhism once attained in India.

b. Not true. The rivalry between Hindu *brahmins* and Buddhists did not lead to violence or suppression.

c. The best answer. Because of their comfortable lives in monasteries, Buddhist monks increasingly lost their passion to communicate their message to society at large as their predecessors had.

8-22. Answer key: pp. 194-95

a. The right choice. Hinduism did not restrict sexual activities. One of principal aims of human life, according to Hinduism, was *kama*—the enjoyment of social, physical, and sexual pleasure.

b. Not a good choice, because the statement is true.

c. Not a good choice, because the statement is true.

Chapter 9

9-1. Answer key: p. 199

a. Yes. In the two epics, the Greeks appeared to be almost as comfortable aboard their ships as on land.

b. Not the best answer. Piracy might be part of their lives, but Homer did not portray them as PROFESSIONAL pirates.

c. No. There is no such description of the ancient Greeks in the two epics.

9-2. Answer key: p. 200-202

a. Not the right choice. The statement is true—the Minoans had a script known as Linear A, while the Mycenaeans adapted Linear A and devised their own script known as Linear B.

b. Not the right choice. The statement is true—enormous palaces have been discovered in Crete, especially at Knossos, built by the Minoans. Massive stone fortresses and palaces were also found throughout the southern part of the Greek peninsula, known as Peloponnesus, built by the Mycenaeans.

c. The best choice. The origin of the Minoans is not clear, while the Mycenaeans were Indo-European migrants to the Greek peninsula.

9-3. Answer key: the whole chapter

a. Yes. The chronological order is correct: Sappho (active during the years around 600 B.C.E.), Socrates (470-399 B.C.E.), Philip II (359-336 B.C.E.).

b. No. The Trojan War was a legend in Homer's epics, which might or might not have been a real historical event.. The Persian War took place before the Peloponnesian War.
c. Wrong order. Sparta was one of the poleis of classical Greece (800-338 B.C.E.), while the Antigonid empire was one of the empires of the Hellenistic era (4th through 1st century B.C.E.).

9-4. Answer key: pp. 203-204

a. No. Many tyrants could be very popular leaders.
b. Yes. The term *tyrant* was used to refer to irregular routes some men took to power.
c. No. Tyrants could be popular leaders, but not all popular leaders were tyrants.

9-5. Answer key: p. 204

a. Not the right choice, because this was indeed part of Spartan life.
b. The right choice. The helots were servants of the Spartan state but technically were not slaves.
c. Not the right choice, because this was indeed part of Spartan life. From this one also should note that because most men were in active military service, women enjoyed greater freedom and power in Spartan society than women in other poleis.

9-6. Answer key: p. 205

a. The right choice. Sophocles was one of the great Greek tragedians during the 5th century B.C.E.
b. Incorrect. Solon was a great democratic reformer of Athens during the 6th century B.C.E.
c. Incorrect. Pericles was a popular democratic leader of Athens during the 5th century B.C.E.

9-7. Answer key: p. 205

a. No. Only adult free males could be citizens. Women and slaves were ineligible.
b. Not really. Solon only abolished debt enslavement. Slavery was still important in Athens.
c. The best answer. To ensure that aristocrats would not undermine his reforms, Solon provided representation for the common classes in the Athenian government by opening the councils of the polis to any citizen wealthy enough to devote time to public affairs.

9-8. Answer key: p. 206

a. Yes. The rocky and mountainous Greek peninsula could not possibly support a large population, and colonization was the primary means of releasing population pressure.
b. Not really. There is no historical evidence for this.
c. Not a good answer. Colonization by the Greeks did not involve military conquests, nor was it guided in a purposeful fashion by any of the powerful city-states.

9-9. Answer key: pp. 207-208

a. Not a good choice. This statement is true.
b. Not a correct choice. Greek colonization in Anatolia led to direct conflict between the Greeks and the Persians.
c. The right choice, because this was not a consequence of Greek colonization. Through colonization, the Greeks were neither weakened nor isolated.

9-10. Answer key: p. 209

a. No. The League was not an Athenian organization, but formed by most poleis of Greece.
b. Yes. The League was created after the Persian War (500-479 B.C.E.) to discourage further Persian actions in Greece.
c. No. The League was actually a strong source of civil conflict within the Greek world because many poleis resented the powerful leadership position of Athens within the League.

9-11. Answer key: p. 209

a. The best answer. The war involved all the Greek poleis, which were divided into two armed camps under the leadership of Athens and Sparta.
b. No. This was not what the Peloponnesian War was about.
c. No. This was not true of the Peloponnesian War, although it more accurately describes later conflict within the Greek world.

9-12. Answer key: pp. 208, 210

a. No. The Persian army led by Xerxes captured and burned Athens in 480, but the Athenians finally triumphed over the Persians at the battle of Salamis.
b. The best answer. By 338 B.C.E. Philip II had overcome all organized resistance and brought Greece under his control.
c. Not the best answer. When Alexander succeeded Philip II in 336, Greece had been unified by his father.

9-13. Answer key: p. 211

a. No. His troops did not stop at Bactria, but proceeded further to the east.
b. Yes. His troops crossed the Indus River and entered into the Punjab.
c. No. Alexander probably did not know of the existence of China.

9-14. Answer key: p. 212

a. Not a good answer. The unification did not make Greece more Hellenistic than before.
b. Not the best answer. It does not explain what the Hellenistic age was about.
c. The best answer. During this age, Greek or Hellenistic culture expanded its influence to Persia, northern India, and Egypt.

9-15. Answer key: p. 213

a. The right choice. This was not true. Alexandria was the capital of Ptolemaic empire. The other two Hellenistic empires had their own capitals.
b. Not the right choice, because the description is true. Alexandria was the most important port of the Mediterranean.
c. Not the right choice. Alexandria was indeed the cultural capital of the Hellenistic world; its museum and library were especially famous.

9-16. Answer key: p. 214

a. No. Quite the opposite was true. Its mountainous terrain and rocky soil were not good for grain farming.
b. No. Mountains and hills made travel and communication very difficult in the Greek peninsula.
c. Yes. This hallmark of Greek geography explains the importance of trade for Greece.

9-17. Answer key: p. 215

a. Yes. Winners would receive olive wreaths and become celebrated heroes in their home poleis.
b. No. Women were not allowed.
c. No. Non-Greeks were not allowed.

9-18. Answer key: p. 216

a. Not a good answer. It was likely for a court to reject such a petition because a husband had the legal right to abandon newborns of his wife.
b. Compared with the other two choices, this is the best one. In most poleis, women could not own landed property even though they could operate small businesses.
c. Not the best choice. Greek society readily tolerated sexual relationships between men, but frowned on female homosexuality. Therefore, it was likely that even homosexual men might frown on lesbians.

9-19. Answer key: pp. 217-20

a. Yes. The Greek philosophers did not rely on divine power or deities, but believed that secular human reasoning would be enough for them to acquire wisdom and construct a just society.
b. Not really. The Greek philosophers relied much more on the senses and logic than on experiment.
c. No. The Greek philosophers took a critical stance toward Greek myths and traditional ethical teachings.

9-20. Answer key: pp. 218-19

a. Not the right choice. This was what his theory of Forms was about.
b. Not the right choice. Plato indeed believed that the best state was one which was either ruled by a philosopher or else by a king who himself was a philosopher.
c. The only choice. Plato never believed in democracy or rule by majority. Philosophers were certainly not the majority in society and Plato believed that they should rule.

9-21. Answer key: pp. 220-21

a. No. Apollo, the god of wisdom and justice, was a subordinate deity under Zeus.
b. Yes. He was the paramount ruler of the divine realm.
c. No. Bacchus was the god of wine, also known as Dionysus, who was celebrated primarily by women.

9-22. Answer key: p. 222

a. Not really. Skeptics gained some popularity among the Hellenistic philosophers but they were not the most respected or influential.

b. No. The Epicureans had some influence in the Hellenistic world but they were less influential than the Stoics.
c. Yes. Unlike the Epicureans and Skeptics, the Stoics did not seek to withdraw from the pressures of the world but taught people to take up social duties. Their thinking became one of the mainstays of the Hellenistic world of philosophy.

Chapter 10

10-1. Answer key: p. 225

a. Not the best answer. He was taken as a prisoner to Rome, although he also might have sought converts there.
b. Yes. He was involved in a local conflict, and knowing that he might be condemned by Jewish leaders, he asserted his rights as a Roman citizen and appealed his case to Rome.
c. No. He had inherited Roman citizenship from his father.

10-2. Answer key: p. 226

a. Yes. He and his brother were raised by a kindly she-wolf. Romulus became the first king.
b. No. The she-wolf nursed Romulus and Remus after they were abandoned by their uncle.
c. No. Aeneas, the father of Romulus and Remus, was a refugee from Troy to Italy.

10-3. Answer key: p. 227

a. No. The Etruscan cities were controlled by kings. City-states did not exist.
b. No. Only after the last Etruscan king was overthrown in 509 B.C.E. was the Roman republic established.
c. Yes. The Etruscan monarchs had political allies and built fleets; they ruled in the city surrounded by defensive walls.

10-4. Answer key: pp. 228-29

a. Yes. The powerful Senate and the two executive consuls made important political decisions and laws, representing the interests of hereditary aristocrats and wealthy classes known as the patricians.
b. Not the best answer. Through their tribunes, the plebeians exercised some political power in the Roman republic, but their power was primarily limited to the right to veto political decisions.
c. No. The patricians made some constitutional compromises with the lower classes but this did not make them democratic leaders.

10-5. Answer key: p. 230

a. Not the right choice. The Romans did these things. Salting the land made it unfit for agriculture.
b. Not the right choice. These possessions became resources for the further expansion of Rome.
c. The right choice. The Romans did these things to the peoples they conquered on the Italian peninsula as a way to secure their control. However, none of these privileges were granted to Carthaginians.

10-6. **Answer key:** pp. 231-32

a. No. They were plebeian tribunes who attempted to limit the landholdings of *latifundia* owners.
b. The best answer. Both brothers worked hard for the interests of the lower classes and advocated land reform in the Roman republic.
c. No. They were not generals.

10-7. **Answer key:** p. 232

a. Yes. General Marius was the first to recruit an army of paid volunteers, mostly landless rural residents and urban workers, whose loyalty to Marius made him a prominent general.
b. No. Following Marius's example, Sulla also recruited a private army.
c. No. Caesar seized power using private armies but he did this a few decades later than Marius and Sulla.

10-8. **Answer key:** p. 233

a. Not a good choice. Caesar confiscated property from conservatives and redistributed it to his army veterans and other supporters.
b. Good choice. Caesar did nothing to abolish slavery.
c. Not a good choice. Caesar made himself a life-time dictator in 46 B.C.E.

10-9. **Answer key:** p. 234

a. Not a good answer. The monarchy was not a disguise, but real.
b. The best answer. Augustus took responsibility for all important governmental functions, but he still preserved the name of a republic for his government.
c. No. Oligarchy and Athenian-style democracy never took root in Roman politics.

10-10. **Answer key:** p. 235

a. The right choice. Neapolis was established by Greek colonists before the rise of Rome.
b. Not the right choice. Both London and Paris (and many other important European cities) were established because of Roman expansion, which apparently quickened the tempo of European urban growth.
c. Not the right choice. See answer b above.

10-11. **Answer key:** pp. 236-37

a. No. The principle of "innocent until proven guilty" was part of Roman law.
b. No. Jury trials were an English innovation many centuries later.
c. The best answer. Judges were allowed to set aside laws that were inequitable or unfair.

10-12. **Answer key:** p. 238

a. Not a good choice. These were indeed part of the attractions of the city.
b. The best choice. All these games were unknown to Romans.
c. Not a good choice. These were indeed part of the city's attractions.

10-13. Answer key: p. 239

a. Yes. The concept of "nuclear family" did not exist in Rome.
b. Not a good answer. *Pater familias* meant "father of the family" or family head.
c. No. This was the policy of the imperial government to provide grain subsidies and spectacular public entertainment in order to keep the masses contented, a policy that had nothing to do with the concept of family.

10-14. Answer key: p. 241

a. Not the right choice. This was true for Roman slaves in the countryside.
b. Not the right choice. This practice was common though not mandatory in Roman cities.
c. The best choice. Slaves were not citizens, and even during republican times, they did not have right to have their own tribunes like the plebeians did.

10-15. Answer key: p. 242

a. No. These were Romans' own deities—Jupiter, lord of the heavens, Mars, the god of war, and Ceres, the goddess of grain.
b. Yes. Juno, the moon goddess, was an Etruscan deity; Cybele was the Anatolian mother goddess; Isis was an Egyptian deity.
c. No. Janus (the household god) and Vesta (the goddess of hearth) were both Roman deities. Cicero was a Roman philosopher who believed in Stoicism.

10-16. Answer key: p. 243

a. Yes. Roman soldiers serving in the Hellenistic world adapted it and they associated Mithras with military values.
b. No. The cult of Mithras did not admit women.
c. No. There was no evidence presented in the chapter to indicate this.

10-17. Answer key: p. 244

a. Not the best answer. They sometimes refused to pay taxes only because the imperial regimes forced them to revere the emperor-gods.
b. Not really. They could respect emperors as secular authorities, not as divine powers.
c. The best answer. Jews were strictly monotheistic revering Yahweh as the only god.

10-18. Answer key: p. 244

a. No. Early Christianity shared many of the same concerns and rituals with the Essenes, but the Essenes were a Jewish sect.
b. Yes. The sect was formed in Palestine during the first century B.C.E.
c. No. The Dead Sea scrolls were Essene writings accidentally discovered by some shepherds in 1947.

10-19. Answer key: p. 244

a. Yes. His followers believed that Jesus was anointed by God, and thus became the savior who would bring individuals into God's kingdom.
b. No. "Christ" did not mean this, although Jesus was believed to be the son of God.
c. No. Jesus was not Buddha.

10-20. Answer key: pp. 246

a. No. Quite to the contrary, Roman imperial authorities launched sporadic campaigns of persecution designed to eliminate Christianity as a threat to the empire.
b. Not really. There was no evidence presented in the chapter to indicate this.
c. Yes. These groups found Christianity appealing because it accorded honor and dignity to those who did not enjoy high standing in Roman society, and it endowed them with a sense of spiritual freedom more meaningful than wealth, power, or social prominence.

Chapter 11

11-1. Answer key: pp. 249-50

a. Not a good answer. Although the intelligence that Zhang Qian gathered during his mission might have contributed to the opening of the silk roads, it was not the purpose of his mission.
b. Yes. This was the single purpose of his mission.
c. No. Chinese viewed the large, strong horses of central Asia as treasures, but to buy horses was not the purpose of Zhang's mission.

11-2. Answer key: pp. 250-51

a. Not a good choice. Long-distance trade became less risky during the classical era than before because classical empires pacified large stretches of Eurasia and northern Africa.
b. Not a good choice. Construction of roads and bridges might have been undertaken for military and administrative reasons, but it also facilitated long-distance trade.
c. The right choice. Imperial policies often encouraged long-distance trade not to obtain foreign slaves or women, but to collect taxes.

11-3. Answer key: p. 252

a. No. Traders generally knew the rhythm of the monsoons and they would not sail when the winds were not right.
b. Yes. The monsoon winds were predictable and thus provided reliable wind power for sailing.
c. No. Hellenistic mariners learned the monsoon rhythm from Arab and Indian seamen whose ancestors had sailed by the monsoons for centuries.

11-4. Answer key: pp. 252-54

a. The right choice. This statement is incorrect because high-quality silk from China was one of the principal commodities exchanged over the roads.
b. Not a good choice. This statement is true.

c. Not a good choice. The silk roads on land and sea DID link much of Eurasia and north Africa into one extensive network.

11-5. Answer key: p. 260

a. The best answer, because merchants traveling from Alexandria in an easterly direction were most likely to bring back these goods (see the illustration on p. 253 in your textbook).
b. No. A ship traveling from Alexandria could not have reached Bactria. If a merchant wanted silk, he could get it from India or directly from south China.
c. No. Ships could not reach central Asia, and horses were not particularly desired by Hellenistic merchants.

11-6. Answer key: pp. 257-58

a. Not the best answer. Compared with merchant believers, imperial sponsorship played a minor role in the spread of Buddhism.
b. The best answer. It was Buddhist merchants who carried their faith along the silk roads to Iran, central Asia, China, and southeast Asia.
c. Not really. Monks did not travel to foreign countries as frequently as merchants did.

11-7. Answer key: p. 258

a. The best choice. Rulers in southeast Asian states called themselves *raja* but they did not shave their heads. Only monks shaved their heads and others who converted to Buddhism did not have to do so.
b. Not the right choice. This was true.
c. Not the right choice. Southeast Asian rulers DID appoint such advisors.

11-8. Answer key: p. 259

a. No. Nestorianism, which appeared in the 5th century C.E., was rejected by Mediterranean church authorities and did not have much influence on Roman Christians.
b. Not a good answer. Confucianism, a Chinese tradition, had no impact on the Christian practices of the Roman empire.
c. The best answer. Some Mediterranean Christians, inspired by ascetic values of Indian traditions, began to abandon society altogether and live as hermits in the deserts of Egypt, the mountains of Greece, and other isolated locations.

11-9. Answer key: p. 260

a. No. Mani did not draw influence from Hinduism but rather from Buddhism, another Indian tradition.
b. Yes. Mani himself was a devout Zoroastrian who drew heavily from Christianity and Buddhism for religious inspiration.
c. No. Both Nestorianism and Daoism were unknown to Mani.

11-10. Answer key: p. 260

a. Not the best answer. These restrictions were only valid for the "elect," not for the "hearers" who were the majority of Manichaeans.
b. The best answer. This stricture applied to both the "elect" and "hearers."
c. Not true. Quite to the contrary, Manichaeism appealed strongly to merchants who adopted the faith as hearers and supported the Manichaean church.

11-11. Answer key: pp. 263

a. Not the right choice. These three diseases were indeed the most destructive.
b. Not the right choice. Population losses (by a quarter to a third) and economic contraction caused by epidemic diseases certainly contributed to the decline of the Han and Roman empire.
c. The best choice. Better off than China, Persia, and the Roman empire, India seems to have escaped epidemic outbreaks and steep population losses.

11-12. Answer key: p. 263

a. No. Nomadic peoples began to establish large kingdoms in north China from the fourth to the sixth centuries C.E., not immediately after the dissolution of the Han empire.
b. Yes. The three large kingdoms were Wei, Wu, and Shu (see the map on p. 264 of your textbook).
c. No. The Sui dynasty unified China in 581 C.E., much later than the dissolution of the Han.

11-13. Answer key: p. 265

a. The best choice. There is no historical evidence to indicate this, although it might have been true.
b. Not the right choice. The collapse of the imperial rule and decline of Confucianism certainly contributed to the spread of Buddhism in China.
c. Not the right choice. Many of the nomadic peoples were Buddhist believers, whose coming into China helped the spread of Buddhism.

11-14. Answer key: pp. 265-66

a. No. The authors do not suggest a single, simple cause, but call explanations of this sort "silly" or "pet theories."
b. No. According to the authors, this is just one of the "pet theories" which cannot be accepted.
c. Yes. The authors' discussion includes internal decay and Germanic invasions that led to the downfall of the western Roman empire.

11-15. Answer key: p. 266

a. The best answer. The sheer size of the empire posed a great challenge for central control, especially when epidemics broke out throughout the empire and its various regions moved toward local, self-sufficient economies.
b. No. The term "barracks emperors" referred to those generals who seized imperial power briefly one after another. Diocletian's aim was to achieve administrative efficiency, thus requiring the suppression of "barracks emperors" rather than their persistence.
c. No. The division had nothing to do with the development of Christianity.

11-16. Answer key: p. 267

a. Not a good choice. These events DID happen.
b. Good choice. In speaking and writing, they used their own language and their social customs were markedly different from those of the Romans.
c. Not a good choice. This was also true.

11-17. Answer key: p. 268

a. No. The last emperor of the western Roman empire was deposed by the Germanic general Odovacer in 476.
b. No. The Huns never reached Rome. The city was sacked by the Visigoths in 410 C.E.
c. Yes. Under the pressures of the Huns, the Germanic peoples began to enter into the western Roman empire and took it over.

11-18. Answer key: p. 268

a. Yes. Through his Edict of Milan issued in 313 C.E., Christianity became a legitimate religion in the Roman empire.
b. Not the best answer. Emperor Theodosius proclaimed Christianity the official religion of the empire in 380 C.E.
c. No. St. Augustine was a bishop of Hippo in north Africa who philosophized Christianity in line with Platonic thought.

11-19. Answer key: p. 270

a. Not really. Altogether there were four patriarchs (of Jerusalem, Antioch, Alexandria, and Constantinople), and their authorities were equal.
b. The best answer. Although the bishop of Rome, also known as the pope, was equal to the four patriarchs in the institutional hierarchy, he enjoyed greater prestige than the others.
c. No. Jesus did not hold any official post in the Christian church for obvious reasons.

11-20. Answer key: p. 270

a. No. The pope alone could not make final decisions about theological controversies.
b. No. The four patriarchs could not make final decisions either.
c. Yes. Church councils consisted of the pope, the four patriarchs, and the bishops of all prominent cities of the Roman empire. The councils would determine which views would prevail as official doctrine.

Chapter 12

12-1. Answer key: p. 279

a. No. The technology of high-quality silk production was from China.
b. Yes. The two monks learned silk production in China and smuggled fine silkworm eggs to the Byzantine empire.
c. No. Procopius did not make this claim although there might have been several routes through which silk production reached the Byzantine empire.

12-2. Answer key: p. 280

a. Not really. The empire takes its name from Byzantion, originally a market town and fishing village, but the Byzantine empire is referred to as Byzantium, a latinized form of Byzantion.
b. No. Constantinople was the capital of the Byzantine empire, which was built on the site of Byzantion.

c.   Yes. Byzantium was a latinized word for Byzantion. To honor the original settlement, the Byzantine empire is also called Byzantium by historians.

12-3. Answer key: p. 282

a.   Yes. This meant that the emperors could use religion to strengthen or legitimize their rule as secular authorities.
b.   No. The Byzantine emperors were all Christians, who could only believe in one God.
c.   No. Christianity held that even emperors were all human mortals.

12-4. Answer key: p. 283

a.   The only right choice. In the Byzantine empire, the color of dark, rich purple was reserved exclusively for imperial use; the color yellow, on the other hand, was reserved for emperors in China.
b.   Not the right choice, because these were part of the court etiquette of the Byzantine empire.
c.   Not the right choice, because these were indeed used in the imperial court to impress foreign envoys.

12-5. Answer key: p. 283

a.   Not a good choice. She was indeed a sagacious advisor to her husband, emperor Justinian.
b.   Not a good choice, because these characteristics describe Theodora before she met her husband, the future emperor.
c.   Good choice. This was not true because Justinian himself was a very ambitious and capable emperor.

12-6. Answer key: p. 283

a.   No. He did not have such a plan. The city was damaged by riots against high taxes, and Justinian then embarked on an ambitious construction program that thoroughly remade the city.
b.   The best answer. Justinian's codification had far-reaching influence on the legal systems of post-classical Europe.
c.   Not really. Under Justinian's reign, general Belisarius reconquered a substantial portion of the former Roman empire, but his accomplishments were far from a complete reconstitution of the Roman empire of the classical era.

12-7. Answer key: p. 285

a.   Not the best answer. "Greek fire" was a very effective weapon against Islamic armies during the 7th and 8th centuries, but it had nothing to do with the constitution of the *theme*.
b.   The best answer. In this way, the free peasantry, backbone of the empire, was strengthened under the *theme* system.
c.   Not a good answer. Generals were also governors of provinces under the *theme* system.

12-8. Answer key: pp. 286

a.   Yes. The Bulgarians were defeated and reportedly 14,000 Bulgarian survivors were blinded by the Byzantine army led by emperor Basil II.
b.   No. European crusades took place in the 12th and 13th centuries.
c.   No. The Muslim Saljuqs, a group of nomadic Turkish people, defeated the Byzantine armies at the battle of Manzikert in 1071.

12-9. Answer key: pp. 288-89

a. Not a good choice. Restriction on landholding was indeed part of government policy from the 6th through the 10th centuries.
b. Not a good choice. To prevent the creation of monopoly, government regulations only allowed individuals to participate in one activity of silk production, such as weaving, dyeing, or selling.
c. The best choice. The Byzantine government did not monopolize trade, although the *bezant* became the standard currency of the Mediterranean basin from the 6th through the 12th centuries.

12-10. Answer key: pp. 290-91

a. The best choice. These were not entertaining at all, nor popular, even though asceticism was practiced by a few devout individuals who contributed to the development of Byzantine monasticism.
b. Not a good choice because these were at the heart of mass entertainment in the city.
c. Not a good choice because these were also part of mass entertainment in the city.

12-11. Answer key: p. 290

a. No. Using colors to represent different armies was a practice of Qing China.
b. Yes. The two factions often engaged in street fights, but on one occasion, they united and mounted a serious uprising protesting high taxes.
c. No. The two colors had nothing to do with gangsters; we have learned nothing of the existence of such individuals from the historical record.

12-12. Answer key: p. 292

a. The best answer. Classical Greek literature, philosophy, and science were at core of the Byzantine educational system.
b. Not really. Before the 6th century, the official language of Byzantium was Latin while local inhabitants spoke Greek. After the 6th century, Greek replaced Latin as the language of government.
c. No. As in classical Greece, the humanities were more important than the natural sciences in Byzantine education.

12-13. Answer key: p. 293

a. Not really. There is no historical evidence to indicate this.
b. Yes. The emperor's concern might have reflected the influence of rational thinking from classical Greek philosophy.
c. No. Iconoclasm was not the creation of a single madman but was supported by many, a campaign lasting for more than a century.

12-14. Answer key: pp. 294-95

a. Not a good choice. Indeed, the earliest monasteries were communities founded by dedicated hermits and ascetics with their disciples and followers.
b. Not a good choice. Monasteries were well supported by the Byzantine laity because monks and nuns provided social services, such as spiritual counsel, famine relief, and medical care to local laity.
c. Good choice. Unlike their counterparts in western Europe and other lands, Byzantine monasteries were not centers of thought and learning.

12-15. Answer key: p. 295

a. Not a good answer. Ritual differences between the east and west existed but these alone did not cause the deep division of Christianity.
b. Not the best answer. Doctrinal or theological debates over such issues as the relationship between God, Jesus, and the Holy Spirit were serious matters, but other issues also contributed to the schism between east and west.
c. The best answer. Differences over ritual and doctrine contributed to the schism, but the authority of the Church was an especially serious matter. The Byzantine patriarchs argued for the autonomy of all major Christian jurisdictions, while the popes in the west asserted the primacy of Rome for all Christendom.

12-16. Answer key: p. 296

a. Not the best answer. Intermarriages alone did not have the power to completely undermine the control of the imperial government.
b. Yes. The decline of the free peasantry meant that the central government could no longer have adequate revenue and military recruits.
c. No. The fights of the fans were a problem in the 6th and 7th centuries, but no longer a problem thereafter.

12-17. Answer key: pp. 296-97

a. The best answer. The crusades were religious wars designed to take holy sites back from Muslim control even though they sometimes lost their original focus.
b. No. To the leaders of western Europe, fighting the Muslims seemed more important and urgent than fighting the Eastern Orthodox church.
c. Not the best answer. Only in the fourth crusade (1202-1204) was the holy mission of the campaign diverted by Venetian merchants to sack Constantinople.

12-18. Answer key: p. 297

a. No. By sacking Constantinople and seizing part of Anatolia during the 13th century, the crusaders weakened the Byzantine empire but did not bring it down.
b. Not really. At the battle of Manzikert in 1071, the Muslim Saljuqs defeated the Byzantine armies and took over much of Anatolia. But Byzantium survived for several centuries after that.
c. Yes. Ottoman Turks captured Constantinople in 1453, and absorbed Byzantium into their expanding realm.

12-19. Answer key: pp. 298-99

a. Not the right choice. This was indeed one consequence of their missions.
b. Good choice. This did not happen.
c. Not the right choice. Their missions, facilitated by the Cyrillic alphabet they devised for the Slavic peoples, stimulated conversion of the Slavic peoples to Orthodox Christianity.

12-20. Answer key: p. 300

a. Not really. He lauded drunkenness and reportedly maintained a harem of 800 women.
b. No. Only much later, in the 16th century, did some Russians begin to claim the imperial mantle of Byzantium by saying that Moscow was the world's third Rome.
c. The best answer. After the conversion, Cyrillic writing, literacy, and Orthodox missions all spread quickly throughout Russia.

Chapter 13

13-1. Answer key: p. 303

a. Not a good answer. The *hajj* drew both men and women.
b. Not the best answer. For centuries before Islam, pilgrimages to Mecca to visit the Ka'ba shrine were an Arabian tradition. Muhammad's visits to the Ka'ba in 629 and 632 changed the pagan shrine into an Islamic holy site.
c. The best answer. For all pilgrims participation in the *hajj* lent new meaning and significance to their faith.

13-2. Answer key: p. 303

a. Yes. It signifies obedience to the rule and will of Allah.
b. No. The word *Muslim* means "one who has submitted" (to Allah).
c. No. The word Allah means "the god."

13-3. Answer key: p. 304

a. Yes. The Bedouin people who lived in the Arabian peninsula were good at herding animals and long-distance trade.
b. Not the best answer. Although the region in which Muhammad was born was covered by desert and had many camels, the phrase "desert society" tells us nothing about the internal characteristics, or the nature, of the society. Scholars, therefore, do not use this term.
c. No. Desert covers most of the peninsula, and agriculture is possible only in the well-watered area of Yemen in the south and a few oases.

13-4. Answer key: pp. 307-308

a. No. He did not purposely found a new religion, but he was instructed by Allah to explain and spread Allah's message to others.
b. The best answer. He referred to himself as the "seal of the prophets"—the final prophet through whom Allah would reveal his divine message to humankind.
c. Not really. Muhammad accepted the authority of earlier Jewish and Christian prophets, but believed that he received a more complete revelation from Allah than his predecessors had.

13-5. Answer key: p. 310

a.   Not a good answer. The Quran is the holy book of Islam, just like the Pible, of which the New Testament is only one part, is to Christianity.
b.   The best answer. The Avesta was the holy book of Zoroastrianism.
c.   No. Yahweh is the Jewish god, not a book.

13-6. Answer key: pp. 307-309

a.   Yes. Literally, the word means "migration"; the date of the *hijra* became the starting point of the official Islamic calendar.
b.   No. *Umma* meant "community of the faithful," referring to the community organized by Muhammad in Medina after the *hijra*.
c.   No. After Muhammad and his followers moved to Yathrib, they called the city Medina, meaning "the city," or "the city of the prophet."

13-7. Answer key: pp. 308-309

a.   Not the best answer. The Ten Commandments, or the Decalogue, were given to Moses but ALL Hebrews were to follow them. Thus, the analogy is not quite right.
b.   Compared with the other two answers, this one is the best. The Noble Eightfold Path calls for ALL Buddhist believers (just as the Five Pillars applies to ALL Muslims) to lead balanced and moderate lives, rejecting devotion to luxury but also extreme asceticism.
c.   No. The Vedas were orally transmitted works, or collections of hymns, songs, prayers, and rituals honoring the various gods of the Aryans. They were not a collection of laws, or prescribed actions, as were the Five Pillars or the Ten Commandments.

13-8. Answer key: p. 309

a.   Not a good choice. Indeed, through the *sharia*, Islam became more than a religious belief, but a complete way of life based on Islamic religious principles.
b.   Good choice. The *sharia* was made by Muslim jurists and legal scholars centuries after Muhammad's death.
c.   Not a good choice. The Quran was the major source of the *sharia*.

13-9. Answer key: p. 309

a.   Not a good answer. Both held paramount power, and it is hard to say which one was more powerful than the other.
b.   No. The word *caliph* means "deputy," not a successor of Muhammad, who had no legitimate successors since he claimed that he was the "seal of the prophets," or the last prophet of Allah.
c.   The best answer. A caliph did not claim divine power, as did pharaohs (hence, the appellation "god-king"), but he was the head of the state, the chief judge, religious leader, and military commander.

13-10. Answer key: pp. 310

a. No. The Shia sect supported Ali, the son-in-law of Muhammad, to become caliph, but the victorious Sunni sect supported the Umayyad clan and established the Umayyad dynasty.

b. Yes. The Sunnis ("traditionalists") represented the majority of Muslims, and became the victorious faction in the struggle over who would be caliph.

c. No. Abu al-Abbas was the man who founded the Abbasid dynasty.

13-11. Answer key: pp. 311, 313

a. Good choice. Instead of maintaining a simple lifestyle, the caliphs devoted themselves increasingly to luxurious living.

b. Not the right choice because this statement is true. The conquered peoples could still observe their religions, but they had to pay *jizya* to the Umayyad government.

c. Not the right choice because this statement is true. Indeed, the Umayyad caliphs showed so much favor to their fellow Arabs that the policy alienated Arabs from non-Arab Muslims.

13-12. Answer key: p. 312

a. No. The founder of the dynasty, Abu al-Abbas, was a Sunni Arab, but he allied with the Shias and non-Arab Muslims to overthrow the Umayyad dynasty.

b. Not really. Abbasid rulers did not show special favor to the Arab military aristocracy, but Arabs continued to play a large role in government.

c. The best answer. Abbasid caliphs were concerned little with the expansion of empire, but learned much about administration from Persian statecraft.

13-13. Answer key: p. 312

a. Yes. *Ulama* were learned officials and *qadis* were judges of Islamic society.

b. Not the best answer. Islam does not recognize priests as a distinct class of religious specialists.

c. No, this is not the best answer because neither of these groups had specific roles as missionaries.

13-14. Answer key: pp. 313-14

a. Not a good choice. These they did.

b. Not a good choice. They were indeed Saljuq Muslims.

c. The best choice. The Saljuq Turks controlled the Abbasid empire for two centuries but retained Abbasid caliphs as nominal sovereigns. The Abbasid dynasty was finally extinguished by the Mongols in 1258.

13-15. Answer key: p. 316

a. Not the best answer. Long before Abbasid times, the Byzantines had learned silk-making techniques from the Chinese. Making fine silk was not an Arabian specialty.

b. Yes. Arab forces defeated a Chinese army in 751 and learned the technique of paper making from Chinese war prisoners.

c. Not really. They might have learned about gunpowder, but only in the late 13th century did the peoples of southwest Asia and Europe began to experiment with metal-barreled cannons.

13-16. Answer key: p. 319

a. Yes. Arab forces conquered north Africa where the nomadic Berbers lived. The latter converted to Islam and conquered Iberia (Spain).
b. No. The Berbers only recognized the Umayyad authorities and claimed independence from the Abbasid dynasty.
c. No. Under the Berber caliphs, al-Andalus actively participated in the commercial life of the larger Islamic world and became a very prosperous country.

13-17. Answer key: pp. 319-20

a. Not a good choice. These were indeed the legal rights of women, at least in theory or by the Islamic holy law.
b. Not a good choice. This was also taught by Muhammad, but in practice, the Quran and the *sharia* could be interpreted in ways unfavorable to women.
c. Good choice. In theory and practice, a woman could take only one husband, while a man could take up to four wives.

13-18. Answer key: p. 320

a. No. The Quran strictly demanded the veiling of women (see the Documentary Evidence below for more on this point).
b. No. Veiling of women was not practiced during the prophet's lifetime or before.
c. Yes. The custom can be traced back to the 13th century B.C.E. in Mesopotamia, and it later spread to Persia and the east Mediterranean lands. When Muslim Arabs conquered these lands, they soon adopted the custom.

13-19. Answer key: pp. 321-22

a. Yes, but not the best answer. The Sufis were kind mystics and led ascetic and holy lives, but they also had other qualities that made them effective missionaries.
b. Yes, but not the best answer. Indeed, they were tolerant of other faiths, and their emotional sermons, passionate singing, and spirited dancing enhanced their charismatic appeal. But these were not the only qualities that made them effective missionaries.
c. The best answer. Because of ALL of these qualities, Sufis became especially effective in attracting converts in lands like Persia and India, where long established religious faiths had enjoyed a mass following for centuries.

13-20. Answer key: pp. 322-23

a. Not a good choice. Persian was the principal language of literature, poetry, history, and political reflection in Islamic society.
b. Not a good choice. Using Hindi numerals, Muslims developed an impressive tradition of mathematical thought, concentrating on algebra, trigonometry, and geometry.
c. The right choice. Greek influence was not long lasting. After the 13th century, Platonic and Aristotelian influences lost favor among the learned and fell increasingly under the shadow of teachings from the Quran and Sufi mystics who held that human reason was too frail to understand the nature of Allah.

Chapter 14

14-1. Answer key: pp. 327-28

a. No. A Buddhist monk did not make the Islamic *hajj*.
b. Yes. Not only did Xuanzang's persistence and determination in pursuing his faith inspire many Chinese, his translations of Buddhist texts also helped spread Buddhism in China.
c. No. Quite to the contrary, he received a hero's welcome and an audience with the emperor despite his violation of the traveling ban.

14-2. Answer key: pp. 328-29

a. Not a good choice, because the statement was true of the Sui dynasty.
b. Not a good choice, because these were indeed done by Sui rulers.
c. Good choice. The Sui was a short-lived dynasty (589-618), and China had not yet achieved high levels of prosperity under the Sui.

14-3. Answer key: p. 331

a. Not a good choice, because this could actually be done in only eight days (rather than three months) by couriers using relay horses.
b. The best answer. Speedy delivery was carried out by human runners.
c. Not a good answer. The Grand Canal was an important mechanism for linking north and south China, but its construction was one of the major accomplishments of the Sui dynasty, not the Tang.

14-4. Answer key: p. 331

a. The best answer. This was the principle on which the equal-field system was established. The working of the system depended on periodic assessments and redistributions of land to individual families.
b. Not the best answer. This was the intent of Tang authorities, but in practice, influential families could always find ways to retain land scheduled for redistribution. The system worked well only for about one century.
c. Not a good answer. The Tang dynasty, especially its early period, was known for its light taxes—only one-fortieth of the annual harvest.

14-5. Answer key: pp. 331-32

a. Not really. Although such families used their influence to place relatives in bureaucratic positions, most positions during Tang times came to be filled by men of intellectual ability.
b. No. The extensive bureaucracy of Tang times could not possibly have been staffed exclusively by the relatively small number of direct imperial kinsmen and relatives.
c. Yes. With few exceptions, most office holders won their posts by passing the civil service examinations.

14-6. Answer key: p. 332

a. Not the best answer, because we do not know how sincere the envoys were in performing kowtow.
b. Yes, this is what the authors meant. Indeed, Chinese authorities did not interfere much with the internal affairs of subordinate states.
c. Not a good answer. Gift-giving was an important part of the system, but this is not what the authors are referring to when they discuss its "fictional quality."

14-7. Answer key: pp. 332-33

a. The best answer. Weak and careless leadership brought about An Lushan's revolt in 755, and the Tang never recovered from this crisis.
b. These campaigns took place before the 8th century and had the effect of strengthening Tang rule.
c. No. Against the will of imperial authority, the equal-field system deteriorated from the early 8th century onward, but the government did not abolish the system.

14-8. Answer key: pp. 333-34

a. Yes. The Song placed more emphasis on civil administration, industry, education, and arts than on military affairs. Its military weakness led to foreign invasions and loss of territory.
b. No. By strengthening the bureaucracy, the Song government was more centralized than that of the Tang.
c. Not right. The Song dynasty was much smaller than the Tang dynasty in size.

14-9. Answer key: pp. 334-35

a. No. By paying large amounts of silk and silver to the Khitan, the Song maintained peace with the Khitan empire.
b. Yes. The Jurchen conquered the Khitan, overran north China, and drove the Song dynasty to the south.
c. No. The Uighurs sacked the Tang capitals and controlled the imperial house for a few decades during the mid-8th century, but they did not invade the Song.

14-10. Answer key: p. 335

a. No. Through military ventures during Sui and Tang times, the Chinese learned about fast-ripening rice from the Vietnamese.
b. Not really. Fast-ripening rice enabled two harvests a year, not three.
c. The best answer. Chinese population increased from 45 million in 600 C.E. to 115 million in 1200 C.E.

14-11. Answer key: p. 337

a. Yes, but not the best answer because it is incomplete. Ancestor worship enhanced the male authority figure in a family because he presided over the rituals and mediated between the living and the dead.
b. Yes, but not the best answer because it is incomplete. Foot binding placed women under tight supervision and control of their husbands and male guardians, one important aspect of Chinese patriarchal social structure.
c. The best choice because both of these practices were typical aspects of Chinese patriarchal social structure.

14-12. Answer key: p. 338

a. Not a good choice. Gunpowder was discovered during the Tang, and the compass was invented during the Song.
b. Not a good choice. Both technologies appeared during the Tang.
c. The best choice. These two technologies already were commonplace a few centuries BEFORE the Tang.

14-13. Answer key: pp. 339-40

a. No. "Flying cash," or letters of credit, appeared in private economic transactions about four centuries earlier than the formal printing of paper money by the Chinese government.
b. The best answer. "Flying cash" referred to the intangible quality of an economic transaction through letters of credit, enabling merchants to deposit goods or cash at one location and draw the equivalent in cash or goods elsewhere.
c. No. Although money may have started circulating more rapidly as trade increased, the term "flying cash" referred not to speed, but to the relatively intangible quality of economic transactions through letters of credit.

14-14. Answer key: p. 342

a. Not a good choice. Religious communities based on these two faiths included both foreign merchants and Chinese converts.
b. Good choice. These two faiths did not leave a mark in Chinese religious history.
c. Not a good choice. Some Zoroastrians fled from Persia to China to avoid Muslim conquerors, while Muslim merchants also came to China and established their communities in commercial cities.

14-15. Answer key: pp. 343-44

a. Not really. Some Buddhist concepts, such as *dharma* and *nirvana*, were cast in Daoist terms, but Buddhist deities were not changed into Daoist deities.
b. The best answer. Monastery life and celibacy certainly posed a serious challenge to Chinese family values, but Buddhists taught that one son in the monastery would bring salvation for ten generations of his kin, a claim that enabled Buddhism to benefit the extended Chinese family.
c. No. Buddhist monasteries were established in China as charitable institutions that paid no taxes.

14-16. Answer key: pp. 345

a. Yes. He was the most influential philosopher of Neo-Confucianism, and his writing reflected the influence of Buddhism.
b. No. He was a holy monk who traveled to India, not a Neo-Confucianist.
c. No. He was the founder of the Song dynasty, not a scholar or theologian at all.

14-17. Answer key: pp. 346-47

a.   The best answer. Although the Korean monarchy sponsored Chinese schools and a Confucian examination system, Korea never established a bureaucracy based on merit such as that of Tang and Song China.
b.   No. They accepted both Neo-Confucianism and Chinese Buddhism.
c.   Not a good answer. The Korean capital was modeled on the Tang capital at Chang'an.

14-18. Answer key: p. 347

a.   Not the right choice. Despite the coming of Confucianism and Buddhism, many Vietnamese retained their own faiths and beliefs.
b.   Not the right choice. The Chinese monarchy and bureaucracy WERE imitated by Korea, Vietnam, and early Japan.
c.   The best choice. If Vietnamese women also had practiced foot binding, they could not have participated so widely in local and regional markets, as they did for centuries.

14-19. Answer key: pp. 348-49

a.   No. The Kamakura (1185-1333 C.E.) and Muromachi (1336-1573 C.E.) periods are considered part of medieval (middle period) Japan.
b.   Yes. Historians refer to the earliest phases of Japanese history as the Nara (710-794 C.E.) and Heian (794-1185 C.E.) periods.
c.   No. Taira and Minamoto were the two most powerful clans fighting for control of Japan at the beginning of the 12th century. In 1185 the Minamoto emerged victorious and established the *shogun*-led government at Kamakura, which signaled the beginning of medieval Japan.

14-20. Answer key: pp. 349-50

a.   Yes. These warriors served the provincial lords and the *shogun*, and enjoyed high privileges and assumed demanding responsibilities in Japanese society.
b.   No. *Bushido*, or "the way of the warrior," was the unwritten but widely observed code of the *samurai*.
c.   No. *Shogun* was the most powerful regional lord who assumed the leadership of the Japanese government under the symbolic authority of the Japanese emperor. His power over other regional lords was rather limited.

Chapter 15

15-1. Answer key: p. 355

a.   Not the best answer, because only **a few** of the stories were about true conditions. For example, one story recounted how a king from north India converted to Islam, and some others reported on Hindu customs, on shipwrecks, and on slave trading.
b.   Yes. Most of the 136 stories were tall tales, telling about such things as giant lobsters, mermaids, sea dragons, and talking lizards.
c.   No. The author, Buzurg ibn Shahriyar, was a Persian sailor from Siraf.

15-2. Answer key: p. 357

a. The best answer. King Harsha's unified rule did not last long, and north India suffered frequent raids and incursions from Muslim forces. Later the rise of Sultanate of Delhi failed to achieve effective control and order in north India.
b. No. Compared with the south, north India was not peaceful and stable at all.
c. Not the best answer because we have not been presented with comparative evidence on the relative levels of wealth and prosperity between north and south.

15-3. Answer key: p. 357

a. Good choice. This is the only one which does not describe Harsha's kingdom. Harsha lived during the first half of the 7th century, while Islam became predominant in north India only from the 12th century onward.
b. Not a good choice. The statement was true. Harsha's forces included 20,000 cavalry, 50,000 infantry, and 5,000 war elephants.
c. Not a good choice. Indeed, when Harsha was assassinated, his kingdom disintegrated immediately.

15-4. Answer key: pp. 358, 375

a. No. Only answer c is correct.
b. No. See answer c.
c. Yes. The three major incursions took place in 711, 1001-1027, and 1206-1526 respectively.

15-5. Answer key: p. 358

a. The best answer. Muslim merchants took their faith to coastal regions in both north and south India, and they established small communities in all Indian port cities.
b. No. Monsoons affected the patterns of trade in the Indian Ocean basin, but in and of themselves had nothing to do with the rise of Islam.
c. Not a good answer. Slavery was not important in Indian society; even if there were a small number of Muslim slaves present, it is unlikely that they would have had a major effect on the spread of Islam in India.

15-6. Answer key: pp. 359-60

a. Wrong. Both were states of south India during the postclassical era.
b. No. The rulers of neither of these kingdoms built tightly centralized state or imperial rules.
c. Correct. These two state were larger than most other kingdoms in south India.

15-7. Answer key: p. 361

a. Not the best answer because both a and b are true. Most of India's rainfall was brought by spring and summer monsoons.
b. Not the best answer because both a and b are true. Irrigation was essential during the dry months, but India's agriculture also relied on monsoon rains.
c. The best answer. Among India's waterworks, the most impressive was the construction of reservoirs which could be as large as lakes.

15-8. Answer key: p. 362

a. Not the best answer. Even though the author discussed commercial affairs, he did not discuss urbanization in comparison with other regions of the world.
b. Yes. The author described Ceylon and south India as great markets which were frequented by ships from lands near and far.
c. No. The Egyptian monk did not discuss these items specifically even though they are part of the terminology used today to discuss commercialization in the Indian Ocean basin.

15-9. Answer key: p. 363

a. Not the best answer because all of the functions mentioned in a and b were true. Answer c thus provides the most correct response.
b. Not the best answer because all of the functions mentioned in a and b were true. Answer c thus provides the most correct response.
c. The best answer. Because of the absence of centralized imperial rule, Indian public life revolved around Hindu temples which served many functions provided by states in other lands.

15-10. Answer key: pp. 365-66

a. The best analogy. Both of these products were used as the basis of a manufacturing industry with products made for export, providing a livelihood for numerous artisans and farmers in the two countries.
b. Not the best answer. Spices were specialized products of southeast Asia, but they did not serve as the foundation for the development of a manufacturing industry and the provision of cash incomes to large numbers of producers.
c. Not the best answer. Although slaves were important commodities of east Africa, they were not the basis of a manufacturing industry.

15-11. Answer key: p. 367

a. Not a good choice. Turkish Muslims in north India gained recognition as distinct groups under the umbrella of the caste system, and within a few generations, their descendants were absorbed into Indian society.
b. The best choice. Guilds of merchants and manufacturers became increasingly important and more powerful than before, but they were not the most powerful castes.
c. Not a good choice. The caste system originated in north India and during the postclassical era, it extended to south India.

15-12. Answer key: p. 368

a. Not a good answer. There was no evidence presented in this chapter to indicate this.
b. Not a good answer. Buddhism was not banned, and it survived as a minor faith in India.
c. The best answer. For instance, in 1196 Muslim forces overran the city of Nalanda, ravaged Buddhist schools, torched Buddhist libraries, and either killed or exiled thousands of monks there.

15-13. Answer key: p. 369

a. The best answer. Shankara mistrusted emotional services and ceremonies and preferred disciplined logical reasoning as the best way to understand the ultimate reality of Brahman. Ramanuja recommended intense devotion to Vishnu in order to win the god's grace and live forever in his presence.
b. Not really. Shankara was a worshiper of Shiva, while Ramanuja was devotee of Vishnu.
c. No. Shankara's theology of logical reasoning was not a help to devotional cults. Ramanuja's thought reflected the deep influence of devotional cults, and his theology inspired their further development throughout India. Even today it serves as a philosophical foundation for Hindu popular religion.

15-14. Answer key: p. 370

a. Not the best answer. Islam did not destroy the Indian caste system, and those who converted to Islam hardly improved their positions at all.
b. Yes. Since Islam recognized the equality of all believers, many members of lower castes converted themselves to the new faith in hopes of escaping discrimination.
c. Not a good answer. There was no evidence presented in the chapter to suggest that lower caste members believed that Allah could do more for them than Shiva and Vishnu in terms of salvation.

15-15. Answer key: p. 370

a. No. Guru Kabir was one of the most famous *bhakti* teachers who lived at the turn of the 15th and 16th centuries, while the *bhakti* movement had already started during the 12th century.
b. No. Hinduism was quite open and tolerant toward other faiths, and there was no nationalistic movement to expel Islam.
c. Yes. *Bhakti* teachers like guru Kabir taught that Shiva, Vishnu, and Allah were all manifestations of a single, universal deity whom all devout believers could find within their own hearts.

15-16. Answer key: p. 371

a. Yes, the only right choice. This alone shows that cultural borrowing from India by people in southeast Asia was rather selective and purposeful.
b. Not a good choice. Indian kingship became the principal form of political authority in southeast Asia, and kings referred themselves as *raja* (the Indian word for "king").
c. Not a good choice. Southeast Asian ruling elites sponsored the introduction of both religions into their courts in order to strengthen their monarchical rule.

15-17. Answer key: pp. 371-72

a. Yes. It was the first state to adopt Indian political, cultural, and religious traditions in southeast Asia.
b. No. The kingdom of Funan lasted from the 1st to the 6th century, a period in which Islam was not yet born.
c. No. There was no state in southeast Asia which was not more or less Indianized.

15-18. Answer key: p. 373

a. Not really. The capital was built with the aid of *brahmin* advisors, and it reflected a Hindu world view. Later in the 12th and 13th centuries, because the Khmers turned to Buddhism, some Buddhist temples were added to the Hindu complex.

b. No. Islamic architecture did not exist in this city.

c. Yes. The city was abandoned by the Khmers in 1431 because of invasions by Thai peoples, and it was rediscovered by French missionaries and explorers in the 19th century.

15-19. Answer key: p. 374

a. Not really. Unlike India, Islam in southeast Asia did not have special appeal to members of lower social classes.

b. Yes. This was so because Islam facilitated their dealings with foreign Muslim merchants, and for the ruling elites, Islam also provided additional divine sanction for their rule. By turning to Islam, the converts continued to honor Hinduism and Buddhism.

c. No. The Venetian traveler Marco Polo during the late 13th century noted that many residents of towns and cities had converted to Islam, while those living in the countryside and the hills retained their inherited traditions.

15-20. Answer key: p. 375

a. No. Originally Melaka was a Hindu state, but it soon became predominantly Islamic as the ruling class converted to Islam about the mid-15th century.

b. No. Confucianism had little influence in this state.

c. Yes. Melakan ruling class enthusiastically sponsored missionary campaigns to spread Islam within the country and throughout southeast Asia.

Chapter 16

16-1. Answer key: p. 379

a. No. This was the name given to an elephant given as a gift to the court.

b. Not the best answer. The albino elephant was born in India and went to the Abbasid court as a present from an Indian king. Later, the caliph gave it to the emperor Charlemagne as a gift.

c. The best answer. Charlemagne dispatched at least three embassies to Baghdad, and the elephant was an important token for Charlemagne's success in establishing diplomatic relations with the Abbasid dynasty.

16-2. Answer key: p. 379

a. No. Historians do not use "mature" to describe medieval Europe because they see this period of European history as one of decline and gradual recovery after the fall of Rome.

b. Yes. The term "medieval" means "middle," and indicates that this period falls between the classical era and modern times.

c. Not the best answer because historians do not see this era as one of "middle age crisis," but rather as a period of slow, and then more dynamic, quickening growth.

16-3. Answer key: pp. 382-83

a. Yes. His conversion to Roman Christianity, which was urged by his wife Clotilda, greatly strengthened the Franks, who became the most powerful of the Germanic peoples between the 5th and 9th centuries.

b. No. After the fall of Rome, many Germanic peoples converted to Arian Christianity, which was condemned by religious authorities in both Rome and Constantinople as heretical. The Franks' conversion to Roman Christianity set an example for other Germanic peoples in western Europe.

c. No. When Clovis converted to Roman Christianity, Islam was not yet born.

16-5. Answer key: pp. 385-87

a. True but not the best answer because b is also true. Charlemagne's son, Louis the Pious, lost control over the counts and other local authorities, and his three grandsons divided the empire into three roughly equal portions.

b. True but not the best answer because a is also true. The Carolingians had no navy, no means to protect valuable sites, and no way to predict the movements of Viking raids. Defense against the Vikings, Magyars, and Muslims rested primarily on local forces.

c. The best answer. Weak leadership plus inability of self-defense brought down the empire.

16-6. Answer key: pp. 387-89

a. Not a good choice. Through these invasions, the Muslims actually cut off the commercial link between western Europe and the Mediterranean basin.

b. Not a good choice. As descendants of central Asian nomads, Magyars were expert horsemen.

c. The right choice. Vikings were outstanding seafarers, not horsemen, and the success of their raids relied on their river-going fleets.

16-7. Answer key: p. 389

a. Yes. The larger realm led by King Alfred was quite effective in fighting against the Vikings.

b. No. This was quite true of Germany and France, but not England.

c. No. The Vikings colonized Iceland and Greenland, and a small group of them even established a colony in Newfoundland in modern Canada. England was not colonized by the Vikings.

16-8. Answer key: p. 390

a. No. The "feud" in *feudalism* does not mean intra-family fights, but refers back to the word "fief," or land grant, given by a lord to his vassal.

b. Yes. This meant that a strong centralized government was not present, and that the feudal lords exercised political, economic, military, and judicial powers in their own domains.

c. Not really. Despite the relative weakness of central institutions, feudal lords were still obliged to obey, respect, and serve the king.

16-9. Answer key: pp. 391-92

a. The best answer. The feudal relationship benefited both lord and vassals.

b. Not a good answer. It is hard to say who exploited whom.

c. Not a good answer. Their relationships involved the lord's discipline and control of vassals, but it would be inaccurate to say that all such relationships were necessarily antagonistic.

16-10. Answer key: p. 392

a. The best answer. The status of serfs was an intermediate category between slaves and free peasants.
b. Not a good answer. The primary role of serfs was not to provide domestic and military service, but rather, agricultural labor.
c. No. Serfs enjoyed more rights than slaves did, especially with respect to farming the land.

16-11. Answer key: p. 392

a. The best answer. But remember that this right was conditional—so long as the serfs fulfilled their obligations to landlords.
b. No. Serfs were not free to move or change lords.
c. Not really. Even a lord did not have such a right. If the marriage involved two serfs of different manors, the couple had to pay fines to their lords.

16-12. Answer key: pp. 392-93

a. The best choice. It was not a plantation, it was not operated by free peasants, and heavy plows were not essential to a manor.
b. Not a good choice. This is one succinct description of a manor.
c. Not a good choice. This is one way to describe a manor.

16-13. Answer key: pp. 393-94

a. Not really. The self-sufficient economy of medieval times in Europe meant that manors had to produce almost everything for their residents. Lack of specialization also meant inefficient and slow economic activity.
b. The best description. Manors were rural communities that relied on agriculture.
c. No. Early medieval Europe had little commercial activity; towns were few and sparsely populated.

16-14. Answer key: pp. 395-96

a. No. There is nothing in the textbook discussion to indicate that this was true.
b. No. The authors' discussion indicates no objections among aristocratic clans to the conversion.
c. Yes. The Franks became deeply committed to Roman Christianity.

16-15. Answer key: pp. 396-97

a. No. Leo III was the pope who crowned Charlemagne in 800 C.E.
b. Yes. He was also known as Gregory the Great, the pope who provided the Roman church with a sense of direction in the late 6th and early 7th centuries.
c. No. Otto I was the king of Germany who received the imperial crown from the pope in 962.

16-16. Answer key: p. 397

a. No. Charlemagne resorted to military force against the Saxons, a pagan people inhabiting northern Germany, and forced the latter to adopt Roman Christianity. He did not do the same in England.
b. No. There was no marriage of this sort.
c. The best answer. Gregory's missionary campaigns focused on the English kings, whose conversion eventually induced their subjects to adopt Roman Christianity.

16-17. Answer key: pp. 397-98

a. Yes. Celibacy and obeying a communal leader (the abbot) were prime virtues of Benedictine monks.
b. No. Accumulation of personal wealth was not encouraged. Rather, poverty was a prime virtue.
c. Not really. Monks were encouraged to do social service beyond their monasteries.

16-18. Answer key: p. 398

a. No. Convents and nuns appeared much earlier than St. Scholastica.
b. Not the best answer. She did not devise completely new regulations for nuns; she based her regulations on her brother Benedict's instructions for monks.
c. Yes. The adaptation meant minor revisions of St. Benedict's *Rule* for monasteries.

16-19. Answer key: pp. 398-99

a. Not a good choice. Such services WERE provided by monasteries.
b. Good choice. These were not part of the social services provided by monasteries.
c. Not a good choice. These were among the important social functions served by monasteries.

16-20. Answer key: p. 399

a. No. There was no imperial government in postclassical India. Rulers of early medieval Europe, except for the short-lived Carolingian empire, did not reinstate an imperial form of government either.
b. Yes. This was one of the major differences between the two societies during postclassical era.
c. Not a good answer. India also suffered from foreign invasions (the Muslims).

Chapter 17

17-1. Answer key: p. 407

a. Not a good answer. The purpose of retelling the story is not to marvel over Guillaume's talents, although his talents as a goldsmith enabled him to enjoy some prestige in the Mongol capital.
b. Not a good answer. The story does not tell us much about how magnificent the capital was.
c. The best answer. Besides Guillaume, the authors have mentioned many skilled captives from various countries working for the Mongol rulers.

17-2. Answer key: p. 408

a. Good choice. The Huns were active and powerful during the 2nd and 3rd centuries, and their migration and raids helped bring down the western Roman empire.
b. Not a good choice. Different groups of Turkish peoples were prominent, and they expanded to Persia, Anatolia, and India during this period.
c. Not a good choice. Mongols were the most formidable nomads during the 13th and 14th centuries.

17-3. Answer key: p. 409-10

a. No. Don't be confused—*kumiss* was an alcoholic drink made of mare's milk, while *yurts* were large tents made of wool. Nomads lived mostly off animal products.
b. Yes. Nomads avidly sought opportunities for exchange of their animal products for manufactured products with settled peoples, and they also were good at long-distance trade.
c. Not a good answer. They believed in shamanism, and many of them converted to Islam, Lamaist Buddhism, and other religions from the 11th through the 15th centuries.

17-4. Answer key: p. 409

a. Yes. The best answer.
b. Not really. During times of war, nobles wielded absolute authority over their forces, and they dealt swiftly and summarily with those who did not obey orders.
c. No. The hierarchy was not rigid. Nobles could lose their status if they did not continue to provide appropriate leadership for their clans and tribes, while commoners could win recognition as nobles by outstanding conduct, particularly by courageous behavior during war.

17-5. Answer key: pp. 410-11

a. The best answer. Cavalry was a great and decisive advantage of nomads over the armies of the settled peoples, which enabled them to conquer many societies during the period from the 11th through the 15th centuries.
b. No. The number of Mongols, for instance, was less than one percent of the Chinese population.
c. Not a good answer. Their equestrian skills, rather than weapons, were surely superior to those of the settled peoples.

17-6. Answer key: p. 411

a. Not the best answer. The Saljuq Turks overpowered the Abbasid caliphs who ruled only as figureheads; real power lay with the Saljuq sultans.
b. Yes. Tughril Beg was the first of many powerful sultans who overshadowed the Abbasid caliphs. He took Baghdad and then extended his power to Syria, Palestine, and other parts of the Abbasid realm.
c. No. The peasants of Anatolia actually welcomed the Saljuq Turks as liberators because they resented their Byzantine overlords.

17-7. Answer key: p. 412

a. No. They were FROM Afghanistan.
b. No. As zealous foes of Buddhism and Hinduism, they severely repressed the two religions and encouraged conversion to Islam in northern India.
c. Yes. They established the Turkish sultanate of Delhi and claimed authority over all of northern India by the late 12th century.

17-8. Answer key: pp. 413-16

a. No. Khubilai Khan was the ruler of China who established the Yuan dynasty in 1279.
b. No. Hülegü was Khubilai Khan's brother who toppled the Abbasid empire and established the Mongol ilkhanate in Persia.
c. Yes. The title meant "universal ruler"; his real name was Temŋjin. Both Khubilai Khan and Hülegü were Chinggis Khan's grandsons.

17-9. Answer key: p. 414

a. Yes. Mongols were known for their ability to travel long distances at a single stretch, and were among the most mobile fighting forces in the premodern world.
b. No. Javelins were unknown to Asian armies.
c. No. No one could shoot that far. The correct answer is 200 meters (656 feet).

17-10. Answer key: p. 415

a. Not a good choice. This was indeed a Mongol method of fighting according to Marco Polo.
b. Not a good choice. This tactic was also recorded by Marco Polo.
c. The best choice. Mongols intended to give the impression that they were fleeing, but in reality, they would turn back to face the enemy at just the right moment.

17-11. Answer key: pp. 416, 418

a. Not really. In Persia, the Mongols showed great tolerance to various religious beliefs. Later Mongol rulers in Persia such as Ilkhan Ghazan even converted to Islam.
b. Yes. The Khwarazm shah ordered the murder of Chinggis Khan's envoys and the merchants accompanying them to Persia to establish diplomatic and commercial relations with the shah in 1219. This event provoked Chinggis Khan's revenge and destruction.
c. No. There is no evidence to indicate this. At the initial stage of conquering China, some Mongol victors made the suggestion to exterminate the Chinese and convert China into pasture land for Mongol horses, but the suggestion was not made into a policy.

17-12. Answer key: p. 417

a. Yes. "Great khan" was the title taken by the rulers of the Mongol khanate in China although these rulers were only nominally superior to the khans of other Mongol empires.
b. No. The Golden Horde dominated south and central Russia.
c. No. The ilkhans ruled Persia, with central Asia ruled by the khans of Chaghatai.

17-13. Answer key: pp. 417-18

a. Not a good choice. Coming from the cold and dry steppelands, the Mongols were not well-adapted to the humid, tropical jungles of southeast Asia, and their horses could not find adequate pasture. Moreover, the Mongol cavalry was ineffective in guerrilla warfare in the jungles.
b. Good choice. Bubonic plague erupted in 1330's, while the Mongol military ventures in southeast Asia and Japan took place in 1270's and 1280's.
c. Not a good choice. The Mongols navies were indeed destroyed by typhoons, which the Japanese called *kamikaze*—"divine winds."

17-14. Answer key: pp. 418-20

a. No. The Mongols had no experience administrating complex societies, and they had a difficult time adjusting to their role as administrators.
b. Not a good answer. After conquests, Mongol rulers were interested in maintaining order and extracting revenue from the conquered peoples rather than simply plundering them.
c. Yes. See the answers for a and b.

17-15. Answer key: pp. 417-20

a. Yes. For instance, they forbade Chinese from learning Mongol language, and they had little interest in Confucianism.
b. No. They ended the privileges of Confucian scholars but did not execute them. Only some among the Mongol elite became interested in Lamaist Buddhism because of its interest in magic and supernatural powers.
c. No. The Mongols rulers created an ethnic hierarchy in China, and intermarriage was outlawed between Chinese, who were at the bottom of the hierarchy, and Mongols, who were at the top.

7-16. Answer key: p. 420

a. The best answer. The Mongols maintained reasonably good order within their realms that allowed merchants to travel unmolested through the four empires.
b. No. Although printed paper money was used in Persia and China, there was no a standardized paper currency circulating between these two societies.
c. Not a good answer. The Mongols did not have such policies.

17-17. Answer key: p. 421

a. Not a good choice. Chinese peasant rebellions drove the Mongols out of China in 1368.
b. Not a good choice. The plague severely weakened Mongol rule.
c. Good choice. Chinese rebels might have believed that Mongol emperors had lost the mandate of Heaven, but it was their military offensive that forced the Mongols out.

17-18. Answer key: p. 422

a. Not the best answer. His contemporaries called him Timur-i lang—"Timur the Lame"—an appellation that made its way into English as Tamerlane.
b. Yes. This was his real name.
c. Not a good answer. Just as Alexander was not born with the title "the Great," Tamerlane was not born with the appellation "the Whirlwind."

17-19. Answer key: p. 424

a. No. They were nomadic Turks who migrated from central Asia to Anatolia after the Mongol conquest of Persia.
b. Yes. They were known as Ottomans, or Osmanlis, because of their charismatic leader Osman.
c. No. Although they rose to power in Persia, they were not native Persians.

17-20. Answer key: p. 424

a. No. Osman was the first powerful leader of Ottomans, active in late 13th and early 14th centuries.
b. No. Tamerlane, who died in 1405, was not the leader of the Ottomans. In fact, Tamerlane's forces crushed the Ottoman army in 1402 and interrupted the Ottomans' expansion.
c. Yes. He was the Sultan of the Ottomans, also known as Mehmed the Conqueror.

Chapter 18

18-1. Answer key: p. 429

a. No. In the long history of Bantu peoples, Islam was rather a late-coming faith, and Muslim scholars were not responsible for the oral tradition.
b. Yes. Professional singers and griots (storytellers) were responsible for transmitting stories, history, and epics.
c. No. Chiefs and diviners had other duties to perform.

18-2. Answer key: p. 429

a. The best answer. The story related the lion prince's tragic childhood, his victorious return from exile, and his establishment of the Mali empire.
b. No. Although the slave trade was important in Mali empire, the story was not about slaves.
c. Not a good answer. Although the lion prince converted to Islam, the story was not about the coming of Islam.

18-3. Answer key: p. 429

a. No. There is no vast desert in central Africa. The Sahara is in the north.
b. No. Sub-Saharan Africa also includes central Africa.
c. Yes. It includes all the regions south of the Sahara desert.

18-4. Answer key: p. 430

a. Yes. The Bantu agricultural economy supported population growth which provided the essential drive for the Bantu expansion.
b. No. Hunting and gathering peoples were eventually absorbed by the Bantu migrants.
c. No. Fishing peoples on coastal areas were absorbed by the Bantu migrants.

18-5. Answer key: pp. 430-31

a. Not a good choice. The use of iron tools meant an increase in agricultural productivity, which in turn supported more population. Moreover, armed with iron tools, Bantu migrants could open new lands more effectively than before.
b. Good choice. Bubonic plague was not a global phenomenon until the 14th century C.E., long after Bantu migrations took place.
c. Not a good choice. The introduction of bananas caused a migratory surge in sub-Saharan Africa because it increased food supply.

18-6. Answer key: p. 432

a. Not really. A number of city-states began to emerge on the east coast during the 11th and 12th centuries.
b. No. The Mali empire emerged during the 13th century.
c. The best answer. Although there were a number of states before the 10th century (e.g., the kingdoms of Ghana and Axum), the dominant form of social organization was still stateless society.

18-7. Answer key: p. 432

a. Good choice. Men monopolized public authority. A village chief had to be a prominent male family-head.
b. Not a good choice. This was the essential feature of a stateless society.
c. Not a good choice. This was true.

18-8. Answer key: p. 433

a. Not really. Unlike some other states of west Africa, Kongo did not participate in the trans-Saharan trade with north Africa. Population pressure and internal conflict might explain the emergence of the Kongo kingdom.
b. Yes. This also indicates that Kongo might have had closer relations with the Indian Ocean basin than with north Africa.
c. No. Kongo was perhaps the most tightly centralized of the early Bantu kingdoms. The king or central administrators could appoint or replace local officials at will.

18-9. Answer key: p. 434

a. Not the best answer. Trans-Sahara communications had been undertaken without camels, though such communications were not frequent.
b. Yes. Camels could travel long distance in the desert, and became the most suitable animals for a trans-Sahara trip which took about 70 to 90 days.
c. No. Elephants were never used for the trans-Saharan trade. After about 500 C.E., camels increasingly replaced horses and donkeys as the preferred transport animals.

18-10. Answer key: pp. 435-37

a. No. Koumbi-Saleh was the capital city of the kingdom of Ghana, while Mansa Musa was the ruler of the Mali empire.
b. Yes. Niani was the capital city of the Mali empire just as Koumbi-Saleh was the capital city of the kingdom of Ghana.
c. No. Koumbi-Saleh was a city while Sundiata was the founder of the Mali empire.

18-11. Answer key: pp. 435-36

a. The best answer. In addition to improving commercial relations, the conversion also brought them recognition and support from other Muslim states.
b. No. In both cases, the rulers did not impose Islam upon their subjects.
c. Not the best answer. The earliest Muslim converts were from African elite society. Although slaves were traded between these two states and other Islamic countries, the majority were probably not Muslims.

18-12. Answer key: pp. 438-39

a. No. Swahili was a Bantu language with some words and ideas borrowed from Arabic.
b. Yes. Swahili is an Arabic word meaning "coasters," referring to the peoples who engaged in trade along the east Africa coast.
c. No. It did not refer to the city-states.

18-13. Answer key: pp. 436, 439-40

a. Not a good choice. They WERE Swahili city-states.
b. Good choice. Ife was a kingdom of west Africa, and Zimbabwe was an interior state of south Africa.
c. Not a good choice. Both WERE Swahili city-states.

18-14. Answer key: p. 440

a. No. The term *zimbabwe* refers simply to the dwelling of a chief or king. Great Zimbabwe was the capital city of the kingdom of Zimbabwe.
b. Yes. It was a city of stone towers, palaces, and public buildings that served as the capital of the kingdom of Zimbabwe.
c. No. There was not such an organization in the kingdom of Zimbabwe.

18-15. Answer key: p. 441

a. No. De Barros was a Portuguese historian of the early 16th century, and when he visited Kilwa, the city-state was a thriving commercial center of the east African coast.
b. No. Neither of these peoples were mentioned in de Barros's account.
c. Yes. A tribe of Arabs had settled among the Kaffirs in early centuries. The Kaffirs were indigenous inhabitants who were Bantu-speaking people.

18-16. Answer key: pp. 442-44

a. Not a good answer. Slave trading and slave holding were prominent features of all sub-Saharan societies.
b. The best answer. Lands were the common property of communities, not the private property of individuals.
c. Not really. Genders and ages played important roles in determining social positions of community members. For instance, men largely monopolized public authority.

18-17. Answer key: p. 444

a. Yes. Previously, the main source of slaves was eastern Europe, which after the 11th century could no longer meet the demand for slaves in the markets of India, Persia, southwest Asia, and the Mediterranean basin.
b. No. There is no evidence to support this point. Quite to the contrary, many slaves were war captives, and many wars were launched just for slave raiding.
c. Not a good choice. See answer b above.

18-18. Answer key: pp. 444-45

a. No. Quite to the contrary, African religion strongly emphasized morality and proper behavior. Failure to observe high moral standards would lead to disorder and would displease deities, spirits, and departed ancestors.
b. The best answer. Diviners were important in African religion but they were relatively unconcerned with theological matters and favored turning their attention to practical matters of explaining, predicting, and controlling the experience of individuals and groups.
c. Not a good answer. Africans believed that the creator god was the source of world order, and failure to observe high moral standards would lead to disorder in the world.

18-19. Answer key: p. 446

a. Yes. Christianity in sub-Saharan Africa had a foothold only in the kingdom of Axum (modern Ethiopia).
b. No. Islam had much more influence in sub-Saharan Africa than Christianity.
c. Not necessarily. Each of these two foreign religions was adopted by Africans for their own needs. Ethiopian Christians, for instance, believed that a large host of evil spirits populated the world, and they used amulets or charms to fight against these menacing spirits, while African Muslims also participated in rituals designed to please nature deities and the spirits of departed ancestors.

18-20. Answer key: p. 448

a. Not really. Efforts to restrict women's activities were unsuccessful.
b. The best answer. Islam had to accommodate African notions of proper relations between the sexes.
c. No. There is no evidence offered to support this point.

Chapter 19

19-1. Answer key: p. 454

a. No. He was excommunicated by the pope, and his imperial authority was challenged by German princes. He regained control only after beseeching Pope Gregory VII's mercy while standing barefoot in the snow.
b. Yes. See answer key a.
c. No. Emperor Frederick Barbarossa came into conflict with the popes over rights to Lombardy, not over investiture.

19-2. Answer key: p. 453

a. Not true. Pope John XII crowned Otto I in 962, thus marking the birth of the Holy Roman Empire.
b. Not a good answer. Although it was true, it was not what Voltaire meant when he made the comment in the 18th century.
c. The best answer. In reality, it was regional state ruling Germany.

19-3. Answer key: p. 455

a. Yes. Moreover, the Capetian Kings also strengthened their authority over feudal vassals through absorbing territories of vassals who died without heirs.
b. No. This was what happened in England after William the Conqueror invaded there in 1066.
c. No. The Capetian Kings did not fight the descendants of Vikings in Normandy during the high middle ages.

19-4. Answer key: pp. 457-58

a. Not a good choice. Indeed, population pressure pushed cultivators to clear forests and swamps, and such an effort was also encouraged by feudal lords for higher taxes.
b. Not a good choice. By using these two simple devices the amount of land under cultivation sharply increased.
c. Good choice. Bananas were a major food crop of sub-Saharan Africa (see Chapter 18), not of medieval Europe.

19-5. Answer key: p. 460

a. Yes. He said that "the road you travel from Tana to Cathay [China] is perfectly safe."
b. No. According to Pegolotti, local lords would claim a merchant's property only when he died on the way and had no relatives or friends to claim the property.
c. No. Here Pegolotti was giving advice about how to use Chinese paper money—don't spend too much simply because the money was made of paper.

19-6. Answer key: p. 461

a. No. The Hanseatic League was a trade network of cities across northern Europe; it had nothing to do with reconquering Spain.
b. No. As a trade network of northern European cities, the Hanseatic League had no direct involvement in curbing the expansion of the Holy Roman Empire.
c. Yes. The League was a trade network which embraced all the significant commercial centers of northern Europe.

19-7. Answer key: pp. 461-62

a. No. The term "three estates" does not refer to these three islands.
b. No. The term had nothing to do with monarchical property or authority.
c. Yes. Social commentators used this term to mean "those who pray, those who fight, and those who work."

19-8. Answer key: p. 462

a. Good choice. There was no connection between long-distance trade and the manners of the nobility.
b. Not a good choice. Christianity encouraged warriors to became cultivated leaders of society. By the 12th century, an aristocratic young man had to pledge his service to God before he entered into the nobility.
c. Not a good choice. A noble was supposed to be romantic, an expectation that was cultivated by aristocratic women through their patronage of troubadours' performances of romantic poetry and song in aristocratic courts.

19-9. Answer key: p. 463

a. The best answer. Beginning in the late 11th century, towns and cities became increasingly jurisdictions of their own, beyond the control of feudal lords.
b. Not the best answer. Cities and town were by no mean egalitarian societies even though they might have been more egalitarian than feudal manors.
c. Not a good answer. Women on feudal manors were also part of the rural workforce.

19-10. Answer key: p. 463

a. Not a good choice. This was something the guilds often did.
b. Good choice. A guild did not have a formal court, although it could solve disputes among its members.
c. Not a good choice. This was something the guilds often did.

19-11. Answer key: p. 465

a. Yes. They focused especially on literature and philosophy.
b. Not really. Reading the Bible was only part of the curricula. Cathedral schools were not geared towards providing only a religious education.
c. Not a good answer. Only some cathedral schools offered advanced courses in law, medicine, and theology.

19-12. Answer key: pp. 465-66

a. No. Popular heresies were a negative response to the power and wealth of the Roman Catholic church, which had nothing to do with Aristotle's writing.
b. Yes. As Aristotle's writings became popular among European scholars, scholastic theologians sought to synthesize Aristotelian philosophy and Christian values.
c. No. The movement of Dominicans and Franciscans was a reform from within the Roman Catholic church, designed to curb its increasingly materialistic tendency.

19-13. Answer key: pp. 465-66

a. No. The Eucharist was one of sacraments during which priests offered a ritual meal commemorating Jesus's last meal with his disciples.
b. No. St. Francis was the co-founder of the order of mendicants, not a scholastic scholar.
c. Yes. St. Thomas was a teacher at the University of Paris and became the most influential scholastic theologian of Europe during the high middle ages.

19-14. Answer key: 466

a. Not a good answer. The Bantus' creator god was equally as omnipotent and omniscient as the Christian God. Moreover, unlike the Christian saints, the Bantu creator god did not intervene or participate directly in the day-to-day affairs of the world.
b. The best answer. Bodhisattvas were Buddhist saints who, like Christian saints, could intervene in the daily affairs of the world.
c. Not a good answer. Mecca was not a saint, but a holy place.

19-15. Answer key: p. 468

a. Not a good choice. Waldensians were among the proponents of popular heresies in medieval Europe, rejecting the Roman Catholic church and organizing an alternative religious movement.
b. Not a good choice. Cathars went even further than Waldensians in terms of heresy. They were ruthlessly suppressed by the Roman Catholic church and Christian knights.
c. Good choice. Quite to the contrary, mendicants worked zealously to combat heterodox movements and to persuade heretics to return to the Roman Catholic church.

19-16. Answer key: p. 469

a. No. The target of the campaign was the Cathars, also known as the Albigensians.
b. Yes. In response to the call of the Roman Catholic church, feudal warriors from northern France undertook the campaign, which ruthlessly crushed Cathar communities in southern France.
c. No. The Albigensians were neither pagan nor Slavic.

19-17. Answer key: p. 470

a. No. The Teutonic Knights were most active in the Baltic region, where they waged military campaigns against the pagan Slavic peoples during the 12th and 13th centuries.
b. No. European crusaders did not march to modern Canada.
c. Yes. Vinland was the name given to modern Newfoundland in Canada, discovered and colonized by a group of Scandinavian seafarers led by Leif Ericsson about 1000 C.E.

19-18. Answer key: pp. 471-72

a. No. Eric the Red was a Scandinavian seafarer who was responsible for discovering and colonizing Greenland in the North Atlantic Ocean at the end of the 10th century.
b. Yes. Roger was a Norman Christian adventurer who, after about 20 years of conflict, took over Sicily from Muslim control.
c. No. Robert was Roger's brother who carved out a small state for himself in southern Italy while his brother engaged in the reconquest of Sicily.

19-19. Answer key: p. 472

a. Yes. This a historical term, specifically referring to the reconquest of Spain from the Muslims, which lasted from the 1060s to the early 13th century. The last Muslim foothold (Granada) survived until 1492.
b. No. Although the term reconquest was also used for efforts to retake Sicily for western Christianity, "the *reconquista*" is usually reserved to refer to the reconquest of Spain from the Muslims.
c. No. The term "reconquest" is not used to describe the efforts launched by crusaders to take back Palestine from Muslim control.

19-20. Answer key: pp. 473-74

a. Good choice. Most crusades failed as military ventures. Although the first crusade took Jerusalem in 1099, the Muslim leader Saladin then took the city back in 1187.
b. Not a good choice. The fourth crusade was manipulated by Venetian merchants, who turned it into an attack on their commercial rivals in Constantinople.
c. Not a good choice. It was true that when Europeans built crusader states in the eastern Mediterranean, they traded eagerly with Muslim merchants of the region.

Chapter 20

20-1. Answer key: pp. 477-78

a. Not a good answer. Diaz COMPARED Tenochtitlan with Venice, and found some similarities between the two cities (for example, both sat in water).
b. Not a good answer. Diaz COMPARED the marketplace of Tlatelolco district favorably to those of Rome and Constantinople.
c. The best answer. This contrast struck them the most and challenged their thinking.

20-2. Answer key: p. 478

a. No. The authors do not make such an argument. Although this might plausibly be argued by a modern scholar, the argument has little to do with Aztec cultural standards.
b. Yes. The authors make this point about human sacrifice in the larger context of Aztec cultural traditions.
c. Not the best answer. It was hardly true that all trading commodities were from tribute; victims of human sacrifices were not exclusively from conquered peoples either.

20-3. Answer key: p. 479

a. Yes. Teotihuacan collapsed in the early 10th century and the Toltecs unified the region and maintained effective imperial control until 1175.
b. No. The Maya were in the Yucatan peninsula, not in central Mexico.
c. Not the best answer. The Mexica (i.e., Aztecs) built a great empire in central Mexico centuries after the collapse of the Toltec empire.

20-4. Answer key: p. 479

a. Yes. The Mexica migrated from the northwestern region to the central region of Mexico, and they remembered *Aztlan* as the home of their ancestors.
b. No. The term *Aztlan* does not mean this, although the migrants of Aztecs had a bad reputation for kidnapping women from nearby communities and seizing land already cultivated by others.
c. No. Because of their constant jostling and fighting with other peoples in central Mexico, the Aztecs sometimes survived only by eating fly eggs and snakes before the early 15th century, but this fact has nothing to do with the term *Aztlan*.

20-5. Answer key: pp. 479-80

a. Not a good choice. Such a rich food source indeed helped the Mexica to settle and survive.
b. Not a good choice. The Mexica dredged rich and fertile muck from the lake's bottom and built it up into small plots of land known as *chinampas*.
c. Good choice. To travel on the marshy land was a great inconvenience. As a matter of fact, the lake served as a natural defense for the Mexica.

20-6. Answer key: pp. 480-81

a. Not true. A small group of long-distance traders served the interests of the ruling elites who needed merchants to take part of their tribute to trade for exotic items. Such traders also served as political and military intelligence about lands they visited.
b. The best answer. The Mexica and their allies simply conquered their subjects and assessed tribute, leaving local governance and collection of tribute in the hands of the conquered peoples themselves.
c. Not true. The Mexica did not keep a permanent, standing army, but they could assemble forces when they launched campaigns. The tributary system depended on military prowess.

20-7. Answer key: p. 482

a. Yes. According to the sumptuary law, burlap-like henequen garments were clothes of commoners.
b. No. Wearing cotton garments was an aristocratic privilege in Aztec society.
c. No. Only celebrated warriors were allowed to don brightly colored capes and adorn themselves with lipplugs and eagle feathers.

20-8. Answer key: p. 483

a. Not the best answer. Only on a few occasions did priests become supreme rulers of the Aztec empire.
b. Not a good answer. Aztec priests did not have elaborate doctrines or moral teachings to preach; when presiding over rituals, they read omens and explained the cosmic forces that drove the world.
c. The best answer. As specialists in calendrical and ritual lore, they could wield considerable influence by giving advice to the rulers.

20-9. Answer key: pp. 484-85

a. No. Tezcatlipoca was "the smoking Mirror," life giver and taker, patron deity of warriors. He was not the one to whom human sacrifices were made.
b. Yes. This was the war god of the Mexica, who could be pleased by human sacrifices.
c. No. This god had a reputation for supporting arts, crafts, and agriculture.

20-10. Answer key: p. 486

a. Not a good choice. They <u>did</u> live in woodlands east of the Mississippi River.
b. Not a good choice. This was true of Iroquois society.
c. Good choice. Only the peoples of the southwestern U.S. and Mexico lived in pueblo.

20-11. Answer key: pp. 488

a.   Yes. Only the peoples of Mesoamerica, such as Mayas and Aztecs, had writing systems.
b.   No. There were no well-developed states in North America and writing systems did not exist.
c.   No. Although the Incas had a well-developed bureaucracy, the officials of the empire used *quipu*, not writing, to keep track of information.

20-12. Answer key: pp. 489

a.   No. The kingdom of Chucuito dominated the highlands region around Lake Trticaca between the 13th and early 15th centuries.
b.   No. The kingdom of Chimu emerged in the lowlands of the modern Peruvian coast in the 10th century, and dominated the region for about one century before the arrival of the Incas in the mid-15th century.
c.   Yes. Only the Inca empire was able to control both the highlands and lowlands of Andean America before the arrival of Europeans in the early 16th century.

20-13. Answer key: p. 490

a.   No. Cuzco was their capital city but there were many other Incas who lived elsewhere in the empire.
b.   The best answer. It also came to refer to all subjects of the Inca empire.
c.   No. Originally, the word referred to the title of the rulers of a small kingdom in the valley of Cuzco, not their residence.

20-14. Answer key: p. 490

a.   No. The Incas did not develop a script.
b.   Yes. An Inca bureaucrat had to learn how to manipulate *quipu* with efficiency.
c.   No. We do not know if the Incas had a calendar or not.

20-15. Answer key: p. 491

a.   Yes. The road system facilitated communication between the central and local governments, and enabled the central government to dispatch large forces rapidly to distant trouble spots.
b.   Not really. The Inca empire was not founded on a market economy, and a large merchant class did not exist.
c.   No. There was little communication between South America and Central America.

20-16. Answer key: p. 492

a.   No. The royal family directly took a share from tribute that was paid to them, not from the storehouses.
b.   Yes. One may say that land distribution by the government, communal life, the lack of a market economy, and their social welfare system made the Inca akin to a socialist system.
c.   No. Government officials were paid directly from tribute, not from the storehouses.

20-17. Answer key: p. 492

a. No. Although the Incas honored Inti as their major god, they also recognized other gods such as the creator god Viracocha.
b. The best answer. The Inca religion involved the concept of sin, punishments and rewards in an afterlife, and rituals of confession and penance. None of these existed in Aztec religion.
c. Not true. Priests of all cults honored their deities with sacrifices, although human sacrifices were rare among the Inca.

20-18. Answer key: pp. 493

a. No. Each individual group had its own myths and deities related to the geographical features of the land around the group.
b. Yes. Because one group's access to food and other resources might be unknown to another group, trade between them became necessary.
c. No. The aboriginal peoples did not settle for agriculture, but led a nomadic hunting and gathering life and engaged in seasonal migration.

20-19. Answer key: p. 496

a. No. *Kapu* meant "taboo" or the sumptuary laws of Hawai'i.
b. No. *Heiau* (or *marae* on other Pacific islands) was the ceremonial precinct and temple structure.
c. Yes. *Ali'i nui*, the high chiefs, commanded enormous respect and power within their societies.

20-20. Answer key: p. 497

a. Yes. This alone set a limit on their ability to exploit the natural environment.
b. No. All the societies with chiefly states were complex societies with sophisticated cultural and religious traditions.
c. Not a good answer. Trade and migration between different islands involved sophisticated watercraft transportation technology even though the Pacific islanders did not have wheeled vehicles or transport animals.

Chapter 21

21-1. Answer Key: pp. 501-502

a. Not the best answer. Although this might be true, it is not the theme of the chapter.
b. Not the best answer. See answer a.
c. Yes. This can be seen even from the title of the chapter—"Reaching Out: Cross-cultural Interactions."

21-2. Answer key: p. 502

a. Not a good choice. Diplomatic missions were quite frequent during this period.
b. Good choice. Cross-cultural tourism was not yet possible; only a few mariners and their crews ventured abroad.
c. Not a good choice. Missionary campaigns, especially those of Christians and Muslims, were very active during this period.

21-3. Answer key: pp. 503

a. The best answer. Silk roads were overland routes. It made sense for light, highly valuable commodities like silk to travel overland.
b. Not the best answer. Sea-lanes were primarily for bulky commodities like steel, coral, or building materials, although luxury goods could also travel by water.
c. Not the best answer. Camels were common animals for transportation only in certain regions.

21-4. Answer key: p. 503

a. Not necessarily. Foreign merchants did not have a preference for specific forms of government; they were primarily concerned that governments maintain order so as to provide safe markets.
b. Yes. Port cities like Melaka, Kilwa, Guangzhou, and Calicut all enjoyed strategic locations.
c. No. Quite to the contrary, excessive customs fees would inhibit foreign trade.

21-5. Answer key: pp. 506-507

a. Not a good answer. There were many foreigners who worked for Chinese governments prior to Marco Polo.
b. No. He did not do either of these. His overland travel to China was still too costly for most European merchants to undertake despite the fact that the Chinese market was always open to them.
c. The best answer. Many European readers were fascinated by Marco's description of China, and in later centuries, European mariners began to explore sea routes to China for direct trade.

21-6. Answer key: p. 507

a. No. Despite the fact that the two sides had the Muslims as the common foe, the Mongols wished to see Europe as a target of conquest rather than as an ally.
b. Yes. The Mongols felt no need to hide this intention from Europeans.
c. No. Events like this occurred involving nomadic leaders and the royal daughters of settled societies, but the Mongol khans were not involved in such marriages.

21-7. Answer key: p. 507

a. Yes. The mission failed because Europeans had no desire to ally with Mongols as long as they refused to convert to Christianity.
b. No. The Europeans refused to offer any military support for the Mongols.
c. Not really. Rabban Sauma actually enjoyed a fine reception from the European leaders although they declined to participate in the alliance with the Mongol ilkhan that he proposed.

21-8. Answer key: p. 508

a. No. At the time of Muhammad, the role of the *qadi* had not yet been established.
b. Yes. The *qadi* played a crucial role in instilling Islamic values among the peoples of newly converted lands.
c. Not a good answer. Recently converted lands might be farther away from Mecca, the ultimate destination for the *hajj*, than the legal scholars' homelands.

21-9. Answer key: p. 508

a. No. Do not confuse *qadi*, Islamic judges, with Sufis, Islamic missionaries.
b. Yes. This he did well. He once sentenced a thief to the loss of his right hand in accordance with the *sharia*.
c. No. He tried hard to persuade the island women to meet the Islamic standard, but he failed.

21-10. Answer key: p. 509

a. Yes. He said in his letter that the great khan "bestows many kindnesses upon the Christians, and these two years past, I have gotten along well with him...."
b. Not true. He said that in two years he had baptized some 6,000 persons.
c. No. He translated it into Turkish, a language commonly used at the Mongol court.

21-11. Answer key: pp. 512-14

a. Not a good choice. Both China and Europe suffered from the demographic disasters caused by the plague.
b. Not a good choice. These regions also suffered devastating population losses, and demographic recovery took much longer in these regions than in China and Europe.
c. Good choice. The plague largely bypassed these regions. India even experienced population growth while other regions suffered population losses.

21-12. Answer key: p. 515

a. No. Later when he became the emperor of the Ming dynasty, Hongwu used eunuchs extensively to carry out governmental duties, but he himself was never a eunuch.
b. The best answer. Emperor Hongwu had been a beggar, an orphan, and a poor Buddhist monk.
c. No. Emperor Hongwu was not a well educated man but promoted Confucian values and restored the civil service system.

21-13. Answer key: p. 517

a. Yes. New taxes levied directly on citizens supplemented the income that rulers received from their feudal subordinates, which enabled the states to equip mercenary forces with gunpowder weapons.
b. No. As soon as gunpowder weapons were in use, the importance of medieval knights as a fighting force began to decline. The states increasingly relied on mercenary forces as standing armies, a measure that greatly strengthened state power.
c. No. It is hard to see how the Renaissance strengthened the states, although many artistic activities of the Renaissance were sponsored by political leaders.

21-14. Answer key: p. 517

a. Not a good answer. Columbus's exploration did not bring fortune to the state.
b. No. The Catholic Kings of Spain were unwilling to make alliances with the Islamic world which they viewed as their arch-enemy.
c. The best answer. The couple, who were known as the Catholic Kings, brought the two wealthiest and most important Iberian realms together as a single state through their marriage in 1469.

21-15. Answer key: pp. 518-19

a. No. Do not confuse burgeoning mercantilism with the cultural activities that scholars have termed the "Renaissance."
b. Yes. The sophisticated urban culture of this period was concerned with individualism and appreciation of Greco-Roman classics, as the works of a multitude of artists and humanists show.
c. No. Although demographic recovery was another aspect of European life during this era, the term "Renaissance" does not refer to this phenomenon.

21-16. Answer key: pp. 519-20

a. Yes. These subjects of learning are called the humanities, and the scholars specializing in them are called humanists.
b. No. At the inception of the use of this term during the Renaissance, advocating universal love was not a major intellectual or moral emphasis.
c. No. The full flowering of the trend toward antireligious secularism came much later in the ongoing evolution of European history.

21-17. Answer key: p. 521

a. Not a good choice. This was one of the purposes of Zheng He's expeditions.
b. Good choice. Remember this question is phrased in the negative. The Ming government wanted to control whatever trade existed, including foreign trade, but Zheng He never ventured as far as Europe. Also, the Ming government had no interest in opening up future opportunities for private merchants.
c. Not a good choice. Zheng He's exhibition of China's naval strength in the Indian Ocean basin was designed precisely to fulfill this purpose.

21-18. Answer key: p. 524

a. Good choice. This could not possibly have motivated European explorers because at the beginning of their explorations, they knew nothing of the existence of the vast continents to their west that stood between Europe and Asia.
b. Not a good choice. To spread Christianity was one of the prime motivations for European explorations, which can be seen from the ambitious campaign of the Portuguese Prince, Henry the Navigator.
c. Not a good choice. Indeed, European merchants were eager to participate directly in flourishing Asian markets through their own sea routes, hoping to avoid those routes already controlled by Muslim and Italian middlemen.

21-19. Answer key: pp. 525

a. No. Vasco da Gama came after the first mariner who reached the Cape of Good Hope at the tip of Africa, sailing far beyond the Cape across the Arabian Sea, reaching to India in 1497.
b. Yes. After Dias reached the Cape of Good Hope in 1488, he could not sail any farther because his crew forced him to return home.
c. No. Columbus was a Genoese mariner, not a Portuguese, and sailed in a completely different direction.

21-20. Answer key: p. 525

a. No. The king of Portugal declined Columbus's petition.
b. Yes. Fernando and Isabel of Spain were ambitious and wealthy enough to make Columbus's dreams into real voyages.
c. No. Although Columbus was from Italy, his voyages were not sponsored by the Italian monarch.

Answer Key, Documentary Evidence

Chapter Nine

9-1. Answer key:

a. Not a good answer. He did not seek any religious teaching or truth for making or justifying his argument.
b. No. He did not cite any political authority to support his idea.
c. The best answer. The passage is a good demonstration of the power of "dialectic," defined in classical Greece as the art of posing questions and giving answers in the process of making arguments. The persuasion was based on human reason.
d. No. There was no feminist movement in classical Greece.

9-2. Answer key:

a. Not a good answer. This has little to do with Plato's reasoning.
b. Yes. Plato set no limit on women's careers.
c. Not a good answer. Although he held that women were the "weaker sex," Plato still concluded that "women will have the rightful opportunity to share in every task."
d. Not the best answer. Plato held that, in comparison to men, women were the "weaker sex."

Chapter 10

10-1. Answer key:

a. Not a good answer. Christians were still a small group of people hated by the elite and misunderstood by the general public "because of their outrageous practices."
b. Not the best answer. It seemed that Nero's cruelty toward Christians only aroused "a feeling of sympathy" among the general public. Should Christianity have become very popular or welcomed by the general public, Nero probably would not have made Christians the scapegoats.
c. The best answer. Tacitus noted that Christianity "received a large following" among "all obnoxious and disgraceful elements."

10-2. Answer key:

a. Not a good answer. Tacitus viewed Christianity as "pernicious superstition" and Christians as "evil criminals," so to punish Christians was not wrong.
b. The best answer. According to Tacitus, Nero did the right thing to punish Christians, but it was wrong to destroy Christians "not for the public good but to satisfy the cruelty of one man."
c. Compared with answer b, this is not the best answer. Tacitus seemed to share the public sympathy, but he also believed that Christians deserved "the worst kind of punishment."